I0096169

The Meanings of Michael Oakeshott's Conservatism

Edited by Corey Abel

ia

imprint-academic.com

Copyright © Imprint Academic, 2010

The moral rights of the authors have been asserted.
No part of this publication may be reproduced in any form
without permission, except for the quotation of brief passages
in criticism and discussion.

Published in the UK by
Imprint Academic, PO Box 200, Exeter EX5 5YX, UK

Published in the USA by Imprint Academic,
Philosophy Documentation Center
PO Box 7147, Charlottesville, VA 22906-7147, USA

ISBN 978 1845403447

A CIP catalogue record for this book is available from the
British Library and US Library of Congress

Full details of additional titles in the Oakeshott Studies series;
www.imprint-academic.com/idealists

Contents

Part I
Religion

Part II
History

Part III
Currents in Philosophy

Part IV
On Being Conservative

List of Contributors

Corey Abel teaches at Metropolitan State College of Denver, and holds degrees from Colorado College, London School of Economics, and the University of Chicago. He rock climbs to relax.

Josiah Lee Auspitz is an independent scholar living in Somerville, Massachusetts.

Todd Breyfogle is Director of Seminars at the Aspen Institute. He is a graduate of Colorado College; Corpus Christi College, Oxford; and the University of Chicago's Committee on Social Thought.

Gene Callahan is an adjunct professor of economics at SUNY Purchase, a charter member of the Michael Oakeshott Association, and the author of *Economics for Real People.*

George Feaver was Professor Emeritus of Political Science at the University of British Columbia. He passed away on May 12, 2008.

Richard E. Flathman is The George Armstrong Kelly Memorial Professor of Political Science, Emeritus, at Johns Hopkins University, and the author of *Pluralism and Liberal Democracy,* which discusses the work of Michael Oakeshott.

Timothy Fuller is Professor of Political Science at Colorado College and past president of the Michael Oakeshott Association.

Michael Henkel, University of Leipzig, works in the fields of political theory and the history of political thought; spends his leisure time with his family – or reading or mowing the lawn.

Ferenc Hörcher, Ph.D., is Chair of the Department of Aesthetics, Pázmány Péter Catholic University, Hungary. His research fields include the history of political and aesthetic thought.

Byron Kaldis is Associate Professor of Philosophy, Hellenic Open University, and contributor of "Oakeshott on Science" in the forthcoming *Cambridge Companion to Oakeshott.*

Leslie Marsh is Assistant Director at New England Institute of Cognitive Science and Evolutionary Studies and Associate Researcher in the Department of Pathology and Laboratory Medicine at the University of British Columbia.

Kenneth McIntyre is an assistant professor of political science at Concordia University in Montreal, Quebec. He is the author of *The Limits of Political Theory: Oakeshott on Civil Association*.

Attila K. Molnár, Professor of the History of Ideas at Eötvös University and Pázmány Péter Catholic University, has written on the Protestant ethic in Hungary, and Edmund Burke. He has two children, and enjoys walking his dog in nearby oak forests.

Ivo Mosley is an independent scholar and freelance writer based in England. His book, on misrepresentations of democracy and freedom in the West, is forthcoming from Imprint Academic in spring 2011.

Jeff Rabin is a Research Associate at Trinity College, University of Toronto, in the Department of Divinity and is working on a book tentatively titled *Barbarians Within the Gates*.

Ian Tregenza teaches political theory at Macquarie University, Sydney. He is the author of *Michael Oakeshott on Hobbes: A Study in the Renewal of Philosophical Ideas*.

Roy Tseng is Professor of Political Theory at National Sun Yat-sen University, Taiwan. He is an admirer of Oakeshott, the MLB pitcher Chien-Ming Wang, and comedian Stephan Chou.

Stephen Turner is Graduate Research Professor of Philosophy at the University of South Florida and a devoted Alfisto. He lives on Pass-a-Grille Beach in Florida.

Memorial to George Feaver, 1937–2008

I met George for the first time in the fall of 1979. I was then a Visitor to the Government Department at The London School of Economics. George was making one of his frequent visits to his old haunts and, in particular, visiting his mentor, Maurice Cranston. We met for coffee in the Senior Common Room, had a friendly visit, and then he was off on his travels. A few years later I met him again in Vancouver. The Canadian Learneds were holding their annual meetings at the University of British Columbia. My friend and colleague, Robert Orr of the LSE, and I had proposed a panel on Hobbes's political philosophy, with assistance from George and from Bill Mathie of Brock University. It was on this occasion that George and I spent time together and began to really know each other. He showed us around Vancouver (my first visit there but the first of numerous trips to Vancouver). George turned out to be a sort of polymath about British politics since the nineteenth century, and a fund of stories about the LSE. This fit well with me since I had written my doctoral thesis on John Stuart Mill, and had become a fan of the LSE Government Department, which was, in my opinion, in its golden age. Like George, I have visited London every year for many years, until 1990 primarily to see Oakeshott, Shirley and Bill Letwin, Ken Minogue, Maurice Cranston, Maurice Cowling at Cambridge, and the others, and I still visit even though most of them are gone from the scene.

Michael Oakeshott, the Letwins, Elie Kedourie, Maurice Cranston, Ken Minogue, Robert Orr, John Charvet, and many others were essential participants in that LSE scene. It was an exciting venue for us political theorists. George and I shared all this in common. Later in the 80s, I was assisting a colleague in the Romance Language Department at Colorado College to inaugurate a program of 'North American Studies'. This was to be a comparative study of Canada, Mexico, and the United States. I taught summer courses comparing Canada and the USA, and eventually took a group of students to Canada in the first of what turned out to be a decade-long program of comparative study excursions. Before that, however, I had invited George to visit Colorado College to give some talks to students about Canadian culture and politics, and we spent a good deal of time exploring the Colorado Rockies. I last saw George at the 2006 meeting of the Michael Oakeshott Association where he delivered a paper, a version of which appears in this volume. We had dinner together and he regaled all of us Oakeshottians with endless stories of the ups and downs of his life which were numerous, a mixture of joy and sadness, and sometimes quite adventurous. I had hoped, alas, to see him at the 2009 meeting of the Michael Oakeshott Association.

George was great fun, an old fashioned citizen of the Republic of Letters and a natural exemplification of the world of liberal learning. I was happy to recommend him for a fellowship to engage in researching the Cranston archive at the University of Texas. He would no doubt have produced a vivid memoir of his teacher had he lived long enough to complete it. I think he also qualifies as a natural "Oakeshottian" in the sense that much of his life seemed to be an unrehearsed intellectual adventure.

Timothy Fuller, Colorado College, January 2010

List of Abbreviations

EM	*Experience and its Modes*
FS	*The Politics of Faith and the Politics of Scepticism*
HCA	*Hobbes on Civil Association* (Liberty Fund, 1990)
HCiv	*Hobbes on Civil Association* (Berkeley, 1975)
LHPT	*Lectures in the History of Political Thought*
MPME	*Morality and Politics in Modern Europe*
Notes IX	British Library of Economics and Political Science, Oakeshott Archives, LSE File 2/1/9
Notes XI	British Library of Economics and Political Science, Oakeshott Archives, LSE File 2/1/11
OH	*On History and Other Essays* (Basil Blackwell)
OHist	*On History and Other Essays* (Barnes and Noble)
OHC	*On Human Conduct*
RIP	*Rationalism in Politics* (Liberty Press, 1991)
RP	*Rationalism in Politics* (Methuen, 1962)
RPML	*Religion, Politics and the Moral Life*
SPD	*The Social and Political Doctrine of Contemporary Europe*
VL	*The Voice of Liberal Learning* (Liberty Fund, 2001)
VLL	*The Voice of Liberal Learning* (Yale, 1989)
WH	*What is History? and other essays*

To be conservative, then, is to prefer the familiar to the unknown, to prefer the tried to the untried, fact to mystery, the actual to the possible, the limited to the unbounded, the near to the distant, the sufficient to the superabundant, the convenient to the perfect, present laughter to utopian bliss.

Michael Oakeshott, "On Being Conservative"

Foreword

This volume is made up of essays that were, for the most part, originally delivered at the Michael Oakeshott Association's 2006 conference, which took place at Colorado College. Tulane University was to have been host in 2005, a plan that was disrupted, like so much else, by Hurricane Katrina. The conference took the fiftieth anniversary of the publication of 'On Being Conservative' as the occasion to explore the question of Oakeshott's conservatism. As this volume demonstrates, interest in Oakeshott's work continues to grow, and his reputation spreads internationally, with scholars in the United States, Canada, and Britain joined by writers in Hungary, Germany, Australia, China, and Greece. While this volume focuses on Oakeshott's conservatism, it reflects Oakeshott's own breadth of interests and distinctive approach to politics and philosophy, in pursuing not a narrowly ideological understanding of conservatism, nor even a strictly political conception, but instead examining the meanings of his reflections on history, tradition, the relation of philosophy to politics and more.

As those familiar with his work know, 'conservative' was not a term Oakeshott normally used to describe his own position. He was not a doctrinaire supporter of right wing ideology, despite what some harsh and hasty critics have alleged. One finds in his work not a Burkean defense of tradition, but rather a Hegelian and Humean critique of abstract reasoning. For Oakeshott, there can be no defense of tradition that relies on characterizing it as the source of wisdom or goodness *against* a deficient present. Tradition is made up of a continuous stream of innovated, spontaneous, dance-like responses of individual agents to their unchosen circumstances. It is not hard to extract an argument about skill in doing that has substantial resonance with Aristotle's thoughts on practical knowledge, nor to see interwoven with it a Paterian argument about living with intensity and winning one's way through to an existence of one's own. Above all, Oakeshott was a philosopher determined to understand the world without feeling pressed to change it, unwilling to compromise with conventional wisdom, a thinker who therefore offends his friends from time to time.

Oakeshott's interest in religion, history and tradition, and the limitation of state power allies him with other 'conservatives,' and yet his approach to these topics often seems anything but conservative. To define the religious disposition as a determination to live in the present, for example, may strike some as decidedly poetic rather than religious, where our thoughts, we are told, should be profoundly and essentially future oriented: hope for salvation and fear of damnation. Instead of subsuming the past ('history') under the single head of tradition, Oakeshott carefully distinguishes the study of the past for its own sake, which he says has nothing to do with the present, and tradition, which is continuous with the present and intimately related to the future; it is, as he says, a sharing of authority between past, present, and future. And rather than make an argument about the size of government, or its limitation to some basic, minimal or 'enumerated' set of responsibilities and powers, he instead develops a novel and striking argument about the *mode of association.*

In his distinction between enterprise association and civil association, the crucial issue turns out to be whether the state is understood as having some identifiable common purpose or not. If it does, Oakeshott argues, it becomes very difficult to argue that government should be limited. On the contrary, government should be vested with as much power as needed to pursue its purpose with as much vigor as possible. The more sure we are about the desirability of the end to be pursued, the less interested we will be in limiting power and the more we will seek ways to make government effective. In extreme cases, this view results in a complete denial of the value of human individuality, political rights, and legal order. Divergence from the common pursuit, hesitancy to commit to the pursuit, or a tendency to arrest the exercise of power for merely 'technical' legal reasons will be seen as burdens, possibly as crimes or even sin. This criticism of the politics of enterprise association applies with equal force to projects of the political right as well as the left. Whether a regime fosters virtue, seeks global democratization, promotes income equality, or strives for social justice here and abroad, it speaks the language of enterprise association. It is possible for a Republican President in the United States to be a good Wilsonian; and defense spending can as easily add to budget deficits as welfare, medicine, or education.

A civil association, by contrast, is, according to Oakeshott 'the only morally tolerable form of compulsory association.' He is aware, in spite of the fact that some critics have missed the point, that the state is a non-voluntary form of association, where the authorities have a right to use coercion. This is true in both civil and enterprise association; in political life in either mode the question of why we are using coercion will always be a focus of concern. In enterprise association, this is always in relation to the end pursued. The justification of power, or what is sometimes called the legitimacy of the regime, hinges on acceptance of the validity or desirability of the end pursued. This makes not just everyday legislative, executive, and judicial activities contentious, but puts the very basis of the association on the same contentious plane. For, in any moderately diverse association of human beings, there will be differences of opinion as to what ends in life are worth seeking. The decision to devote the resources of the state to the pursuit of one or a few such ends necessarily excludes a significant portion of what a substantial part of the 'city' opines to be their goods. They will be imposed upon for the sake of others' private visions.

In civil association, power is used on an 'as needed' basis. In a large state with a complex economy and social life, we should not be dismayed to find the size of government to be larger than that in a small, less complex country; but in a large state that understands itself as a civil association, we should be surprised to find a desire to use the state's power to mold or transform society. A conservative, Oakeshott says, does not lightly surrender known goods for unknown betters. Civil association will seem most compelling and appropriate whenever we are able to focus on the enjoyment of known goods. When we face crises, feel an overpowering need to address great evils, or respond to external threats, the simple pleasures of living peaceably and commodiously with our neighbors fade, and enterprise association restates its argument, always ready for accomplishment.

Oakeshott's dispositional, non-doctrinaire conservatism is tied to his sensitivity to the poetic dimension of life. It is in 'On Being Conservative' that Oakeshott makes his famous complaint that Rationalism denies 'the poetic character of all human activity' It is an essential part of Oakeshott's conservatism to remind us of poetry and of all those forms of experience that are enjoyable for their own sakes – friendship, play, and non-instrumental modes of association, including non-instrumental political association. It is highly significant that after laying out the basic characteristics of the conservative disposition, Oakeshott makes the point that this disposition is, ultimately, a disposition to enjoy certain kinds of activities. Oakeshott's conservatism is really the attempt to refocus our attention upon activities in which we do not seek constant improvement or innovation because the nature of what is being done does not depend upon the pursuit of results. In defending these kinds of activities, in which the end is in the activity itself, he is of course harkening back to Aristotle and putting himself in opposition to a trend in modern thought about human conduct, which denies that such non-instrumental activity is even possible. However, Oakeshott would argue, with Aristotle, that there is an important difference between activities that have some purpose extrinsic to the activity, typically ones that produce some product or other measurable outcome, and those activities that are ends in themselves. This latter kind of activity has an end in a strikingly different way than activities that produce external ends. The activity is inherently enjoyable; non-necessary; intimately related to the highest human capacities; self-sufficient; and intimately connected to human happiness.

The disposition to enjoy the present, to delight in it, to laugh, implies that the given world as we find it is worth affirming, has much good in it, and may be delightful. And indeed, we find in Oakeshott the affirmation of ordinary human experience that is quite at odds with jeremiads of both the left and right. In spite of being able, at times, to pronounce gloomily on the 'dark ages' we seem in danger of falling into, he never made 'crisis' the central motif of his thought, including his diagnoses of modern ills. Instead, he says:

> In any generation, even the most revolutionary, the arrangements which are enjoyed always far exceed those which are recognized to stand in need of attention, and those which are being prepared for enjoyment are few in comparison with those which receive amendment: the new is an insignificant proportion of the whole.

It may be that this comes down to one's position in some arcane theodicean debates, or perhaps it could be settled by appeal to moral intuition, possibly even to some empirical measurement. In any case, Oakeshott found he could enjoy the world, in spite of living 'after Auschwitz' and in the midst of 'the crisis of modernity.'

On a different plane, Oakeshott's appreciation for civil association also comes from a deep and sensitive reading of the history of political thought, especially in its medieval to modern period, but going all the way back to the ancient Greeks. While the non-purposiveness of civil association has been criticized as unrealistic, we find, especially among those political theorists involved in the modern liberal tradition, a set of ideas, miscellaneous, to be sure, concerning the proper basis of authority, constitutional checks on the use of power, rights and privileges of citizens, governance by rule of law, electoral devices serving both accountability and representation, the application of law to the rulers, and so on, none of which would be very meaningful if the point was to understand how best to empower a government to pursue a common purpose. For, as others have noted, many of these devices make effective and energetic rule more difficult, not easier, and ensure that a state will not stay long upon a single course. It may be that the underlying logic of a major stream of modern thought is to rid governance of the characteristics of purposive activity.

Here, we can resort to a kind of empirical check on Oakeshott's reading. His oft-noted 'preference' for civil association is never framed as a merely moral or political preference. It is a claim about what in the modern world is the dominant ideal – the ideal of individualism. Oakeshott's list of proponents of civil association includes an impressive line-up of major thinkers: Pico della Mirandola, Marsilius of Padua, Montaigne, Hobbes, Pascal, Hume, Kant, Burke, Blake, Locke (usually), the American Founders (in spite of their often 'enterprising' rhetoric), Nietzsche, and of course, Hegel. No doubt, the assertion that such a long list of thinkers belongs to an identifiable tradition, and that it is the tradition of conversation, civility, non-instrumentality, individualism, and play is an extraordinary claim. To put it mildly, there should be material enough for many generations of doctoral studies, should anyone feel it worth their while to sort and sift Oakeshott's reading of the tradition of Western political thought.

While we are imagining Oakeshottian research programs, we need not confine our investigation to modern theorists. Oakeshott argues that civil association is a modern phenomenon, and that ancient and medieval polities are not properly understood as enterprise associations. The yearning for a common enterprise rests in part upon a nostalgic yearning for solidarity that the ancient world is believed to have enjoyed; but this yearning, Oakeshott says, is best understood as a reaction to the modern idea of civil association. What the ancients had was neither civil nor enterprise association, although we can detect traces of both modes in authors quite remote from our own times. A simple example might be Aquinas' denial that human law should suppress all vice (*Summa Theologiae*, 96.2), which might lead one further to deny that the state's power should be used to impose a vision of the good life. More subtly, it might lead one to ask whether a 'common good' is possible where such a vision is pursued. Some versions of enterprise association might even be indicted for impiety. Another interesting example would be Aquinas' great forebear, Aristotle.

Aristotle frames his discussion of political rule by distinguishing it from mastery, and returns to this theme again and again throughout *The Politics*. Late in the book, he deploys a peculiar device in his discussion of the best life: the isolated or single city. His aim is to identify what is essential to politics, again to distinguish political rule from mastery, and to determine to what extent war making is essential to politics, while asking what sort of life is best. If a city existed in isolation, would it still be a city; would it still have something essentially political about it, or does 'politics' occur only in the context of war and the acquisition of power over one's neighbors? Would such a city be 'active'? Aristotle answers that such a city would be active, as god and the philosopher are active; that is, there would be internal activity, activity that has its end in itself. Moreover, he concludes that war making is for the sake of peace, not peace for the sake of war making. The aim, it seems, is to be a self-contained city with good laws, and with nothing to pursue other than to maintain itself in its own character.

Akin to Aristotle's single city, one of the qualities of civil association is its essential non-belligerence. By contrast, enterprise association is 'inherently belligerent; its already purposeful disposition invites that of a state of war.' War is one of the commonest examples of mobilization for a common end. The end is clear, single, and undeniably important: our very survival as a people may be at stake. Other political enterprises often adopt the language of war: a war on poverty, a war on drugs, a war on terror, a *campaign* to reduce illiteracy, a *mission* to protect the environment. In 'The Universities,' Oakeshott takes Sir Walter Moberly to task for adopting war as his image of educational reform. According to Moberly, 'The analogy of wartime experience suggests that to get the most out of a university, it must be enrolled in the service of some cause beyond itself.' Oakeshott's response is worth quoting at length:

> We cannot too often remind ourselves that in politics, and in every other activity, war offers the least fruitful opportunity for profitable change: war is a blind guide to civilized life. In war all that is most superficial in our tradition is encouraged merely because it is useful, even necessary, for victory. Inter arma silent leges is an old adage which can support a wide interpretation; not only are the laws suspended, but the whole balance of the society is disturbed. There are many who have no other idea of social progress than the extrapolation of the character of a society in time of war – the artificial unity, the narrow overmastering purpose, the devotion to a single cause and the subordination of everything to it – all this seems to them inspiring: but the direction of their admiration reveals the emptiness of their souls. Not only is a society just emerged from a shattering war in the worst possible position for making profitable reforms in the universities, but the inspiration of war itself is the most misleading of all inspirations.

With Oakeshott's reminders – about the value of poetry and friendship, the dangers of war as an analogy for political activity, the possibility of delighting in the present – we are invited to reflect on the meaning of conservatism, rather than to be told what conservatives must or must not do. With Oakeshott, this reflection goes well beyond conservatism in the narrow political sense, and leads into the heart of what it means to be associated politically, how we are to understand our relationship to the past and future, and how the modes of human experience compose a multivocal conversation. Oakeshott has been called a nihilist, a romantic, a Burkean, a liberal, a republican, and a conservative. He has been called nicer things, too. It may be that he is a Tory upon Whig premises. His conservatism does not fit today's political categories. Above all, Oakeshott is a philosopher; those looking for an ideology will find him hard going. But those who want a fresh and profound perspective on the most persistent problems in political theory and philosophy will find much in him to enjoy.

This volume brings together a rich collection of essays on several dimensions of Oakeshott's conservatism, without any pretension of comprehensiveness. Although Irving Kristol at one time found Oakeshott too secular others have found in his work a rich vein of reflections on religion: Corey Abel compares Oakeshott's early plan for a work of apology with his thoughts on religion across his career; Todd Breyfogle examines the links between Oakeshott's thoughts on language in poetry and religion; Byron Kaldis explores the 'antinomies' of religion and aesthetic experience in politics; and Ian Tregenza takes up Oakeshott's radical religious modernism. History and tradition play an important role in Oakeshott's thought, and these are discussed deftly in treatments of Oakeshott's approach to the history of political thought, focusing on the idea of law in Greece and Rome by Josiah Lee Auspitz, a critique of Jared Diamond's use and abuse of history by Gene Callahan, and an in depth comparison of Oakeshott with Otto von Gierke by Michael Henkel. Oakeshott has been most often studied in the United States by political theorists, but he has a great deal to offer to contemporary philosophy, and here we have comparisons of Oakeshott, Arendt and Cavell on the theme of education and conversation by Richard Flathman, Oakeshott and Hume on skepticism by Timothy Fuller; Rorty and liberalism by Jeff Rabin; and Oakeshott's place in relation to Romanticism and the Enlightenment by Roy Tseng. Leslie Marsh lays out for us a detailed analysis of the 'knowing how'/'knowing that' distinction in Ryle and relates this to Oakeshott's distinction between technical and practical knowledge; and Stephen Turner explores the precautionary principle. Finally, several authors explore Oakeshott in relation to more directly political concerns, though these are also highly varied: George Feaver discusses Oakeshott in relation to English identity; Ferenc Hörcher traces the ideals of conversation and poetry in relation to classical and modern theories of rhetoric and morals; Kenneth McIntyre examines Oakeshott's place in the charged debate over the character of American politics and American conservatism; and Ivo Mosely reminds us of Oakeshott's capacity for trenchant criticism of the modernity whose friend he claimed to be.

George Feaver passed away before this volume could be completed, but after having approved the near-final version of his essay. Subsequent changes were restricted to minor points of proofreading. As an editor, it was a pleasure to work with George, on both this volume and on *The Intellectual Legacy of Michael Oakeshott*, for which he contributed a fine piece on Oakeshott and representative democracy. He appreciated the effort to refine a piece of writing, and always strove to keep the conversation going. May he rest in peace.

Corey Abel
Denver, Colorado, 2010

I

Religion

Ian Tregenza

Skepticism and Tradition: The Religious Imagination of Michael Oakeshott

Introduction

While Oakeshott is usually described as a philosopher of conservatism for, among other things, his defense of tradition against rationalism, and for his defense of the tradition of limited government, his thought often went in surprisingly non-conservative, even radical directions. He made the claim in his essay 'On Being Conservative' that it is not 'inconsistent to be conservative in respect of government and radical in respect of every other activity.'[1] In the very next sentence he invoked the names of some of the great early modern sceptics – Montaigne, Pascal, Hobbes, and Hume – as best exemplifying the conservative disposition that he favored. As many commentators have noted there is a close connection between Oakeshott's political conservatism and his philosophical skepticism. Oakeshott was a consistent skeptic and it conditioned all aspects of his thought, including his account of religion and tradition.

Along with his Idealist predecessors Oakeshott sought to defend religious experience from some of the exaggerated claims of scientific naturalism as well as the 'critical history', which shaped the theological debates of the late nineteenth and early twentieth centuries. But he did this by making sharp modal distinctions between realms of human experience, and rejecting the teleological interpretation of world history that was a feature of much earlier Idealist thought. Religion, for Oakeshott, completes the world of practice, but it is distinct from history, science, and philosophy. Religion is practical life itself whenever it reaches a certain level of intensity and satisfaction, whereas science, history and philosophy involve an escape from the demands of the practical mode of experience. Likewise, Oakeshott's elaboration of the idea of tradition in the middle period of his career is closely related to his early claim that the world of practice is an autonomous mode of experience. The search for 'rational' foundations, in the form of fixed

---

[1]   Oakeshott, *Rationalism in Politics and other essays, new and expanded edition*, ed. Timothy Fuller (Indianapolis: Liberty Press, 1991), 435. Hereafter: *RIP*.

rules or principles, for ethics, politics or religion – a code of conduct, a bill of rights, a creedal statement – not only involves a failure to appreciate the invariably traditional nature of human experience, it denies the integrity of the practical mode of experience.

In theological circles the themes of tradition and scepticism are not usually run together. Those who defend tradition often do so either because it is said to contain within it the essence of Christianity or because, more generally, it is the vehicle through which truth is revealed. For instance, Jaroslav Pelikan, who has devoted much of his scholarly career to describing the development of the Christian tradition, defends this latter view when he writes that for a tradition not to become a mere idol it must seek to grasp the universal truth of which it is a particular manifestation.[2] In Oakeshott's formulation by contrast, since religion belongs wholly to the practical mode of experience the truth it discloses is conditioned by practical imperatives. Indeed, in his belief in the essentially practical import of religion and religious ideas – God, immortality, salvation – Oakeshott's account has much in common with the anti-metaphysical thrust of much twentieth century theology, from Albert Schweitzer and Rudolf Bultmann to Don Cupitt. The aims of this paper are twofold. The first is to establish the connections between one of the best-known themes of Oakeshott's writings – the concept of tradition – and his less well-known religious writings. The second aim is to identify some links between these writings and broader trends in modern 'radical' theology.

Religion And The End Of 'Faith In History'

Oakeshott's radical distinction between the different modes of experience is usually described in terms of tendencies within the tradition of British Idealism. That is, he takes over from writers such as Bradley and Bosanquet the idea of orders or degrees of reality but he pushes their separation further than any of his predecessors. An equally important source of this modal separatism comes from his engagement with early twentieth century theological debates centered on the relationship between history and Christian belief.

Much of Oakeshott's early writing addresses theological matters, and reflects the key concerns of church historians and theologians of the time. Of particular concern was the relation between history and Christianity. As is well known, during the latter part of the nineteenth and in the early twentieth centuries many church historians were obsessed with questions concerning the historical Jesus and searching out the essence of Christianity. These were the concerns particularly of liberal theologians who saw themselves as continuing the work of the Reformation, by stripping away the accretions of the centuries to return to a pure form of the faith. It was believed that the more sophisticated historical methods that scholars had developed in the nineteenth century provided the means for a more penetrating analysis of such questions. And with typical nineteenth century optimism historians set about the task of discovering the historical Jesus and with it the essence of

---

[2] Jaroslav Pelikan, *The Vindication of Tradition* (New Haven and London: Yale Univ. Press, 1984), 56.

Christianity. The purpose of all these endeavors was not primarily historical – at least in Oakeshott's sense of seeking to understand the past for its own sake – but was shaped by practical concerns. This was true not only of liberal theologians but also of someone like John Henry Newman whose turn to the history of the early church resulted in a significant change in his religious practice. Pelikan describes Newman as both rediscovering tradition intellectually, as well as recovering it for existential reasons.[3] But this optimism about what historical studies could reveal about the past in order to inform current religious practice was coming under attack in the first two decades of the twentieth century.

Two important figures in this are Ernst Troelstch and Albert Schweitzer, who, in different ways, could be understood as signaling the exhaustion of this endeavor, what might be called the loss of faith in history. Schweitzer did this by revealing a Jesus completely unlike the liberal/humanitarian of the liberals' projection:

> The Jesus of Nazareth who appeared as the Messiah, proclaimed the kingdom of God, established the kingdom of heaven upon earth, and died in order to consecrate his work – this Jesus never existed. It is a figure sketched by Rationalism, enlivened by Liberalism, and dressed up by modern theology in the clothes of historical science.[4]

Far from revealing a Jesus who would confirm the optimistic ethical sensibilities of the nineteenth century, Schweitzer discovers a Jesus who is a stranger to us, a tragic figure whose expectations of the coming supernatural Kingdom were not realized. 'The study of the life of Jesus,' says Schweitzer,

> has had a curious history. It set out in quest of the historical Jesus, believing that when it found Him it could bring Him straight into our time as a Teacher and Saviour.... But He does not stay; He passes by our time and returns to His own. What surprised and dismayed the theology of the last forty years was that, despite all forced and arbitrary interpretations, it could not keep Him in our time, but had to let him go. He returned to His own time, not owing to the application of any historical ingenuity, but by the same inevitable necessity by which the liberated pendulum returns to its original position.[5]

Don Cupitt suggests that the paradox of liberal Christianity is that it failed at the moment of its own success.[6] The attempt to discover, through historical method, the Jesus of history, and therefore the essence of Christianity (being realized in modern humanitarianism) was to discover a Jesus completely alien to the modern world.

Schweitzer himself shared with the liberals a faith in history's capacity to reveal the true Jesus. But 'after him,' says Cupitt, 'it was no longer possible to identify faith's approach to scripture with that of critical reason. After him, faith and reason drew apart: it was one thing to study the New Testament in a strictly critical and

[3]   Pelikan, *Vindication of Tradition*, ch. 2.
[4]   Albert Schweitzer, *The Mystery of the Kingdom of God*, cited in E. N. Mozley, *The Theology of Albert Schweitzer* (London: Albert and Charles Black, 1950), 10, 11.
[5]   Schweitzer, *Quest of the Historical Jesus*, cited in Mozley, *Theology of Albert Schweitzer*, 12, 13.
[6]   Don Cupitt, *The Sea of Faith: Christianity in Change* (London: British Broadcasting Corporation, 1984), 106.

objective spirit, and it was another thing to make a faith-judgement in response to what you had read.'[7] Moreover, post-Schweitzer, there is no way of determining the right interpretation of scripture, no divinely packaged truth in scripture, no 'true' Jesus. There is rather, a 'challenge to religious creativity.'[8]

Like Schweitzer, Troeltsch tried to combine the role of the historian with that of the Christian apologist. He believed that the historian would view Christian history differently if he thought it had a future. Where Schweitzer sought to discover the historical Jesus, Troeltsch sought to discern the essence of Christianity. Troeltsch's historicism leads to the conclusion that Christianity is simply one tradition among many. Moreover, the essence of Christianity is shaped by historical development and will in fact be different in different epochs. The effect of this is to undermine the idea of essence. Karl Barth thought he was the last theologian of the nineteenth century – the culmination of liberal theology.[9] Others have seen him as the first theologian of the twentieth and as paving the way for post modernism.[10] The main point to stress here is that Troeltsch's turn to historical method, which was meant to solve certain problems in theology and apologetics, raised as many questions as it settled.[11]

So Oakeshott writes his early essays on religion, and his first major philosophical treatise, *Experience and Its Modes* in the light of these developments: We might call it the crisis of faith in history, or at least the point at which history and theology, or history and religious thinking part company. After Schweitzer and Troelstch theologians were more circumspect about what history could recover, what could be claimed about history. One response was to turn away from history towards dogmatic theology. Karl Barth is representative of this move. Another response is represented by what might loosely be called radical theology – some key figures here are Bultmann, Tillich and, more recently, Cupitt. Here the aim is to save religious experience in the wake of the loss of faith in history, and indeed metaphysics. To put it in more positive terms, the end of history or the end of metaphysics is sometimes thought of as providing the opportunity for discovering a more authentic understanding of religious experience – authenticity being a key word particularly for existentialists such as Bultmann and Tillich.

Earlier Idealists such as T.H. Green, Edward Caird, and Henry Jones defended religion by making an ally of the new critical history and science. Such developments were understood in teleological terms, as the products of the unfolding of mind, which, far from destroying religion, pointed in fact to the spiritual nature of the universe. By the 1920s – post World War I, and post-Schweitzer – this optimism about the unity of knowledge and specifically about the possibility of

---

[7]   Cupitt, *Sea of Faith*, 110.
[8]   Cupitt, *Sea of Faith*, 112.
[9]   See Garrett E. Paul, 'Why Troelstch? Why Today? Theology for the 21st Century,' available at: www.Religion-online.org. Accessed on 30 May 2006. First published in *The Christian Century*, (30 June–7 July 1993): 676–81.
[10] Max L. Stackhouse, 'A Premature Postmodern,' *First Things*, 106 (October, 2000): 19–22.
[11] For a discussion of these themes, see S. W. Sykes, 'Ernst Troeltsch and Christianity's Essence,' in John Powell Clayton ed., *Ernst Troeltsch and the Future of Theology* (Cambridge: Cambridge Univ. Press, 1976).

history delivering practically useful judgments about religion was not so easy to maintain.[12]

In various places in the late 1920s Oakeshott is critical of the faith in history that had characterized the recent past. In his 1928 essay, 'The Importance of the Historical Element in Christianity' Oakeshott mentions Troeltsch's *Der Historismus und seine Probleme* and Schweitzer's *Civilization and Ethics* as works that represent this tendency to overstate the importance of history for religion. A faith in what he calls the *prima facie* historical or the historical as such, is not necessary to religion, and is the product of a particular *Weltanschauung*. This has, no doubt, been part of Christian history, particularly in recent years, but he thinks it is on the wane. 'As far as our civilization is concerned,' he writes, 'so much belief in history seems to be working its own ruin; the intellectual energy of our generation is turning in other directions, and the power to stand on the point of the present is returning.'[13] We get in this essay an early articulation of Oakeshott's life-long interest in distinguishing the practical from the historical pasts.[14] Not only does religion not need history; it is better off without it. 'What religion demands is not a consciousness of the necessity and individuality of past events, but a consciousness of the individuality of present experience … religion is nothing if not contemporary' (*RPML*, 72).

One of the effects of this bracketing of history, the separation of history from practice, is to undermine any teleological reading of history. History is not heading towards a necessary goal or end point. We therefore do not turn to history to discover a guide to present behavior. We can turn to the past for guidance, but not to history. To make too much of history for religious experience is a form of idolatry (*RPML*, 72). In his 1929 essay 'Religion and the World' he says that 'conscience has made cowards of some generations, history and tradition of others, but a generation which would be religious must be courageous enough to achieve a life that is really contemporary' (*RPML*, 36). The practical past provides a resource whose value is to be traded in the present.

---

[12] Some later Idealists, such as R. G. Collingwood and Clement C. J. Webb, continued to defend a unified conception of knowledge up to the Second World War. For some discussion see my, 'Collingwood, Oakeshott and Webb on the "Historical Element" in Religion,' *Collingwood and British Idealism Studies*, 13, no. 2 (2007): 93–117. The following three paragraphs draw on this article.

[13] Oakeshott, *Religion, Politics and the Moral Life*, ed. Timothy Fuller (New Haven and London: Yale Univ. Press, 1993), 69. Hereafter: *RPML*.

[14] In his early piece, 'An Essay on the Relations of Poetry, Religion and Reality' which Luke O'Sullivan dates at 1925, Oakeshott did not yet make a distinction between the practical and the historical pasts. Indeed, he says he borrows from Schweitzer's view (which in turn is similar to Croce's) that the purpose of understanding the past is to make it live in the present. 'Chronicle is dead history: if we wish to get at the truth we must make it live. The only true source of our knowledge of the life of Christ lies in actual communion with Him at the present time. We must experience the facts of history before we can win from them their truth,' in *What is History? And other essays*, ed. Luke O'Sullivan (Exeter: Imprint Academic, 2004), 111 n. 102. In many ways this piece bears the hallmarks of the absolute idealism of an earlier generation. Philosophy and Poetry are described as different ways to reality, which is conceived in monistic terms. For a discussion of the development of Oakeshott's idea of modality during the 1920s see Efraim Podoksik's 'The Idealism of Young Oakeshott' in James Connelly and Stamatoula Panagakou, eds., *Aspects of Idealism: Selected Essays* (Oxford: Peter Lang, forthcoming).

A similar claim is made in another early piece called 'Culture and Despotism.'[15] Here Oakeshott defends a view of culture as personal, as opposed to one of mere acquisition, either of information (the crude encyclopedic view), or of Matthew Arnold's more sophisticated idea of culture as 'the best that has been thought and known in the world.' The encyclopedic view sets up a distinction between Culture and Ignorance and the 'classical' view opposes Culture to Anarchy. In the view of culture that Oakeshott recommends, 'nothing is essential but an integrated self whose purpose is not to remember, adopt or assimilate, but to live a life contemporary with itself. The past and future are nothing to it except in so far as they come alive in the present.' Only this third view, Oakeshott thinks, has an adequate answer to mortality. It does not lead to a feverish activity, nor to a desire for a 'classic' permanence, but to a determination to find an altogether extemporary satisfaction in life. What is valued is not the fruit of experience, but the flower – something we know only in a present enjoyment and cannot garner. Death is not outrun; it is denied, dismissed.

He goes on to say (in providing an exposition of J. C. Powys' work, *The Meaning of Culture*, which articulates this view), 'Culture is then, a way of life, a religion. It does not imply that we consider our own path the noblest or the wisest, but simply that we know it to be our own and value it as such.' This view of Culture is opposed, not to Ignorance or Anarchy, but Despotism – the despotism of mankind's accumulated achievements[16] or an imagined external standard of perfection.

The sources of Oakeshott's concern with present subjective experience at this time are no doubt many. Podoksik suggests that it is a reflection of the 'life philosophy' that was then current in European (and especially German) intellectual circles.[17] Oakeshott mentions in passing both Epicurus and Montaigne as holding to something like the view of culture he outlines. Perhaps we can also add the name of Walter Pater whose work Oakeshott greatly admired and whose two historical novels (*Marius the Epicurean* and *Gaston de Latour*) are centered on characters who engage with the ideas of Epicurus and Montaigne in their quests for spiritual understanding. There are indeed some suggestive parallels between Pater and Oakeshott. *Gaston de Latour* was one of Oakeshott's favorite novels and he identified with the book's protagonist[18] – a priest who loses his faith and who seeks out the company of Montaigne. Pater himself identified with Marius and *Gaston de Latour* was written as a sequel to the earlier work – 'a sort of Marius in France.'[19] *Marius* itself was written as a rather thinly disguised autobiographical defense of Pater's notorious conclusion to *The Renaissance* where he had outraged

---

[15] Oakeshott, 'Culture and Despotism,' *The Cambridge Review*, 51 (May 2, 1930): 367–8.
[16] Or what C. S. Lewis referred to as 'the fatal serialism of the modern imagination – the image of infinite unilinear progression that so haunts our minds.' *The Abolition of Man* (Oxford: Oxford Univ. Press, 1943; Glasgow: William Collins Sons & Co., 1978).
[17] Podoksik, 'Idealism of Young Oakeshott.'
[18] Timothy Fuller mentioned this at the Third Plenary Meeting of the Michael Oakeshott Association, in Colorado Springs, CO, June 2006. See also his discussion in 'An Introduction: Michael Oakeshott's Achievement,' *The Political Science Reviewer*, 21 (Spring 1992): 1–15.
[19] Walter Pater, 'Letter to Mrs. Humphrey Ward,' cited in Michael Levey, 'Introduction' to Walter Pater, *Marius the Epicurean* (Harmondsworth: Penguin, 1985), 13.

many with his 'hedonistic' and 'subjectivist' calls to live in the present with a 'sense of the splendor of our experience and of its awful brevity.' The appropriate response to the tyranny of time is to engage in activities that carry their own intrinsic reward at the moment in which they occupy us – 'some mood of passion or insight or intellectual excitement is irresistibly real and attractive to us, – for that moment only. Not the fruit of experience, but experience itself, is the end.... To burn always with this hard, gem-like flame, to maintain this ecstasy, is success in life. In a sense, it might even be said that our failure is to form habits.' For Pater it is in artistic experience that this sensibility is most intensely felt, since 'art comes to you proposing frankly to give nothing but the highest quality to your moments as they pass, and simply for those moments' sake.'[20]

The idea of forms of experience that carry their own intrinsic reward is one of the central features of all of Oakeshott's thought, and his early writings on religion and culture in particular convey a Pater-like mood. Podoksik makes the point that the writings from the late 1920s are marked by 'pathos,' a 'lack of irony' and even a kind of 'religious narcissism' that would disappear in Oakeshott's later work.[21] Perhaps he came to recognize the same limitations of this 'subjectivism' that Pater himself identified when he suggested in relation to Marius' development, that

> Cyrenaicism is ever the characteristic philosophy of youth, ardent, but narrow in its survey – sincere, but apt to become one-sided, or even fanatical. It is one of those subjective and partial ideals, based on vivid, because limited, apprehension of the truth of one aspect of experience (in this case, of the beauty of the world and of the brevity of man's life there) that it may be said to be the special vocation of the young to express.[22]

The concluding paragraph to Oakeshott's 1956 essay 'On Being Conservative' strikes a similar tone. If we read this autobiographically it looks as if Oakeshott is revising some of his earlier enthusiasms:

> Everybody's young days are a dream, a delightful insanity, a sweet solipsism. Nothing in them has a fixed shape, nothing a fixed price; everything is a possibility, and we live happily on credit.... The world is a mirror in which we seek the reflection of our desires.... The allure of violent emotions is irresistible.... We are not apt to distinguish between our liking and our esteem; urgency is our criterion of importance; and we do not easily understand that what is humdrum need not be despicable. We are impatient of restraint; and we believe, like Shelley, that to have contracted a habit is to have failed.

But this way of being in the world cannot last and 'for most,' Oakeshott continues,

---

[20] Pater, *The Renaissance: Studies in Art and Poetry*, ed. Adam Phillips (Oxford: Oxford Univ. Press, 1986), 152–3. For further discussion of the relationship between Oakeshott and Pater see Elizabeth Campbell Corey's *Michael Oakeshott on Religion, Aesthetics and Politics* (Columbia and London: University of Missouri Press, 2006), 67–71 and 120–1.
[21] Podoksik, 'Idealism of Young Oakeshott.'
[22] Pater, *Marius the Epicurean*, 181.

[T]here is what Conrad called the 'shadow line' which, when we pass it, discloses a solid world of things, each with its own point of balance, each with its price; a world of fact, not poetic image, in which what we have spent on one thing we cannot spend on another; a world inhabited by others besides ourselves who cannot be reduced to mere reflections of our own emotions. (*RIP*, 436–7)

The point he is making here is that the 'virtues' of youth are not those that are suitable for politics. But perhaps implicit in this passage is the idea that in the quixotic character of youth there is a special religious insight. Where politics demands a consequentialist attitude to the world, religion is concerned primarily with a certain kind of sensibility that reconciles us to the 'dissonances' of human life. This is developed at greater length in the distinction that he would develop in *On Human Conduct* between self-disclosure and self-enactment. The former entails intentions to bring about change in the world, the latter is not directly related to external consequences, but to an agent's self understanding – 'conduct released from its character as a response to a contingent situation.' 'Here,' Oakeshott continues, 'doing is delivered, at least in part, from the deadliness of doing, a deliverance gracefully enjoyed in the quiet of a religious faith.'[23]

While there is little trace in Oakeshott's later writings of the 'pathos' that marked his youthful religious reflections, there is no fundamental change in his understanding of religion as a particular kind of experience centered on the present and indifferent to worldly achievement.

Tradition, Religion, and the Identity of Christianity

As mentioned earlier, both religion and tradition are closely connected in Oakeshott's account of practical experience. In *Experience and Its Modes* he wrote that religion 'is not a particular form of practical experience; it is merely practical experience at its fullest.'[24] Further, '[t]here is no exact point in the conduct of life at which religion can be said to begin. Religion differs from other forms of practical activity, not in kind, but in degree; it is characterized everywhere by intensity and strength of devotion and by singleness of purpose' (*EM*, 295). So religion is in fact synonymous with practical experience at its most satisfying level – the level at which there is as much coherence as possible between 'what is' (fact) and what 'ought to be' (value).

Likewise, tradition is very closely related to the concept of practice in that it largely takes the place of the practical mode of experience in Oakeshott's post war writings. W. H. Greenleaf for one sees Oakeshott's use of tradition as another way of describing the concrete universal – 'a concrete entity which, like the historical individual, continues in some sense the same through all the changes it

---

[23] Oakeshott, *On Human Conduct* (Oxford: Clarendon Press, 1975), 73–4. Hereafter: *OHC*. Oakeshott suggests that a certain nonchalance in the face of uncertainty in achieving our goals was strong in Epicureanism and Stoicism (*OHC*, 73 n. 1).

[24] Oakeshott, *Experience and Its Modes* (Cambridge: Cambridge Univ. Press, 1933), 292. Hereafter: *EM*.

undergoes.'[25] Here Oakeshott's idea of traditional behavior as involving the pursuit of intimations is very similar to the account in *Experience and Its Modes* of practical experience as the never ending endeavor to make the world of 'what is' conform to the world of 'what ought to be'.

For someone who has been described as a traditionalist, Oakeshott in fact says surprisingly little about tradition; and, it is certainly not treated with the sort of reverence characteristic of someone like Burke. Traditions are simply the inescapable context for all current action.[26] They are not to be worshipped or venerated. They do not reveal the ways of providence, nor do they embody Wisdom or Reason – 'there is no sovereign purpose to be perceived or invariable direction to be detected; there is no model to be copied, idea to be realized, or rule to be followed' (*RIP*, 61) – but they do provide us with a set of resources on which we can draw. When too much, or the wrong sort of emphasis is accorded tradition then we have what might be called 'traditionalism'. And Oakeshott would undoubtedly endorse Pelikan's claim that 'tradition is the living faith of the dead, traditionalism is the dead faith of the living.'[27] Indeed, they both invoke the same lines from Goethe's *Faust* to underline the importance of appropriating tradition for present purposes:

Was du ererbt von deinen Vätern hast,
Erwirb es, um es zu besitzen.
(What you have as heritage,
Take now as task;
For thus you will make it your own!)[28]

Traditionalism in this sense is not unlike what Oakeshott refers to as worldliness – the belief that things have value apart from the insights they bring to the present experience of individuals. For the worldly a successful life is measured in external results and achievements, and in the contribution it makes to the stockpile of goods or knowledge. On this view, 'history and tradition ... acquire an exaggerated importance, and the legacy of the past is often appropriated mechanically, as one might inherit an incipient disease or a volume in a foreign language' (*RPML*, 31).

Where tradition in the modern world is usually counterposed to change and innovation, for Oakeshott and Pelikan[29] a stagnant or ossified tradition is a contradiction in terms, a mere simulacrum of a concrete manner of living. For Oakeshott the mutability of tradition is linked to the way that the practical mode of experience is conceptualized. Whereas the worlds of science and history,

[25] W. H. Greenleaf, *Oakeshott's Philosophical Politics* (London: Longmans, 1966), 55.
[26] Luke O'Sullivan makes a similar point in *Oakeshott on History* (Exeter: Imprint Academic, 2003), 112.
[27] Pelikan, *Vindication of Tradition*, 65.
[28] Oakeshott cites these lines in his essay 'Religion and the World' (*RPML*, 33); Pelikan in an epigraph to *The Vindication of Tradition*. (I have borrowed Pelikan's translation.) Oakeshott uses the following two lines as well: Was man nicht nutzt, ist eine schwere Last,/Nur was der Augenblick erschafft, das kann er nutzen.
[29] Cf. Alasdair MacIntyre, *After Virtue: A Study In Moral Theory* (London: Duckworth, 1985), ch. 15.

for instance, assume 'a world of facts that does not change or move,' practical experience presupposes change. 'The world of fact in practice is the world of 'what is' at this moment; it is the present as such. What cannot change cannot, for practice, be a fact' (*EM*, 263). Likewise, a tradition of behavior 'is neither fixed nor finished … [though] some parts of it may change more slowly than others … none is immune from change … everything is temporary, but nothing is arbitrary' (*RIP*, 61). This understanding of human life as temporal or evanescent is central to the way that Oakeshott theorizes both religion and tradition. Religion provides us with a means by which we can be reconciled to this condition,[30] whereas tradition offers a degree of stability amidst the change and with it resources to negotiate this change.

In perhaps his most well known passage on the nature of tradition Oakeshott mentions the Christian religion as an example of what he has in mind (*RIP*, 61 n). What he has to say here about the identity of tradition in general clearly echoes his earlier reflections on the identity of Christianity. Later in his career it is developed further in his account of the historical characters civil and enterprise association. Here I want to focus on the earlier work, and in particular on the implications that his view of the identity of Christianity has for its current practice. While the passage on tradition in 'Political Education' is well known, the following passage on the identity of Christianity in an earlier review is not. It is worth quoting at length as much of it is subsequently worked into his account of tradition:

> i. The notion that there has been no development or change is indefensible both historically and logically. ii. The identity of a historical phenomenon cannot be preserved by mere adherence to a fixed original datum, because (a) there can be no identity without a real change of some sort, and (b) there is no fixed original datum for us to adhere to. iii. If there has been change and development there must also be an identity, for without an identity there can be no change. Christianity is neither a bottle filled once and for all time, nor one into which anything may be poured so long as the label is retained. iv…. What we must keep hold of is the fact that we are discussing the development of a world of ideas, and consequently any 'physical' analogy is bound to be misleading. Ideas are not like bricks to be added one above another, nor are they like the pieces of a jig-saw puzzle merely to be replaced by one another. The first idea we have is in no sense the 'foundation' of all that grows from it; nor may a later stage be tested by comparing it with a former. In the development of a world of ideas a former stage, as such, is always lost in a later, and there can be no returning. v. We must give up speaking of the 'essence of Christianity' if that means merely 'the most important part of Christianity'. Whatever Christianity is it is not its 'essence' unless that be taken to mean the whole of it.[31]

Here Oakeshott is making a philosophical or theoretical point about historical identity, and thereby how best to come to grips with the identity of Christianity. When he writes about tradition in 'Political Education' he has a more practical

---

[30] In *On Human Conduct* he would describe the 'central concern' of religion as reconciliation to the 'futility' of the human condition, a 'reconciliation to nothingness' (*OHC*, 83–4).

[31] Oakeshott 'Review of G. G. Atkins, *The Making of the Christian Mind*,' in *Journal of Theological Studies*, 31 (1930): 203–8, at 207–8. I have also discussed this passage in my *Michael Oakeshott on Hobbes: A Study in the Renewal of Philosophical Ideas* (Exeter: Imprint Academic, 2003), 141–2.

agenda – to combat the mistake of Rationalism.[32] Nevertheless, this view of the identity of Christianity is not without practical implications. After all, at different times he describes Christianity as our tradition, our way of life, or our civilization. How we think about what has historically been described as an historical religion cannot but affect our practical understanding of religion. What are the implications?

Oakeshott is here dismissing the whole endeavor of the nineteenth and early twentieth centuries to discover the historical Jesus as well as the essence of Christianity. The principle of a tradition (or historical identity) is continuity. There is nothing behind or before a tradition. Indeed, as church historians have known for at least one hundred and fifty years, the gospels themselves are a record of traditions about Jesus. As Pelikan puts it: 'Tradition there certainly was, even before and within the Bible and not simply after the Bible: tradition was in Grelot's phrase, the "source and environment of Scripture".'[33] Though it has been popular since the Reformation to make a distinction between gospel and tradition, this is a mistake. In the beginning was not 'the word'. In the beginning was tradition and this means interpretation – 'no line is possible between what has come to men and their interpretation of what has come to them.'[34] 'Christianity' Oakeshott argues, 'cannot be simply Jesus' religion because at present, it involves ideas or beliefs about Him and about His death.'[35] Not only is there no original datum on which a tradition is based, there is no core or essential element lying behind the various historical manifestations of Christianity. There is no distinction between essence and accident (*RIP*, 61–2).

In a book very much in the 'tradition' of radical theology called *God in Us*,[36] Anthony Freeman asks whether his reinterpretation of Christianity involves a repackaging of the same faith as his ancestors or whether it is a different faith, and he comes to the conclusion that he offers not 'just a different *interpretation* of the same essential core, but a *different faith*. This is because there is no essence or inner core. Re-interpretation is not like peeling the layers off an onion: the interpretation goes all the way down. All is interpretation. That *is* the essence.'[37]

This is consistent with Oakeshott's view of historical identity, which implies both change as well as difference. Indeed, he claims that 'identity, so far from excluding differences, is meaningless in their absence, just as difference or change depend upon something whose identity is not destroyed by that change.' 'On this view of identity,' Oakeshott continues,

---

[32] It has to be said that the distinction between practical and historical traditions is not always clearly delineated in Oakeshott. See O'Sullivan *Oakeshott on History* (Exeter: Imprint Academic, 2004), 113.

[33] Pelikan, *Vindication of Tradition*, 9.

[34] This line from F.J.A. Hort's *The Way, the Truth and the Life* Oakeshott uses in his discussion of Hobbes's treatment of scripture. See Oakeshott, *Hobbes on Civil Association* (Indianapolis: Liberty Fund, 1975), 53.

[35] Oakeshott, 'Review of Atkins, *Making of the Christian Mind*,' 205.

[36] Anthony Freeman, *God in Us: A Case for Christian Humanism* (London: SCM Press 1993; Exeter: Imprint Academic, 2001).

[37] Freeman, *God in Us*, 59.

[T]he characteristic of being Christian may properly be claimed by any doctrine, idea or practice which, no matter whence it came, has been or can be drawn into the general body of the Christian tradition without altogether disturbing its unity or breaking down its consistency. This means that an idea or practice may properly be Christian which, in part at least, runs counter to much that had previously been regarded as Christian. It means, also, that the identity of our religion is maintained, not in spite of, but because of, differences and changes (*RPML*, 67).

The theological implications of this principle of qualitative continuity are in fact quite radical. While some parts of a tradition or an historical identity will change slowly and other parts more rapidly, nothing 'is immune from change' (*RIP*, 61). Over time the concrete detail of a tradition may in fact change completely. His argument then is that 'we can change much without ceasing to be Christian' (*RPML*, 70). The concrete expression of Christianity may be completely different today than that of, say, primitive or medieval Christianity, but it is no less Christian.

Early Christianity, Radical Theology

This view of the Christian tradition provides great scope for creativity. Indeed, in the passage on tradition from 'Political Education' Oakeshott writes that 'nothing that ever belonged to it [a tradition] is completely lost; we are always swerving back to recover and make something topical out of even its remotest moments' (*RIP*, 61). In his early religious writings in particular, Oakeshott is engaged in a work of excavation of this sort.

The most notable example of this can be found in his essay 'Religion and the World,' where Oakeshott returns to the experience of the early church for inspiration. The early Christian community was united in a belief in the imminent return of Jesus, a belief that has no necessary claim on us. Yet this awareness of living at the end of time gave the early Christians a heightened sensitivity to the immediacy of existence and the transience of the present order of things, a sensitivity that we need to recover, Oakeshott thinks, if we are to live religiously. Oakeshott's recovery of the spirit (though not the essence) of primitive Christianity for a present understanding of faith is very much in keeping with twentieth century radical protestant writers including Schweitzer, Bultmann, and Cupitt.

Though undoubtedly there are important differences between these writers, they all have an interest in recovering something of the spirit of early Christianity for the present conduct of faith. For Bultmann this famously involved 'demythologizing' the gospels in order to discern the authentic early Christian experience, which, he thought, could be described in the terms of contemporary existential thought. For Schweitzer it entailed an appreciation of the role that the idea of the Kingdom of God played in the early Jesus movement, and translating this into a modern idiom without its supernatural connotations. Schweitzer describes the contemporary relevance of the idea of the Kingdom as follows:

[O]nly as it comes to be understood as something ethical and spiritual, rather than supernatural, as something to be realised rather than expected, can the Kingdom of God regain, in our faith, the force that it had for Jesus and the early Church. Christianity must have a firm hold of this, if it is to remain true to itself, as it was at the beginning, – religion dominated by the idea of the Kingdom of God. What the Kingdom of God is in reality is shown by the part which it plays in the life of faith. The precise conception which is held of its coming is a matter of secondary consideration.[38]

The challenge for faith today, according to Schweitzer, is to affirm life in the face of the non-arrival of the Kingdom, whether the Kingdom refers to belief in the literal rule of God on earth or a providential understanding of history.

More recently Cupitt has described what he terms 'Kingdom theology' which he thinks is truer to the spirit of Jesus and his early followers than ecclesiastical or church religion. Cupitt's reading of church history, like Oakeshott's, owes much to Schweitzer. For Cupitt, Kingdom theology is immediate, non-dualist (whether sacred/profane or natural/supernatural), belief-less, and shaped by a sense of the transience of existence. Ecclesiastical religion, which is mediated and focused on the afterlife, came about, says Cupitt, in response to the non-arrival of the Kingdom. At first Jesus was said to be hidden with God and he would reveal himself and usher in the Kingdom. Over time the Kingdom is 'deferred so far into the future that it effectively vanishes over the horizon of history.' The church becomes permanent and establishes sacraments that must be performed and doctrines that must be believed if one is to secure one's salvation at the end of time. This present life becomes little more than the waiting room for future reward in the afterlife. 'You are not preparing for [Jesus] to come to you: you are preparing yourself to go to him. Life is spent in readying oneself for death.'[39] It is time, Cupitt thinks, for Christianity to overturn ecclesiastical, mediated religion and return to Kingdom religion – 'the reformation of Christianity must proceed by going back to the beginning in order to go forwards.... The Kingdom is purely of this present world; it is a new ethic, and a new way of relating oneself to life.' 'Kingdom religion,' he writes,

> is simply a way of living, which is popularly described as living life to the full, or to its fullest.... In its contemporary form it passionately loves what is living and only transient, *just for being transient*. Church religion is ulterior, long-termist and thinking ahead, whereas Kingdom religion is intensely focused upon the Moment, the here and now, and is oblivious of everything else. It hasn't time even to *think* about cosmology: it lives at the end of the world. Church religion thinks and waits patiently. Kingdom religion *burns*: it is in a hurry because it understands that we are already in our last days. There is not much time left.[40]

For Cupitt, as for Oakeshott, the early church's sense of living at the end of time meant that present experience was infused with a special significance. If the end was near at hand it was futile to be too prudent, too calculating, too future oriented. For Oakeshott, this belief 'in the coming dissolution of the world was as

---

[38] Schweitzer, 'The Conception of the Kingdom of God in the Transformation of Eschatology,' in Mozley, *The Theology of Albert Schweitzer*, 102.

[39] Cupitt, *Reforming Christianity* (Santa Rosa: Polebridge Press, 2001), 7.

[40] Cupitt, *Reforming Christianity*, 54.

much the expression of a certain scale of values as it was a crude expectation of an historical event. Fundamentally he [the Christian believer] believed that history and the natural world must be held subservient to him, his life and his purposes' (*RPML*, 30). The point for us is to learn to live with the sort of immediacy that characterized the early Christian experience, rejecting the world's criteria of success – achievement, career, contribution to the stockpile of knowledge – and replacing it with a conception of human life which carries 'in each of its moments its whole meaning and value' (*RPML*, 32). Where the world sees immortality in 'some far distant, future perfection of the race' or in 'the hoarded achievements of men,' and asks us to spend our lives in its service, a religious view of life finds immortality revealed in present experience (*RPML*, 37).

We find another reference to early Christianity in Oakeshott's 1948 essay 'The Tower of Babel.' In keeping with the shift in mood noted earlier, this essay is more somber than that of his essays from the late 1920s and early 1930s where he detected the awakening of a new religious sensibility. 'The Tower of Babel' has what might be called a therapeutic aim. He says in concluding the piece that 'the only purpose to be served by this investigation of our predicament is to disclose the corrupt consciousness, the self-deception which reconciles us to our misfortune' (*RIP*, 487).

In this essay he is interested in uncovering the origins of a view of morality understood as the 'self-conscious pursuit of ideals.' He suggests that our current obsession to find a 'foundation' for our moral life in a set of principles or codified rules can, in part, be traced back to the second and third centuries of the Christian era, where there was a translation of Christianity as a way of life or a set of customs, to a grammar of belief – 'a conversion parallel to the change from faith in a person to belief in a collection of abstract propositions.' It came about for a variety of reasons including collapsing customs, barbarian invasions, the need to have a package of beliefs that could be 'exported' to those who had no experience of Christianity as a tradition (*RIP*, 484–6). The European moral consciousness has, ever since this time, been infected by the belief that a moral life based on explicit rules and precepts is superior to a tradition of moral conduct.

Conclusion

No doubt there are many points where Oakeshott and Cupitt would disagree on which parts of the Christian tradition are worth preserving or reviving. For instance, Oakeshott was a great admirer of Augustine, whereas for Cupitt, Augustine is one of the chief culprits in the establishment of ecclesiastical Christianity. There are also clearly parts of the Christian tradition – such as Pelagianism and Gnosticism – that Oakeshott sees as harmful and as resurfacing in modern times in the form of Rationalism. Yet at least on Oakeshott's view of historical identity, Pelagianism and Gnosticism are no less Christian than the Christianity of the early Jesus movement. When we do away with the idea that a tradition has an essence or an inner core holding it together, then we also have to give up on the idea that there is a historical or a rational basis for preferring one expression of the tradition to another. For many Christian or religious believers this is no doubt a disconcerting prospect, but it also opens the space for great religious creativity. On this view tradition is not a hindrance to individual self-creation or self-fashioning, but a valuable resource, which provides no fixed anchor but it does provide depth. To learn how to become an individual, or to 'become a Christian in Christendom' (as Kierkegaard put it), is at the same time to learn how to draw on a tradition, to make it live in our present experience. This is a creative endeavor not so different from the activity of the artist or the poet. The Australian poet A. D. Hope, who was himself known as something of a traditionalist, expressed this relationship between tradition and creativity in the following terms:

> Yet the myths will not fit us ready made,
> It is the meaning of the poet's trade
> To re-create the fables and revive
> In men the energies by which they live,
> To reap the ancient harvests, plant again
> And gather in the visionary grain,
> And to transform the same unchanging seed
> Into the gospel-bread on which they feed.[41]

---

[41] A. D. Hope, 'An Epistle from Holofernes' (1960), in *Selected Poetry and Prose*, ed. David Brooks, (Sydney: Halstead Press, 2000), 50. Three recent studies that deal at length with the relationship between poetry and religion in Oakeshott are Elizabeth Campbell Corey, *Michael Oakeshott on Religion, Aesthetics and Politics*; Glenn Worthington, *Religious and Poetic Experience in the Thought of Michael Oakeshott* (Exeter: Imprint Academic, 2005); and Andrew Sullivan, *Intimations Pursued: The Voice of Practice in the Conversation of Michael Oakeshott* (Exeter: Imprint Academic, 2007).

2

Corey Abel

Oakeshott's Wise Defense: Christianity as a Civilization

What we must do now is to follow, like good conservatives, the generations before us and make our Christianity as they made theirs.[1]

— Michael Oakeshott

I

Here we have the essence of Oakeshott's conservatism – to make the world one's own. This is the time-honored practice of earlier generations, of our fathers, and forefathers, and of their fathers before them.

We also have here an aspect of Oakeshott's intellectual character of which very few have been aware. Thanks to the recent work of Elizabeth Corey,[2] Glenn Worthington, and Introductions and essays by Tim Fuller and others, it is becoming more widely recognized that Oakeshott was concerned with religion, that he even had, in Ian Tregenza's words, 'an attitude to experience which could be termed religious.'[3] The notion of Oakeshott as an apologist, however, must strike most readers (as it struck me), as even stranger than the novel assertion that Oakeshott characterized conduct 'in terms of the good life.'[4] Is Oakeshott as Christian apologist far too strong, even wildly off-center? Yes it is, if you mean by that what is usually meant. There is no Oakeshottian analogue for *Mere Christianity*. But just as Oakeshott suggests making our own Christianity, he has his own approach to apologetics, noting, at one point, 'the entirely different approach of today than of yesterday' (*Notes XI*, 7).

In *Notes XI*, which the archivists at LSE date between 1924–1935 (there being no date on its cover, as with most others), Oakeshott sketches a work treating present Christian doctrine and practice under the heading of 'Modern Christianity.'[5] He

[1] Oakeshott, *Notebook XI*, n.d. (c. 1924–35), LSE File 2/1/11, 11. Hereafter: *Notes XI*.
[2] Elizabeth Campbell Corey, *Michael Oakeshott on Religion, Aesthetics and Politics* (Columbia: Univ. of Missouri Press, 2006).
[3] Ian Tregenza *Michael Oakeshott on Hobbes: A Study in the Renewal of Philosophical Ideas* (Exeter: Imprint Academic, 2003), 130.
[4] Glenn Worthington, *Religious and Poetic Experience in the Thought of Michael Oakeshott* (Charlottesville, VA: Imprint Academic, 2005), 9, passim.
[5] 'By temperament,' Oakeshott writes, 'I should be disposed to throw over [? out] what I

identifies this as 'a work of <u>Apologetic</u>; but, with a new principle of apology –
i.e., to admit everything that must be admitted, ... To reconstruct rather than to
buttress; to rebuild rather than to reconstruct; to reform rather than to rebuild'
(*Notes XI*, 13).[6] A few pages prior to this he has questioned whether the 'notion of
<u>defending</u> Christianity' might be 'out of date,' and thinks that what is called for is
to 'defend Christianity by defining it, by understanding it.' But, he adds, 'perhaps
beyond this, <u>defense</u> is still needed' (*Notes XI*, 8).

In his reformative apologetic, Oakeshott envisions 'an attempt to restate the
doctrines of Christianity for the contemporary mind, and see where the Christian
festivals, worship, prayer, etc. fall into place. Popular theology – to remove from it
that appetite for absurdity which Hume found there' (*Notes XI*, 7). In subsequent
writings, Oakeshott does not dwell at length on doctrines, nor on festivals, though
he does write compellingly about religion in terms of its being an 'otherworldly'
orientation to living in the world, or a 'scale of values' that is opposed to the ethos
of success, productivity, and what he later came to call the achievements of self-
disclosure. Oakeshott remains attentive to religious concerns in a non-doctrinaire
way, and even late in life, said that he wanted to write a 'post-Montaigne, post-
Pascal, post-Blake version of *Cur Deus Homo*.'[7] This is a project which, if he had
undertaken it, would certainly have led him to revisit the most basic doctrine of
Christianity, the Incarnation. As I will suggest below, it is not a stretch to think that
the Incarnation was central to Oakeshott's thinking, even though he never wrote a
properly 'theological' work.

Oakeshott seeks to articulate an understanding of Christianity that faces squarely
the intellectual condition of the age; not, as he says, one that defends merely
because it is attacked; not one that defends 'too much,' or 'what is indefensible,'
or 'what is irrelevant' (*Notes XI*, 7v). This means defending Christianity '(i) where
it is attacked <u>now</u>, not where it <u>was</u> attacked, (ii) where it needs defense, even if
it is not attacked there.' This he calls a 'wise defense, not a conventional defense'
(*Notes XI*, 8). And, just as modality is in so many ways central to his thinking, we
should not be surprised to find that he thinks of the apologetic task partly in terms
of the modal plurality of modern knowledge. 'Science and history has [sic] shot
their bolt – under their influence, Christianity has been cleansed of irrelevancies

---

could not understand and build for myself a religion freed from the trammels of tradition.
But the circumstances of my education set my feet upon another track, and prevented me
from dismissing from my mind, what no one who is not eaten up with prejudice or pride can
altogether forget – the history of Christianity' (*Notes XI*, 7).

[6] Note the implicit order: buttress; reconstruct; rebuild; reform. The middle two terms may
represent a distinction 'more subtle than accurate', but the notion of first trying to shore up;
next, to re-do; and then, more subtly, to reshape represents, of course, a profoundly conservative
dialectic of responsive possibilities to a situation recognized to call forth some remedy. But
at the same time, the layering of these terms around 'rather thans' suggests it is really with
the least conservative of these that Oakeshott is ultimately concerned: reform. To get beyond
buttressing by reconstruction, beyond reconstructing by rebuilding, and beyond rebuilding by
reforming. Again we see the project is to 'make our Christianity as they made theirs;' and the
mere 'shoring up of fragments' is the least interesting prospect.

[7] Letter from Oakeshott to Patrick Riley, quoted in Riley's 'Michael Oakeshott, Political
Philosopher,' *The Cambridge Review*, 112 (October, 1991): 113.

– but, by the nature of these studies – it has not been reconstructed for the modern mind' (*Notes XI*, 8).

In another notebook, Oakeshott again resolves that the truly religious thing to do is face squarely the current age, not withdraw into a 'monastic' posture of separation from the world or into resignation. Oakeshott quotes lines from Whitehead's *Science and the Modern World*, in which the latter notes that 'for two centuries religion has been on the defensive', and that [Oakeshott, paraphrasing] 'Each new development has found religious thinkers unprepared.' Below this he responds, 'But what is religion? How far does this unpreparedness show them to have been not 'religious thinkers'?'[8]

Thus, his is no attempt to turn back the clock, to reject modernity's awful turn to life-endangering knowledge. Indeed, he is, as Efraim Podoksik has argued, a defender of modernity's epistemological plurality. Characteristic of his whole attitude, we find the line, 'To accept historical facts upon insufficient evidence is not faith, it is incredulity' (*Notes XI*, 8v). This is across the page from a remark bearing on the historical criticism of the Gospel. 'Instead of asking about the reliability of this-or-that passage of the N.T., we ought to enquire into the general character of the N.T. What the N.T. says, and what it is silent about; and the value of these, depends upon the general character, the purpose for which its books were written. Etc.' (*Notes XI*, 9), and after some interesting thoughts on the problems of continuity and the self-conscious introduction of change in a tradition, Oakeshott outlines what it is he is thinking of doing:

> What I propose then, falls into two independent or semi-independent parts. First, an exposition of the general nature of religion and Christianity to show the necessity and the ground of change. And a consideration of the limits of change consistent with the retention of identity.
>
> Secondly, a project for the reform of Christianity based (i) upon this view of Christianity; (ii) upon the present situation of Christian doctrine and practice.
>
> I may be wrong in supposing that the time is ripe for this second project; and what I have to say under that head, depending as it does upon so many and so various contingencies, is less certain than what I have to say in the first part – which is a question of logic and definition.
>
> The second part should contain a review of the present situation; showing particularly that the attacks on Christianity of the last century have mainly been irrelevant, and the defenses misconceived. (*Notes XI*, 12–3)

Among the many interesting points in these passages is the recognition of 'irrelevance' as an error not only in epistemology, but as having practical effects. On the one hand, Christianity has been purged of irrelevancies, but on the other, Christianity has been attacked irrelevantly. While Oakeshott says little or nothing to explain what Christianity needed to be purged of, there might be some clues to the irrelevancies of the attacks upon it in certain passages of *Experience and Its Modes*, where the problem of religious 'authorities', the historical character of

---

[8]   Oakeshott, *Notebook IX*, January 1927, LSE File 2/1/9, 15. Hereafter: *Notes IX*.

Christianity, 'God' as an explanatory principle, and the practical conception of Nature are touched upon, among other things.

However, I do not propose to look at these issues here.[9] Suffice it to say, while Oakeshott is aware of the dangers to Christianity posed by critical history and science, he is also aware that these are bodies of experience with legitimate truth claims to make in their own spheres, and that they cannot be dislodged by appeal to out-dated visions of the world, nor resolved into a single world of experience. Practical life cannot be reduced to science, nor science to practical life, and history, while it can explain the past of both practical life and science (as well as of history itself) is also no substitute for either.

Rather than explore Oakeshott's theory of modality then, what I wish to do now is simply to ask whether, and how far, he pursued his two part project.

Does his work in any sense provide a defense of Christianity?

Again, if we are looking for *Against Heresies*, we are likely to be disappointed. But anyone familiar with Oakeshott's work should have no trouble recognizing that the first of the two parts of his project is carried out, especially in the essay 'The Importance of the Historical Element in Christianity.' It may be that Oakeshott had something much more ambitious in mind. Yet that essay does at least three things: It gives a view of Christianity as being able to incorporate anything that does not cause a complete rupture, addressing the necessity and ground of change, and considering the (very broad) limits of change consistent with retaining identity; it addresses the problem of 'credulity' by asking in what sense is Christianity 'historical' and what is the place of history in the religious imagination of Christians; and, it takes up the general nature of religion and of Christianity, suggesting that a religion must satisfy the actual minds and needs (emotional, spiritual) of a people. So it would appear that he at least began in a serious way to make his 'exposition' of these basic points.

What about the second part, the 'project for the reform of Christianity'? This is subtler, but I do not think it a wild claim to say he did, across his numerous writings on politics, the moral life, and religion, at least outline such a project.

In many essays, such as 'Religion and the Moral life,' and 'Religion and the World,' 'The Nature and Meaning of Sociality,' as well as in his treatments of religion in *On Human Conduct*, his many references to religion throughout *Rationalism in Politics*;[10] and again in his retelling of the Tower of Babel story there is a pervasive concern with religion. This might be construed as the beginnings or fragments of the second part of the project. Of course Oakeshott never, strictly

---

[9] I have discussed this modal principle behind Oakeshott's 'apology' in light of his theory of modes of experience, and related this to the current debates between evolution and religion elsewhere. See Corey Abel, 'Oakeshottian Modes at the Crossroads of the Evolution Debates,' *Zygon: A Journal of Religion and Politics*, 44, no. 1 (March 2009): 197–222.

[10] Oakeshott, *Rationalism in Politics and other essays*, new and expanded edition, ed. Timothy Fuller (Indianapolis: Liberty Press, 1991). Hereafter: *RIP*. These references and allusions appear more and more frequent as one starts to look for them: A quick glance, for example, turns up: the declining belief in Providence as a factor in Rationalism's rise; the morality of the Rationalist as 'idolatry'; Rationalism as *superbia*; the rationalistic turn of medieval Christianity; the Humean acceptance of a national church; etc.

speaking, addresses the contemporary state of Christian belief and practice – even his notebooks offer only sketchy clues here. But there is, unmistakably, in both his published and unpublished works, an attempt to characterize the 'present situation,' a characterization that very often has a religious flavor. This is what has been picked up by other commentators, and elaborated along with Oakeshott's religio-aesthetic sensibility, or what Elizabeth Corey calls, 'being otherworldly in the world.' Further, his characterization of the present situation, and of religious experience, is very much based on his view of Christianity as sketched in 'part one' – it is a Christianity for which there is 'nothing essential, no detail, doctrine, moral or religious' (*Notes XI*, 11).

Of course, the sensible thing to do would be to look for *Against Heresies*, or some equivalent, find it lacking, and declare that Oakeshott either forgot to defend Christianity (as he is said to have forgotten to include 'Masses in Representative Democracy' in the first edition of *Rationalism in Politics*), or fell away from the faith and no longer cared to give it a defense. The possibility of his forgetting cannot be dismissed, but it is not a very interesting thesis, so I leave it to one side. The possibility of his falling away from the faith is complicated by (at least) two factors: first, a profound skepticism is already present in these early notebooks. Indeed, in the late 1920's he is already willing to imagine a Christianity shorn of anything that cannot stand up to the criticism of modern knowledge, a Christianity infinitely adaptable and almost devoid of doctrine. He is even, in anticipation of his radical declarations in *Experience and its Modes*, ready to confess that religious 'truths' may be nothing more than presuppositions necessary for life.[11] Second, in spite of a profound skepticism from the beginning of his career to the end, there is a profound acceptance and appreciation for 'real presences,' to use Steiner's phrase for the *Logos* that John said pervaded our experience; an assurance that at least some notional whole provides the ground of meaningful and intelligible experience. This never disappears from his work, in spite of some signs of decreasing concern with grand philosophical themes. As I have already noted, in the waning days of his life he re-read all the works of St. Augustine, and wished 'to extend those brief pages in *On Human Conduct* into a [modern] version of *Cur Deus Homo*.' One cannot imagine a John Rawls, say, perhaps not even an Alysdair MacIntyre, contemplating such a project. One is too busy building towers, the other too busy critiquing the design. Let me try to press this a bit further to see in what sense Oakeshott's writings contain some defense or reform of Christianity.

II

If you can tell anything about a person from his choice of insults, then Oakeshott's repeated attacks on 'Pelagians' and 'Gnostics' might indicate a religious (and orthodox) turn of mind. However, these very attacks, or rather, the use of these

---

[11] See, for example, *Notes IX*: p. 50, on immortality; p. 54–6, on the philosophy of 'as if'; p. 47 & 55, on 'the atheist'; p. 46, Pascal's 'common error'; p. 46 v, on Nietzsche, that it is 'desirable that as few people as possible should reflect about morals'; etc. These are but fragmentary hints of matters that would run far afield of my present project. Also, for example, the frontispiece to 'Essay on the Relations of Philosophy, Poetry, and Reality.'

terms to criticize aspects of a world which is in profound respects, as Nietzsche already pointed out, decidedly post-Christian, raises the question begged by the argument of both the notebooks and 'The Importance of the Historical Element,' i.e., that nothing is essential. Indeed, Oakeshott's stance appears as an extreme version of Justin Martyr's view that 'Whatever things are rightly said among all men are the property of us Christians.'[12] If nothing is essential, why is Gnosticism wrong? Why not Pelagius?[13] Moreover, is Gnosticism wrong because it is utopian, because it is a manifestation of spiritual pride, because it is *hubristic*, or because it is a doctrine denying the divinity of Jesus Christ? It can, of course, be wrong for all these reasons, but accepting the fourth reason puts one in a rather more exclusive metaphysical camp than the first three. One yearns for some comment from Oakeshott on what has been 'rightly said among all men.' This is all that 'we Christians' would wish to appropriate.

Now, the reason for dredging up Oakeshott's plan for an apology and for raising questions about the divinity of Christ, is that in the present best treatments of Oakeshott's 'religious' view of experience, there is some want of energetic criticism.[14] Oakeshott is taken pretty much at his word as being a good Augustinian. There is great value in both Corey and Worthington's works, and much that I agree with. So, with no pretense of giving a fair and balanced view of their work (nor of the subtle but important differences between them), I will be ungratefully succinct: The aspects of Oakeshott's view of experience that are 'playful', non-instrumental, contemplative, are all deftly brought out. The disposition to enjoy rather than use; his liberal allusions to Augustine and the *civitas peregrina*, and his view of the limitations of human reason and the endless frustrations built into the logical structure of practice are examined. The bearing of these on his political theory is duly noted, and civil association is depicted as a place where the absence of communal solidarity is compensated by the provision of conditions in which real friendship between individuals can emerge – the *civitas* is a place where we can enjoy one another because we are not preoccupied with imposing our private dreams on one another. And civil association would seem to be calculated to accommodate the categorical imperative, except that association in terms of the rule of law is based on an imaginative appreciation of the inherent worth of persons and activities, rather than a tortured internal monologue driving relentlessly and undramatically to a foregone conclusion.

Elizabeth Corey is better in this respect than Glenn Worthington, more critical and questioning. She notices, for example, that Oakeshott's view of tradition and religion as almost infinitely flexible 'opens the door to what might be seen as a more gradual corruption of Christianity.'[15] She also finds 'Oakeshott's central

---

[12] Justin Martyr, quoted in Jaroslav Pelikan, *Christian Tradition, A History of the Development of Doctrine, Vol. 1, The Emergence of the Catholic Tradition (100–600)*, (Chicago: Univ. of Chicago Press, 1971), 62.

[13] Indeed, Oakeshott associates Hobbes with the 'Fideism' of Pascal and Montaigne (*RIP*, 237) and identifies the 'speculative audacities of Abelard [and] venturesome heresy' (*OHC*, 239) as among the signs of the emergent modern disposition of individuality.

[14] Corey, *Micahel Oakeshott on Religion*, and Worthington, *Religious and Poetic Experience*.

[15] Corey, *Michael Oakeshott on Religion*, 90.

religious insight' in the view 'that human life and its satisfactions are unavoidably transient;' and, though she recognizes this to be 'a clear-sighted assessment of the universal human condition,'[16] she does not speculate on its possible origins in the doctrines of, say, Epicurus. In fact, there is a good deal to suggest that this is precisely a clear-sighted, that is, philosophic, and not religious view. In other words, why call this a particularly 'religious' insight, if it is not derived from a revelatory tradition?

Despite his 'transposed Augustinianism' Corey notes, 'Oakeshott's reformulation of the "two cities" seems to lack the kind of external ordering principle that makes Augustine's view intelligible. In short, Oakeshott's religious man does not appear to need God ... there seems to be nothing to bolster Oakeshott's religious man beyond his own hard-won self-understanding.'[17] It is true that Oakeshott never 'confesses' a belief in God, at least not in print; it is also true, as I suggested above, that he had an inborn disposition to question, to reflect, and not to accept anything 'on faith'. And it is true that he has a more sophisticated reply to Augustinian dualism than I can enter into here. It may be that Oakeshott's religious man has no external support, because as a good Hegelian, Oakeshott would hold that there is nothing external to the whole of human experience within which we find ourselves.

A different approach is this. Corey notes that 'Augustine's mature view is remarkably similar' to Oakeshott's view of our condition in the *civitas peregrina*. She links Oakeshott's view of our universal predicament with Cochrane's account of Augustine's understanding of '*the* problem of life' as 'the problem of consciousness.'[18] The great question this poses, and the indirect way of getting to the question of just how closely we can link Oakeshott and Augustine (or any other 'Christian writer'), is: *what weight can we put on accumulated allusions*? As I have mentioned, Oakeshott's work is surprisingly full of such allusions, things a casual reader might easily pass over, or someone interested in narrowly political questions could forgive himself for leaving aside, which most have done.[19] Oakeshott (along with Voegelin) can call aspects of the modern world 'Gnostic;' can identify 'pride' or even the Latin '*superbia*' as a fundamental problem in political life; can pledge allegiances and affiliations with Pascal against Descartes, with Augustine and Montaigne against Bacon, can even praise Catholic political thought,[20] however qualifiedly. But what does it all add up to? To take one more example, Corey writes, following Oakeshott's suggestions, that 'Rationalism depends upon a view of morality that is both Gnostic and perfectionist in character, a view that at once

---

[16] Corey, *Michael Oakeshott on Religion*, 94–5.
[17] Corey, *Michael Oakeshott on Religion*, 227.
[18] Corey, *Michael Oakeshott on Religion*, 24.
[19] There can be no excuse, however, for the willful ignorance and distortion of Gertrude Himmelfarb, who attacked Oakeshott as a basically anti-religious thinker. See Himmelfarb, 'The Conservative Imagination of Michael Oakeshott,' *American Scholar*, 44, no. 3 (Summer 1975): 405–20. It is impossible to guess where, even on the hastiest reading of Oakeshott, she got her ideas.
[20] See Oakeshott, *The Social and Political Doctrines of Contemporary Europe* (Cambridge: Cambridge Univ. Press, 1939). Hereafter: *SPD*.

denies the uncertainty of existence and tries to arrange all of experience into logical, 'rational' categories.'[21] But arranging experience into logical categories is what all philosophers do; and perfectionism can be faulted apart from any particular religious beliefs. So why does Oakeshott choose to express his criticisms in the idiom of Christian orthodoxy, as anti-Gnostic? Why Pelagius; why not Prometheus? (Oakeshott does of course, mention him, as well as other 'classical' figures, like the famous tyrant Ozymandias.)

To show that I am not stingy in my stingy criticism, let me point somewhat unfairly, to a single line in Worthington's study which raises a similar problem of what to make of an accumulated mass of allusions (should we ask, is there some 'illative sense' to it all?). After mentioning the letter I have cited from Oakeshott to Patrick Riley, Worthington writes, quite boldly, 'It is my contention that there are enough references to religious experience in Oakeshott's work to establish more than a glimpse of what his post-Montaigne version of *Cur Deus Homo* would look like.'[22] A single bold line is pardonable, even if it is questionable. When I read the line I was astonished – in part because I have thought that an interesting project (although one running a bit too much toward that of Pierre Menard, author of *Don Quixote*), would be to explore Anselm's work in an Oakeshottian light, to see what could be made of it, an Oakeshottian commentary, one could say. And I have not found it easy to get even a glimpse, much less a clear outline of just what such a commentary would say. However, I agree with Worthington that there are a plethora of references to religion in Oakeshott's works; far more than are usually acknowledged. I have alluded to some of them. There are also numerous saintly, sinnerly, theological, and philosophical figures cropping up – Varro, Irenaeus, Erastus, Erigena, Boethius, to mention only a few – so that even if Oakeshott relegates them to a cryptic aside, a footnote, or a parenthesis, one is provoked to wonder why he mentions them at all. There are footnotes, like the one noting that the understandings of Cicero and St. Augustine of the civil condition were not altogether different.[23]

Two problems confront the interpreter who would weave a cloth from these disparate threads; first, there is the question of what to make of them each individually; how much weight to place on them and how to assess their relation to the rest of what Oakeshott says; second, there is the fact that there are equally numerous, if not more numerous references to writers who do not obviously fit in a work of apologetic – Rabelais, Rimbaud, Rousseau, Blake, Rex Warner, Harriet Martineau; and again, with these, the task of assessing each one's weight and relevance.

Since I have no time to sift all of Oakeshott's allusions here (it would require several volumes of intertextual analysis), I would suggest the following as a possible way of understanding Oakeshott's 'apology.' The accumulated mass of allusions points us to a deeper-than-textual, deeper-than-creedal conviction of the

---

[21]   Corey, *Michael Oakeshott on Religion*, 189.
[22]   Worthington, *Religious and Poetic Experience*, 79.
[23]   Oakeshott, *On Human Conduct* (Oxford: Clarendon Press, 1975), 213 n. 1. Hereafter: *OHC*.

coherence of the world, the meaningfulness of experience.[24] This is also attested by Oakeshott's vocabulary, quite aside from his patterns of allusion. I mentioned above Oakeshott's conviction that there are 'real presences' in human experience. For example, human experience is a 'conversation'; morality is a 'language' of utterance and response; activities occur in 'idioms'; and actions 'evoke' responses from agents; that is, actions call forth (*vocare*) other actions, which are utterances, exhibitions of understanding, in a great 'affirmative flow' of tradition. Moreover, we are said to be 'faithful' to the knowledge of how to conduct ourselves in various practices; *cives* 'keep faith,' and have a bond of loyalty to one another; the considerations of self-enactment might be ultimately expressed as a 'graceful' acceptance of the evanescence of every element of worldly life; we have a 'world of meaning;' and so on. All of this points to a view of human experience as fitting within some frame of intelligibility, one in which language, thought, and meaning are profoundly intertwined at both literal and figurative levels, across all forms of experience. But is it in any meaningful sense 'Christian'? For this, we need God and we need his becoming man.

Let me approach by another indirect path, with Worthington's glimpse of an Oakeshottian *Cur Deus Homo*. The difficulty may be expressed this way: One of the features of Oakeshott's intelligible universe is that he finds it possible to translate endlessly the ideas of other thinkers into his own language, a language borrowed, modified, and improvised from traditional materials, but a language distinctly his own. He has a universal hermeneutics without the usual hang-ups. Thus, to take one notable example, he writes of an Aristotelian agent's *'eudaimonia'* as 'continuously disclosing an enacting himself in his own chosen actions while subscribing adequately to considerations of moral propriety or worth' (*OHC*, 118–19), that is, in *exactly* the terms in which Oakeshottian agents are described. And he renders Hegel's political philosophy, and Hobbes', and many others' in his own idiom. Nor am I the first to notice this feature of Oakeshott's appropriations.

When you open *Cur Deus Homo*, even for just five minutes, what you find is a linguistic challenge of an altogether different order. For, what shall we say of God and His becoming man? That he was 'enacting and disclosing Himself in His own chosen actions'? This might make him a happy god, but would it make him Flesh? Would it make him suffering, substituting, reconciling, atoning or otherwise saving? (Does God, by the way, subscribe to considerations of moral propriety or worth, thinking of himself as he should while behaving as he ought?) Let Him be self-enacting; but there is a quite specific range of meaning that this particular Agent intends. Can this adequately be captured in the language of human conduct? To put it differently, Aristotle, Montesquieu, and Augustine can be linked, woven together in an Oakeshottian tapestry because their concerns – or rather Oakeshott's concerns with them – are worldly. They are, loosely speaking, anthropological and political concerns relating to human beings and the terms of human association.

We should recall though, that Oakeshott also writes that the greatest thinkers

---

[24] [Todd Breyfogle's essay in the present volume, 'Language and the Conservation of the Religious Disposition' evocatively and carefully explores key aspects of this relationship. – *Ed.*]

need to be considered in the context of eternity. He often invokes *the* predicament of mankind, or links what he knows are diverse epochs and cultures, for example, by saying that aesthetic experience as he defines it has *always been known*, even if it was relatively neglected and undeveloped in ages past (*RIP*, 530). So, his 'worldy' concerns are not merely worldly. And we must not forget, in thinking of what it would mean to describe the actions or intentions of God in the language of human conduct, that the language of human conduct is what we have always had, and all that we have ever had, to speak about the divine. And, even mischievous gods have taken the trouble to speak to human beings in their own languages, and to appear in recognizable shapes, as swans, as whirlwinds, as a man.

The deeper difficulty, of course, is not so much that the language of human agency might not 'fit' the divine. This is what poetic magnificence is for; why the prosaic is sometimes all that we have got to deal with. The deeper problem is that to speak of why God became man would require Oakeshott, even in his most ironically detached, horizon-fusing mood, to take up some position on precisely those theological questions he is so wont to avoid. It would return him to doctrine. For, it makes some difference, particularly if you are rumbling with the Gnostics in your neighborhood, whether or not God *was* man, or only appeared to be so; whether, in becoming man he ceased to be God, or, becoming Incarnate left heaven vacant; whether or not he died and rose again, or simply died, or lived through his crucifixion; whether he rose after a descent into Hell; whether or not the Holy Spirit proceeds from the Son and the Father, or the Son but not also the Father; indeed, it might even matter whether 'God' is a fourth entity superior to and manifest in the more familiar anthropomorphized persons. It makes some difference because error in respect to these large questions is reputed to be one of the major sources of error in respect to the moral and political issues of perfectionism. As Elizabeth Corey notes, Pelagius thought it a duty, and not merely a possibility, that human action could play a significant role in human salvation. And it would seem to matter to Oakeshott too, because he chooses to call his intellectual opponents (among other things) Gnostics and Pelagians.

This leads me to another dimension of the problem of accumulating allusions. Augustine was quite clear about why human action alone, indeed, even in any significant degree, could not contribute to human salvation. And this was in part because of sin, and in part because of the Being with whom our relationship sin severs. I need not rehearse the steps of his familiar arguments here. It is enough to ask whether Oakeshott ever asserts that our 'fugitive adventures' belong to a 'fallen' world, or that we are powerless to achieve salvation without Grace. Here, of course, it is easy enough to point out that Oakeshott never asserts a doctrine of sin. He mentions Augustine's doctrine always favorably and never negatively. He discusses the ways in which Hobbes reconfigured the 'myth' of pride and sin. But he takes no stand himself, unless vicariously, in these pledges of affiliation. 'Sin' appears to be unnecessary as a postulate of conduct. But if it is not necessary, we still have the fact of evanescence, the fact of frustration, the fact of human inability and powerlessness. These do appear to be symptoms or analogues of sin, the sorts of things someone who believes in sin might stress as evidence, or by way of explanation. If silences could be made to speak, one might suspect Oakeshott of leading us to conclude that there must be some doctrine of sin underneath it all. After all, a doctrine of human imperfectability would gain cogency if it could be shown, *contra Rousseau*, that our miseries are not merely historic accidents of our own creation. But aside from the difficulty of making muteness vocalize, there is the rhetorical consideration that Oakeshottian agency, although under a dim veil of finitude and contingency, is also repeatedly and beautifully figured as an adventure; as setting sail (with Democritus no less); as a carefree dance on a May morning. And in tone, if not in content, this is very far indeed from the medieval altar decorated with skulls and bones.

What I would like to suggest all to briefly, is that there is no direct path to an Oakeshottian apology, because, if he did not forget and did not despair, he may very well have been daunted by the 'many and various contingencies' which he has identified as a stumbling block at the outset. However, this is not a very interesting thesis either – he did not do it because the task was too great.

There is, I think, a very oblique manner in which Oakeshott's work might be seen as an apology for Christianity. But it must be clearly stated, this has nothing to do with conventional apologetics. And if it is too much to conceive Christianity shorn of doctrines, then we have to conclude that Oakeshott had no such apology. I have tried to show how far Oakeshott is from entering into any debate on the doctrine of the dual nature or the trinity, or any discussion of soteriology. For these, if we are interested, we must look elsewhere. And in these familiar senses, Oakeshott is very far from being a 'religious thinker,' even if he has a 'religious' view of human life. Nonetheless, without being a defense of doctrine, Oakeshott's oblique apologetics might be very much to the point and directly relevant to Christianity's central claims, if we are able to see these in what may be called a civilizational context.

III

I have noted already that Oakeshott's view of tradition, specifically of the Christian religion as a changing tradition, seems like an extreme version of Justin Martyr's saying that 'Whatever things are rightly said among all men are the property of us Christians.' The sense in which it may be possible to speak of Oakeshott's work as fulfilling the second part of his early-sketched 'project' is in the notion of Christianity as a civilization, a civilization with a specific content. Paradoxically, what this means is that in spite of the near identity in many people's minds between Christianity and a basket of doctrines, 'Christianity', for Oakeshott, is precisely 'not-doctrine'. It is life itself. But this denial of doctrine also means that the most appropriate way of recollecting us to the values of a 'Christian' civilization may be through a re-telling of the O.T. story of the Tower of Babel, or simply rehearsing and recollecting the most important aspects of a religious 'scale of values' in works not specifically concerned with religion, thus, writing on play, poetry, friendship, and a mode of association in which fellows citizens treat each other as ends only.

In his notebooks, Oakeshott considers a problem, one critics have pressed against his view of tradition, of how to decide what belongs and what does not; whether, in his chosen idiom, 'a certain growth belongs to the main stem, or whether it is parasitic' (*Notes XI*, 14). And a few lines later he wonders if the metaphor is misplaced. It is misplaced he decides, because it turns out the problem is not that of purity – not that of 'main stem' versus 'parasitic growth,' not, 'apple tree' versus 'mistletoe.' The problem is how anything can fail to be admitted to the whole. As he puts it:

> All religious and moral ideas which have currency in Western Europe are somehow attached to or derived from Christianity; ours is a Christian civilization in that its formative conceptions, its atmosphere, etc., are derived from Christianity. I do not mean that every idea we have can be traced back to a definite source; I mean that the whole to which our ideas belong is dominated by the [unclear word: 'name'?] Christianity. And those who have rejected the particular brand or phase of Christianity preferred by their generation are not less influenced by it, than those who accept it. (*Notes XI*, 14)

If this is true, then defending a doctrine is decidedly beside the point. How could the defense of one proposition or set of propositions stand in the balance with a whole way of life, with hundreds of generations of actual, lived experience? More precisely, if as Hegel and others observed, the event of Christianity transformed the world, it may have rendered itself, by virtue of its very success, both indefensible and unassailable; aside from some new revelation that would 'transvalue' all values.

Well, some would-be apologists like T. S. Eliot have fretted that Christian Europe was, in the early twentieth century, being re-paganized. Is there anything in the 'whole' we call our civilization that is distinctly Christian or in defending it are we defending civilization only in some generic sense? What in short, are the values of 'Western Europe' that would justify Oakeshott's assertion of its 'Christian' character?

Here, Oakeshott's Hegelianism needs to be redisplayed, not in terms of the liberal-communitarian squabbles, but in terms of Hegel's own comments on Christianity having given birth to a new civilization. The best terse example of how Hegel sees the modern West as 'Christian' may be in his Remark to *Philosophy of Right* §124:

> The right of the subject's particularity, his right to be satisfied, or in other words the right of subjective freedom, is the pivot and centre of the difference between antiquity and modern times. This right in its infinity is given expression in Christianity and it has become the universal effective principle of a new form of civilisation. Amongst the primary shapes which this right assumes are love, romanticism, the quest for the eternal salvation of the individual, &c.; next come moral convictions and conscience; and, finally, the other forms, some of which come into prominence in what follows as the principle of civil society and as moments in the constitution of the state, while others appear in the course of history, particularly the history of art, science, and philosophy.[25]

---

[25] G. W. F. Hegel, *The Philosophy of Right*, trans T. M. Knox (Oxford: Oxford Univ. Pres, 1967), §124, Remark.

And for an explanation of why Hegel might think so, if we needed to go outside of Hegel himself, we might turn to one of his most insightful interpreters, Michael Foster, with whom Oakeshott more than once signaled his agreement by positive references and reviews, and who explained at length how the doctrine of creative will, which Hegel too harshly attacked Plato for not grasping, was introduced into Western civilization through the Biblical tradition.[26]

At least one scholar has explored Oakeshott's thought in terms of the core Christian idea of the Incarnation. In an APSA conference paper in 2001, Joshua Mitchell wrote on Oakeshott as an 'Incarnational' thinker.[27] Mitchell is clear that Oakeshott takes no position on dogma, as I have stressed. But Mitchell justifies his use of this term by drawing on Hegel's early theological lectures, to suggest that Oakeshott's concentration upon the 'concrete universal' reflects a sensibility and opens up intellectual and moral possibilities that are distinctly Christian in the sense that, for example, the interiority of romantic love and the demands of modern subjectivity were, if not first 'discovered' in Christian experience, at least most profoundly liberated and nurtured there. More recently another young scholar from Georgetown has delved into a comparison between the ideas of Reinhold Niebuhr and Michael Oakeshott, suggesting fruitful possibilities for more research along these lines.[28]

Also relevant to this notion of a civilizational Christianity would be some of Charles Taylor's discussions of the 'sources of the modern self', in particular his arguments about the centrality of St. Augustine to modern European experience.[29] Relevant, too, would be Steiner's *Real Presences*, *Grammars of Creation*, and other writings in which he laments the loss of a belief in the Word, in intelligibility.[30] Oakeshott, however, is considerably more sanguine about our situation than Steiner, in spite of characterizing the modern situation at times in dark terms – a 'dark age of barbaric affluence', for example. But throughout his career he continued to write on the assumption that philosophy could still say something, that the world was full of intelligibility, that meanings were everywhere.

In this quick survey of possible sources for grasping what Oakeshott's defense of a 'civilizational' Christianity might look like, I would be remiss if I failed to mention Remi Brague's discussions of European identity in terms of his concepts of 'secondarity' and 'Romanity', and his effort to link this identity with major strands of Christianity. In particular, Brague points to the controversies against Marcion, in respect to the unity of tradition; that instead of denying the validity or importance of what is past and discarding it as false, as a fulfilled and no longer

---

[26] Michael Foster, *The Political Philosophies of Plato and Hegel* (Oxford: Clarendon Press, 1935).

[27] Joshua Mitchell, 'Incarnational Thinking in the Early Writings of Michael Oakeshott' (paper presented at the annual meeting of The American Political Science Association, San Fransisco, CA, 31 August–4 September, 2001).

[28] Matthew Sitman, 'Politics after Babel: Michael Oakeshott, Reinhold Niebuhr, and the Theological Defense of Modernity' (paper presented to the Fifth Plenary Meeting of the Michael Oakeshott Association, Baylor University, Waco, TX, 12–14 November, 2009).

[29] Charles Taylor, *Sources of the Self: The Making of Modern Identity* (Cambridge: Harvard Univ. Press, 1989).

[30] George Steiner, *Real Presences* (Chicago: Univ. of Chicago Press, 1991); and *Grammars of Creation* (New Haven: Yale Univ. Press, 2001).

useful prophecy, Christianity established a principle of continuity by canonizing the O.T. This seemingly arcane matter has direct analogues in Oakeshott's critique of Rationalism, which, like the Marcionites, attempts to deny the importance of the past, rejecting continuity in the name of starting over anew with a truth. Brague does not mention Oakeshott in his discussion of 'Historical Marcionism,' but it is of some interest that he mentions the other great twentieth century political philosopher who chose to confront modernity in terms of its 'Gnosticism', Eric Voeglelin.[31]

In addition to this, Brague's thesis concerning the way the European identity has involved not the insistence upon its own originality but upon its relation to a complex past, a relation he calls secondarity, is deeply resonant with Oakeshott's ideas on how we always relate to the past but never simply to imitate or repeat it; rather we make it our own. Brague deals with this in terms of the recurrent renaissances in European history; Oakeshott's implicit hermeneutics seem to call for a continual, universal renaissance of the past being mediated by present action into the future. And, like Brague's Europe, Oakeshott's appropriations range not just across Judeo-Christian sources but Greek and Roman as well. His view, one might say, is thoroughly catholic – small 'c'.

Naturally, I cannot do more here than hint at the ways Oakeshott's work might be placed in the context of a view of European civilization as 'Christian.' The key is that it is not a matter of doctrine, Church attendance, affiliations, or even public recognitions of any church or creed. It is not a matter of theology, nor of Oakeshott's own beliefs. I hope I have put enough evidence forward from Oakeshott's early and unpublished notebooks, early published writings, and writings throughout his career to show that this is no fanciful project.

In Oakeshott's famous essay 'On Being Conservative,' he repudiates the idea that to be conservative in politics one must hold certain religious beliefs, or believe in a natural law. He even takes a swipe at T. S. Eliot, by noting wryly 'the "conservatism" of an Englishman has even been connected with Royalism and Anglicanism' (*RIP*, 423). Thus, one Englishman to another. But his point turns out to be that the conservative (among many other things) distinguishes crime from sin; that the conservative is, in the language Oakeshott elsewhere develops, a defender of civil as against enterprise association. But then he turns, strangely, and points out that his view does not require the elimination of religion from public life; that it might even be consistent with an established church, provided that church was not trying to run society as its enterprise. Conservatives, he writes,

> might even be prepared to suffer a legally established ecclesiastical order; but it would not be because they believed it to represent some unassailable religious truth, but merely because it restrained the indecent competition of sects and (as Hume said) moderated 'the plague of a too diligent clergy'. (*RIP*, 435)

And in his essay, 'The Tower of Babel,' in which, Hume-like, he attacks moralities

---

[31] Remi Brague, *Eccentric Culture: A Theory of Western Civilization*, trans. Samuel Lester (South Bend, IN: St. Augustine's Press, 2002), 182.

of abstract reflection and defends moralities of habit, he dilates for six and one-half pages, the whole of section five, on the transformation of Christianity in the third and fourth centuries from being a morality of habit, a lived practice, grounded in 'faith in a person,' into an abstract 'grammar.' From around the third century, he writes, 'a Christian habit of moral behaviour (which had sprung from the circumstances of Christian life) was swamped by a Christian moral ideology, and the perception of the poetic character of human conduct was lost' (*RIP*, 485).

It cannot be a mistake that he also takes the time to add:

> Every significant attack upon Christian morality (that of Nietzsche, for example) has been mistaken for an attack upon the particular moral ideals of Christian life, whereas whatever force it possessed derived from the fact that the object of attack was a morality of ideas which had never succeeded in becoming a morality of a habit of behaviour (*RIP*, 486).

This line seems to say that attacks upon Christianity have only been successful when they have attacked what Oakeshott himself is attacking. That attacks upon Christianity have not really attacked Christianity, but only a deformed, 'idealized' version of it. That the relevant attack (and defense) would be centered on the lived habits of Christian life, and not its consciously formulated, rationalistic ideals. Oakeshott is not only critiquing the critics; he is pointing out that in being defended against attack, the ideals of Christianity became 'rigid and exaggerated' (*RIP*, 485–6), thereby offering his own implicit critique of what Christianity has come to believe itself to be, a creedal community.

One cannot help being reminded of what Oakeshott called his 'wise defense': to defend Christianity '(i) where it is attacked <u>now</u>, not where it <u>was</u> attacked, (ii) where it needs defense, even if it is not attacked there' (*Notes XI*, 8). And one cannot help being reminded of the second part of Oakeshott's apologetic project, one which I have been exploring indirectly: 'The second part should contain a review of the present situation; showing particularly that the attacks on Christianity of the last century have mainly been irrelevant, and the defenses misconceived' (*Notes XI*, 12–13). This might allow us to give some weight to an apparently useless introductory phrase near the beginning of one of his most famous essays, 'Rationalism in Politics.' 'If we except religion, the greatest apparent victories of Rationalism have been in politics' (RIP, 8). Oakeshott's motive for eschewing a direct confrontation with religion and deciding to focus on politics in his characterization of the present situation must remain for now a matter of speculation. But his saying that political Rationalism has enjoyed 'apparent' victories, and that these are the greatest aside from its victories in religion, would seem to suggest Rationalism has indeed made some victories in religion, and that these are perhaps greater, while perhaps being less apparent, than those in politics.

So it would seem that the least we can say is that Oakeshott had a view of Christianity that was deeply implicated in the way he thought about history and tradition; reason; and moral, political, and poetic experience. We might not be unjustified in thinking that his views on tradition and history, reason, morals, politics, and aesthetic experience were, in turn, deeply implicated in his thoughts on Christianity.

3

Todd Breyfogle

Language and the Conservation of the Religious Disposition

'There's something fishy about describing people's feelings,' said Hugo. 'All these descriptions are so dramatic.'

'What's wrong with that?' I said.

'Only,' said Hugo, 'that it means that things are falsified from the start. If I say afterwards that I felt such and such, say that I felt 'apprehensive' – well, this just isn't true.'

'What do you mean?' I asked.

'I didn't feel this,' said Hugo. 'I didn't feel anything of that kind at the time at all. This is just something I say afterwards.'

'But suppose I try hard to be accurate,' I said.

'One can't be,' said Hugo. 'The only hope is to avoid saying it. As soon as I start to describe, I'm done for. Try describing anything, our conversation for instance, and see how absolutely instinctively you...'

'Touch it up?' I suggested.

'It's deeper than that,' said Hugo. 'The language just won't let you present it as it really was...'

.... I was puzzled by this myself. I felt that there was something wrong in what Hugo said, and yet I couldn't see what it was. We discussed the matter a bit further, and then I told him, 'But at this rate almost everything one says, except things like 'Pass the marmalade' or 'There's a cat on the roof', turns out to be a sort of lie.'

Hugo pondered this. 'I think it is so,' he said with seriousness.

'In that case one oughtn't to talk,' I said.

'I think perhaps one oughtn't to,' said Hugo, and he was deadly serious. Then I caught his eye, and we both laughed enormously, thinking of how we had been doing nothing else for days on end.[1]

I

This passage from Iris Murdoch's *Under the Net* was for a long time understood, I am told, to be a portrait of Michael Oakeshott. Some recent findings have called that into doubt, though it is known that Murdoch and Oakeshott knew each other. Even if 'Hugo' is not in fact based on Oakeshott, this passage discloses a series of

---

[1]   Iris Murdoch, *Under the Net* (London: Penguin, 1960), 59–60.

understandings about language that may be termed Oakeshottian: the complexity of the art of translation, the impossibility of past description, the concessions we make to communicate, the way 'the language just won't let us present something as it really was.'

For Oakeshott, language bears a peculiar relationship between the present, the past and the future. For Oakeshott, as for Augustine and T. S. Eliot, there is only the present; any speech is, therefore, necessarily a mediated and partial – perhaps necessarily deceitful, but certainly imperfect – disclosure of the present. As an imperfect mediation of past and future in the present, language bears significance for what it means to have a disposition which is both conservative and religious. My aim in this paper is to suggest some ways in which Oakeshott's understanding and use of language help us understand the conservation of the religious disposition.

Religion is, for Oakeshott, if I understand him rightly, a special case of, but not reducible to, the moral life. As such, it may be analyzed in two distinct yet inseparable forms: '*a habit of affection* and *conduct*' and '*a habit of reflective thought*.'[2] As a habit of affection and conduct, the moral life is 'nothing more than the unreflective following of a tradition of conduct in which we have been brought up. And such moral habit will disclose itself as often in *not* doing, in the taste which dictates abstention from certain actions, as in performances' (*RIP*, 468). The moral life is, then, inherently conservative, and Oakeshott introduces a revealing comparison: 'We acquire habits of conduct, not by constructing a way of living upon rules or precepts learned by heart and subsequently practiced, but by living with people who habitually behave in a certain manner: we acquire habits of conduct in the same way as we acquire our native language' (*RIP*, 468).

In Oakeshott's understanding, the moral life – and with it, religion – is understood in terms of a practice, a performance, analogous to the learning and speaking of a language. A moral and religious act Oakeshott frequently refers to as an 'utterance' – a particular performance at a particular time; a moment of self-enactment, which is not the 'application of rules to a situation' (*RIP*, 469). In this it is distinguished from the moral life understood as a habit of reflective thought – the *ex post facto* theorization of a practice and a set of performances, their reification into a code or set of rules and precepts. Let us follow the comparison through. Religion as a habit of affection and conduct is to theology as language is to grammar. Neither grammar nor theology can substitute for the activity of speaking or the living of a life religiously, nor can either speaking or a religious life be reduced to grammar or theology. The grammar killeth, but the language giveth life.

Oakeshott's essay on the 'Tower of Babel' concerns itself with making clear the ways in which the theorization of the moral life (and with it religion) has taken the place of the moral life itself as a habit of affection and conduct. This codification

---

[2]   Oakeshott, *Rationalism in Politics and other essays, new and expanded edition*, ed. Timothy Fuller (Indianapolis: Liberty Press, 1991), 467. Hereafter: *RIP*. This essay, 'Tower of Babel,' deals with different understandings of moral life, and should not be confused with the essay of the same name published in *On History and other essays*, in which Oakeshott re-tells the story of Babel in his own idiom.

or theorization is a kind of abridgement and, by extension, a misconceived short-cut epitomized by the myth of the Tower of Babel. Our predilection for a single language, a single voice, propels us to look at the scattering of languages and people at Babel as a misfortune. 'The view dies hard, that Babel was the occasion of a curse,' writes Oakeshott at the outset of the 'Voice of Poetry in the Conversation of Mankind' (*RIP*, 488). In fact, Babel is a reminder – a safeguard – that the conditions of human understanding and utterance are plural; in this plurality lie the possibilities of freedom and delight.

Both the acquisition of language and the diversity of languages of whose origins the myth of Babel seeks to give an account underscore the essential conservatism of the moral and religious life. The moral and religious life is learned necessarily, and inevitably, from that which remains of what has gone before; living morally and religiously is learned as a practice before the codes of morality and religion impinge upon us; such life is learned in communities of practice; and, its change is slow. But as a practice, the moral and religious life is not static; it does change. 'Intellectual error with regard to moral ideas or opinions does not compromise a moral life which is firmly based upon a habit of conduct. In short, the stability which belongs to this form of the moral life derives from its elasticity and its ability to suffer change without disruption' (*RIP*, 470). Like language, the religious life is always in motion, never at rest: 'its history is one of continuous change' (*RIP*, 471). The resilience of the religious life as a habit of affection derives from its unreflective embrace of its inheritance and the freedom and innovation of its emerging practice.

Beneath his skeptical and reticent style, Oakeshott makes clear that he is defining what human beings do. He makes the strong claim that his understanding is only what is inescapable to anyone who really looks into the matter. Just as he argues elsewhere that Rationalism arises from a mistaken view of mind, he says tradition cannot be ignored even if we feel trapped by it or dislike it. We cannot even cogently criticize tradition without already being a part of it. Nonetheless, our prevailing notion of the moral and religious life is that it is nothing other than the 'reflective application of a moral [or religious] criterion,' whether this involves 'the self-conscious pursuit of moral ideals,' or 'the reflective observance of moral rules' (*RIP*, 472). In this form, education in the moral life requires the detachment of moral ideas from their expression, training in the art of the 'intellectual management of these ideals,' as well as training in the 'art of translation' – note the linguistic metaphor – 'and in the art of selecting appropriate means for achieving the ends which our education has inculcated' (*RIP*, 474). Religion in this form, no less than the moral life, is susceptible to the dubious pursuit of 'virtue as the crow flies' (*RIP*, 475) and so admits to the same thoroughgoing critique of rationalism that Oakeshott bestows upon politics.

Both forms of the religious life – to reiterate – are necessary and inevitable, but the excessive dominance of the form of reflective application over that of the habit of affection and conduct is what erodes and dissolves a coherent moral life. Oakeshott's clear preference is for language over grammar, action over theory, a form of moral life that will 'offer to a society advantages similar to those of a religion which has taken to itself a theology … but without losing its character as a way of living' (*RIP*, 478). We have here, by double analogy – language and the moral life – a picture of what the religious disposition is at its healthiest.

Like the practice of a moral life more generally, the healthy religious life offers a bulwark against the radical defect of the extreme form of rationalist morality – 'its denial of the poetic character of all human activity' (*RIP*, 479). Without equating religion and poetry here, we may nonetheless assert that religion and poetry share an affinity or a common disposition. At the very least, Oakeshott indicates that 'what is true of poetry is true also, I think, of all human moral activity' (*RIP*, 479). This affinity is at the root of the absence of translation:

> A poem is not the translation into words of a state of mind. What the poet says and what he wants to say are not two things … they are the same thing; he does not know what he wants to say until he has said it. And the 'corrections' he may make to his first attempt are not efforts to make words correspond more closely to an already formulated idea or to images already fully formed in his mind, they are renewed efforts to formulate the idea, to conceive the image.' (*RIP*, 479)

In this sense, the religious life, like poetry, is an engagement of performative image-making, an unrehearsed utterance in speech or action with its own, impractical valence. It is not the translation of a mystical experience, or the rendering of the meaning of religious symbols, or the expression of a feeling of comfort or awe. It is an action of wonder and delight and, perhaps, of worship, but certainly an act of spontaneous gratitude.

If Oakeshott's critique of Rationalism in religion in 'Rationalism in Politics' is muted by the explicit subject of politics in that essay, in the 'Tower of Babel' Oakeshott is appropriately more explicit about 'the form of the moral life of contemporary Christendom' (*RIP*, 481). The dominance of 'the self-conscious pursuit of moral ideals' leaves us 'dizzy' and desirous of filling 'the hollowness of our moral life' which merely 'covers up the corruption of consciousness' and 'moral distraction' – a 'pitiless wedding which we have celebrated with our shadowy ideal of conduct' (*RIP*, 481–2).

Both moral ideology and moral life spring from the moral world of Greco-Roman antiquity and that of Christianity, in Oakeshott's analysis. Christianity, for Oakeshott, encountered a Greco-Roman world in which 'the old habits of moral behavior had lost their vitality' (*RIP*, 483). The moral life formed by Christian community and practice in the first three centuries came to be, for various reasons, 'converted into the self-conscious pursuit of formulated moral ideals' (*RIP*, 484). Christians needed to define themselves, but the Christian way of life needed to be 'translated' into a form which could be appreciated by those coming to the Christian life from outside of it, those who 'having to learn their Christianity as a foreign language, needed a grammar' (*RIP*, 484). When the Christian life was 'swamped by the Christian moral ideology … the perception of the poetic character of human conduct was lost' (*RIP*, 485).

Oakeshott's account of religion and the moral life in the 'Tower of Babel' essay may be seen as a kind of bridge between 'Rationalism in Politics' and the 'Voice of Poetry in the Conversation of Mankind.' In this Babel essay, there is a more explicit, if still muted, attention to religion as a way of life and thought than is the case in 'Rationalism in Politics,' while the link between the religious and poetic dispositions is suggested more strongly (and with greater clarity) than in the 'Voice of Poetry.' Similarly, 'Babel' complements the account of the emergence of rationalist individualism in 'Rationalism in Politics' by suggesting the much earlier introduction of what we might call moral rationalism, which Oakeshott attributes to the classical-Christian moral ideology of at least the third century A.D. The failure of the moral and religious life to withstand the dominance of a morality of reflective application – the supercession of language by grammar – has diminished the possibility of perceiving the poetic character of life.

If this is the appropriate reading of Oakeshott's position, then the defense of poetry may be seen as the prelude to the possibility of recovering a more balanced language of the moral and religious life. Oakeshott's 'Voice of Poetry' essay is, famously, a correction to a misstatement in *Experience and Its Modes*, while reinforcing one of the central features of that great, early book – the plural structure of the languages and voices which make up the conversation of mankind. Without suggesting that Oakeshott meant 'Voice of Poetry' to be 'about religion', it is possible to shed light on his view of religion by holding fast to his remark about the poetic character of all experience, and then by looking closely at what the essay on poetry says about experience, about language, and by extension, about moral and religious life.

The vitality of the poetic voice is both a reminder of the plurality of voices and of the possibility of a voice that partakes of a purely performative language. To be clear, the poetic voice is not the voice of religion as a habit of affection and conduct; that said, the recognition of poetry opens up a space for perceiving that which is not merely the reflective application of moral criteria to a practical end. Put another way, the defense of poetry can be understood to be the defense of religious *language* against religious *grammar*.

In the 'Voice of Poetry' essay, the language Oakeshott uses to describe the defect to which the voices are subject is strikingly similar to that of the 'Tower of Babel.' Some of the voices, he writes, suffer from 'a loosening (even a detachment) of what is said from the manner of its utterance, and when this takes place the voice appears as a body of conclusions reached (*dogmata*), and thus, becoming eristic, loses its conversability' (*RIP*, 492). This separation of content from form and the consequent attention to content echoes the separation of theological grammar from the Christian life. Just as the form and content of a poem constitute a single, inseparable performance, so too a properly Christian life unites form and content in a manner of acting which binds together its disparate, particular acts, a singleness that might in a traditional idiom be called piety, or virtue.

If this account of the affinities between poetry and religious life is accurate, then we are forced in reading the 'Voice of Poetry' essay to confront the status of religion as a symbolic language. The business of practical life, writes Oakeshott, is conducted in a symbolic language of agreed upon signs which have 'relatively fixed and precise usage.... Speaking here is expressing or conveying images and is not itself image-making' (*RIP*, 503). In this, religion and poetry would seem to part company dramatically, for religion is, at first glance, a commerce in images of fixed and precise usages. By contrast, poetry is 'the activity of making images of a certain kind and moving about among them in a manner appropriate to their character' (*RIP*, 509). This activity, for Oakeshott, takes the form of 'contemplating' or 'delighting' in images which are merely present, provoking neither speculation nor inquiry. As objects under contemplation, these images have no history (*RIP*, 510), nor are they oriented toward a purpose. 'Contemplation does not use, or use up or wear out its images, or induce change in them: it rests in them' (*RIP*, 510).[3]

For religion to be understood as a species of poetry, it must be shown to be a form of non-representational image-making conducive to contemplative rest. Put in this way, the trajectories of religion and poetry begin to converge. For religion – if we understand here a language or way of life as distinct from its reflective grammar – is full of images which, like poetry, 'positively provoke a contemplative attitude' in part because of their 'resistance to being read symbolically' (*RIP*, 517). To be sure, religious worship – and particularly religious art – is full of strict symbolic language, but when that language seeks only to discern and to translate the symbolic images into dogmatic content, it has ceased to be contemplative, and, like the language of the literary critic, has entered into a non-contemplative mode; the images 'have merely ceased to be poetic images' (*RIP*, 528). To engage symbols religiously is to treat them like a poem – a performative utterance whose value lies exclusively in its presence, and not in its usefulness as something conveying information, or affirming a state of mind, or confirming a truth beyond its present performance. Religious truth (or the truth of ritual), no less than Oakeshott's description of 'poetic truth' (*RIP*, 521) is a field of unique and incommensurable valence.

How can this be so? The religious life is not primarily a grammar to be analyzed but a language to be spoken, one that, when spoken, both enacts and changes the language which has been inherited. ('Poetry, then begins and ends as a language' [*RIP*, 527].) In the act of worship or ritual, or in religious contemplation, the images are properly not objects of reflective application or translation. On the contrary, the religious disposition re-creates or recapitulates the images in a moment of self-enactment. In this sense, religious ritual is a dramatic action of absolute presence in which form and content are one and the image and its creator are understood as a 'perpetually extending partnership between the contemplating self and its images' (*RIP*, 513). In the religious and liturgical utterance, unlike in its scientific or practical counterpart, '*what* is said and *how* it is said, doctrine and activity' are indistinguishable (*RIP*, 539). Perhaps this is the 'something more' which is enjoyed, perhaps obliquely, when one enjoys 'the momentary release' and 'brief enchantment' of the voice of poetry (*RIP*, 540).[4]

---

[3] The relationship between rest, contemplation, and religious worship becomes clear in Josef Pieper, *Leisure, The Basis of Culture* (Indianapolis: Liberty Fund, 1999).

[4] For an extensive, explicit theological exploration of these same themes, see Hans Urs von Balthasar's magisterial, five volume *Theo-Drama: Theological Dramatic Theory* (San Francisco: Ignatius Press, 1989–1998).

So far our account has addressed only the solitary activity of the religious life, though it has acknowledged the origins of its language in communal practice. Yet, religious activity expressly does not view others in terms of the common relationships of practical activity. Rather, the religious disposition of poetic imagining views others as persons to be delighted in, to be enjoyed for their own sakes in friendship and in love (*RIP*, 537). Indeed, because living religiously is an adverbial, not a substantive condition, the one who lives religiously is more prone to bestow himself graciously on others because he is unpreoccupied with abstract ideals. In this, religion is a kind of 'truancy' from the practical life; but its truancy is the truancy of the sacred from the mundane, an intimation of the truancy of the eternal from the temporal, an absence which restores us, if only momentarily, to a rich and restful presence in life.[5]

The distinction between religion as a feature of the moral life understood as a habit of affection – as distinct from a habit of reflective application – helps render more intelligible Oakeshott's tantalizingly brief but rich remarks on religion in *On Human Conduct*.[6] There, Oakeshott's treatment of religion is a brief interlude in his discussion of moral conduct, and in particular a detour within his elucidation of the difference between self-disclosure and self-enactment (a distinction I have already anticipated here in describing the character of the religious life). Self-disclosure Oakeshott identifies as 'choosing satisfactions to pursue' with respect to acknowledged conditions to which one subscribes. Self-enactment he describes as 'choosing the sentiments in which to act' where conditions are 'intimated in a language of moral conduct' (*OHC*, 76). The vocabulary of moral self-disclosure and virtuous self-enactment constitute a single language for Oakeshott, yet 'they concern different things' (*OHC*, 77). Significantly, Oakeshott emphasizes what we might call the linguistic aspect of morality.

> A morality, then, is neither a system of general principles nor a code of rules, but a vernacular language. General principles and even rules may be elicited from it, but (like other languages) it is not the creation of grammarians; it is made by speakers. What has to be learned in a moral education is not a theorem such as that good conduct is acting fairly or being charitable, nor is it a rule such as 'always tell the truth', but how to speak the language intelligently. (*OHC*, 78–9)

In this context, Oakeshott describes religious faith as 'a gift ... of a reconciliation to the unavoidable dissonances of a human condition ... a mode of acceptance, a 'graceful' response' (*OHC*, 81). A man's religion, 'like the language he speaks and the poetic utterances evoked from it' is historically contingent; a man is 'fortunate where he has a religion, a *traditio*, of notable imaginative splendour to draw upon' (*OHC*, 81). Here, it would seem, a man who acts religiously is one who enters into a necessarily conservative fund of historically contingent images and finds

---

[5]   See further Josef Pieper, *In Search of the Sacred: Contributions to an Answer* (San Francisco: Ignatius Press, 1991).

[6]   Oakeshott, *On Human Conduct* (Oxford: Clarendon Press, 1975). Hereafter: *OHC*.

in them a contemplative splendor which unites the present with eternity. To act religiously is not an act of self-disclosure but rather of self-enactment that abates 'the unresolved and inconclusive character of human conduct' (*OHC*, 84). This enacted self is a 'fugitive' – Augustine might call him a pilgrim – understood as having a performative or 'dramatic identity' (*OHC*, 84). The religious imagination, like the poetic imagination, pictures human life in terms of mutability and the intimations of that which does not change. Religious faith is, for Oakeshott, 'the evocation of a sentiment … to be added to all others as the motive of all motives in terms of which the fugitive adventures of human conduct, without being released from their mortal and their moral conditions, are graced with an intimation of immortality' (*OHC*, 85). Theology may provide the grammar and vocabulary of a religious life, but only a human being can speak it; only when the language of self-enactment is spoken religiously can the human life embark on its encounter with eternity. 'A man may enact himself religiously,' writes Oakeshott, 'but there are no religious actions' (*OHC*, 86). The religious life is a creative or re-creative performance of reconciliation and graceful acceptance, whose dignity depends upon – and transcends – the poetic quality of the images, rituals, observances, and offerings that invite us to restful contemplation in which one is most fully present.

The purpose of religion as a language of self-enactment is not, for Oakeshott, to communicate the feeling of transcendence or the symbolism of divine love. Rather, religion is for him one significant, fugitive means by which we enact ourselves in performative utterances of poetic delight, reconciliation, and presence. To look for the content in Oakeshott's account of religion is to make a categorical mistake; for Oakeshott is concerned with the *form* of religion – not mere form, but the adverbial condition of what it means to enact oneself religiously in an attitude of reconciliation and graceful acceptance.

The natural conservatism of the religious disposition may mitigate some of the pernicious effects of moral and political Rationalism. The defense of poetry may preserve the possibility of a religious disposition, for language conserves the religious disposition in two ways: first, by reminding us that we inhabit a world of historical contingency in which our inheritance must be claimed in each present moment or it will be lost; and second, by illustrating the poetic – that is, performative – imaginings of which religion is a special case.

Hannah Arendt once described free, virtuosic human action (akin to Oakeshott's self-enactment) as the miraculous possibility of something new.[7] The religious disposition preserves this sense of the miraculous by permitting a creative, sacred imagining. The religious disposition may of necessity be inclined to silence. Like Hugo in Iris Murdoch's *Under the Net*, there are moments when perhaps *we oughtn't to talk*. Religious utterances may be largely silent utterances; to act religiously may simply be *to be present* in a way that speech cannot disclose. And, were speech to attempt such a disclosure, the religiously enacted performance itself would be falsified.

---

[7] Hannah Arendt, 'What is Freedom,' in *The Portable Hannah Arendt* (New York: Penguin, 2003), 460.

III

The words of Murdoch's Hugo suggest Oakeshottian echoes in another literary character, one not based on Oakeshott yet still comprehensible through an Oakeshottian lens: the bishop in Willa Cather's novel *Death Comes for the Archbishop*. 'Where there is great love there are always miracles,' says the Bishop to his dearest friend.

> One might almost say that an apparition is human vision corrected by divine love. I do not see you as you really are, Joseph; I see you through my affection for you. The Miracles of the Church seem to me to rest not so much upon faces or voices or healing power coming suddenly near to us from afar off, but upon our perceptions being made finer, so that for a moment our eyes can see and our ears can hear what is there about us always.[8]

These miracles are acts of supreme image-making possessing their own truth, both in themselves and in how they fashion our perceptions of others. Oakeshott speaks of religion as 'simply life itself, life dominated by the belief that its value is in the present, not merely in the past or the future'; the religious life is 'synonymous with life itself at its fullest.... [T]here can be no revival of religion which is not a revival of a more daring and more sensitive way of living.'[9] In his formal account of the religious disposition, Oakeshott has helped us to see that the mystery of the human person – and of eternity – is not disclosed, it is enacted anew by concentrating in each present moment a lifetime's gift of love.

---

[8]   Willa Cather, *Death Comes for the Archbishop* (New York: Vintage, 1990), 50.
[9]   Oakeshott, *'Religion and the World,'* in *Religion, Politics and the Moral Life*, ed. Timothy Fuller (New Haven: Yale Univ. Press, 1993), 34–5. Hereafter: *RPML*.

4

Byron Kaldis

Religion and Art: Modal Formalism and Political Antinomies

I

Becoming immersed in actual political life, religion and art are led to transgress their boundaries as 'reclusive' or *'anchoritic'* special modes of experience. In losing their unique and integral *formalism* these modes exhibit a certain antinomy. This antinomy has to do with the paradoxical or unexpected positioning of religion versus art in actual political life along the spectrum of what is ordinarily understood as political conservatism. Despite initial convergence in terms of the absence from both of 'technical' reason, art and religion may turn out as internally contradictory and externally antithetical in their respective conservative or progressive qualities when, in shedding their authentic Oakeshottian character, they embrace 'social-engineering' or 'technical' *raisonnement* appropriate to political argument and ideology, for such an *ésprit de geometrie* is foreign to both of them. The 'mechanized control' that the sovereignty of rationalist technique hopes for, according to Oakeshott's well-known critique, aims at the triumph of the homogeneous employment of reason. Yet, I wish to claim that this over-confidence for the homogeneity of rationalist technique across domains founders in the case of religion and art when these enter into politics. Political reason generates political antinomies.

My argument extends ideas left implicit by Oakeshott himself, but adds to his theory of modality by exploring the specific problems arising from a forced political relevance for religion and art. This idea of an antinomy of political reason 'corrupting' these particular modes of experience by inhering in them, thus removing them from their pristine separateness is not of course found precisely as such in Oakeshott's texts; but I claim that his writings furnish us with the instruments of such a diagnosis. As to their precise status as 'modes' I have to postpone this until the last section. Officially he treats neither art nor religion under such a status, although the number of areas of experience to be regarded as modes is left open explicitly. It is therefore worth our while to ask to what extent they could be considered as special modes on a par with those he examines. However, whatever the final verdict is, as to their status what I claim is – and must remain – special to religion and art compared to the other Oakeshottian modes, according to my reconstruction, is that the dichotomy between self and world (in Bradleyan terms) or inquiry and object thereof or form and content is absent only in their case (see end of section 4).

An antinomy is understood to be, in the manner made prominent by Kant, a contradiction in the sense of a conflict of two antithetical series of philosophical syllogisms about a certain metaphysical issue, both equally valid. I am employing Kant's idea in order to bring forth the diagnosis of a contradiction in which both art and religion get ensnared, once they begin acquiring a political voice. Each can equally turn out to be both politically conservative and anti-conservative at the same time and on the same grounds provided by a technical/rationalist argumentation – analogous to the two equally valid antithetical series of philosophical positions in Kant's scheme. In our case, it is political 'technical' reason in its social-engineering capacity that is responsible for the antinomies. In the case of pure reason, Kant has famously spoken of four specific antinomies whereby a thesis and an equivalent antithesis about, for example, causality and freedom or the cosmological beginnings of the world, emerge as unavoidable logical pairs when pure reason refuses to get the benefit of a philosophical disciplinary restraint offered by the only philosophical position capable of doing so, i.e. Kant's own transcendental idealism. Kant speaks revealingly of the otherwise natural tendency of the human mind to opt for an 'architectonic' of reason.[1] This 'architectonic' takes the side of the theses while it is denied by the antitheses, the role of the latter being precisely this: to unsettle such a tendency towards a neat mental self-structuring on the part of the human subject of knowledge. The 'architectonic' expresses reason's confidence that parts of knowledge can (or cannot, for that matter, as the recalcitrant antitheses reveal) form, in unison with the rest of the segments of knowledge, a coherently unified, systematic building. For Oakeshott, too – hailing, however, not from a Kantian but from a neo-Hegelian point of intellectual origin – the entire spectrum of the modes of experience seen without the unavoidable arrest or abstraction each imposes on the totality of experience in its concreteness, can also be considered as such a sought-for, yet constantly evanescent, architectonic tower. Oakeshott castigates the moral equivalent of the human tendency to such an 'architectonic'. He points out that such a penchant for a resolution of actual moral plurality, wrongly 'understood as so many contingent and regrettable divergencies from a fancied perfect and universal language of moral intercourse' is not surprising: 'human beings are apt to be disconcerted unless they feel themselves to be upheld by something more substantial than the emanations of their own contingent imaginations.'[2] But such an urge for an 'architectonic' resolution of opposite moral theses or for effacing difference and silencing polyphony should prove both fruitless and frustrating and, what is more, even dangerous in distorting the character of religion and art, in the case of technical reason's politicizing effect on them – as I wish to show.

---

[1] Immanuel Kant, *Critique of Pure Reason*, trans. Norman Kemp Smith (London: Macmillan, 1929), A475/B503; Cf. on antinomy F. H. Bradley, *Appearance and Reality* (Oxford: Clarendon Press, 1897), 232.
[2] Oakeshott, *On Human Conduct* (Oxford: Clarendon Press, 1975), 80. Hereafter: *OHC*.

For Kant these 'antithetics', as he calls the tug-of-war internal to pure reason, get resolved by transcendental idealism, whereas in the discussion that follows nothing of the sort is being attempted. On the contrary, while retaining Kant's general inspiration about the predicament of reason (or parallelly, of an Oakeshottian mode) overstepping its boundaries, as well as his idea of the natural yet dangerous tendency towards building the parts of knowledge in unison with each other, I want to claim that an Oakeshottian diagnosis does not of course aim at a resolution *via* something playing the role of transcendental idealism. Rather, it underlines the need for retaining the distinctions between the modes, even in conversation, while coming to terms with the necessarily partially-built, fragmentary field of knowledge (repudiating the illusion of an alleged self-completeness that technical/ rationalist knowledge arrogates to itself, a completeness appropriately lacking in the case of practical/traditional knowledge he embraces instead [*RIP*, 16–7]). This is one feature of Oakeshottian thought we need to employ here.

An additional one is, I claim, equally significant yet seemingly at odds with the unavoidably partial character of our cognitive building: this other feature which my discussion below will attempt to bring forth has to do with the idea of *presentness* and *timelessness* central to Oakeshott's thought on matters such as aesthetic contemplation and the religious attitude. It is clear at first sight that the two features do not harmonize with each other, not at least on their own: If human knowledge is informed by a generally skeptical attitude favoring necessary incompleteness translated into an ongoing construction through time, then to search for a metaphysical locus in which the permanent is present, time defied, contingency abated, and transience suspended is tantamount to denying the former position against the 'architectonic' of finished outcomes.[3] So these two Oakeshottian features ask to be reconciled. While Kant therefore tried to reconcile the theses with the antitheses thus eradicating the antinomies, the case I am here presenting points to a conflict that cannot be overcome without reconstruction.

This involves two levels or claims: one is the idea that completeness or epistemological closure is unattainable due to some of Oakeshott's well known strictures against the profligate demands of Rationalism's 'technical' reason plus his insistence on keeping the modes of experience apart; on the other level, or meta-claim, the separation of modes is not adequate to the task of avoiding the antinomies, in fact, this appears not to be the issue anymore. What we now get involved in is quite another predicament even if, that is, we were careful enough to keep the modes unadulterated. Now the new and at first sight insurmountable obstacle is successfully to honor both of the two Oakeshottian demands or features identified here. It is not immediately apparent how, while accepting incompleteness and contingency immersed as we are within time thus rejecting essentialism, teleology or once-and-for-all technical reason with its '*monistic yearnings*', we can go on searching nevertheless for timelessness such as the 'reconciliation to the

---

[3]   It is no accident that Oakeshott thought of the instance of youth and the period spent by one in university education as Paterian lived-in moments of an otherwise sought-for but never attained metaphysical presentness.

unavoidable dissonances of the human condition' that Oakeshott conceives the 'gift of religious faith' essentially to consist in (*OHC*, 81).

That is, I want to stress that the Kantian-type of antinomy of thesis vs. antithesis is present at two levels here according to my argument: it appears both at a meta-level as well as at the particular level of religion and art. In the former, there is an antinomy in the generic account of knowledge informed by both these two Oakeshottian features identified here as antithetical but equally valid epistemic demands held in tandem, i.e. the antinomy appears within Oakeshott's thought itself. At the same time it is manifested at the specific level of religion and art when these two domains of experience acquire simultaneously politically contradictory attributes as a result of these two features getting mixed up in this specific case: that is, we must decide whether the contradictory political positioning of art and religion is a result of their losing their modal separateness or whether it is the result of seeking, in vain, a permanence and timelessness in them.

Of course, Oakeshott himself was well aware of this discord between the two features without, of course, identifying or naming them explicitly as such. He thus paid considerable attention to re-defining one of the central protagonists here, namely, contemplation, traditionally an activity related to the second feature of timeless permanence yet having to do with time-bound human conduct, without falling into contradiction, i.e., by keeping the two features or 'antithetics' reconciled in this case (I shall come back to this in more detail at the start of the next section). He also underlined that religious and artistic self-enactment capture presentness (the second feature) without contradicting epistemic incompleteness (the first one) – or without making the elementary mistake, as he himself is quick to point out in a remarkable note in *Experience and its Modes*,[4] of mixing up the possibility of successfully engaging in contemplative moments or philosophizing with a hapless withdrawal from mundane practical activity.

The problem, rather, is one for *us*: how is it that *we* shall employ two Oakeshottian methodological strictures or generic epistemic features in order to make the diagnosis of antinomies cogent. Is art paradoxically aligned with conservative political activity due to the loss of modal independence or modal firmness, abandoning its pristine locus outside politics and getting mixed with it (feature one becoming predominant), or is it due to the loss of the mystical timelessness of contemplative experience in taking the didactic turn (feature two getting relinquished)? Similarly for religion, is its anti-conservative placement a function of its loss of modal separateness or is it a matter of the violation of the timelessness of its central activity, namely faith? What all this questioning comes to is this: can Oakeshott supply us with consistent tools for our diagnosis? And if this is not a problem for him since he was interested in questions different from the one we are posing, it is certainly a problem for any one of us who wishes to employ his ideas in a coherent way. I shall avoid making an argument as to whether this may turn out in the end to be a problem for Oakeshott's thought as such; that is, that we can find a tension between two central streaks (the two features identified

---

[4]   Oakeshott, *Experience and Its Modes* (Cambridge: Cambridge Univ. Press, 1985), 310 n. 1.

here) yielding antithetical results or at least inviting opposite treatments. But as regards his or any important thinker's significance for us when we wish to posit questions other than the ones he cared to raise or when we wish to bring to light problems distinct from those that engaged his interest by employing his most central methodological ideas, we certainly face a problem. Anticipating my result, though, I believe that we do not in fact have such a problem when we enter Oakeshott's thought in order to accomplish fruitful work of our own; his insights do not conflict when we wish to employ them for our own purposes.

One indication of Oakeshott's consistency is relevant to my present theme. Though I am not interested in precise exegesis of Oakeshott's texts, or discovering a pattern of development in his thoughts on religion and art, I nevertheless subscribe to the view expressed by Timothy Fuller, that the themes of *self*-understanding, of the importance of presentness and the non-teleological approach, and of the transcendence of the self in losing oneself in God, all these themes stayed with him throughout his life.[5] Similarly the common element shared by religion and art is revealed early on in his thought and is retained until the end, namely their joint juxtaposition against, or their placement outside, the practice of political activity. Politics is clearly mundane, even if unavoidable, and certainly never 'poetic', 'mystical,' or 'reflective' in the way that art and religion are despite their different modalities – or despite the unique mode of being practical in a different non-mundane way that religion exhibits as a kind of 'consummation of practice' (*EM*, 292). It appears then that at the meta-level the presence of the second epistemic feature is both central and not incongruent to the other one. My own concern here is, however, the entanglement of these features in the specific cases of religion and art, worlds of experience in which the second feature ought to be prominent (as we just saw) yet reconciled with the first one. Failing to structure this reconciliation in the right away as I shall try to do in what follows is responsible – I wish to argue – for the appearance of political antinomies at the heart of a distorted and politicized religious or aesthetic attitude. What turns out to be crucial is the precise meaning of 'practical' as we shall see. So in answer to the questions of the previous paragraph as to where the deforming tendencies come from – is abandoning feature one responsible, or is surrendering the demands of feature two the source of the antinomies – I would say that the common element in both I wish to pinpoint is the illicit use of technical reason in overextending itself. Therefore, behind either a wrongly overflowing modal barriers inundating religion or art in the vain hope of an architectonic or behind the loss of the ideals of timeless and permanence, lies the non-legitimated overdose of political-cum-engineering rationalism.

To substantiate my argument, I show first in the section that follows how this reconciliation of epistemic features may be effected – within certain limits and under certain conditions – by philosophy as understood by Oakeshott in a very specific way adding to this my own reconstruction and a hermeneutic strategy. In this we get a first route towards our theme, that is, the danger of deforming religion and art.

---

[5] Timothy Fuller's 'Introduction' in Oakeshott, *Religion, Politics and the Moral Life*, ed. Timothy Fuller (New Haven: Yale Univ. Press, 1993), 3, 10. Hereafter: *RPML*.

Section 3 carries further the theme of the anti-political-rationalist critique and its relevance for our two areas and the resulting antinomies while Section 4 examines in detail religion and art, separately, each one in terms of its distinctive apolitical authenticity and distinguishes three senses of 'practical' a distinction crucial to my project. Finally Section 5 offers the concluding considerations.

II

A number of high quality scholarly works have focused recently on the combined theme of aesthetic experience and religious attitude, as Oakeshott understood them – sometimes in an admittedly unusual if not eccentric way.[6] However, my treatment of this theme and the combination of these two 'modes of experience' I am putting forward issues from a different standpoint. I am doing the reverse of what Efraim Podoksik articulates, especially when he comes to Oakeshott's later ideas and finds them ambiguous with respect to the place of art on the margins of society. Podoksik describes correctly how Oakeshott is forced to qualify the absolute irrelevance of poetry to practice thus ending up with an ambiguous position.[7] My approach, rather, is to show that this ambiguity, which an exegesis is bound to discern in Oakeshott's earlier and later views, though correct, is at the same time part and parcel of my central thesis: namely, that religion and art get distorted or exhibit the ambiguity of antinomies if they are allowed to assume the role of another mode, that of politics. Our topic, I want to emphasize, is reflected in the building blocks themselves, the ideas we borrow from Oakeshott, which scholars have found ambiguous. This ambiguity in Oakeshott's own ideas is not carelessness on his part; rather it is a proof of my diagnosis.[8]

---

[6]   See Glenn Worthington, *Religious and Poetic Experience in the Thought of Michael Oakeshott* (London: Imprint, 2005); Worthington, 'Michael Oakeshott and the City of God,' *Political Theory*, 28, no. 3 (June 2000): 377–98; Worthington, 'Poetic Experience and the Good Life in Writings of Michael Oakeshott,' *European Journal of Political Theory*, 4, no. 1 (2005): 57–66; Worthington, 'Michael Oakeshott on Life: Waiting with Godot,' *History of Political Thought*, 16, no. 1 (Spring 1995): 105–19. While I agree on many points with Worthington, my standpoint is different than his. Also, see Elizabeth Campbell Corey, *Michael Oakeshott on Religion, Aesthetics and Politics* (Columbia: Univ. of Missouri Press, 2006). Corey's book-length treatment is excellent though I have no space to express some of my disagreement with her verdicts in chapters 3 and 4. Finally, see Corey Abel, 'The Theological Analogue of the Civil Condition' presented at the Third Plenary Meeting of the Michael Oakeshott Association, Colorado College, Colorado Springs, June 3–5, 2006, which shows how Oakeshott's view of religion together with his unique understanding of conservatism may be responsible for his being in principle unable to compose a post-Montaigne Christian apology. Abel's points are relevant to what I say below in section 4.

[7]   Efraim Podoksik, 'The Voice of Poetry in the Thought of Michael Oakeshott,' *Journal of the History of Ideas*, 63, no. 4, (2002): 717–33, esp. 729.

[8]   It is all to the good for a hermeneutical approach (see next paragraphs) that Oakeshott, not only pursues reflective thinking as an ongoing activity that shuns both teleological and essentialist final truths waiting to be discovered (and in this sense his peculiar brand of Idealism is his most forceful point); but also that, as a remarkable stylist of precisely this kind of reflective mental activity, which he never tires of championing, his texts contain ambiguities that invite multiple interpretations. He was not even remotely interested in being finicky about strictly logical argumentation or detailed analysis (though rigor was never sacrificed) and he was thus happy to include ideas that would, logically speaking, not sit in purely deductive comfort with others a few pages below. In fact it is indicative of this tendency that in one of his texts he talks about

What I am doing falls within the philosophical genre described at the very start of the Preface to *On Human Conduct*,[9] where Oakeshott says, 'Philosophical reflection is ... the adventure of one who seeks to understand in other terms what he already understands.... Its most appropriate expression is an essay where the character of the utterance (a traveler's tale) matches the character of the engagement, an intellectual adventure which has a course to follow but no destination' (*OHC*, vii). Such a philosophical *essai* is also called a 'continuous voyage' or 'unbroken descent.[10] These metaphoric figures remind us of a subtle point Oakeshott insists on repeatedly: the necessity to keep unconditional and continuously critical or subversive reflection – i.e. philosophy unfettered by 'facts' – linked with its subject matter, in the case at hand, the world of politics (cf. my point about his re-defining contemplation in the previous Section). 'Radical reflective subversiveness' must find a way to stay in touch with, or 'moored', as he says, in its mundane subject–matter instead of losing itself in unfettered speculative flight. The best way to understand how philosophical reflection is responsible for fixing whatever permanent character political activity may be seen to have (paralleling the two features above: permanence vs. incompleteness) is, I propose, by means of the model of a *hermeneutics* of text and context (*RPML*, 151–2). This is why I would disagree with some interpreters who try to link Oakeshott's criticism of a *per impossibile* philosophical politics with something like Bradley's or Strauss' moral and political pronouncements on the eternal causes of the changing world of contingency, which philosophy is supposed to have discovered. Oakeshott does not claim that philosophical reflection sees things *as they truly are*, meaning anything essentialist by it, as the usual interpretation of 'eternal causes of contingency' would unavoidably push him to; rather, his claim is to be taken, I suggest, in the sense of a hermeneutics which is moderate and intellectually humble enough to be able to 'read' meanings by means of a continuous interpretative enterprise, rather than impose substantive goals onto the activity, i.e. politics, that it reflects upon.

---

the self very much in the spirit of Hume's image of a bundle of sensations while placing all this in a context of a Berkeley-type of idealism. The fecundity gained by re-reading Oakeshott's texts is well attested by anyone familiar with them. Re-reading Kant's texts may give us better or more coherent arguments but no new theses, whereas coming back to Oakeshott one always gains new inspiration and fresh ideas. Engaging in an Oakeshottian mode of reflection on a certain predicament is something that he himself urges us to do (as he does in the closing paragraph of 'The Tower of Babel,' *RIP*, 487): clear the misconceptions that are part and parcel of our interminable efforts at understanding, not in order to get rid of them automatically, as soon as they are seen as such, or denounce them conclusively, but at least to know what lies beneath, to think not in order to conclude, but in order to begin thinking anew. [A similar view is to be found in Debra Candreva's 'Oakeshott and Plato: A Philosophical Conversation,' in Corey Abel and Timothy Fuller eds., *The Intellectual Legacy of Michael Oakeshott* (Thorverton, Exeter: Imprint Academic, 2005), 2–20, in which she argues that Oakeshott understood himself as, and may plausibly be construed as a Socratic thinker. – *Ed.*]

[9]   Of course thinking as an on-going activity that cannot cease without thereby terminating itself echoes Hobbes's famous image of death as the cessation or absence of all motion. Cf. section 4 below for the same idea.

[10] 'Political Philosophy' (*RPML*, 153); on page 139 of the same essay Oakeshott clearly indicates a hermeneutical stance that he wishes to adopt naming it *'dialectical'*. On the idea of 'unbroken descent' in some early writings of his see *RPML*, 153, and for that of 'unconditional theorizing' and 'radical subversive reflection' *RPML*, 24, 127, 136, 142, 149, 150, 155.

These considerations on the precise nature of philosophical reflection ('subversive yet moored') as well as my proposed hermeneutic stance allow us to see how we should understand the authentic nature of artistic and religious experiences, and how it is lost once they get attached to politics, becoming surrogates of political activity, i.e. when they lose their necessary *formal* distance from it. I wish to make an analogous case here, too. Just as subversive unconditional theorizing 'does not mount on wings' (*RPML* 153) but rather it must be kept complementary to its practical object so that philosophical discourse could successfully talk about, and reflect genuinely upon, a definite something rather than an indefinite nothing so, too, art and religion must keep a subtle balance of distance-*cum*-engagement with practical activity (without of course becoming surrogate moral voices, either).[11] In both instances this subtle balance, a 'dialectic of reflection' (*RPML*, 152) is, I believe, furnished by means of having philosophy in the one case, and art and religion in the other case, accomplish this acrobatics of distance-and-touch. Oakeshott's 'unbroken descent' from the upper strata of thought to mundane action can best be seen as a hermeneutics of sorts, whereby what philosophy or art and religion do – the former as reflective thought, the two latter as special 'non-theorem bound' modes of experience – is to capture the cluster of meanings (cf. his idea of philosophical definition providing a 'greater economy of concepts' [*RPML*, 131]) constituting their practical opposites, i.e. the world of contingency, without, however, losing themselves in it or adopting its technical or social engineering style of reasoning. Once they err towards the latter, religion and art get involved in antinomies of political reasoning.

My hermeneutic approach to Oakeshott is connected to the careful contrast he draws between conditional and unconditional understanding. To escape[12] the arrests of experience (imposed unavoidably by the separate modes) with the help of a critical reflection both on the conditionality or abstractness of these modes and on the resulting partiality of experience (the first epistemic feature) does not simply obliterate the modes or lead one to an immediate vision of the whole (the equivalent of the second epistemic feature). Disclosing any conditional theorizing as such, exhibiting its conditionality or its presupposed postulates (e.g. of a certain scientific field), does not thereby issue in an entirely unconditional surrender of the sought-for absolute or concrete totality to our philosophical reflection. Rather, Oakeshott stresses the continuous *activity* of philosophizing (or theorizing), its ascending steps of inquiring into the conditionality of conditions, and this is how the link between reflection and its object is exhibited. Reflection discloses, for instance in the case of the practical activity of human conduct, the conditional self-understandings of practical agents involved in their give-and-take, as well as the understandings of inquirers within modally confined disciplines trying to explain

[11] Guarding against religion becoming morality is a preoccupation of much of Oakeshott's early work, while preventing art from becoming an ethical-social consciousness is a theme of the mature *OHC* and other essays, most famously, 'The Voice of Poetry in the Conversation of Mankind' in *Rationalism in Politics and other essays*, new and expanded edition, ed. Timothy Fuller (Indianapolis: Liberty Fund, 1991), 488–541. Hereafter: *RIP*.
[12] On 'escape' see *EM*, 3, 297, 355. Cf. 'The Voice of Poetry in the Conversation of Mankind' (*RIP*, 535).

this conduct (e.g. sociology, psychology, political history, etc.). Some of these understandings (theoretical explanations) are in terms of theorems, or concepts, such as 'cause-effect' or 'human nature', but they are theorems nonetheless that remain implicitly accepted within a given 'world' of experience on the basis of postulates, i.e. epistemic conditions. The subversive radicalism of philosophy is not to magically obliterate these preconditions; it is not to achieve a *per impossibile* unconditional stepping-up to a hoped for 'top of the tower'; it is rather confined to a modest yet pertinacious questioning: 'what constitutes its unconditionality is the continuous recognition of the conditionality of the conditions' (*OHC*, 11). The modest 'self-consciously conditional theorist' must not 'offend' by surrendering to the 'deplorable character' of the 'theoretician' who is aiming at imposing 'correct conduct' and 'substantive ends' from without (*OHC*, 26). We see in this a first way of how we can soften the demands of the second epistemic feature – total permanence and timelessness or radical unconditional reflection – by not misunderstanding its precise nature and letting it overshoot its mark; and thus we can further see how we may be able to reconcile it with those of the first. That is, start reconciling the recalcitrant 'antithetics'.

When self-reflection or understanding by theorems begins to be the principal way in which the 'modes' of religion and art articulate their domain, it is salutary that a voice like Oakeshott's is warning us against a logically *prior* misplaced philosophical reflection on politics. If philosophy is shown to be out of place when it turns political, it is *doubly* so when art and religion turn first 'reflective' and then 'political'. Barring the wrong engagement of philosophy with politics prepares the way for blocking art and religion from being politicized. Given this, there are two routes we can take or two questions to ask. What I wish to do here is to introduce the idea of modal formalism in an attempt to re-work further the second epistemic feature.

(a) Being sceptical about philosophical politics, that is, the politics of the wrong kind imposing a rationalist-deductive style of understanding on, and attempting to interfere with, political life from an *a priori* foundation (be that contract theory or Natural Law or what not), and acknowledging that reality ('as such', as it were) outstrips our comprehension forever in the constant unresolved movement of thought and its object, it is natural to ask whether there may be a field – other than such a misplaced and misnamed 'political philosophy', itself an oxymoron – where an error such as this political Rationalism or Gnosticism is not committed. Is there really another means by which we can attain 'truth' in the special sense of what modes of experience can offer? Historically, artistic creation and religious sentiments are two classic candidates for this role and, what I wish to point out, the Oakeshottian analysis, suitably reconstructed by smoothing out the 'antithetics' of the its features above, can explain why.

(b) Authentic politics (in contrast to that of technical rationalism) has to do with *respublica* – a system of purely *authoritative* rules, 'not a system of theorems' – demanding civil obligation appropriate to such a *formally* defined civil association or 'moral condition,' which eschews substantive ends or advantages: 'there cannot be an obligation to acknowledge the truth or the falsity of a theorem or a doctrine' (*OHC*, 171) The politics of civil association exhausts itself in the 'subscription to conditions formulated in rules indifferent to the merits of any interest' (*OHC*, 172). It does not commit the error of providing, in the form of a political *philosophy*, a superior 'substitute' for the supposed nescience of the lower levels of any conditional understanding such as social-scientific understanding ('map-making' or 'diagnosis') or the self-understanding of actors themselves engaged in everyday political conduct (*OHC*, 26–9). The 'self-authenticating' property of *respublica* (*OHC*, 150), which in this aspect is not unlike Kant's Categorical Imperative, needing no legitimation outside itself and its *Grundnorm* is, I claim, akin to what Oakeshott identifies as fabricating *par excellence* accomplished only in art. There is a certain analogy in the non-purposiveness of both civil association and aesthetic experience. Creation of the finished art product has its self-contained meaning inherent in it, not in an external or future response by other agents, as ordinary fabrication or the cycle of economic production necessarily involve, i.e. the constant agitation of the world of 'doings' and *'pragmata'* in the language of later Oakeshott (*OHC*, 35-6, and see also below page 21). Thus art, authentically, is not – must not be – a species of 'performing.' When, however, art becomes entangled in the world of means-ends substantive pursuits of ordinary conduct, it loses its own distinctive identity that unites Content and Form; in thus losing its soul, supposedly gains the world as when, similarly, 'Practical Experience, to gain the whole world, must lose its own soul' (*EM*, 310) – that is, a partial mode of abstraction can never attain concreteness by deluding itself into struggling to become less defective and more concrete while retaining its specific (non-concrete) identity, be that practice or art. Art becomes sadly eligible for wholesale assimilation to politics understood in terms of the lowest common denominator: who gets what, when and how.[13] But the analogy to the formal character of civil association helps us guard it against such a deformation and its attendant antinomy.

Similarly, the union of Form and Content may be seen also in the field of religion in a parallel sense, as 'a release from the bondage of contingent circumstance' (*OHC*, 76). This refers to the feature of *presentness* that I and others identify as central to the Oakeshottian conception of religious experience. This presentness is epitomized in the deliverance 'from the deadliness of doing,' i.e. from neverending activity chasing after substantive ends or desires. This deliverance, Oakeshott writes, may be 'gracefully enjoyed in the quiet of a religious faith' (*OHC*, 74) away from the interminable succession of episodes of activity aiming at a certain satisfaction. But note that this is a matter of self-enactment (see below) and of faith (*vide Interimsethik*), not one of joining an organized religious community with which civil association proper should never be confused (*OHC*, 119). The *formal* ontology characterizing a civil association in terms only of *lex*, which to the vexation of many critics seems to call for a political serenity akin to Oakeshott's image of religious deliverance, has its counterpart in the formal properties responsible for keeping

---

[13] Though I disagree with his overall point, cf. Wendell John Coats, Jr., 'Michael Oakeshott and the Poetic Character of Human Activity' in Corey Abel and Timothy Fuller eds., *The Intellectual Legacy of Michael Oakeshott* (London: Imprint Academic, 2005), 312–13. For the underestimation of the intellectual element in religion on the part of Oakeshott see Kevin Williams, 'The Voice of Religion in the Conversation of Mankind,' *Doctrine and Life* 38 (1988): 395–404.

religion and art as unique modes of experience separated from the contingency of ordinary socio-political engineering: neither is religion to be identified by means of a communal grouping-enterprise in the service of a substantive belief (in a supreme being or what not), nor is art to be identified by the substantive ends of a fabricating that asks for responses from external observers. Oakeshott's insistence on artistic contemplative delight must be linked to what he says in a footnote about Aristotle's *eudaimonia*; namely, that it must not be misunderstood as a 'substantive condition of things' (*OHC*, 118–9 n. 1). The key is in the *formalism*.

III

With the exception of the historical instance of natural or rational religion (and perhaps deism) religion and art have been traditionally identified as modes of experience explicitly inimical to, or implicitly dissociated from, rational-*cum*-instrumental thought. Either stemming from doctrinal considerations or the pre-eminence of emotions that were part and parcel of religious belief or artistic creation, instrumental rationality has been construed as foreign to them, or rather as something that would contaminate their distinctive character. Recent intellectual fashions such as postmodernism have, to a large extent, given additional credit to this traditional disjunction of reason on the one hand, and art or religion on the other, by emphasizing the legitimacy of sceptical and relativist attitudes against all sorts of essentialist talk.

One crucial methodological point is in order here. The previous paragraph is phrased in Oakeshottian terms, i.e. in accordance with a characterization of art and religion as 'ideal' types or characters or as abstracted modes of experience, not as concrete historical realities accurately described. One such viewpoint is the typology of early Christianity seen with Oakeshott's eyes as in his early papers, collected in *Religion, Politics and the Moral Life*, while Plato's treatment of art as a kind of divine madness in the *Phaedrus* is another. I follow, that is, Oakeshott's approach in terms of *'form,'* as in the 'Tower of Babel:' his own topic there is the form of morality, not its actual historical occurrences. Of course what Oakeshott says about early and later Christianity as a move from a morality of habit to a self-consciously reflecting, abstracting, defining morality of ideals – i.e., a move from a form of morality as a way of living, of being a member of a community, to a form of morality best called 'moral ideology' – all this does not contradict the picture of religion I am presenting. For the introduction of 'reflection', abstraction and substantive ideals as a 'grammar', to use Oakeshott's revealing phrase, did not mean that the place of initial non-reflective experience in the case of religion (or the *Phaedrus*-like irrationalism in the case of artistic creation) was thereby taken up exhaustively by reason itself. In becoming self-reflective, morality does not necessarily become rational in its ends, too, in the sense of having also a fully rational *content* (beyond a rationalized *form*). Similarly, considered in this formal mode and not as historical facts, religion or art may be consistently seen to retain their non-rational contents or ends (e.g., an otherworldly hypostasis to be prayed to, or artistic contemplative delight) while being clad within a rationalist exterior.

Let us now come to the description of the antinomies.[14] Let us recall what we said at the start that the antinomies here are generated against, and what is more, *despite* technical/rationalist self-confidence in the homogeneity of reason's control over all domains of human conduct. Notwithstanding this convergence in terms of the initial absence of 'technical' reason in them, art and religion can turn out as antithetical and internally contradictory *on the same grounds* when they come to be seen from a politicized perspective stressing their conservative or anti-conservative features.[15] This alternative perspective draws its inspiration and its elements of criticism from social and political thinking. It indicates that for a number of reasons religious beliefs and practices are naturally predisposed to be conservative both in terms of their doctrinal interior as well as in terms of the non-critical social 'voice' they allow themselves, at least in some historic periods, to enunciate. By contrast, artistic creation appears at first as inherently anti-conservative, both in terms of its constitutive elements defining aesthetic style historically as well as in terms of the explicitly politically 'engaged' or so-called 'anti-establishment' character of its active involvement in social practices and issues, again in certain periods. Thus, while in dissociation from 'technical' rationality, religion and art lead to opposite ideological positions along the socio-political scale, each the representative *par excellence* of either conservative or progressive stances.

Paradoxically, however, their roles begin to be *inverted*. Antinomies appear as a result of political reason taking over. Religion sheds its monolithic conservatism whereas art acquires conservative qualities. Certain religious voices urge respect for science while castigating its political abuses especially in the case of environmental crises; others urge tolerance and doctrinal and intercultural understanding while they press for far-reaching changes in liturgical and related practices. Art, for its part, has started showing signs of relativistic parochialism and acceptance of anti-cosmopolitan ideas or enmity or disrespect to non-human life forms that get exhibited in tortured forms while, especially in Europe, its erstwhile avant-garde forms of expression, though not abandoned as such, are no longer associated exclusively or primarily with the expression of progressive social and political ideals. Religion transforms itself into a kind of doctrinally hopeful mode of experience whereas art becomes a kind of emotional pessimism. The homogeneity of 'overall mechanical control' by reason is lost. Reason issues in contradictory political statements.

The Oakeshottian version of the anti-rationalist character of what I treat here as two modes of experience assumes the following form: In the case of Religion, the absence of reflective 'theorems' and rational understanding amounts to mystical experience and timelessness (as expounded in *On Human Conduct*, as well as in earlier writings). Art is identified with delight in the contemplating of

[14] For a different but interesting mentioning of 'antinomies' see J. L. Auspitz, 'Individuality, Civility and Theory: The philosophical Imagination of Michael Oakeshott,' *Political Theory*, 4, no. 3 (August, 1976): 266.

[15] I use the term 'conservatism' not in the strict Oakeshottian sense, i.e. as a disposition and not as a doctrine, but in the ordinary political sense (despite its variety of historical and theoretical strands that I, of course, acknowledge). To make it more precise, in my text I focus on types of social voices or activities that art and religion are asked to enunciate or perform.

images amenable neither to the 'fact' vs. 'non-fact' distinction, nor to that between usefulness and uselessness, nor between ulterior ends and effective causes (*RIP*, 509–10). This is what it means for the non-rational to be characteristic of these modes: 'Experience' in these modes is non-discursive and non-deductive, more like *emanation* in a universe understood in terms of Neo-Platonist metaphysics. Once they become self-reflective,[16] in the sense of a theorem-bound inquiring carried out by 'technical' or 'social-scientific' reason, or equivalently, in Oakeshottian terms, once they lose their *timelessness* or *permanence*[17] and become ideological or 'telic', placed within time – the time of science and the time of political activity – they turn into kinds of 'meta-discourses' losing their identifiable difference and separateness from either *scientia* or practice. We can see this, for example, when Christianity abandons its early phase and becomes a self-conscious moral ideology, or when religion now competes with science for an identical understanding of the world of nature, or when art competes with political action in the form of social movements as artistic activism that postmodernism exhorts some of these to be. Religion and art begin to merge with these two other modes of experience by adopting their postulates, especially their ethico-political ones. As a consequence we end up with the antinomies of adopting conservative and non-conservative positions at the same time *on the same grounds* (as the Kantian 'antithetics of pure reason'). In other words, the conservative idioms of religion are employed to utter the radical slogans, while art's contemplative vocabulary is put in service of facticity. If, moreover, in becoming self-reflective religion and art imitate philosophy's effort to dictate its style of reflective thinking, quite inappropriately, to politics, then they commit the same error at *second remove*, as I explained above.

IV

In discussing religion in this section I follow an inverted chronological route that allows the hermeneutic understanding I espouse. It is in the early Oakeshott of *Experience and its Modes* that we find the means to understand his later views in a non-contradictory way. Moreover, Oakeshott, throughout his life, develops four themes for what we discuss here: religion as intimation of the eternal, religion as a special mode or completion of one, art as special fabricating, and art as contemplative delight (also as intimation of the timeless). These strands are interlaced and for the purposes of this paper I treat them in an interconnected way. Reducing them to a more or less neat classification, we should say that there is an approach to understanding the separateness of religion and art from politics or practical life, that stems from their being treated as having a special feature *qua* modes, on the one hand, and on the other, there is an approach in terms of the absence of reason and being apolitical.

---

[16] What it means concretely to turn self-reflective can be understood by the example of contemplation which, from a state of non-propositional suspense, turns into the specificity of conditional understanding which may lead, for example, to a self-study in terms of evolutionary biology, or cognitive psychology, or other fields of scientific inquiry.
[17] A metaphysics of the *present* is the appropriate type of philosophical discourse allowing us to discover this.

It is not without significance that the context in which Oakeshott places his mature views on religion, has to do with the understanding of human conduct and with idioms of theorizing appropriate to it. Here there is an instance of the special case where doing and understanding assimilate to each other. Oakeshott's analytical tools are furnished by his preceding analysis in *On Human Conduct*: in 'self-disclosure' (moral idiom) actions are performances in response to contingent situations for the achievement of imagined outcomes; in 'self-enactment' (idiom of virtue) actions are conceived in terms of a self-understanding, that is, motives or sentiments in which the agent permits himself or herself to act. Self-disclosure is placed within the transient facticity of contingency. In self-enactment contingency is absent in a way: 'doing is delivered – at least in part – from the deadliness of doing' (*OHC*, 74).[18] I shall presently employ this duality of distinct modes of self conduct in elucidating religion and its securing a balance between the two features we started with.

Religion may evoke a reflective consideration of its postulates in the form of theology (or, we may add, of 'sociology of religion'), but a theoretical understanding of faith is not itself faith.[19] Consequently 'Doing' (here *qua* believing) and 'Understanding' are not assimilated any more. Oakeshott offers a three-tiered description of religious belief in ascending importance. First, religion is to be understood in terms of a 'reconciliation' offered to people living as they are within constant dissonances (multiple moral voices). In contrast to the urge for an 'architectonic' against antinomies I discussed at the very start, this reconciliation provides repose without a resolution of the predicaments of temporal existence. At a second level, religion offers a rejection of the fatality of sinning, of the 'irreparability of sin,' sin being categorically distinct from human offence, or mere calamity, or injustice.[20] But what is more important in religious belief is at a third level the 'reconciliation to nothingness' it offers against this 'less contingent dissonance in the human condition' (*OHC*, 83; cf. " 'Man is time's eunuch'," [*OHC*, 84]). Contrasted with the chain of incessant episodes that a series of particularized actions amounts to – where we have the unresolved and inconclusive character of a self-disclosed human conduct – religion evades the dualism of the evanescent versus the eternal by being understood in terms of self-enactment, as 'an *echo* of an imperishable achievement' (*OHC*, 84, italics added). But, let us notice: only an 'echo' of such 'durability' or unconditionality, an 'image' of the presentness of a perfect self-enactment, not an authentic one. Within a world of inevitable mutability,

---

[18] Cf. *EM*, chap. 5 section 5, for a view that places valuation and morality in relation to – though not identical with – the world of practical facts or instability (*EM*, 262) and thus within contingency.

[19] Oakeshott's urging for an 'imaginative,' in the sense of non-rational, return to religion's Augustinian mode or 'grammar' is, I claim, reminiscent of Kierkegaard's deriding those who seek proofs, or his castigation of those who have to 'think' of Jesus suffering rather than feel it: 'as if Christ had been a professor and as if the Apostles had formed a little professional society of scholars.' Kierkegaard, *Concluding Unscientific Postscript*, ed. and trans. H. Hong E. Hong (Princeton, NJ: Princeton Univ. Press 1992), 215.

[20] St. Anselm offers an elaborate rationalist defense of the redemption of sin and its particular appropriate form in his *Cur Deus Homo* (bk. 1, chs. 14, 17, 20, 22–24, and bk. 2, chs. 5–8, 17–18) that is the exact opposite of what Oakeshott understands by reconciliation.

religious faith is the evocation of a higher sentiment whereby mortals, still sallying forth on 'fugitive adventures,' may find themselves 'graced with an intimation of immortality,' or may enjoy 'encounters with eternity' (*OHC*, 85). But if even self-enactment, the special case of moral conduct, is itself the victim of temporality, it is only religion (and art) that can escape contingency – even if only as intimations of the wholeness of Reality. But when they fail to do so by becoming political they, too, fall into the antinomies of practical conduct regulated by technical utilitarian reason, or by necessarily conflicting motives of multiple self-disclosures.

In the end, though, contrary to his dictum against all monistic yearnings in morality, Oakeshott allows religion to furnish us with 'a motive of all motives' (*OHC*, 85) – reminiscent, I would suggest all too briefly, of Paul Tillich's celebrated idea of 'total commitment,' or 'ultimate concern' articulating a special kind of foundational symbol, God, being 'the character of ultimacy and the nature of faith. That which is the true ultimate transcends the realm of finite reality infinitely.'[21] Although the early Oakeshott denounces the view that 'religion is not a body of practical, but of ultimate knowledge' (*EM*, 293), he holds a view that in its subtlety advances further than the one he rejects. By differentiating the various modes, as well as broadening the range of practical human concerns to include religion, Oakeshott moves toward a firmer view of the exalted position upon which religion should stand, without, however, reducing religion to the mundane sense of 'practical life' and its petty concerns. Instead of confronting our routine and drab existence with otherworldly 'truths' and rather than make religion the handmaiden of a self-help culture, Oakeshott tries to redirect attention to the irruptive character of the lived experience of divine fullness. Religion does not instruct us about the world; much less does it fix our problems. It makes us more alive and provokes us to live more fully and perfectly our mortal lives. Hence we must not hastily say that there is a contradiction in his views, even if we notice the difficulty a metaphysical monist faces in dealing with religion in the Biblical idiom. A reconstructive reading of the passages of *Experience and its Modes* dealing with religion will help clarify his views further.[22]

First we note that he describes religion as fulfilling the tendency of all practical activity towards unrequited integrity, completeness, intensity and coherence, which practice *ex hypothesi* can never attain. As a kind of lynch-pin or *summa* of the continuous process of chasing after satisfactions of the active life itself as self-disclosure, religion offers the sought-for comprehensiveness and completion. But we must note something important here. The actual phrasing Oakeshott uses (*EM*, 293, 295) is no different from how he has already described the totality of experience in its concreteness at the start of *Experience and its Modes*, that is, before the arrests of the various modifications take over. Religion is thus seen as *formally* replicating the concrete totality of experience (revealed only to, and by, philosophy proper), having its timelessness secured in this way and not merely or less subtly by postulating a supernatural being. In fact the latter, we note as we go on (*EM*, 345–6), as the object of single-minded devotion, is not itself adequate to the task of

---

[21] Paul Tillich, *Dynamics of Faith* (New York: Harper & Row, 1957), 76.
[22] See *EM*, 293–5, 309–13, 345–9.

elevating religion to the status of ultimate truth; not, that is, from the standpoint of the totality of experience which retains for ever its Hegelian-like supremacy as a criterion. We may still fall into the error of missing the fact that religion, despite its closeness to the non-practical, philosophical zenith of experience, is itself an arrest of experience. We may thus substitute one type of abstraction with a less obvious one like religion (or art) the deceptive character of which may easily lead us along a slippery route confusing it with absolute reality, namely, the totality of concrete experience or the Buddhist-like 'open sea of experience' (*EM*, 346). The latter, the 'whole' of earlier idealism or the 'presentness' of the metaphysics of presence, needs no contribution from any partial modification including that of religion, even if the latter is situated closer to it. Therefore, again, the only wholeness or presentness or timelessness that religion can secure for itself as a special mode is by means of this intimation of the original whole. Religion, the completion of practical experience at its most intense, falls short of the totality of experience while only formally sharing the criterion of concrete or total experience, namely, completeness.

The error of confusing the two (totality and a modification of it) is compounded by inattention to the different senses of 'practical' I now wish to bring forth. Three meanings of 'practical' must be distinguished in order to make sense of what Oakeshott says about modes in *Experience and its Modes*; one of these meanings must be isolated as responsible for the deformation of the authentic character of religion and art.

(1) In the first sense, 'practical' means something so general that every sort of human conduct or action can be such, including contemplative activity or even the life of a mystic or an anchorite. It is this sense that Oakeshott points to by speaking of 'practices' in his later work, rather than 'practical experience'. In the idiom of the 'Voice of Poetry,' the 'practical', although comprising the 'pragmatic', facticity and everyday desire or aversion, if interrupted or fallen into lethargy, may offer its images to contemplative activity; thus becoming a foil for the artistic moment in which a 'loaf of bread in a bucket of paint' (*RIP*, 515) brings delight rather than aggravation.

(2) In a second, narrower, yet exalted sense, 'practical' covers only what religion becomes as a 'consummation of practice'[23] 'characterized everywhere by intensity and strength of devotion' (*EM*, 295); it also covers art as an exceptional type of fabrication exhausted in the creation itself – both of these being intimations of the ultimate. Here, practical experience still encompasses human conduct, but the criterion of concrete or total experience – wholeness or the tendency towards an 'integrative state of mind' – is intimated, a reference point set off from our diurnal *aventures*.

(3) In a yet narrower sense – this being the breeding place of antinomies – 'practical'[24] means 'political' in the pejorative sense, that of technical-utilitarian

---

[23] Cf. passages describing religion as 'simply life itself,' 'synonymous with life at its fullest,' and 'its value is in the present' (*RPML*, 34, 35).

[24] Cf. *RPML*, 154. Here, Oakeshott employs the narrow sense of 'practical' to discuss reflective activity the whole object of which is politics in the sense of a technical knowledge in the service of desires generated in this world – not the 'making' of contemplative images as in aesthetic experience.

rationalism in politics, or ideology, which, when religion and art get assimilated to it, explains why they begin exhibiting contradictory political features. Thus religion and art can be practical at three levels that must be carefully distinguished.

In the idiom of the 'The Voice of Poetry' a similar set of distinctions is drawn between degrees of 'practice'. In a sense (our first, here), all image-making including the special one of poetry is 'practical' *qua* activity of a sort. But *à propos* of laying down a similarity between contemplative aesthetic activity and the special relationships of friendship and love, we are given a second sense of 'practical', like the second sense I noted above, but in a new idiom. These special activities or relationships if 'they are not properly speaking contemplative activities, they are at least ambiguously practical activities which intimate contemplation' (*RIP*, 538). Similarly, there is a third sense of 'practical' erroneously applied to aesthetics only to end up silencing it, a sense that mirrors the third sense of 'practical' as exclusively equivalent to modern rationalist politics (cf. *RIP* p. 493-4 n. 2). To speak of 'being practical' as when the *homme d'affaires* contemns the scholar, corresponds to the demand that art be 'a devise of formulating judgements' (*OHC*, 79). This demand loses sight of the ambiguity inherent in an art work or poetic image: this fecund ambiguity stems from the fact that an art work may be considered from both the practical, utilitarian point of view as well as the contemplative. For example, a building is capable of being both a space of utility and a work of art. A poetic image is at the same time isolated in its contemplative mode but, revealingly, and a little cryptically, Oakeshott comments, 'this remoteness of poetic utterance no doubt accounts for the disposition to assimilate it somehow or other to the idioms of science and of practice' (*RIP*, 536), thus generating political antinomies at the heart of art transformed into a social critic.

In their authentic mode, religion is the consummation of practice and art the idealization of fabricating *par excellence* or contemplative delight, i.e. ideal completions of otherwise abstracted experience, which, of course can never be – as we saw above – equivalent to the truly complete totality of concrete experience revealed only in and by philosophical thought. When they lose their totalizing quality or tendency even one 'at second-remove' ('practical' in the second exalted sense), and get absorbed into practical *qua* 'political' experience in the third sense (e.g. when religion converses politically about biotechnology or the environment, or art turns into a social movement), they end up talking of specific varieties of living within the world of practical experience. They talk about this or that form of practical-political life, but not in the totalizing generality they can afford by staying practical in the second exalted sense: about the form of life as such.

When Oakeshott writes against taking the truths of religion 'to belong to the world of concrete truth,' i.e. to the totality of concrete experience (*EM*, 309), thus shedding its practicality and modality, he wishes to retain, for instance, the psychological, practical contribution religious beliefs may offer. He stresses, correctly, that any erroneous identification of the total truth with a modification of it is tantamount to having the practical value of religious truths 'at once disappear.' Just as Oakeshott maintains that philosophy errs when it dictates necessary propositions or unconditional truths to the partial, necessarily conditioned, abstract modes – 'Ultimate truth must always be irrelevant to an abstract world of experience as such' (*EM*, 313) – I would suggest that the religious truths, too, may be wrongly employed in the political sphere, even if both religion and politics are 'practical' but failing to heed the different senses as distinguished above.

When religion becomes a moral ideology or follows the political demands of a rationally calculating technique, it is robbed of its tendency to evade abstractness or partiality as much as it can by turning into a 'completion' or high-point of conduct; it thus becomes even more abstracted from the whole of concrete experience and is turned away from any chance of playing the role of a 'consummation'. When the practical value (in the second proper sense) of religious or artistic ideas becomes wrongly twice practical by becoming also explicitly political or ideological in the third sense, religion and art are absorbed entirely by practice-as-politics where political reasoning ends up distorting their character of being intimations of timelessness. Their specially defined practical value is distorted by political antinomies.

In the special case of art considered in terms of contemplation, Oakeshott's analysis, though following a quite different approach by means of 'self', 'voice' and 'language', also helps us see the same conceptual error of mixing art's intimations of timelessness with political temporality. This problem can be seen in Oakeshott's choice to write about art in terms of both image making and in terms of a (sketchily laid out) theory of language which, when we notice it, also incidentally makes sense out of Oakeshott's shift from the early scheme of modes to the later image of voices in conversation. Art's intimation of timelessness emerges in part from the non-symbolic character of artistic discourse as well as from its being essentially an idealization of fabricating *per se* as we encountered above. Artistic images, Oakeshott insists, are not signs or symbols that point beyond themselves; they point only to themselves and are thus unrepeatable *individua*. If they cannot point to some-*thing* else, they also do not point to some-*place* else, or some-*time* else. This places them beyond practice, (and also beyond science) beyond the world of desire and striving, which postulates objects and ends external to the self and later in time – out 'there' in the future, to be attained. It also places them outside the moral vocabulary part and parcel of practice thus showing up artistic moralizing as another oxymoron. As we said above, only when pragmatic utility, desiring, facticity and moral approval or disapproval, essential functions of practical activity, turn lethargic or get interrupted some of their (especially ambiguous) images may serve as an opportunity for activating aesthetic contemplation. Moreover the language of desire/aversion used in practice is a representational language of fixed signs and rules, a symbolic language operating as a medium of communicating, where words point to things and things mediate or deliver states of satisfaction, which have varying durations. The language of art, by contrast, is one with no synonyms or representational function (*RIP*, 527), hence when art is mistaken for the representation of practical (preeminently political) desires, rather than authentically as contemplation and image-making activated only during a stage of necessary interruption of practical activity, it begins to promulgate social ideals as extensions of its own discourse.

The dislocation of language into a realm of non-representation opens the space for conversation, for making sense of an epistemologically fragmented world, in a unique way. Conversation does not reduce art to a political arbiter with simultaneously conservative or anti-conservative theses; rather it keeps the voices distinct.[25] How can this happen? First we should recall that contemplation emerges during certain specified in-between moments of other types of imaging (i.e. interruptions of imaging appropriate to practice or science). It needs, though, to be activated at such intervals that are nevertheless not devoid of all activity, are anything but episodes of *ennui*, for an entirely pure *vita contemplativa* would be impossible for this task – let alone suitable for a conversation – and in the end not unlike the image of frozen perception being equivalent to death used by Hobbes.[26] Also, images, in general, are not merely mental pictures ready to be entertained by any 'voice' but specific to each case. At times Oakeshott is ambiguous as to what makes them specific: there is a lingering ambiguity (*RIP*, 518) when he says of a work of art as an image that it is protected from 'falling' into practical or scientific viewing, leaving it unclear whether the difference between images lies in their distinct metaphysical type, each hailing its provenance from a separate mode, or in their differing manner of being perceived. He insists nevertheless that 'images of one universe of discourse are not available (even as raw materials) to a different mode of imaging – only diminished or interrupted activity in one mode' the latter generating an opportunity for the appearance of images by another voice (*RIP*, 516). When he says a work of art is an image protected from falling into practical or scientific experience, he seems to be insisting that they possess their own modality.

This is important, for it says a lot about what kind of 'conversation' Oakeshott has in mind. I claim that the kind of conversation that such an analysis would allow is one where the self is passing from one state to the other. This is crucial for it does not allow for art's voice to be heard as that of politics without contradictions.

Images in artistic contemplation as I hinted above, are merely *present*: they provoke neither speculation nor inquiry but only delight. (Likewise, the other side of aesthetic activity, namely authentic artistic creation is, as we saw, fabrication *par excellence* and thus also self-contained having an inherent meaning – not an external one, equivalent to an 'ought to be' awaiting practical application or political endorsement.) Hence 'contemplative' images cannot serve, *ex hypothesi*, as practical maxims of action. This cannot be overstressed. These images are not within a causal series and have no history; they are 'not episodic' (*OHC*, 184). They have the appearance of being *permanent* and *unique*: permanent in the sense that no change or destruction is possible; unique in the sense that no other image can

---

[25] 'The obvious outcome of our total experience is that the world can be handled according to many systems of ideas, and is so handled by different men ... science and religion are genuine keys for unlocking the world's treasure house. Neither is exhaustive or exclusive of the other's simultaneous use. And why, after all, may not the world be so complex as to consist of many interpenetrating spheres of reality?' William James, *The Varieties of Religious Experience* (New York: Prometheus Books, 2002), 122. This type of pragmatism is not what Oakeshott means by voices or modes.

[26] See also, n. 9 above

take the place of an artistic image in contemplation. The latter is an activity that can obviously not be inferential or argumentative.[27] I spoke above of resonances of Neo-Platonism in the use of the image of emanation; there are more of these present here when it is said that aesthetic contemplative activity does not use-up or wear-out its images (also reminiscent of the Thomistic conception of the common good).

'Poetry' is 'a language without a vocabulary' (the equivalent of a 'vernacular' in *On Human Conduct*), a language empty of synonyms where no sign can be substituted for another. The remoteness of poetic language forces people, wrongly, to assimilate it somehow to the other idioms (recall the architectonic tendency and the 'monistic yearnings'). We saw above how confusion of the three senses of being 'practical' is responsible for this. In addition, as in the case of religion above, the only thing we can say to make a conversation among voices possible is that there may be an *intimation* of moral life or a form of moral life – love or friendship – that by its obliquely aesthetic character may lure us into being attentive to the special images of artistic contemplation. Art and Religion are two kinds of 'conduct' that do not involve 'doings' that engage the world of what Oakeshott calls *'pragmata'*.[28] Hence they themselves are not exhibiting (and are not supposed to exhibit) the separation between inquiry and the object thereof: a separation – to use Oakeshott's terminology – between 'theoretical understanding' and performance of actions or human conduct in the case of practical experience or the analogous separation found in the cases of Science or History, the latter having, by definition, external objects separate from them as their domains of study. And while their non-inquiring character is obvious enough to keep religion and art in clear distance from either scientific or historical inquiry, Oakeshott's strictures on imaging and the conversational ideal, are crucial tools needed for keeping them away from practical-cum-political conduct, too, and its theoretical understanding (carried out by social-scientific disciplines) by blocking religion and art from being susceptible to the low demands of 'practice' in the third sense.

V

Modal formalism, rich in its multifarious aspects explored in the preceding sections, encapsulates what is special about religion and art in their authentic status. Once this is lost, political antinomies ensue. Let me finish with three methodological points and one final claim positioning Oakeshott's treatment of religion and art within his oeuvre.

(1) The first point brings together the two ingredients of modal formalism. In *Experience and Its Modes*, modes of experience are partial and defective from the point of view of the concrete totality of experience, in their being abstractions or modifications of such totality. At the same time they are self-contradictory: from their internal point of view they posit a coherent world of ideas in which experience is represented through them, but seen from the external standpoint of

---

[27]   Cf. Bradley, *Appearance*, 152, 409; and Appendix, 493.
[28]   See also above, page 50.

the whole, all modality is equivalent to a statement asserting its incompleteness; it is a falling short of a fully coherent world of ideas (and as such, modality must be destroyed by being superseded). Therefore strictly speaking, we must not conceive of religion and art as ordinary modes of experience if there is anything special to be acknowledged in their constitution. Identifying religion with something supernatural will not do the trick. Similarly art, though a contemplative activity of special images, acquires a voice in conversation not in, or as, politics. Science, History and Practice – the three major modes Oakeshott chooses to discuss in detail as being the most developed, but not the only ones – are temporalities par excellence. Religion and art must therefore be expected to be different to the extent that they can represent or symbolize, but only formally, a placement outside time. Yet they are also 'practical' in a quite special sense (as I distinguished above) that will allow them such complementary roles of ultimacy and practicality or contemplation and dialogue (paralleling the two generic epistemic features we started with). I wish to claim that what Oakeshott does with respect to civil association, namely delineate its formal character, is also what, by means of a formal isomorphism with presentness and timelessness, religion and art, too, are shown to have. There is in all these descriptions of three principal domains of human conduct a deliberate expulsion of any substantive content that self-confident rationalism may furnish them with. Their formalism ensures their a-temporality and thus the political antinomies have no place to be realized as long as this formalism is respected. My argument is that the only worldly analogue of the a-temporal that Oakeshott can allow is his description of Civil Association, where moral neutrality (*OHC*, 175) and formal conditions of lex do not permit us to deduce the content of political life from substantive ends. Certainly neither religion nor art can play the role of an analogue of such formalism by being timeless, eternally present culminations of experience if they become transformed into social critics.

(2) It is further revealing that what Oakeshott does, in his reading of Hobbes,[29] is to distinguish Reason in the sense of a hypostasized entity à la Plato or Spinoza from 'reasoning' which he, of course, accepts: the Hobbesian 'saviour' is not an external remedy or a 'god-like power of Reason come to create order out of chaos,' there is 'no break' between the state of nature and its remedy. It is, I claim, when there is such a break, whereby hypostasized Reason is introduced to religion or art, that we get political antinomies.

(3) Religion and art in their authentic states, though still operating within a mode of experience, that of practice, either as its 'completion' or as an ideal form of fabrication, respectively, nevertheless operate as a kind of 'meta-mode' similar to that of philosophy. Oakeshott warns that philosophy is not the historical terminus of abstract modalities but 'the concrete and complete whole implied and involved in every modification of experience' (*EM*, 349–50). Analogously, according to my proposed reconstruction, religion and art emerge in their authentic states not as implying the concrete totality, but as intimations or forms of the concrete whole since, and as long as, they echo timelessness and presentness.

---

[29] See, Oakeshott, 'Introduction to Leviathan' (*RIP*, 256).

My final claim. The aesthetic dimension appears to be superior to the religious one in Oakeshott's later writings. In dealing with art (especially in 'Voice of Poetry') Oakeshott places his discussion of it within a clearly idealist context right from the start – one in which Self and Not-Self are an integral activity, a whole, rather than a substance and its external world. In other words, Oakeshott's effort, in 'Voice of Poetry' is, however we may judge its success, an attempt to rethink and reformulate his whole system of thought. Its scope and context is experience as a whole, and art is seen as one state of being active, amongst others, in which the polarity 'Self vs. Non-Self' is situated in terms of familiar, but reconfigured modes, now voices: Art, Science, Practice. Art is thereby accorded pride of place within an exalted context, one that could be fairly described as a metaphysics of the mind, i.e., viewed from an elevated standpoint: imaging is not a condition of thought, as he points out, 'in one of its modes it is thought' (*RIP*, 497). When it comes to religion, though, in his later writings, Oakeshott introduces it while he is speaking of human conduct, i.e. from a level lower down the scale; that is, viewed from the standpoint of practice in which Oakeshott feels he must integrate religious experience in a special way.[30]

---

[30] Timothy Fuller is absolutely right when, in pointing to what most other commentators miss, he underlines the suffusion of Oakeshott's political outlook with a religious character that, nevertheless, is not principally motivated to construct doctrinal propositions: 'The Poetics of the Civil Life,' in J. Norman, ed., *The Achievement of Michael Oakeshott* (London: Duckworth, 1993), 73-4. It is salutary that Fuller reminds us (74) that far from being his main interest, for Oakeshott politics was not at the heart of his life where 'the encounter with eternity' was central.

II

History

5

Josiah Lee Auspitz

What is Political Thought?
The Example of Law in Greece and
Rome in Oakeshott's London
School of Economics Lectures

Though Michael Oakeshott was an influential scholar and teacher, he understood scholarship and teaching as activities distinct from doing philosophy. Nevertheless, his introductory lectures to undergraduates at the London School of Economics combined the callings of teacher, scholar and philosopher. In his opening sentence and in the typescript he circulated, he described them as *A Study of Political Thought*.[1] There were at various times thirty to thirty-three lectures. They comprised a survey course in which students read both classics of political theory and secondary sources. The lectures are at once learned and accessible. They provide an introduction to three thousand years of Western political history and serve to introduce Oakeshott himself. Their distinctive virtue, however, lies elsewhere: They show how a genuinely philosophical mind can elevate a pedagogical exercise into a theoretical inquiry. Oakeshott used his course not merely to organize introductory material but also to pursue a question: *What is political thought?*

The lectures dwell on four important episodes in the political experience of European peoples: Greece, Rome, medieval Christendom, and the modern European state. Their idiom is mostly historical, but in Oakeshott's hands historical exposition is enriched with philosophical reflection and shafts of aesthetic insight.

Oakeshott concentrates on four episodes in European experience not from any ethnocentrism but because he sees politics as a largely Western contribution. It is, as he puts it, 'Europe's somewhat embarrassing gift to the world' (*LHPT*, 38). Political life, as its name reminds us, begins in the Greek *polis* with the confluence of three conditions: a diversity of persons, a unity of rule, and the belief that ruling is an activity to be chosen and justified by human deliberation. Politics is that activity in which diverse persons deliberate over the conditions of their

---

[1] Oakeshott, *Lectures in the History of Political Thought*, ed. Terry Nardin and Luke O'Sullivan (Exeter: Imprint Academic, 2006), 31. Hereafter: *LHPT*. Throughout, all page references are to this work; see Endnote.

own government. The same government may also hold sway over those who are excluded from politics. It is thus possible to be governed without participating in politics, but not to conduct politics without government.

Politics in this sense is perhaps never wholly absent in any regime. But the political element will be weak where persons are lacking in diversity, as in homogeneous tribal groups; where rule is fragmented and ill-defined, as in the overlapping feudal arrangements that followed the collapse of the Roman Empire; or where an entire society is seen as the household of the king, as in Oriental despotism, or as so deeply rooted in received or revealed truths as to make the idea of deliberation and man-made legislation impious.

The four European episodes overlap. Rome was for several centuries contemporaneous with the Greek *polis*. The seeds of medieval Christendom were planted during the Christian conversions and barbarian infiltrations of the declining Roman Empire. The modern state emerged fitfully from feudal realms. Ideas and practices from one experience are drawn upon and reinterpreted in another. For Oakeshott everything emerges slowly and imperceptibly from accumulated experience. But none of this, as Oakeshott sees it, forms a continuous political history. Politics is not a baton in a relay race handed from the Greeks to the Romans to the medieval bishops and kings to the parliaments and prime ministers of modern Europe. And the reflection upon political experience does not form a connected history of political thought. 'I cannot detect anything,' Oakeshott says, 'which could properly correspond to the expression '*the* history of political thought'' (*LHPT*, 32). Each experience has its peculiar epochal character, its distinctive political vocabulary and its manner of reflection.

And in each, Oakeshott discerns at least two – and sometimes three – levels of political thought. At the everyday level there is the practical vocabulary in which people organize and express their thoughts about politics: their legends and myths, their workaday notions of law, rule, citizenship, and so on. This political vocabulary, evident in their rhetoric, is open to adaptation, innovation and improvisation as new circumstances arise.

There is a more systematic level of thought that revises, criticizes, informs and orders the prevailing political rhetoric. Sometimes Oakeshott annexes this to the practical, rhetorical level, sometimes, as in Rome where it was rigorously developed, he portrays it as a second, intermediate level of political thought. He finds its systematic expression in the more refined discussions of lawyers and jurisconsults. This is, properly speaking, a rigorously structured, generalizing kind of practical thinking – involving what he would later call 'practical theorem-making.' It makes the practice of politics – and particularly of law – systematic, coherent, self-critical and self-validating.

Finally, at a genuinely theoretical level one encounters attempts to explain politics in an idiom removed from that of contemporary debates. Here Oakeshott puts what he elsewhere analyzes as two explanatory 'modes' of discourse, history and philosophy. History in the proper sense is to be distinguished from the legends, myths, factoids and fictions drawn from the past that appear in political rhetoric and legal citations of precedent and authority. Political philosophy in the proper sense is still more rare: it arises when some combination of new experiences and new canons of understanding sparks an attempt to re-explain politics; in so doing it calls forth a purely conceptual achievement that may endure beyond its historical context.

To give a flavor of Oakeshott's approach let me suggest with a few vignettes from the lectures how his sense of the three plateaus of political thought informs his discussion of law in ancient Greece and Rome. In Greece, the practical and the philosophical levels of thought are the two he sees as most noteworthy. In Rome, he pays more attention to the intermediate level, where a doctrinally grounded kind of legalistic theorem-making gives continuity and stability to practice.

The Greek Experience With Law

The Greeks, as Oakeshott presents them, were notable for their rhetorical and speculative achievements. Loquacious and inquisitive, they developed for their politics both an eloquent practical vocabulary and a subtle theoretical one. Oakeshott uses their notions of law and justice to show how political thought emerged from mythologically grounded tribal custom into highly sophisticated rational thought that ultimately took wing into genuine philosophy, and then relapsed into a quasi-religious doctrine of consolation when the *polis* declined.

He takes their three terms for law – *themis, thesmos, nomos* – to mark the emergence of the first true politics, while he notes how a continuing term for justice – *dike* – changes to accommodate each new conception.

At first, the closest thing to law was *themis*, a deified embodiment of clan custom. Justice, *dike*, was visited upon the law-breaker by the offended deity, or by some human acting in her stead. At this stage there is no distinction between law and taboo, or between law-breaking and offense to the gods. And in the dramatic rendering of this view Dike (justice, in the sense of ordered relations among men) is, appropriately, the daughter of Themis by Zeus. Violate Themis, what is right and proper, and Dike, the restoration of ordered relations, follows from the gods with the severity of a daughter avenging her affronted mother.

As various clans came together in the polis the *themistes*, the household deities of each, were collected in one place, the *sceptron* of the king. This scepter was not only a symbol of authority but also a sort of magic wand with which the king would, as Homer puts it, 'extract *themistes* from Zeus' (*LHPT*, 75). The king did so after consultation, with a council of nobles, with priests, or with an assembly of the people. Where the king failed to follow good counsel, he, as well as his subjects, could expect a bad fate. In the person of the king, the *themistes* had a unified human focus, but still lacked the notion crucial to politics that human agency was their source.

So long as the common ground among the clans could be located in the court of a king, there was no need to go beyond the essentially household conception of law as *themis*. But the relations of the *polis* increasingly called for superimposing upon the life of the clans a level of activity conducted outside household precincts, in a public space, the *agora*. Here from an assortment of tribal customs, common traditions emerged, and a new term for these became current, *thesmos*. Oakeshott takes the use of the term *thesmos* to mark a further stage in the development of Greek thought towards an unwritten common law uniting diverse clans. The pivotal moment in the history of each *polis* comes when these *thesmoi* are committed to writing.

The man who accomplished this act of codification was the thesmothete (*thesmothetes* in Greek), a term usually translated as lawgiver. But Oakeshott understands him not as legislator but as judge and anthologist. The thesmothete selected and reconciled the best of tribal custom. He did justice or *dike* to the customs of the several tribes. Justice in this context consists in the appropriateness of the *thesmoi* to a shared sense of what is right and proper for all those conducting affairs in the *agora*. Like *themis*, *thesmos* still derives from divine wisdom, so that it entails no fundamentally new conception of law.

The example of the thesmothete, however, does introduce a new element that Oakeshott thought more important than the substance of the customs codified. By selecting and reconciling the *themistes* of the several tribes, the thesmothete engages in an essentially judicial activity. Henceforth it is plausible to think of law as something elicited rationally by judicious human beings from human customs, rather than magically by kings, priests and prophets from divine will. This marks a crucial juncture in the movement to man-made law.

In Athens *thesmos* was the term used by Draco in the 7th century B.C. Solon in the next century used the term *nomos*, which Oakeshott takes to mark the further transition to law as a conscious, man-made phenomenon. Solon frankly states the basis for his legislation as knowledge of the nature (*physis*) of the *polis* and its peoples. The criterion for justice is now the fitness or appropriateness of law to nature (or *nomos* to *physis*). Moreover, the *nomoi* now proceed from human agency – from a person, a dictatorial nomothete in the case of Solon, or from human institutions specifically empowered with judicial and legislative authority. With the establishment of man-made law, politics in the proper sense emerges. There is now a unified public sphere of diverse persons some number of whom form their own laws for living together as a polity.

The polis-experience of man-made law, however, presents conceptual problems that require further intellectual response. First, there is the problematical meaning of justice. The accretion of meanings to *dike* embraces, as we have seen, a range associated with *themis* or taboo-sanctioned custom for each person and household, *thesmos* or an unwritten common law of several clans, and *nomos* or obedience of the subject to man-made law. Can a single notion of justice cover all these three? Can we speak of justice in the soul of man, the management of a household, and the deliberations of the city? Second, *nomos* or man-made law transfers the effective source of legal authority from divine will to human judgments about nature. This introduces into politics the question of man's place in the cosmos. How do law and politics reflect man's nature or *physis*?

Oakeshott reads Plato's *Republic* as an inquiry into the first problem – the question of justice – and Aristotle's *Ethics* and *Politics* as an inquiry into the second – the problem of the political nature of man. These questions are closely related, but very differently posed by the two writers. Oakeshott is concerned to show how each writer's approach to the *polis* is of a piece with deeper philosophical concerns. Both Plato and Aristotle he treats as primarily theoretical writers because their main purpose is not to advocate some policy but to explain the basis of polis-life as such on terms that are adequate to explanation as such. Of his nine lectures on the Greeks, he devotes four to an account of these two writers. And for each he concentrates the larger part of his exposition on philosophical arguments and methods that go well beyond the subject matter of politics.

Thus, Oakeshott devotes an entire lecture to elucidating Plato's theory of ideas. He then shows how, in the opening book of Plato's *Republic,* the general theory is used to lead us inexorably to an archetypal idea of justice as criterion both for the soul of man and the regime of the city. Justice for Plato is a regulative principle; it requires ultimately that the rational part of the soul should control the courageous part and the desiring part. Plato's tripartite view of the soul has passed into the common parlance of Western thought: reason, as we might now say, must govern will and desire. Plato illustrates this tripartite idea at the macro-scale where it is easier to grasp. Whence the Republic, a model polity ruled by philosophers, who, being governed by reason, can design systems of law and education to bring justice to those who are not so governed. The raw material for Plato's inquiry is five centuries of Greek sentiments, beliefs and ideas surrounding the notion of *dike* as what is right and proper for man, the household and the city. Yet Plato turns all this into an enduring and genuinely philosophical discussion (as opposed to a merely anti-democratic tract) by using *dike* to illustrate and develop a theory of ideas in which every sense experience reflects an Idea or archetype that has greater reality than its tangible manifestations.

Similarly, Oakeshott presents Aristotle as bringing a ramified conceptual apparatus to bear on the experience of polis-life at the very moment when the *polis* was to be submerged in empire. Aristotle portrays polis-life as a defining mark of humanity itself. His dictum that man is a political animal (*zoon politikon*) is not, of course, an empirical generalization but a statement about human potential. It draws upon a more general philosophy of nature as purposive, and upon a logical rule of definition as elucidating the differentiating attributes specific to the thing defined. Man is defined as that animal having within its nature the capacity to deliberate upon and choose the form of its life with others. Only in the *polis* has this potential been actualized, and hence only those living the polis-life as citizens can achieve the sociability that is truly distinctive to humankind. By coming together with others, outside the household, and sustaining a *polis* man becomes more fully human.

As with Plato, the best-regulated *polis* follows the principles that hold for a person. The principle of the mean in Aristotle's *Ethics* – a moderate life that avoids excess – recurs in the *Politics* as an endorsement of a moderate or mixed regime that maintains a healthy balance among classes and between rulers and ruled. In combining theory and advice Aristotle's *Politics* is itself 'a mixture of several different modes of thinking:' philosophical reflection, the rudiments of both a 'history' of the *polis* and a political 'science' anticipating Montesquieu and Weber, as well as a quasi-medical diagnostic 'science' describing political pathologies and recommending cures. 'We must get used to this sort of mixture,' Oakeshott writes, 'because it is common enough in the literature of European political reflection. But getting used to it does not mean failing to recognize the important differences between these modes of thought' (*LHPT*, 115).

In all, Aristotle shifts the basis of the long-standing Greek view of their superiority to the barbarians: to him their virtue lay not in birth but in a political life that fulfilled the nature of man. He thus transmutes the Greek pride of race into a justification of polis-life that has endured to summon men and women to civic engagement long after the experience from which it derived receded into memory.

As the *polis* declined Aristotle's view of it had to be rethought. In 338 B.C. Philip of Macedon subjugated the Greek mainland. Its free and independent cities became municipal appendages to empire. If the Greek was a polis-forming animal, what was he without a fully self-governing *polis*? A barbarian, or worse, a brute?

Oakeshott reads the political doctrines of Zeno, the Stoic, (c. 300 B.C.) as a consoling response to this question. Zeno saw the *cosmos* itself as a *polis*, with an ordered nature as its *nomos*. Every human being was in effect a potential citizen of this Cosmopolis. To exercise his citizenship, he needed only to assure that the rational element of his nature governed the passionate. He would then live by ordering his life in accordance with a reasoned obedience to the law of nature. Such a universal, natural law was also the criterion for the laws of empires; it assured every person a citizenship that transcended worldly governments. In the cosmopolis of the Stoics, 'an ideal citizenship replaced a lost actual citizenship and an ideal law of nature replaced a lost actual legal system' (*LHPT*, 168).

Oakeshott does not see this universalization of the *polis* and its laws as moral progress, but as a symptom of sad times. It never, in his view, reaches a philosophical standard (Natural Law would not in his view receive a properly philosophical treatment until Aquinas), and should be read as a doctrine of comfort to those deprived of meaningful politics.

> In the subsequent history of Europe there have been not a few occasions when the circumstances of third century Greece have been reproduced – circumstances when a traditional morality and a traditional politics have disappeared. When this has happened there has often been a recourse to the teachings of Zeno. (*LHPT*, 168)

Roman Legalism

Now, if one were writing a continuous history of political thought, one might pass the torch at this point to the Romans who in due course took up the notion of Natural Law not as consolation but as a doctrine for a self-aggrandizing legal system. But this is not what Oakeshott has in mind. His discussion of the Greeks has already made clear that he views political thought as, so to speak, local. When the Romans seize on terms and concepts from the Greeks, the contexts and purposes are specific to their own experience. 'In most respects,' he says, 'the political experience of the Romans is utterly unlike that of ancient Greece. The expression 'the Ancient World', which puts Greeks and Romans together, is one of the most misleading generalizations ever made' (*LHPT*, 176).

Of course, Rome also begins in a coming together of clans and tribes, in this case on the seven hills. It, too, has terms to distinguish custom (*fas*), emergent common law (*jus*), and man-made law (*lex*). But the Roman polity was the product of a very different sort of people – a people in many ways less attractive to Oakeshott who sees them as limited in their capacity for speculation, more disposed to action than palaver, and self-absorbed in a family-oriented religiosity.

The Romans worshiped their ancestors, their founding, and, in effect, themselves. They saw themselves as a chosen people and made the *Populus Romanus* a self-perpetuating legend. Their belief in their own destiny gave them the tenacity and self-confidence to sustain civil order for a millennium. Oakeshott holds no political experience in higher esteem. He sees the Romans as having successfully addressed the central practical problem for law and politics: the reconciliation of stability with change.

He writes: 'Law, even in the most conservative societies, never stands still for very long. Any society which is to understand itself must have an understanding of legal change. And this has often proved the most difficult aspect of human association to understand.' And further, 'There will of course be small adjustments to take account of new circumstances.... But there is, usually, great reluctance to believe that genuinely 'new' law is being made: the laws are too important to the stability of a society to be thought of as being merely at the disposal of each succeeding generation' (*LHPT*, 79).

The political genius of the Romans, on Oakeshott's account, is to have developed a capacity for great changes within a stable legal order and to have preserved withal a durable political vocabulary. Whereas the Greek city-states were convulsed with upheavals of constitution and regime, Rome even as it was transformed from monarchy to republic to empire never conceded a break in authority. And the conceptual apparatus with which the Romans maintained their sense of stability was so durable that it lived on to shape in different ways the categories of the Roman Catholic Church and those of the newly founded American Republic. It was a powerful alchemy of crude myth and highly sophisticated legalism.

Unlike the Greeks, whose politics gave rise to philosophical works of astonishing refinement, the Romans produced no philosopher worthy of the name. Their ideas about government were never put into systematic theoretical form. Yet underlying their laws and their political culture was a 'remarkably firm and profound intellectual organization' (*LHPT*, 208) – the work of lawyers, poets and historians rather than philosophers – a doctrinal rather than a theoretical achievement.

At its core was a myth of the Roman founding, for which Oakeshott finds a modern parallel only in the United States. The Founding Father of Rome, Romulus, was *auctor* or initiator of the *Populus Romanus*. The Roman People, in turn, saw themselves almost poetically as a family, bound by treaties to their gods and to other peoples, but to each other by a family solidarity transmuted into law.

As in Greece, Roman law had three stages, but each departed significantly from the Greek parallels. At every stage, the Greek notion of *dike*, right and proper conduct, was in Rome replaced by a strong emphasis on legality – that is, on a purely formal element. Thus, the Roman *fas*, a religious prohibition like *themis*, differed from the Greek notion in being the product of a covenant with the relevant god, judged by the priest of the shrine where the god was believed to be in residence. At the second stage of emergent common law, the original Roman notion of *jus* (which later took on other meanings) stemmed from formal agreements or treaties among the tribes and clans, and not from the more elusive selection and reconciliation that characterized the Greek thesmos. Finally, the Roman *lex*, unlike *nomos*, emphasized the institutional basis of legislation, not simply the fact that it was man-made: *Lex* was defined as the product not of wise counsel or knowledge of nature, but of a formal, authorized procedure, 'a known process of making law' (*LHPT* 244) whereby custom could be replaced by statute. At every stage the emergent Roman political culture was marked by elements of negotiation and contract.

So thoroughgoing was Roman legalism that the notion of justice itself became a matter of legal judgment. Here the Romans reached their most speculative level, the appropriation of a vulgarized Stoic notion of natural law. Justice to them was simply the application of another, higher kind of law, which served as a criterion for existing statute. The judge applied the law, *lex*, to cases. The legislator applied the law to lex-making. The critic of their efforts applied another set of laws, the *Lex Naturalis*. Thus, the entire legal system was encompassed in a single, self-validating, purely juridical mode of thought. The narrow focus on legality was reinforced in the law-abiding character of the Roman people: the City of Rome, Oakeshott reports, had no police force and no death penalty for nearly seven centuries.

The Roman conception of a legal system pursued in the name of the *Populus Romanus* alone served as a powerful tool of political order and empire. Employing statute where others relied on ancient custom, it was able to penetrate many other relations. Within Rome, law rather than location defined the line between public and private. The notion of 'public space' is Greek, not Roman. In Athens public business was conducted in the *agora*, private affairs in the household. The Roman notion, by contrast, is of *res publica*, or public concern, a legally defined matter that need accept no boundaries. The *res publica* could be extended into the family, as in the laws of intermarriage between patrician and plebeians or the laws of adoption that prolonged the familial basis of Roman politics. Law itself defined the line between public and private.

It was this same legalism that enabled the Romans to extend their *imperium* more durably than any other conquering people of ancient times. Alexander consolidated his conquests by toleration of local custom. Roman legality was more ambitious: the *Populus Romanus* did not simply conquer new territories; it gave them *libertas*; it liberated them. By a variety of municipal, gubernatorial, treaty and agency arrangements the law of the *Populus Romanus* was extended to subjugated peoples, incorporating their customary practices by reference into the Roman legal structure (as *jus gentium*). This gave Romans the sense not of *dominium*, a term they used for household relations of master to slave, but of *imperium*, a term synonymous with bringing the *libertas* of Rome to other lands. In their own eyes, for example, the Romans 'liberated' Athens by replacing Macedonian despotism (the parallel Greek term for *dominium*) with Roman law. Abroad, as in Rome itself, 'liberty' did not consist in active democratic participation in the making of laws, but in being subject to laws enacted and to powers executed in the name of the *Populus Romanus*. Only rarely, as Oakeshott once remarked on the problem of Judea, did the Romans meet a religiously grounded legalism so resistant to their own union of *religio* and *lex* as to require decimation and ultimate depopulation.

Oakeshott most admires the legal improvisation within the constitutional order of Rome itself. The Romans pioneered fine distinctions between the power to accomplish one's projects (*potentia*), the powers inherent in an office (*potestas*) and the prestige to initiate new collective undertakings (*auctoritas*). They thus had three concepts where modern thought uses only two: 'power' and 'authority'. They understood perfectly the distinction upon which modern rule-of-law society rests between the enumerated powers of a legally defined office and the informal means of enforcing one's will. The *potestas* of a magistrate inhered, as with us, in the office rather than the person. But in a practice for which we have no exact parallel, the prerogatives of office might also be invested for a time in someone who did not occupy it. For example, by a formal act the Senate might invest its *auctoritas*, derived from that of the *auctor* of Rome himself, in a non-Senator, without alienating that attribute from the existing Senate. And this was the device whereby, with no change of constitutional form, Republican Rome invested all executive, judicial, legislative and advisory powers in an Emperor for life. *De facto* the Republic abolished itself, but *de jure* nothing changed.

How was a political culture capable of such subtle artifice also able to sustain the crude conquering legions of empire? Why did it not become more quickly desiccated, or tied up in its own legalism? For Oakeshott the answer lies in the union of religion and politics, which enabled the Romans to hold fast to a few simple doctrines even as their legal system multiplied distinctions over an expanding *imperium*.

The *Populus Romanus* as the font of all legitimate rule was the crucial doctrine, and it was bolstered by a religion centered on the family and its household gods. The *Populus Romanus* was seen as a family extended by law. Just as the father of a family joined the household gods upon his death, so, too did Caesar Augustus become deified. (Oakeshott takes it as a sign of *religious* corruption when in the second century A.D. the emperor was deified during his lifetime.) In this continuity between ancestral and civil religion, as in the constitutional continuity between Republic and Empire, resourceful adaptation shielded the Romans from conceptual change.

By such improvisations, by treaty and by adoption of diverse foreigners into prominent Roman families, the myth of a single Roman people was prolonged. But the religio-political system did not survive the formal extension of Roman citizenship to the subject peoples of the empire. As citizenship was broadened, the familial basis of Roman politics became implausible and a universal religion seemed necessary to preserve the doctrinal basis of Roman politics. Unfortunately for the continuity of the *imperium*, Christianity, the most serviceable sect at hand, had tenets that undercut the deepest, self-worshipping Roman beliefs about the ultimate unity of the political and religious realms. And by the time of its official adoption Christianity also had an organizational structure of its own that, having profited from Roman examples, could compete in the political arena. Both doctrinally and institutionally, Christianity, on Oakeshott's account, did more to subvert than to support the union of religion with politics that characterized the vigor of Rome. Nevertheless, in various forms the nostalgia for a Roman fusion of politics and religion or at the very least a diarchy of primates and kings continued to haunt Western political thought long after Rome had been sacked.

The need to re-explain politics on Christian grounds gave rise in time to genuine philosophy – a re-casting of Roman categories in an enduring form that Oakeshott elucidates in his lectures on the medieval experience. It is in this context that he discusses Augustine's *De Civitate Dei* and Aquinas' views on Natural Law.

The Character of Political Thought

We need not, however, pursue here Oakeshott's lectures into the medieval period. Our samplings of his discussions of law in Greece and Rome, though they cannot hope to capture the richness of his presentation, still less the complexity of the underlying subject matter, do suffice to evoke the main lines of his approach to political thought overall.

What, then, is political thought? And how on Oakeshott's considered view does it proceed from the activity of politics?

Politics for Oakeshott, as we have seen, has three preconditions: a diversity of persons, a unity of rule, and the belief that rule is to be shaped by conscious human deliberation. These conditions give rise to obvious questions, which he poses in this way:

- What sort of political community do we compose?
- What is ruling and being ruled?
- What is the authority of rulers, and how do they acquire it? What are the rights of subjects, and how are they acquired?
- What is law? (*LHPT*, 237)

Answers are given at three levels – at the everyday, practical level of political discourse, at the more organized level of systematic doctrine and practical theorem-making, and at the purely explanatory levels of history and philosophy. The Greeks are noteworthy for their originality at the first and third levels – for having invented politics and developed the first philosophical reflection upon it. The Romans are remarkable for their unsurpassed achievement at the second level in sustaining both intellectually and institutionally a rigorously organized answer to the question: What is law? In these and all cases the conduct of politics and reflection upon it, whether practical, praxiological or jurisprudential, whether historical, scientific or philosophical, is inescapably contextual. We are in Oakeshott's view always thinking about politics from within a present context, even when we write the history of ancient times.

Oakeshott's own approach in these introductory lectures though mainly historical is disciplined by a philosopher's insistence upon distinguishing genuine theorizing from advocacy and advice. He is acutely aware that even philosophical reflection on politics is rarely pure. Indeed, his view on the mixture of modes in Aristotle's *Politics* bears repeating, for it is central to his teaching in the lectures overall: 'getting used to it [the mixture of modes] does not mean failing to recognize the important differences between these modes of thought' (*LHPT*, 115).

His is not an obsessive mind. He does not find it illuminating to see politics everywhere. He sees it as an historically limited cultural achievement that is sustained with difficulty. Only where political experience has been continuous, does it make sense to speak of political thought. Without political experience, political thought is unthinkable. As a living activity politics is carried on within a tradition. Philosophical and historical thought may serve to locate, to criticize, and to understand such a tradition on other terms, but politics moves forward on its own terms in a practical idiom; it is the product of sustained intelligence, in which knowing and doing – articulated political thought and tacit political experience – are inextricably intertwined in patterns peculiar to each epoch and culture.[2]

This is why Oakeshott insists in his essays in *Rationalism in Politics* that politics consists not in the application of general, theoretical knowledge to human affairs, but in deliberated conduct drawing intimations from shared experiences. This is why in *Experience and Its Modes* he distinguishes history and science as modes of experience from practice. In the historical and scientific modes, doing (the activity of being a scientist or historian) is put at the service of knowing; in the practical mode the reverse is the case, but as his discussion of Rome testifies, he does not underrate the systematic intellectual element in practical affairs. Finally, his sensibility to the intertwining of the several varieties of knowing and doing peculiar to each tradition explains why in these lectures he rejects the notion, not uncommon among his contemporaries, that we can write a continuous 'history of political thought' as if from a closed canon of approved philosophical and didactic writers.

Some historical moments do indeed encourage genuinely philosophical writers to examine politics, but as the examples of Greece and Rome suffice to show, the quality of the philosophy is no measure of the genius of the practice. And the specificity of the practice to its context requires us to learn the political vocabulary of each tradition.

The benefit of Oakeshott's approach is to help us discern quickly the character, integrity and provenance of various kinds of discourse. When, for example, a philosopher or scientist or historian pronounces upon public affairs, we know not to expect the utterance to have integrity as philosophy, science or history. At the same time we understand that from within any political tradition there will be

---

[2]   Though Oakeshott does not discuss the traditions of rhetoric in Greece and Rome, their differences serve to underline his point about the Roman focus on the intermediate level of political thought. In Greece, the professional and practical disciplines, including legal procedure, were not considered part of the training of the rhetor, whereas in Roman rhetoric, as propounded by Quintilian, a grounding in law, economics, architecture and other practical sciences was considered essential.

disciplined ways of making arguments and coming to judgments, and that these may require intellectual gifts of a high (but non-theoretical) order. We are thus encouraged to admire achievements – and perhaps even to pursue achievements of our own – on the grounds appropriate to them.

Politics is to be admired for sustaining a tradition of civic life in which human beings can form their own characters and institutions under a durable rule of law. The life of the mind, even when it takes law and morals as topics for reflection, has other standards.

Endnote

This essay is adapted from a talk delivered at the Robert M. Olin Colloquium in Political Philosophy at Columbia University on November 26, 1991. Professor David Sidorsky, who directed the Olin program at Columbia, scheduled this lecture and a subsequent talk by Shirley Robin Letwin to commemorate the first anniversary of Michael Oakeshott's death.

The original talk relied on an unpublished typescript of Oakeshott's LSE lectures entitled *A Study of Political Thought*, made available to me by John Lingner, a former student to whom Oakeshott had given a photocopied version, and by Stuart Warner, a member of the Philosophy Department at Roosevelt University, who, with Lingner had deciphered Oakeshott's hand-written additions. In January 2006, Imprint Academic published the lectures as Volume 2 in its projected six-volume series *Michael Oakeshott: Selected Writings* (Luke O'Sullivan, General Editor) under the title *Lectures in the History of Political Thought*. Volume 2 is edited by Terry Nardin and Luke O'Sullivan, with an introduction placing the lectures in their academic setting, so that one can imagine oneself, à la Collingwood's view of history, being there at the LSE as Professor Oakeshott speaks.

In the foregoing essay all the quotations from Oakeshott are given page references and (sometimes emended) wording and orthography to conform to the Imprint Academic volume. I have, however, consistently retained Oakeshott's capitalization of *Populus Romanus*, and where appropriate of Natural Law, and I have also departed from the printed edition in preserving Oakeshott's title, A Study of Political Thought, to underline my theme that the presentation goes beyond the historical. In the first sentence of his opening lecture, where Oakeshott announces 'a study of political thought,' he also proposes a characteristically modest alternative: 'aids to the study of political thought' (*LHPT*, 31).

There have been published since 1991 several discussions of Oakeshott in relation to the Greek and Roman thinkers and topics treated here:

Part one of *The Intellectual Legacy of Michael Oakeshott*, ed. Corey Abel and Timothy Fuller (Exeter: Imprint Academic, 2005), is devoted to 'Oakeshott and the Ancients' with the following three essays: 'Oakeshott and Plato: A Philosophical Conversation,' by Debra Candreva, pp. 2–20; 'Platonic Themes in Oakeshott's Modern European State,' by Eric S. Kos, pp. 21–36; 'Appropriating Aristotle,' by Corey Abel, pp. 37–61. Debra Candreva has in addition compared Oakeshott and Plato at book-length in *The Enemies of Perfection: Oakeshott, Plato, and the Critique of Rationalism* (Lanham, MD: Lexington Books, 2004). Also, Eric Kos has recently added *Michael Oakeshott, the Ancient Greeks, and the Philosophical Study of Politics* (Exeter: Imprint Academic, 2007).

The relation of *On Human Conduct* to the Roman republican tradition was broached by Wendell John Coats, Jr., in a 1992 article, 'Some Correspondences Between Oakeshott's Civil Condition and the Republican Tradition, *The Political Science Reviewer*, 21 (Spring): 99–115. David Boucher, writing on a similar republican theme in 2005, provides the first article since 1991 to make extensive use of the Lectures in 'Oakeshott, Freedom and Republicanism,' *British Journal of Politics and International Relations*, 7, no. 1 (February): 81–96. Luke O'Sullivan touches on the Roman lectures and their bearing on Oakeshott's late legal philosophy in *Oakeshott on History* (Exeter: Imprint Academic, 2003), 184–5.

The availability of the Lectures will doubtless give rise to further work. It is worth noting the suggestion of Nardin and O'Sullivan in their 'Editors' Introduction' that the Imprint Academic publication encourages one to compare Oakeshott's exposition for undergraduates of the vocabulary of Roman legalism to the Latin terminology he later used in the essay 'On the Civil Condition' in *On Human Conduct* (and one should add, in 'The Rule of Law' in *On History and Other Essays*). Did Oakeshott see himself as the philosopher of law that Rome never produced?

6

Michael Henkel

A Conservative Concept of Freedom: Otto von Gierke's 'Genossenschaftslehre' and Oakeshott's Philosophy of Practice[†]

The idea of comparing the political philosophy of Michael Oakeshott with Otto von Gierke's history and theory of law and state suggests itself on account of the obvious parallels and convergences in their conceptions. These similarities are sometimes mentioned,[1] but with the exception of David Runciman and Luke O'Sullivan's books[2] the relationship between Oakeshott and Gierke is nowhere discussed in detail. It is neither my intention nor is it possible to present such a detailed interpretation here. What I want to do is to direct attention to some aspects of Oakeshott and Gierke's common views and to some points concerning a conservative concept of freedom.

To compare Oakeshott and Gierke does not mean to search for an influence of Gierke upon Oakeshott. We know that the latter was an attentive reader of Gierke's works: Oakeshott reviewed Ernest Barker's English edition of (portions from) volume 4 of Gierke's *Genossenschaftsrecht*[3] and occasionally he names the German jurist and gives explicit and implicit hints to his reception of Gierke's works in his own texts.[4] But instead of searching for an influence I want to look for objective congruencies and parallels between their concepts, points of views, and their arguments. While speaking of congruencies, parallels, and convergences, I remain cognizant of the serious divergences and differences between Gierke and Oakeshott.[5] Runciman and O'Sullivan properly underline these differences, and

---

[†] I would like to express my gratitude to Corey Abel for his help in editing this paper, both with respect to content and style.
[1]   See, for example, Robert Grant, *Oakeshott* (London: Claridge Press, 1990), 90.
[2]   David Runciman, *Pluralism and the Personality of the State* (Cambridge: Cambridge Univ. Press, 1997); Luke O'Sullivan, *Oakeshott on History* (Exeter, Charlottesville: Imprint Academic, 2003).
[3]   Oakeshott, 'Review of O. Gierke, *Natural Law and the Theory of Society*,' *Cambridge Review*, 56 (1934): 11–2.
[4]   See, Oakeshott, *On Human Conduct* (Oxford: Clarendon Press, 1975), 203, 205. Hereafter: *OHC*.
[5]   One of the main sources of those differences seems to be the fact, that on the one hand, Gierke,

the following exposition cannot and will not ignore them. But in respect to the concept of freedom I hold it to be more fruitful to accentuate the similarities.

Gierke and Oakeshott On Association and The Modern State

What Oakeshott and Gierke principally have in common is an historical approach to politics, law, and the state on the one hand, and a reflective theoretical position on the other hand. Both endeavored to extract their theoretical views and concepts from historical materials.[6] Whether and to what extent they succeeded in the realization of this intention – and first of all, what such an intention means – is an independent question. In every case both thinker's views and concepts depend on some conceptions of a philosophy of history. For Gierke, whose *Genossenschaftslehre* (i.e. his theory and history of fellowship and of the law of fellowship)[7] I want to discuss here in more detail than Oakeshott's theory, European and especially German history is shown as an evolutionary process of a gradual unfolding of an initial idea, the idea of freedom. This process, which is also a process of differentiation, has, for Gierke, reached its end in the modern constitutional state, the *Rechtsstaat*, which Gierke imagined as a constitutional monarchy but not as a democratic republic. In accordance with the liberal tradition of the eighteenth and nineteenth century, Gierke sees an inherent tendency in democracy to become a tyranny of the masses.[8]

---

as a member of the Germanist section of the Historical law school is without doubt a specific German thinker, whose work is closely related to the German politics of his times, to German history, and to German academic traditions and usages. See Ernest Barker, 'Translator's Introduction,' in, Otto Gierke, *Natural Law and the Theory of Society 1500 to 1800*, with a Lecture on *The Ideas of Natural Law and Humanity* by Ernst Troeltsch, trans. with an intro. by Ernest Barker (reprint of the 1934 two volume ed. in one vol., Cambridge: Cambridge Univ. Press, 1950), l–lvi. Oakeshott, similarly, is a specific English scholar and is – like Gierke – a son of his times, his country, and its university traditions. On the other hand, both scholars are expressly concerned with revealing a common European political tradition, its unity, and specific nature. An essential feature of this European tradition is that it is a one-in-many and a many-in-one, a pluralist tradition that can be viewed from different perspectives and be described in different idioms, but time and again shows the same essential features – the most important of which is freedom, the central subject of Gierke's as well as of Oakeshott's studies.

[6]   Anthony Black explains, 'Philosophy and history are intimately connected in Gierke's understanding of the world and of law, in his analysis of both the phenomena and the concepts of *Recht*.' Anthony Black, 'Introduction' to *Community in Historical Perspective*, by Otto von Gierke (a translation of selections from *Das deutsche Genossenschaftsrecht* [The German Law of Fellowship]; principally from vol. 1: *Rechtsgeschichte der deutschen Genossenschaft* [The Legal and Moral History of the German Fellowship]), trans. Mary Fischer, sel. and ed. Anthony Black (Cambridge: Cambridge Univ. Press, 1990), xvi.

[7]   For an introduction to Gierke's thought in English see the following 'classical' texts: Frederic William Maitland, 'Introduction' to *Political Theories of the Middle Age*, by Otto von Gierke, trans. Frederic William Maitland (Cambridge: Cambridge Univ. Press, 1913), vii–xlv; Barker, 'Introduction' to *Natural Law*; Sobei Mogi, *Otto von Gierke: His Political Teaching and Jurisprudence* (London: P. S. King and Son, 1932); John D. Lewis, *The Genossenschaft-Theory of Otto von Gierke: A Study in Political Thought* (Madison: Univ. of Wisconsin, 1935), a very careful and reliable study; as well as – more recently – Black, 'Introduction' to *Community*; and Runciman, *Pluralism*, 34-63, passim.

[8]   That Gierke's theory nevertheless is not inherently antidemocratic can be seen in the work of his disciple Hugo Preuss, who was the chief draftsman of the republican Weimar Constitution. Preuss elaborated a decisively pluralistic and democratic theory on the basis of Gierke's

The specific nature of the historical process – as Gierke presents it – lies in the dialectical interplay and struggle between two main principles of the organization of social and of public life: the principle of fellowship (*Genossenschaft*) and the principle of lordship (*Herrschaft*). Gierke's European history reveals many variants of these principles and finds them effective in different institutions, legal concepts, historical contexts, and under different names, but the respective core of these principles essentially remains the same throughout the centuries.

Fellowships are voluntary associations 'based on the free association of its members.' The members of fellowships are considered to be equals, which is a characteristic every bit as important as fellowships' assertion of 'an independent dominant group identity over their members.'[9] Gierke traces this concept of fellowship as a specifically German concept or rather, a specific concept of German law and its history.[10] The respective historical claims, at least as far as they tend to a kind of more or less ideological 'Germanism' are of course problematic; and in addition, historical research has shown that a considerable part of Gierke's claims in this connection are considered to be falsified.[11] But besides those historical aspects there remains a theoretical content of the concept of fellowship; and here its merit consists in its capacity to grasp the autonomy and self-government of groups as well as in grasping the aspect of group personality. This latter aspect is of great importance in Gierke's theory: Fellowships are able to constitute a group personality as a collective personality. Group personality indicates as a general term a state of common consciousness of the members of the same *genossenschaftliche* group, a consciousness that works as the basis for collective thinking and acting as one corporate person (or as a unit). In a narrower sense, the term indicates the recognition of the group personality by law.[12] It is of great importance to realize that this quasi-collectivist concept is nevertheless a liberal concept. Fellowships as collective personalities remain *free* associations because they are 'truly willed and therefore truly free forms of association.'[13] As examples of fellowships (taken from all centuries since Teutonic times and the early middle ages) Gierke discusses guilds, craft guilds, medieval cities, city leagues such as the German *Hansa* or, with respect especially to nineteenth century Germany, the varied forms of *Vereine*, co-operatives, joint-stock companies, and producers' cooperatives – and many more. Those examples not only mark the wide range and the plurality of forms of fellowships, but also show that Gierke does not without further ado accept the sharp distinction between private and public associations claimed especially in the

---

Genossenschaftstheorie, cf. esp. Hugo Preuss, *Gemeinde, Staat, Reich als Gebietskörperschaften: Versuch einer deutschen Staatskonstruktion auf Grundlage der Genossenschaftstheorie* (Berlin: Verlag von Julius Springer, 1889). In essential respects Gierke did not consent to Preuss' further development of his theory.

[9]   Gierke, *Community*, 6.

[10] For the concept of fellowship as a specifically German concept, see Otto von Gierke, *Geschichte des deutschen Körperschaftsbegriffs* [= *Das deutsche Genossenschaftsrecht*, vol. 2] (Berlin: Weidmann, 1873), 865–923 ('Der Genoßenschaftsbegriff'). A few portions of this chapter are to be found in Gierke, *Community*, 241–3.

[11] Black, 'Introduction' to *Community*, xx–xxi, xxviii–xxx.

[12] Barker, 'Introduction' to *Natural Law*, lvii–lxxxvii.

[13] Black, 'Introduction' to *Community*, xix; cf. Gierke, *Community*, 63.

Roman law tradition. One specific example – the modern state – will be discussed later. Before doing so, we have to take a look at the other principle of social or public order, the principle of lordship.

It is the inherent equal freedom of fellowship that determines its decisive difference from its counterpart: lordship. The concept of lordship first of all marks a 'form of human community, in which one individual is the bond of all,'[14] or broadly, in which an individual, group, or institution is vested with independent rights from which it gets its competence to order the community at its own discretion. Such a community therefore is essentially characterized by the relation of lordship and service. It is a hierarchical order of inequality. On one side we find the master or ruler, and on the other side the serving subjects, whose rights are not rights of themselves as members of the community, but are unilaterally granted by the sovereign powers (*Obrigkeit*) – and in some historical cases are not more than acts of mercy. A prominent example of lordship is the feudal system of the middle ages.[15] In the modern industrial era, Gierke insists on the lordship character of 'capitalist business enterprises of all kinds.'[16] In the light of these examples, we again notice that for Gierke the conceptual distinction between the public and the private sphere cannot be definitive, which results in some important consequences upon which I will touch later.

For now we have to call to mind that for Gierke the course of history presents a struggle between the principles of fellowship and lordship. This struggle produces many different forms of social and public order in which we find different combinations of the realization of the principles and also various forms of relations between the different forms of groups and associations. Gierke discusses a vast number of historical forms and their evolution, but I want to concentrate just on one of those forms, namely the modern state. To understand Gierke's concept of the state, we have to take into account that he differentiates between two main forms of modern statehood, namely the absolutist state and the constitutional state.

First, the absolutist state is the modern state as lordship, as *Obrigkeitsstaat* or sovereign power, realized in Western Europe and not least in the 'benevolent despotism' of the so called *Policeystaat* (supervisory state) of sixteenth to eighteenth century Germany. Gierke describes the idea or concept of *Obrigkeit* in a passage worth quoting here at some length, not least because it leads us to Oakeshott:

> The *essence* of this concept, however great the difference in other respects between Luther's demand for obedience, the '*l'état c'est moi*' of Louis XIV, and Frederic the Great's 'first servant of the state', has remained the same in spite of progressive clarification and intellectualism. Indeed it applies equally to all the diverse political constructs of the philosophers of the seventeenth and eighteenth centuries and to the idea of the state found in the French Revolution. The characteristic feature of this concept is that it sees the state as something apart from the people. In the abstract formulation of this state, it concentrates the sum total of all public power within a distinct sphere, territorially and personally enclosed. It concentrates the Right and duty to represent the common

---

[14]   Gierke, *Community*, 10.
[15]   Gierke, *Community*, 15–7.
[16]   Gierke, *Community*, 212.

interest (*salus publica*) against special interests ... to create Right and public order, and to regulate the relationship of member to whole in a necessary unity, to such an extent that sovereign power becomes the visible representation of the abstract concept: apart from the state there can only be individuals.[17]

This concept of *Obrigkeit* – despite some parallels[18] – contrasts with the concept of fellowship community and (as a result) especially with the concept of *Rechtsstaat*, or the constitutional state. In a comparative description, Gierke confronts the two forms of public organization:

In community all had a share in the representation of the unity; in the sovereign state, unity is represented only by an individual, or in exceptional cases a group of individuals. Thus in community, unity is collective, dwells in the collectivity and finds its highest expression in the collective will; whereas in the sovereign state, unity is alien to the collectivity. Therefore, while the communal constitution [*Gemeinheitsverfassung;* MH] determines the organization by means of which the collectivity *governs itself*, the sovereign constitution contains within itself the organization by means of which the collectivity *is governed*. The concept of *citizen* unites political rights and political duties, lordship and obedience, active and passive participation in the common life: the *subject* is a legal subject only in the sphere of private law, in public law he is merely the object, he is to the state as the layman is to the church. The common life demands that the citizen participate in administration, adjudication and legislation, and inclines towards the principles of election, collegiality and majority voting; sovereignty strives towards the exclusion of subjects from public life and favors centralizing administration by means of nominated unitary agencies. If, then, the principle of sovereignty strives towards the realization of the *absolute state*, it is at the same time a *supervisory* state [*Polizeistaat*]. For, since the concept of the *public good* is regarded as supreme, concern for the public good or positive intervention [*Polizei*] are bound to count as the functions of the state, for the sake of which all other functions exist. If, then, existing law comes into conflict with the public good, it must give way unconditionally; even state treaties, privileges and well-established rights become invalid where they are prejudicial to the public good. Since the representative of the public welfare – the sovereign – has the exclusive right to verify and decide whether such is the case, the principle that *salus publica lex suprema est* (public safety is the supreme law) is a convenient argument for justifying all breaches of law [*Recht*] .... Sovereignty as the representative of *Polizei* recognizes no limitations on, or even protection against, its powers in Right. Rather, the sovereign state increasingly moves *above* and *beyond* Right and becomes the opposite of the *constitutional state* [*Rechtsstaat*] foreshadowed in the communal system [*Gemeinwesen*], which exists within the law and accepts that law sets limits on its freedom of movement – its organism itself is law – and which strives as its ultimate goal for the unity of state and Right. The sovereign state not only wants to control all powers, it wants to control them exclusively. The recognition, implementation and protection of what is required for the common good is not simply its Right and duty, but the *monopoly* of the sovereign. The subject as such may see to his own individual affairs, but he is neither capable of keeping universal affairs [*das Allgemeine*, i.e. strictly speaking: common affairs; MH] under his control, nor empowered to do so, unless he is endowed with the superior insight, common sense and

---

[17] Gierke, *Community*, 109.
[18] Gierke, *Community*, 109–10.

political authorization by a state office.... Even private affairs are supervised, restricted and regulated wherever they encroach on the public interest – and whether or not this is the case is adjudicated at the direction of the sovereign power. It is the Right and duty of the state to prescribe, enforce or restrict, in every detail, the economic activity of the individual for the increase of national wealth, to standardize trade and commerce by means of statutes, taxes and regulations, to tax unproductive consumption by means of sumptuary laws, to prescribe the country's manner of building by cultural decrees [*Kulturmandate*; MH], and to prevent idleness or the incorrect use of labor by threats of punishment. In the same way it attempts to be the guardian of economic life, it seeks also to be the guardian of the life of the intellect [*das geistige Leben*; MH], to prescribe its direction and to limit its own vitality. Indeed, if at all possible, the subject is to be regulated even in his social and recreational activities, each one's rank and entitlements being determined by the sovereign power. From this it emerges that the authoritarian state is a *tutelary state* [*Bevormundungsstaat*], and also that it inclines toward bureaucratic over-government, centralization and standardization.[19]

Thus, while Gierke's paradigm of lordship for modern times obviously is the German *Policeystaat*, i.e. the pre-1789 welfare-state,[20] Gierke is not only aware that there was a further development of the modern state after 1789, but it is first of all this development that he concentrates on in his debate with some contemporary German scholars to which his sharp critique is directed. The development led to the nineteenth century sovereign state of which the dualism of state (or government or ruler) and society is characteristic.[21] This further development is now to be observed in a comparative discussion of Oakeshott and Gierke: On account of Gierke's – so to speak – 'ideal-typifying' characterization of the two principles of fellowship and lordship extracted from specifically modern examples, his explanation shows very clearly the congruencies to which I want to direct attention.

Gierke's characterization of *Obrigkeit* corresponds with decisive aspects of what Oakeshott characterizes in various works as the politics of faith and as enterprise association. This becomes obvious when we remember for instance Oakeshott's claim that 'the politics of faith understands governing as an endlessly proliferating activity, integrating all the activities of the subject, and ... always at the end of its tether.'[22] What Oakeshott thus describes in an abstract manner is for him, as it is for Gierke, a historical phenomenon that entered the stage of European history in the sixteenth century under certain conditions which were the very first to enable such a politics of faith (*FS*, 48-51). An association characterized by the prevalence of what in the 1950s he calls a 'politics of faith' is described by the late Oakeshott as an 'enterprise association'. I want to bring to mind just two features of such

---

[19] Gierke, *Community*, 110–1. In this and subsequent long quotations, I have made slight alterations to the translation, indicated by my initials 'MH'.

[20] This was not in the twentieth century sense an authoritarian state (or a dictatorship), but nevertheless an authoritarian state pursuing an interventionist and supervisory policy usually in the name of 'welfare'. Cf. Michael Stolleis, *Geschichte des öffentlichen Rechts in Deutschland*, vol. 1, *Reichspublizistik und Policeywissenschaft 1600–1800* (München: C. H. Beck Verlag, 1988), 334–93, as well as Black's remarks and references in Gierke, *Community*, 257–8 n. 3.

[21] For the historical background of this dualism see the remarks in Gierke, *Political Theories*, 73.

[22] Oakeshott, *The Politics of Faith and the Politics of Scepticism*, ed. Timothy Fuller (New Haven, London: Yale Univ. Press, 1996), 28, 46–7. Hereafter: FS.

an association. First, the management character of its pursuing of the common purposes that are at the root of the association is a typical feature of enterprise associations.[23] Its understanding of rules is a second feature. In an enterprise association, rules are to be understood as instrumental (although they may be 'contingently connected with the purpose' [*OHC*, 117] of the association). Their basic character is that of commands rather than orienting norms. What Oakeshott describes in this way are the features that prompt Gierke to qualify the sovereign state – in accord with a long tradition of political thought – as a mechanism or a machine.[24]

Of course, Oakeshott and Gierke are very skeptical regarding a human association understood as an enterprise or as a machine. The decisive point for both scholars is in this connection that a politics of faith or a politics of an *obrigkeitliches* government undermines and at last tends to destroy the freedom of its citizens by treating them as immature subjects. Both identify from their understanding of such a politics a specific tendency of political development in modern times. The politics of faith as well as of the *Obrigkeitsstaat* tends in practice (as it implies in theory) toward a dualism of government on the one side and more or less isolated individuals on the other side, 'to achieve, alongside the absolute state, *absolute individuality.*'[25] This means that such politics foster the disintegration of intermediate social associations, institutions or groups at least in so far as those are not constituted or approved by the government itself,[26] the latter of which Gierke terms *Anstalt* (institution).[27]

Of course Oakeshott and Gierke do recognize the benefits of this process which are to be seen principally in an increase of freedom understood as personal independence, and of equality among individual citizens.[28] But these benefits have another side. Under conditions of a sovereign state with a prevailing politics of faith and especially in the context of a modern economy, such freedom and equality tends to lack a freely chosen content. Therefore under such conditions persons are condemned to remain subjects instead of freely self-determined citizens. To denote this ideal of freely self-determining citizens, Oakeshott uses the term *'civis'*. This term gives the cue to come back to the form of social and public organization that is opposed to enterprise association. This is the association of *cives* or 'civil association' (*OHC*, 108–184, *passim*) and it is paralleled in Gierke's scheme by the

---

[23] For the concept of enterprise association, see (*OHC*, 114–117, *passim*); on the management aspect of enterprise association (*OHC*, 115-6). 'An enterprise is a 'policy', and enterprise association is a managerial engagement' (*OHC*, 115).

[24] Cf. Barbara Stollberg-Rilinger, *Der Staat als Maschine: Zur politischen Metaphorik des absoluten Fürstenstaates* (Berlin: Duncker und Humblot, 1986).

[25] Gierke, *Community*, 112; cf. Gierke, *Political Theories*, 87–8.

[26] Cf. *FS*, 49-50, and Gierke, *Community*, 111-3.

[27] 'The *Anstalt* … is created from above and resembles the 'authoritarian union'; the *Genossenschaft* or *Körperschaft* is created from below or within a group' (Lewis, *Genossenschaft-Theory*, 60 n. 21).

[28] Gierke considers this to be 'one of the greatest deeds of history' carried out by the absolute state and just reached at the end of nineteenth century. He also holds this to be 'an immense step forward [*unermeßlicher Fortschritt*; MH] from medieval guild-state' (Gierke, *Community*, 113).

'communal system' understood as a fellowship association. Gierke stresses the lawful character as the decisive feature of such an association, and Oakeshott does the same with respect to civil association, which is virtually defined as the association of *cives* who are 'related solely in terms of their common recognition of the rules which constitute a practice of civility' (*OHC*, 128). The decisive difference that identifies such an association consists, then, in the character of the respective rules that are qualified by Oakeshott as *lex* (*OHC*, 127–30, *passim*). The *corpus* of *lex* stands in contrast to rules as understood in an enterprise association, and it stands for rules 'which prescribe the common responsibilities (and the counterpart 'rights' to have these responsibilities fulfilled) of agents and in terms of which they put by their characters as enterprisers and put by all that differentiates them from one another and recognize themselves as formal equals – *cives*' (*OHC*, 128). Here it becomes obvious that the civil condition is essentially a state of freedom and equality: the rules of *lex* assume the citizens to be free agents and at the same time release them to free agency. And the status of recognizing the conditions of such free agency set by the rules of *lex* is what Oakeshott calls a *respublica*, a commonwealth of equally free citizens (cf. *OHC*, 147–58, 164–73).

Taking up two Roman law concepts, Oakeshott now calls a modern state understood in terms of civil association a *societas* (or *civitas*, *OHC*, 203), and in contrast he calls a modern state understood as an enterprise association a *universitas* (*OHC*, 199–206, passim).[29] He emphasizes that any *actual* modern state is never characterized only by one of the two 'dispositions represented by the words *societas* and *universitas*' (*OHC*, 201), but on the contrary is always of an ambiguous nature as a *societas cum universitate*. Similarly, politics has an ambiguous character, determined by the tension between the politics of faith and the politics of skepticism.

At this point we have a decisive correspondence of Gierke with Oakeshott: Gierke describes the modern constitutional state as a unity of fellowship and lordship, and this has much in common with the *societas cum universitate*.[30] This parallel is at the same time the source of quite a lot of differences, which will be discussed shortly. At first we will look at the parallels. They are to be seen in Gierke's description of the *Rechtsstaat* as an essentially lawful state. It is only its lawful character that guarantees it to be a state of freedom and equality; and, this lawful character lies in the fellowship-aspect of such a state, just as for Oakeshott

[29] Gierke deals at great length with the Roman law concepts of *universitas* and *societas*, their reception in jurisprudence and natural law theory, and the changes in their meanings (cf. esp. the discussion of Roman law concepts and their 'reception' in Otto von Gierke, *Die Staats- und Korporationslehre des Alterthums und des Mittelalters und ihre Aufnahme in Deutschland* [= *Das deutsche Genossenschaftsrecht*, vol. 3], (Berlin: Weidmann, 1881), but unlike Oakeshott he does not adopt them as theoretical concepts (for Gierke's interpretations see Maitland, 'Introduction' to *Political Theories*, xviii–xxvi; Lewis, *Genossenschaft-Theory*, 47; Runciman, *Pluralism*, 34–40). Here is not the place to discuss the problems of Oakeshott's use of the concepts in comparison to Gierke's discussion.
[30] Gierke, *Community*, 162–3. Runciman notes: Gierke's *Rechtsstaat* 'is a synthesis of the two ideas which Oakeshott takes to divide up European conceptions of the state,' *Pluralism*, 53–4. A critical discussion of a statement of Anthony Black is given in *Pluralism*, 54 n. 39. Runciman sees rightly that Gierke's conception has some features in addition to this synthesis.

the modern state as an association of free and as such equal citizens lies in its *societas*-aspect. What Gierke here has in mind is the idea that law can not be made simply by the state's issuing commands, but is instead the expression of the convictions of the citizens: 'Law is not the common will that something shall be, but the common conviction that something is.'[31] This conviction is, of course, an ethical conviction representing a form of public life that came down to the citizens through the course of their common history and that is coining their mentalities, virtues, and practices. Because for Gierke those convictions are the, so to say, 'sources' of law and although the modern state is of course lawgiver, it cannot be the state that creates law.

> Law, whether manifested directly in usage or declared by a social organ appointed for this purpose, is the conviction of a human society [*Menschengemeinschaft*; MH] that in it there are external rules for the will, that is, limitations of freedom which are externally binding and by hypothesis [*ihrer Idee nach*; MH] enforceable. The State as lawgiver not only acts to a great extent as that which bears and determines the legal consciousness [*Träger und Feststeller des Rechtsbewußtseins*; MH], but also completes the formation of all law with its command and enforcement. Yet if the common will commands that that which is law shall be obeyed, the law is not thereby created but merely confirmed. And if it is only through a supreme Might that the enforceability posited in the idea of Law can be perfectly realized, yet the law is still law even though in a particular case its enforcement fails or is imperfect or even impossible in default of a competent superior Might, if only there is still a general conviction that enforcement would be right if it were possible or if a competent power were at hand. And likewise the State no longer appears to us as a mere legal institution that exists for the law alone; yet among all its functions the legal purpose presents itself as the specific and indispensable purpose of the State, just because its full realization is possible only through the supreme Might. And while we regard the Law for its own part as primarily an instrument to serve the purpose of the state's life, yet its functions are very far from being exhausted or bounded by this. When lastly, on the one hand we set the State not above and beyond but within the Law, so that even its own freedom is bounded by the legal order, and on the other hand we set the Law not above and beyond but within the State, so that the formal omnipotence of the sovereign power prevails even against the Law, we thereby admit indeed the possibility of a conflict between material and formal law. But he who denies the possibility of such a conflict denies the very idea of Right.[32]

The *Rechtsstaat* thus is thought to be a 'living unity'[33] integrating a foundation of fellowship and a sovereign peak or summit (*Spitze*) – as the necessary authority for the proper realization of law – in a dialectic or, as Gierke calls it, organic manner.

---

[31] Otto von Gierke, *The Development of Political Theory*, trans. Bernard Feyd (1880, reprint; London: Allan and Unwin, 1939), 329; cf. Lewis, *Genossenschaft-Theory*, 69–70.
[32] Gierke, *Development*, 329–30; cf. Gierke, *Political Theories*, 73: The 'old Germanic idea' of the *Rechtsstaat* 'was the idea of a State which existed only in the law and for the law, and whose whole life was bound by a legal order that regulated alike all public and all private relationships.' The modern *Rechtsstaat* is different from this old one on account of its containing the feature of sovereignty. The above quoted passages of Gierke, *Development*, can be found in another translation in Gierke, *Natural Law*, Appendix on 'Gierke's Concept of Law,' 223–6.
[33] Gierke, *Community*, 163.

Therefore, Gierke conceptualizes the *Rechtsstaat* as an organism instead of as a mechanism, as a corporation instead of as an institution (*Anstalt*), as, finally, a *reale Verbandspersönlichkeit*, a real group personality which is acting on its own and which is in itself the 'subject' of sovereignty.[34] The merit of this concept lies for Gierke not least in the overcoming or – in a Hegelian sense – in the sublation (*Aufhebung*) of fruitless dualisms like that of sovereignty of the ruler *versus* popular sovereignty, or even the dualism between fellowship and lordship. For Gierke, the constitutional state is thus a 'higher unity' and a 'harmonious unity.'[35] This does not mean a unity without social conflicts and tensions, nor does it mean that the state as such is an entity somewhere above the individuals; it is instead a one-in-many and many-in-one. One of the effects of this concept is the decentralizing and civilizing of power by law because of the fact that the constitutional state as an organism is a whole, but nevertheless, as a consequence of its fellowship-aspect, a whole that comprises a manifold of other private and public associations, corporations, and group personalities in their own rights. As a whole the state is built up by all other such groups and is in its own personality defined through the totality of its legal relations – the totality of law. Thus in many cases its power is qualified and it is prevented from taking on the character of a 'sovereign state' (*Obrigkeitsstaat*). Remarkably, it is also the qualification of the difference between the private and the public sphere that has a decisive effect, as Runciman observes.

> It does not follow from this [concept of *Rechtsstaat*; MH] that the distinction between the public and the private breaks down altogether – the external relations of persons within the state, whether individuals or groups, must remain private so long as such persons are capable of acting in their own right, as will be the case, for example, whenever they contract with one another. But it does follow that no distinction can be drawn between persons on the basis of the sphere – public or private – to which they belong. All persons in the *Rechtsstaat* are public parts as well as private wholes, and so no person can either be denied a public function (i.e. be reduced to the level of a subject), nor claim the whole of public right as their own (i.e. be raised to the level of a sovereign).[36]

This reveals indeed a synthesis of *societas* and *universitas* in Oakeshott's sense, which at the same time leads us to recognize a key difference between Gierke and Oakeshott's conceptions of a modern state. The concept of the state as a group personality or as an organism has no parallel in Oakeshott's theory, and Oakeshott's *societas cum universitate* is surely not the same as such an organism. Indeed, unlike

---

[34] On the difference between *Subjekt* and *Objekt* in German, see the explanatory note by Maitland, 'Introduction' to *Political Theories*, xx n. 1. Maitland also gives a clear – if somewhat 'biological' – statement on the character of a state understood in terms of fellowship: The 'German Fellowship is no fiction, no symbol, no piece of the State's machinery, no collective name for individuals, but a living organism and a real person, with body and members and a will of its own. Itself can will, itself can act; it wills and acts by the men who are its organs as a man wills and acts by brain, mouth and hand. It is not a fictitious person; it is a *Gesammtperson*, and its will is a *Gesammtwille*; it is a group-person, and its will is a group will.' 'Introduction' to *Political Theories*, xxvi. Cf. Lewis, *Genossenschaft-Theory*, 54–62.

[35] Gierke, *Community*, 163.

[36] Runciman, *Pluralism*, 53.

his compatriots Maitland and John N. Figgis who welcomed Gierke's concepts,[37] Oakeshott explicitly distances himself from these concepts (*OHC*, 198–9, 205). This distance has its roots in different understandings of the concept of will (especially common will) just as in different ideas of common purposes.[38] In this light it becomes obvious that what on the one hand offers considerable parallels, shows some fundamental divergences on the other hand. While O'Sullivan and Runciman discuss these differences in some detail, I do not want to do so here; suffice it to say that I am convinced that the theories, in spite of certain differences, do not principally contradict one another.

There is just one difference I wish to emphasize: Gierke and Oakeshott had markedly divergent theoretical intentions. Gierke's concept of organism is in the end an attempt to give a 'sociological' explanation of the *'cum'* in the *civitas cum universitate*; Oakeshott undertakes above all a philosophical analysis of the twofold composition of the modern state, *civitas* here, and *universitas* there. Although the concept of the state as an organism is of course a problematic one – which, by the way, Gierke did anything but ignore[39] – I hold that Gierke's theory at least opens the possibility for a somewhat deeper or broader understanding of the nature of the modern state than Oakeshott's theory, if we are willing to follow his theoretical intention and put the concept of organism under critical revision. Several German political and legal scientists undertook such a revision and critical reformulation in the 1920s, so especially by Hermann Heller (1891–1933). Thus, setting aside the status of a reformulated concept of 'organism', it can be said that Gierke opens up the possibility of fruitfully exploring the modern state as it actually appears. Oakeshott acknowledged the state to be an ambiguous mixture of two opposed dispositions, but his theory analytically disambiguates the phenomenon so fully that the gain in definitional clarity is offset by a loss of descriptive or sociological value.

A Conservative Concept Of Freedom

Now I want to discuss three aspects of the concept of freedom that are common to Oakeshott and Gierke's respective understandings of it. The first two aspects can be treated briefly because they have been explained at some length above. What in my opinion essentially qualifies Oakeshott and Gierke's ideas of freedom as conservative is the third aspect, which will be discussed in more detail.

Gierke and Oakeshott's idea of freedom is conservative first of all because of the

---

[37] Cf. Maitland, 'Introduction,' in Frederic William Maitland, 'Moral Personality and Legal Personality' (1903), printed as 'Appendix D' in David Nicholls, *The Pluralist State: The Political Ideas of J. N. Figgis and his Contemporaries*, 2d ed. (Houndmills: Macmillan, 1994), 173–9.

[38] Although Gierke surely would on the whole have agreed with Oakeshott's description of *respublica*, he would not have approved without reservations Oakeshott's statement that '*respublica* does not define or even describe a common substantive purpose, interest, or 'good'' (*OHC*, 147); for Gierke's point of view see Barker, 'Introduction' to *Natural Law*, lxxxvi-lxxxvii).

[39] Otto von Gierke, 'The Nature of Human Associations' [= trans. of parts of Otto von Gierke, *Das Wesen der menschlichen Verbände*, 1902], in: Lewis, *Genossenschaft-Theory*, 145–6. In his latest texts, however, Gierke leans toward an increasingly uncritical use of the concept of organism.

meaning as well as the importance of the state for the realization of freedom. For Gierke as well as for Oakeshott the state in modern times emerges as a necessary condition of freedom, not just as an unavoidable instrument for the satisfaction of private wants, but also as a qualified mode of association or of public life. Hence, for them, the state is not simply a necessary evil or a necessary but temporary evil. For them, a liberal as well as a socialist or a Marxist hostility against the state represents a somewhat naive point of view. But as we have seen, this does not prevent them from recognizing the possible endangerment of freedom that is given with the modern state, which is not least a consequence of an inadequate understanding of the state. This endangerment is named in the concepts of the benevolent despotism of an *Obrigkeitsstaat* or of the state as an enterprise association or as *universitas*. In this context Gierke and Oakeshott are undoubtedly liberals on the one side, but they remain conservative liberals insofar as they are skeptical of the possibilities of a rationalistic politics of faith understood as a policy of managing a society, or a policy of ordering the public sphere *via* rules of command that prescribe substantive behavior.

This somewhat general point gains some more substance when focusing on the second aspect of the concept of freedom. What makes the state a free association of citizens is its being a lawful association. Here, of course, all depends on the meaning of the concept of law, of which essential characteristics have been outlined above. What seems to be the decisive feature of the rules that constitute the body or system of law, is the ethical or, as Oakeshott usually calls it, moral character, i.e. the non-instrumental and non-prudential character that is required for those rules to be law in a proper sense: *lex*. What is coming into view is that the concept of law (although both have in mind positive law alone), for Gierke as well as for Oakeshott is essentially a concept of the terms of relationships that define 'the practice of being 'just' to one another' (*OHC*, 128), i.e. a concept of justice. Law is concerned with ordering the coexistence of free agents on the basis of an endeavor of the citizens themselves to give to everyone what is his right.[40] The subscription to the rules of law means thus the recognition not of purposes but of rights, and exactly this recognition is what civilizes life *inter homines*. Gierke no less than Oakeshott therefore contrasts the 'idea of Justice' that determines his *Rechtsstaat* with 'the idea of social utility as well as' any 'idea of collective might.'[41] And here, in my opinion, we reach the core of Gierke and Oakeshott's understandings of law. While this concept of law again is obviously in accord with traditional liberalism, it is at the same time more than a liberal concept because of its view of the origins or 'sources' of rights and law. This third aspect not only qualifies the concept of law, but also the vision of a free association of citizens as a conservative concept.

---

[40] It is of course true that Gierke as a leading representative of the Germanist section of the Historical Law School was in many respects (but not absolutely) opposed to Roman law concepts. Nevertheless, his idea of justice is in full accordance with the famous Roman law formula of Ulpianus that justice is to be defined as *'constans et perpetua voluntas ius suum cuique tribuendi.'* It goes without saying that *'ius suum cuique tribuendi'* is different from *'suum cuique tribuendi,'* and that *'ius'* here marks the decisive difference, i.e., between a *Policeystaat* and a *Rechtsstaat.*

[41] Gierke, *Development*, 329.

The origins of rights and law for Oakeshott and Gierke are not to be sought – and thus not to be found – in an idea of natural law or a natural law concept of human nature, but in the specific character of human practice. The point here is that the practice of living together means the creation of the forms of this living together. These forms are two-sided: With regard to the external aspects of behavior they consist in 'recommendations' for the proper performance of conduct which, in being actualized, form the habits, mentalities, usages, traditions, etc., of the participants. And with regard to the inner aspects of behavior they coin the beliefs, knowledge, understandings, even the wants and purposes of the participants. So the forms of practice have, so to say, an objective aspect in constituting orders of action (social institutions in a wider sense) and a subjective aspect in constituting the personality or character of the involved persons. The forms of living together entail, of course, ideas of right and wrong, and it is from such concepts that law arises. Such an idea is not opposed to the idea that law is to be fixed by means of legislative acts of the state. Neither Oakeshott nor Gierke deny that the modern state is lawgiver. What is decisive here is that the state is for them not the final source of the 'normative content' of the law, of the underlying ideas of right and wrong. This final source is to be seen in the forms of the living together of persons. This is one point concerning the nature of human practice that needs to be underlined.

The other is the previously mentioned aspect of the constitution of personal character by means of practice. Outside social practices a person cannot exist, and it is only in partaking in social practices (conduct *inter homines*) that an individual becomes a unique personality, that a person's intelligence arises. It is Oakeshott who describes such proceedings at length and in detail (*OHC*, 36–45), and in some opposition to psychological and sociological ideas. Gierke, by contrast, gives only a few, but still sound indications. The first sentence of volume 1 of his *magnum opus*, which presents 'the theme of the whole study,'[42] tells us, 'man owes what he is to union [*Vereinigung*, which would better be translated here as *association*; MH] with his fellow man.' In talking of what man *is* Gierke has in mind first of all that man is essentially an historical being, a concrete, rather than an abstract being. Being 'historical' means standing in history and creating history through practice. Such history, for Gierke, is the history of unfolding freedom and as such at the same time the history of processes of unification, especially of evolving group personalities, which tends to produce 'at some time in the remote future' an organized unity of mankind. 'But,' Gierke carries on,

> this development from apparently insurmountable complexity to unity represents only one facet of social progress. All the life of the intellect, all human excellence would atrophy and be lost if the idea of unity were to triumph alone to the exclusion of all others. The opposing principle forges its path with equal power and necessity; the idea of the plurality that persists within every all-embracing unity, the particular within the general, the principle of the rights and independence of all the lesser unities which go to make up the greater whole, down to the single individual – the idea of *freedom*.[43]

---

[42]   Lewis, *Genossenschaft-Theory*, 26.
[43]   Gierke, *Community*, 2.

What is of particular interest for us is that Gierke links freedom with plurality, i.e. with the existence of a plurality of traditions, groups, associations, corporations, and so forth. This conception has, especially in respect to the modern state, important consequences. It stands in contrast to the conception of a dualism between the state (the 'machine' of government and administration) and the society of individuals, in which individuals are conceptualized as removed (or 'abstracted') from all historically contingent circumstances and conditions. For Gierke, such abstract individuals do not exist; and Oakeshott, following a tradition of British idealist thought,[44] defends the same position. This becomes obvious especially in a review of a book by John D. Mabbott, wherein Oakeshott criticizes Mabbott's concept of the 'private individual.' Oakeshott writes:

> The 'private individual' as I understand him is an institution, a social, indeed for the most part a legal, creation, whose desires, emotions, ideas, intelligence, are social in their constitution. Nothing, I take it, is more certain than that this individual would collapse, like a body placed in a vacuum, if he were removed from the 'external' social world which is the condition of his existence. This does not mean that he is part of a collective mind; but it does mean that the last word has not been said by calling him 'private'.[45]

Despite the fact that Gierke is willing to accept a concept of collective mind – though for him this does not negate the individual's individuality and freedom, or the private aspect of its existence – he offers a parallel consideration.

> What we learn by external experience is verified by internal experience. We find the reality of the community in our personal consciousness as well. The association of our ego with a social institution of a higher order is a personal experience for us. We feel ourselves to be self-sufficient beings, but we also feel ourselves to be parts of a whole, which lives and acts within us.... Were we to think away our membership in a particular people and state, a religious community and a church, a professional group, a family, and numerous other societies and associations, we should not recognize ourselves in the miserable remainder.[46]

That the individual as such evolves from its living *inter homines* in an historical society constituted by a plurality of associations has nothing to do with collectivism or with a normative disregard of individuality. On the contrary, the historical or situated condition of the individual is one of the essential conditions of genuine individuality. In Oakeshott's case this becomes obvious almost in every sentence he has written; and, although the late Gierke sometimes seems to overrate the value of the social whole, this is not the necessary consequence of his theory, which always can be read as a strong defense of individuality.[47]

---

[44]   Nicholls, *The Pluralist State*, 58, 77-8.
[45]   Oakeshott, 'Review of J. D. Mabbott, *The State and the Citizen,*' *Mind*, 48 (1949): 386.
[46]   Gierke, 'Human Associations,' 150.
[47]   For Gierke the history of the unfolding of reflection in German law (*Rechtsbewußtsein*) is 'the long process through which the association is differentiated from its individual members and *the individual eventually freed from the bonds of the collectivity.*' Lewis, *Genossenschaft-Theory*, 36, italics added. Cf. 'Es beginnt der große Proceß, der die Allgemeinheit von ihren individuellen

Now, this concept of the individual person advocated by Oakeshott and Gierke is also the core of the concept of a citizen: Only by living *inter homines* do we learn to accept rules (of *lex*) or to take responsibility not only for our own actions but also for communal, including public affairs, affairs of the *civitas* (the *rei publicae*). And, of course, the other side of responsibility for actions is the freedom of such actions, because only an agent that is supposed to be free is confronted with the responsibility for its actions. And all this is learned not in a society of abstract individuals but in historical communities, which are destined by historical contingencies and therefore of a specific historical character.

When I mention that this conception stands in a contrast to the conception of a dualism between the society of individuals and the state, it does *not* imply a strict opposition to or rejection of that point of view. In the case of Gierke, I just remarked that he welcomed the personal liberation of the individual in modern times, and, needless to say, so did Oakeshott. But what it implies is a rejection of a reductionist understanding of this dualism as can be attributed to most liberal as well as to socialist positions, which meet in their atomistic or radical individualism and as a consequence in this dualism. And, of course, this dualism represents a basis of the despotic regimes especially described by Gierke. He emphasizes the tendency of a radical individualism to change into what he calls absolutism (and *vice versa*); and he sees the respective positions represented in the natural law theories of social contract.[48] The dualism of state and the society of individuals for Gierke parallels another one, the dualism of two paradigmatic ideas of sovereignty, namely the idea of the sovereignty of a ruler on the one hand and the idea of the sovereignty of the people on the other hand. And, of course, there are two paradigmatic theories of the modern state that correspond to those ideas and to the underlying dualism with its despotic tendencies, namely the theories of contract from Hobbes and Rousseau. It is not my concern here to compare Gierke and Oakeshott's respective interpretations of these two classics, but it is obvious that above all their interpretations of Hobbes are very different. But apart from this, Gierke does claim - as we have seen - to have out grown these dualisms in his theory of group personality. For Gierke, thus, the state as such a group personality is sovereign. This means that no natural person or authority or office of the state and in the state can be understood as sovereign, that sovereignty has no fixed place *in* the state but nevertheless is a necessary characteristic *of* the state. But all this is not to be elaborated here. Rather I want to go back to the dualism of state and society.

While Oakeshott and Gierke not only accept but also advocate and defend modern individualism, they remain skeptical of the tendency to reduce the variety of forms of common life, of association, into a two-sided relation between the institutionalized organs of 'state' or 'government' and the amorphous collective of 'individuals'. They remain skeptical because of their esteem for freedom. The reason for this skepticism is their understanding of the human person outlined above. The

---

Trägern entbindet und das Individuum von den Banden der Gesammtheit befreit.' Gierke, *Geschichte*, 14.

[48] Gierke, *Natural Law*, 114, 310 n. 119.

individual is accordingly in need of autonomic groups, associations, corporations, etc., for becoming an individual and for learning what it means to be a *civis*. But the commonplace liberal and socialist views of individualism – no matter whether they understand the individual as only a private individual or as the representative of the species (a *Gattungswesen* in the Marxian sense) – obscure the threat to freedom that lies in the emergence of what Oakeshott calls the individual *manqué*, the anti-individual, and, finally, the mass man,[49] an emergence that is only the other side of the emergence of the individual, of modern individualism, and its ethics. Gierke is no less aware of this threat than Oakeshott, although he describes it in another idiom. What Oakeshott calls the individual *manqué* and the anti-individual is for Gierke, first of all, the deprived person not as a character type but – at least for a decisive part – as the result of circumstances that do not allow such a person to become an individual in an emphatic sense. In this respect Gierke stands in his analysis much closer to Marx than Oakeshott would and could ever be able to do.[50] But be this as it may, with relation to the nineteenth and early twentieth century, both have at first the figure of the worker in mind, the member of the proletariat, and at least Oakeshott's description additionally aims at what can be described as the proletarized middle classes.

The threat of freedom that is represented in the despotic tendencies implied in the mentality of such persons in the individualistic society was in another but related context explained by Hannah Arendt. Arendt describes in her famous study on totalitarian dictatorship that the masses of atomized individuals – Oakeshott's anti-individuals – are characterized by their lack of ties to a common world, represented, for example, in 'political parties or municipal governments or professional organizations or trade unions.'[51] At least this observation – regardless of other parallels or differences – undoubtedly expresses what our authors have in mind when speaking of the individualized society that always tends to be a collectivistic society.[52] The counter-model of such a society of atomized ('anti-') individuals is the concept of a pluralistic society of *cives* or a state understood in terms of *societas*, which Oakeshott characterizes in his concise interpretation of Bodin (in *On Human Conduct*) with the following words: 'A state ... is persons, families, groups, corporate associations, etc., each pursuing its own distinct and different purposes and all related to one another in the recognition of a sovereign authority.... It is relationship in terms of civility, association in being just to one another' (*OHC*, 253). That this passage describes not only Bodin's ideas but also Oakeshott's own becomes obvious when we compare it, for example, with the following passage from 'The Political Economy of Freedom' (1949), where he states that 'the secret of [our society's] freedom is that it is composed of a multitude of

---

[49] Oakeshott, 'The Masses in Representative Democracy' [first published in German, 1957], in: Oakeshott, *Rationalism in Politics and other essays, new and expanded edition*, ed. Timothy Fuller (Indianapolis: Liberty Press, 1991), 371-83. Hereafter: *RIP*. See also, *OHC*, 274-9.

[50] Black, 'Introduction' to *Community*, xxv-xxvi.

[51] Hannah Arendt, *The Origins of Totalitarianism*, 3d printing of the 2d ed. (New York: Meridan Books, 1960), 311.

[52] Arendt's analysis of 'the masses' (Arendt, *Origins*, 305–26) has especially much in common with Oakeshott's analysis in *RIP*, 363–83.

organizations in the constitution of the best of which is reproduced that diffusion of power which is characteristic of the whole' (*RIP*, 389).

So, I think that this sphere of associations, corporations, etc., that lies 'between' the private or atomistic individual on the one side and the state or government on the other side is for Oakeshott as well as for Gierke the source of human freedom, but that those associations alone do not define the sufficient condition of freedom as such. This condition has to be completed by the authority of the sovereign *Rechtsstaat*, which has first of all to guarantee the law and to secure the rights of the citizens (if necessary against the demands of particular groups, associations, etc.) but also to guarantee the rights of those particular groups, associations, and so forth. The pluralist society and citizens in turn condition the sovereign authority. Because of this view I hold the concept of freedom that is essentially common to Oakeshott and Gierke to be a conservative one: It stands in contrast to liberal and socialist theories which in the end are atomistic and therefore in danger of transforming into despotic concepts, despotic not necessarily in the sense of totalitarianism, but still in the sense of a gentle despotism like Tocqueville feared, or an authoritarian regime.

One point remains to be mentioned. In his treatment of the emergence of the anti-individual and the mass man, Oakeshott holds that the realization of the political demands, purposes, and intentions of those men gives rise to a politics of faith corresponding to the understanding of the state as an enterprise association. The politics of mass society is characterized by Oakeshott as 'active government' (*RIP*, 376–7), as an administration of the community's public life in the manner of an enterprise. It is the policy of an *Obrigkeitsstaat*, of a benevolent or enlightened despotism (cf. *RIP*, 371) and in its extreme forms, of totalitarian regimes. In other words, it is a policy that destroys freedom and paves the 'road to serfdom'. There can be no doubt that Oakeshott is strictly opposed to such a policy, which is represented not least in the welfare policy of post-war Labour governments in England and elsewhere, and it is no secret that his writings are in their practical dimension to be understood as a strong critique of those policies. In this respect, Oakeshott holds undoubtedly a classical liberal position (*RIP*, 384–406), that is comparable for instance to Hayek's, to whom Oakeshott indeed is sometimes compared.[53]

However, in squeezing social policies into the dualism of enterprise or civil association, Oakeshott tends to overlook some conclusions which can be drawn from his own premises, but which do not fit into his dualisms. Gierke, on the other hand, draws these conclusions in carrying out a theory of social policy that is not in contradiction to the principles of civil association and that leads to the concept of a 'social' *Rechtsstaat* (*sozialer Rechtsstaat*) – a term that is not used by Gierke who nevertheless formulates the concept of it. This concept (which is today a juridical concept of German constitutional law) starts with the realization of the ambivalence of freedom, especially of the ambivalence of the freedom of contract and of liberal property rights in an industrial economy. In this respect, Gierke is

---

[53]   See, for example, Grant, *Oakeshott*, 113–4.

aware that the political demands of the working masses are not simply a result of a personal character, but at first of an objective situation of economic, social, and cultural exclusion that is essentially caused by the exercise of economic freedom by entrepreneurs. In accordance not least to Marx, but also to 'bourgeois' political scholars such as contemporaries like the liberal conservative Lorenz von Stein (1815–1890) or the conservative liberal Robert von Mohl (1799–1875), he accepts the analysis that the mechanisms of a capitalist economy produce in fact dependence and bondage as a result of exercised liberty. But as the principle of the *Rechtsstaat* or the state as *societas* is freedom, such a state cannot accept the lack of freedom of a great number of his citizens. This means that the state for the sake of freedom, and as a consequence of the claim of justice is forced to execute a policy that secures general conditions that are in a capitalist economy necessary conditions of actual freedom. Such conditions are not only the rules of law but especially educational and certain material conditions as well. Lorenz von Stein, to whom, as a disciple of Hegel, the state is the actualization of freedom, wrote in a famous and influential book on the socialist movement in early nineteenth century France, 'Freedom is actual freedom only for him who owns the conditions, the material and intellectual goods that are the prerequisites of self-determination.'[54] So we see here a postulate of the political responsibility of the state to ensure general conditions, especially educational and material conditions, to enable the citizens to realize their rights and to partake in a life *inter homines* under their own responsibility. In the end, this is in principle what Gierke, too, is advocating,[55] and the argument formulated by von Stein is also the basis of Gierke's proclamation of the social responsibility of private law.

In a speech on the social duties of private law from 1889, Gierke therefore contends with famous and often quoted metaphorical words (which do not translate well into English) that 'In our public law there must be a taste of the natural law doctrine's scope of freedom, and through our private law must run a drop of socialist oil.'[56] In a later passage Gierke offers, in the course of a discussion of freedom of contract in property law the following explanation.

If modern law here realizes the principle of freedom of contract, then this does not possibly mean arbitrary freedom but only reasonable freedom: freedom that on account of its ethical purposes has its measure in itself, freedom that at the same time is commitment. Unlimited freedom of contract must destroy itself. A terrible weapon in the hands of the strong, a useless tool in the hands of the weak, it becomes a device for one's suppression by the other, for an unsparing use of intellectual and economic superiority. The law that as a consequence of inconsiderate formalism accepts the willed

---

[54] Lorenz von Stein, *Geschichte der sozialen Bewegung in Frankreich von 1789 bis auf unsere Tage*, [originally pub. 1850], ed. Gottfried Salomon, vol. 3, *Das Königtum, die Republik und die Souveränität der französischen Gesellschaft seit der Februarrevolution 1848* (München: Drei Masken Verlag, 1921), 104: 'Die Freiheit ist erst eine wirkliche in dem, der die Bedingungen derselben, die materiellen und geistigen Güter als die Voraussetzungen der Selbstbestimmung besitzt.'
[55] Cf. Gierke, *Community*, 211–4.
[56] Otto von Gierke, *Die soziale Aufgabe des Privatrechts* [1889] (Frankfurt am Main: Klostermann 1948), 10: 'In unserem öffentlichen Recht muß ein Hauch des naturrechtlichen Freiheitsraumes wehen und unser Privatrecht muß ein Tropfen sozialistischen Öles durchsickern.'

or the supposed results of the free legal transaction legalizes the *bellum omnium contra omnes*, giving it the impression of an order of peace. More than ever the private law of our times has the duty to defend the weak against the strong, the interest of the whole against egoism.[57]

Gierke's concept of social policy (*Sozialpolitik*) that results from this argument must not, of course, be confused with the welfare policies of the *Obrigkeitsstaat*; the *soziale Rechtsstaat* is neither the pre-1789 welfare state of a benevolent despotism, nor is it the same as what in the English speaking world of our times is called a welfare or nanny state. It has nothing to do with paternalism; it does not postulate a common purpose (in Oakeshott's sense), and therefore its rules are not designed to promote such a purpose and are not substantive commands. However, while Gierke's theory accepts the judicial division of public and private law,[58] it does not accept a division of public and private spheres as a political dogma, not least because for Gierke the sharp division lacks a sociological basis or justification.[59] It is only on the basis of a qualified division of the private and the public sphere that a social *Rechtsstaat's* policy is possible as a policy of actual freedom.

Both the concept of social policy in Gierke's sense and the realization of such a policy raise, of course, their own problems that I cannot discuss here. The important points are that Gierke's concept has its place beyond liberalism and socialism, and that Gierke opposes his concept explicitly to both of them.[60] In Oakeshott's theory, in contrast, no conceptual parallel exists to such a concept, and it seems that for Oakeshott a social policy assumes and implies *per se* the understanding of the state as an enterprise association. So Oakeshott does not exhaust the theoretical potential of his own premises, especially of his concept of freedom, although he is anything but principally hostile to a social policy in Gierke's sense. An example of this can be seen in Oakeshott's advocating political regulations of the market for

---

[57] Gierke, *Soziale Aufgabe*, 22–3: 'Wenn das moderne Recht hier den Grundsatz der *Vertragsfreiheit* durchführt, so kann doch auch hier nicht willkürliche, sondern nur vernünftige Freiheit gemeint sein: Freiheit, die kraft ihrer sittlichen Zweckbestimmung ihr Maaß in sich trägt, Freiheit, die zugleich Gebundenheit ist. Schrankenlose Vertragsfreiheit zerstört sich selbst. Eine furchtbare Waffe in der Hand des Starken, ein stumpfes Werkzeug in der Hand des Schwachen, wird sie zum Mittel der Unterdrückung des Einen durch den Anderen, der schonungslosen Ausbeutung geistiger und wirthschaftlicher Übermacht. Das Gesetz, welches mit rücksichtslosem Formalismus aus der freien rechtsgeschäftichen Bewegung die gewollten oder als gewollt anzunehmenden Folgen entspringen läßt, bringt unter dem Schein einer Friedensordnung das *bellum omnium contra omnes* in legale Formen. Mehr als je hat heute auch das Privatrecht den Beruf, den Schwachen gegen den Starken, das Wohl der Gesamtheit gegen die Selbstsucht der Einzelnen zu schützen.'

[58] 'The clear, fundamental opposition [of public and private law; MH] is unimpeachable to us' ['Der scharfe, grundsätzliche *Gegensatz* ist für uns unantastbar'], Gierke, *Soziale Aufgabe*, 9.

[59] See above, 'Gierke and Oakeshott on the Modern State'; cf. Lewis, *Genossenschaft-Theory*, 71–4.

[60] Cf. e.g. the following concise passage: 'The denationalization [*Entstaatlichung*] of public law in the sense of an individualism as held by the natural law doctrines results in disintegration and death; the nationalization [*Verstaatlichung*] of private law in the sense of socialism results in unfreeness [*Unfreiheit*] and in barbary' ['Die Entstaatlichung des öffentlichen Rechtes im Sinne des naturrechtlichen *Individualismus* bedeutet die Auflösung und den Tod, die Verstaatlichung des Privatrechts im Sinne des *Sozialismus* bedeutet die Unfreiheit und die Barbarei'], Gierke, *Soziale Aufgabe*, 9–10.

the sake of freedom even in a context of an argument designed to defend liberal principles of economy (*RIP*, 384–406). In *On Human Conduct*, Oakeshott recognizes that even a civil association may contingently deploy the state's resources for the sake of social welfare or environmental protection, but these are deviations from what the ideal type would seem to call for. Of course, Oakeshott would say his ideal types are not intended to describe actual political conduct, but to clarify the postulates of association. In other words, Oakeshott no less than Gierke represents the tradition of a theory of actual freedom, but unlike Gierke he does not draw all the consequences of this concept. The concept in itself, including its institutional consequences, was paradigmatically formulated in the practical philosophy of Hegel, which, in different ways stands in the background of both of our scholars.[61]

---

[61] In respect to Gierke's relation to Hegel, see Lewis, *Genossenschaft-Theory*, 92–5; Runciman, *Pluralism*, 54–8, 62; and in respect to Oakeshott's, see Paul Franco, 'Oakeshott's Relationship to Hegel,' in Corey Abel and Timothy Fuller, eds., *The Intellectual Legacy of Michael Oakeshott* (Exeter, Charlottesville: Imprint Academic, 2005), 117–31.

7

Gene Callahan

Geography Cannot Replace History

Introduction

Jared Diamond, a professor of geography and physiology at The University of California, Los Angeles, has suggested in his works that he has, for the first time, sketched an outline of the research program that will transform history from a mere liberal art into a true science. In this paper I will examine Diamond's claim, focusing particularly on his book, *Guns, Germs and Steel: A Short History of Everybody for the Last 13,000 Years*, a work presenting an extensively developed exposition of his views.

Guns, Germs and Steel is a fascinating, erudite, and eloquent expression of Diamond's meditations as to how geography has influenced human history; indeed, it is a cornucopia of interesting facts concerning plausible explanations of the intimate relationships of history and geography during at least the most recent 13,000 years of humankind's past. However, even though the many genuine insights scattered throughout the book offer a more than ample return to its readers, it still must be judged a failure, at least if it is measured against the author's aspirations for his intellectual progeny. In this paper, I will argue that the gulf separating what Diamond actually – and quite admirably – has achieved, and what he more grandiosely claims to have achieved, is due to his ignorance of the character of historical understanding.[1]

To support that contention, I will compare Diamond's concept of history with what I regard as a more coherent formulation of the character of the discipline, a formulation drawn primarily from the works of R. G. Collingwood and Michael Oakeshott. The latter view sees the *differentia* of historical enquiry in its quest to make the occurrence of a unique and unrepeatable episode of mankind's past more intelligible by displaying its genesis in the particular circumstances and actions preceding it. This understanding of history does not rule out attempts to

---

[1] Here, I do not intend to enter into a dispute over title to the *name* 'history.' It would be relatively unproblematic if Diamond claimed the name 'history' for his geographical studies and what is now considered history were to be called cliology. My central concern is with Diamond wanting to *replace* history with geographical and environmental laws.

comprehend the human past by reference to general laws or recurrent patterns; it only insists that such efforts are distinct from history proper, and that, as they aim at an entirely different type of explanation than does history itself, they are in no position to supersede it.

Diamond's 'Scientific History'

The central theme running through *Guns, Germs and Steel* is that the course of history (broadly speaking!) is determined neither by individuals' choices and actions, nor by the different characteristics of particular cultures, nor by genetic variations among tribes, nations, or races. For Diamond, history primarily has been the inexorable outcome of the inequality of the environments into which various human groups stumbled by luck, good or bad. The migrants who happened upon a locale offering a variety of plants and animals suitable for domestication, or one that made acquiring domesticated species and new technologies from other societies relatively easy, or, most favorably, came to a place with both of those advantages, wound up having a decisive edge over less fortunate groups. When the geographically chosen people subsequently re-encountered their long-lost cousins it was almost a foregone conclusion that the former would absorb, enslave, or exterminate the latter. So we can see, claims Diamond, that it is geography, rather than greater inventiveness, superior culture, or racial traits that provides the 'ultimate explanations' of what has gone on in history.

Having gotten this far, it is worth mentioning, in passing, an accusation that some of Diamond's critics have lodged against him: they contend that he lets the perpetrators of wars of aggression, genocides, slavery, and other crimes against humanity off the hook, since (as these critics understand his thesis) 'geography made them do it.' In response, Diamond quite correctly distinguishes between *understanding* why some event occurred, and *justifying* the actions that led to it. As he notes, 'psychologists try to understand the minds of murderers and rapists … social historians try to understand genocide, and … physicians try to understand the causes of human disease.'[2] But they do not do so in order to justify murder, rape, genocide, or disease – indeed, their efforts to explain such phenomena are frequently motivated by the hope that understanding the cause of some evil might help in the fight against it.[3]

Diamond's Evidence

One would not expect any serious scholar to forward a bold and sweeping claim, such as ascribing to geography the primary causal role in history, without presenting evidence in its support. And, in fact, the bulk of Diamond's recent work presents historical events meant to demonstrate the soundness and explanatory scope of his hypothesis.

---

[2]   Jared Diamond, *Guns, Germs and Steel: A Short History of Everybody for the Last 13,000 Years* (London: Vintage Press, 1998), 17.

[3]   See Gene Callahan, 'Historical Explanation and Moral Justification,' *LewRockwell.com*, October 8, 2001, http://www.lewrockwell.com/callahan/callahan60.html.

The first step Diamond must take in making his case is to find characteristic geographical differences, and ones that are plausibly significant, between the homelands of history's conquerors and its conquered. He exerts tremendous ingenuity towards that end, achieving some success but nevertheless falling far short of what he ambitiously claims to have accomplished.

Diamond concentrates his efforts on trying to solve the puzzle of why the descendants of those who occupied Eurasia[4] 13,000 years ago today exercise rule over most of the Earth's inhabitable land. Why, he wonders, did not the American Indians or sub-Saharan Africans colonize Europe, rather than the reverse? The answer he proposes is that the Eurasian people's superior technology, coupled with the deadly diseases they brought to foreign lands, made that outcome inevitable. (Thus, the 'guns, germs and steel' in the title of one of the books under discussion.) He calls those factors the 'proximate causes' of the present Eurasian dominance of the world. But, quite understandably, he is not satisfied to halt his inquiry there. Why, he goes on to ask, did Eurasians come to possess better technology than the inhabitants of the other continents? And why did Europeans carry germs so deadly to American Indians that many Indian nations were wiped out even before having any direct contact with Europeans (through disease transmission from Indian tribes that did have direct contact with colonists)? Why was it not the Europeans who were falling in droves to diseases they contracted from Indians?

Diamond begins his quest for deeper causes by noting that the pace of technological development in a society depends heavily on its ability to create a food surplus. Once the typical member of a society can procure significantly more food than is needed simply to keep him alive, then some individuals need not devote themselves to securing their own sustenance; this enables them to specialize in some craft such as pottery or tool making. And that situation generally emerges only after a group of people starts to deliberately produce its food supply through farming and herding, so that it no longer relies on nature to provide food that it must hunt down, dig up, or pick.

Diamond presents a convincing case that all modern humans (*homo sapiens*), given enough time living in one place, will tend to discover how to domesticate any of the indigenous plants and animals that are suitable for agriculture in that locale. (For example, there are nine widely separated places on the globe – the Fertile Crescent, China, Mesoamerica, the Andes, the African Sahel, tropical West Africa, Ethiopia, and New Guinea – where agriculture seems likely to have arisen independently.) However, it happens that Eurasia was blessed with far more species suitable for domestication than any other continent. Most of the leading food crops in the world today originated in Eurasia, and of the fourteen mammals over one hundred pounds that humans have domesticated, every one of the 'major five' (cattle, sheep, goats, pigs, and horses) is Eurasian.[5] And Diamond offers strong

---

[4]   Diamond prefers to regard Europe and Asia, with which he includes North Africa, as a single large region, a choice that appears quite reasonable when one considers a map of the world as well as the durable and significant cultural connections between European, Asian, and North African cultures.

[5]   Diamond, *Guns, Germs and Steel*, 159.

evidence against the suggestion that those facts can be explained by positing that Eurasians were simply the most clever people when it came to domesticating the local flora and fauna: Even though Eurasians have colonized every inhabitable continent, even though the practice of agriculture has seen tremendous technological advances during the last several centuries, and even though our understanding of genetics and breeding far exceeds that of earlier times, no new species of major agricultural importance have been domesticated in any of the new lands where Eurasians settled.

Besides its edge in the number of native species suitable for domestication, Diamond argues that the 'east-west axis' of Eurasia, as opposed to the 'north-south axis' of the Americas and Africa, also plays a large role in explaining the Eurasians' current global dominance. Because the long axis of the European-Asian landmass runs from east to west, Eurasia encompasses a vast stretch of lands with roughly similar climatic conditions, so that agricultural innovations spread widely, resulting in an enormous area of shared agricultural practices and common crops extending over the 6000 miles between Ireland and Japan. In contrast, the crops and the agricultural techniques developed in tropical West Africa could not spread south into the Mediterranean climate of South Africa or north into the Sahel. The species domesticated in the Andes never reached central Mexico, nor visa-versa, because they were useless in the intervening tropics of Central America. Although Mexican corn eventually was cultivated in eastern North America, it took millennia to spread there, because of the two regions' different climates and the arid stretches separating them.

It is not terribly difficult to imagine that an advantage in food production can result, over time, in a technological advantage as well, because it permits a greater division of labor, as discussed above. But how can Diamond account for the fact that the diseases European colonists carried to the Americas and Australia were so much deadlier to the peoples they met than were the natives' diseases to them? Quite cleverly, it turns out. He first posits the very plausible hypothesis that epidemic, or 'crowd,' diseases, such as influenza, measles, smallpox, and bubonic plague, cannot easily sustain themselves among small bands of hunter-gatherers. Microbes of that kind tend to wipe out the entire population of any such groups that they infect, which, unfortunately from their point of view, leaves them without hosts, doomed to immediate extinction. Only a large human population, particularly one in close contact with other populous groups nearby, opens up the possibility of epidemic diseases existing in a sustainable relationship with their hosts. In a large population the likelihood of a few individuals having natural immunity to the disease is greater. Also, the microbes can shift back and forth between neighboring groups, surviving dormant, among people that recently have acquired immunity to it, until it can jump to another, more susceptible population nearby.

But from where do such microbes first arrive among human hosts? It seems unlikely that they simply conjure themselves into existence out of thin air once there are enough people living in one place. Diamond argues that the only plausible genesis of human epidemic diseases is that they are mutations of microbes adapted to life amidst dense populations of other mammal species, specifically, among the herd animals, several species of which humans domesticated and came to live with in close quarters. If Diamond is right, then agriculture provided the necessary conditions for the survival of epidemic diseases among humans, and animal domestication, especially of herd mammals, supplied the source of microbes able, through a minor mutation, to make the adjustment from being hosted by cows or pigs to being hosted by humans. As a result, when Europeans first encountered American Indians, it was the Europeans, and not the Indians, who carried the deadly crowd diseases.

Diamond offers, as evidence for his case, several historical episodes, including some relatively unfamiliar to readers whose education focused on Western European history, such as the Austronesian expansion, first from Taiwan to the Philippines, next to Indonesia and Malaysia, and then westwards to Madagascar and eastwards across the Pacific, eventually reaching Hawaii and Easter Island.

Given the intelligibility of his explanatory scheme and its apparent applicability to a variety of actual events, Diamond has presented a good argument for entertaining the following ideas, which are certainly significant, but not revolutionary:

(1) When any two societies first encounter each other, the one that is more technologically advanced will frequently eliminate or absorb the less advanced;

(2) Technological progress is greatly accelerated once a society can create a food surplus, which generally follows its adoption of agriculture;

(3) The extent to which some particular people could turn to an agricultural way of life, before the advent of world-wide commerce, was determined largely by the number of species in their territory that were suitable for domestication, plus the species that easily could be acquired from neighboring cultures sharing a similar climate;

(4) Agriculture and the domestication of herd animals were also prerequisites for the emergence of epidemic diseases among humans; and

(5) Therefore, agricultural, animal-herding societies will carry deadlier germs than will hunter-gatherers or people that farm only plants.

If Diamond had been satisfied with the very real achievement of drawing our attention to the explanatory power of those important patterns, I would have nothing but praise for his work. But he is not so satisfied, and attempts to climb on his results to heights well beyond those where they can support him. Based on having had a few successes at abstracting his ideal types from real historical events in a way that seems to increase our understanding of them, he becomes infatuated with the fancy that he has become the first 'historical scientist.' He sets his sights on transforming the subject of history from its current, 'pre-scientific' condition into a natural science that discovers deductive-nomological[6] explanations for events, a discipline seeking 'ultimate causes' of historical happenings, rather than the merely 'proximate causes,' such as the ideas and decisions of the people involved,

---

[6]   The deductive-nomological model of science claims that a genuinely scientific explanation of an event consists in deducing the occurrence of the event from a set of empirical laws and initial conditions. It is also called the 'covering law' model.

which have sufficed for historians up until now. In adopting that grandiose project, Diamond turns what would have been an enlightening and sound exposition of some common historical patterns into a deeply flawed attempt to reform a subject he does not really understand.

The first problem Diamond's assault on history encounters is that, in order to jam the real course of events into his conceptual scheme and thereby demonstrate his 'laws,' he frequently has to lop off inconvenient facts. For instance, in groping for a law explaining why the Vikings did not successfully colonize the New World while the Spaniards and the other Europeans who followed in their wake did, he writes, 'Spain, unlike Norway, was rich and populous enough to support exploration and subsidize colonies.'[7] But Norwegians *did* successfully explore the North Atlantic, and *did* successfully colonize the Faeroe Islands and Iceland. If Diamond were true to his project of turning history into a deductive-nomological science, he ought to proceed to formulate a quantitative law governing just how far from its mother country a colony can survive, given any particular amount of wealth and any number of residents in the homeland. However, simply to state that requirement is to expose the attempt to stuff human history into a deductivist framework as the absurdity that it is.

Another instance of forcing the facts to fit the theory is Diamond's 'law of history' asserting that agricultural societies will inevitably come to dominate their non-agricultural neighbors. He ignores the multitude of instances where settled farmers were conquered by nomadic horsemen: the Hittite conquest of the ancient Middle East, (arguably) the invasion of Greece by the Dorians, the successive movements of the Celtic and Germanic people across Europe, the Aryan migration into India, the Turkish conquest of much of the Muslim world that began in the eleventh century, and the vast Mongolian conquests of the thirteenth and fourteenth centuries. In fact, such examples led both the political theorist Albert Jay Nock[8] and the economist Murray Rothbard[9] to posit an historical ideal type that is almost the reverse of Diamond's: They suggest that states are born when some nomadic people, who have been repeatedly raiding a nearby society of relatively peaceful farmers for some time, finally realize that it will be more profitable to settle right in the farming community as rulers, thus enabling them to continually raid the productive population by way of taxation. It is quite beside this paper's point to speculate as to how states came to be, or to examine whether the pattern of conquest proposed by Diamond is more or less common than the Nock-Rothbard scenario. Nor do I contend that any possible counter-examples make nonsense of Diamond's observations, much less that they demonstrate a 'law of history' such as 'nomadic horsemen will always defeat settled farmers.' I have introduced this alternate and conflicting ideal type only to suggest that the complexity of history seems likely to thwart all attempts to deduce universal laws from its labyrinthine

---

[7]   Diamond, *Guns, Germs and Steel*, 373.
[8]   Albert Jay Nock, *Our Enemy the State* (New York: William Morrow & Company, 1935), available online at http://www.lewrockwell.com/orig3/nock1.html.
[9]   Murray Rothbard, *For a New Liberty: The Libertarian Manifesto* (New York: Macmillan, 1978), and available online at http://www.mises.org/rothbard/newlibertywhole.asp.

patterns. It is only by 'cherry picking' his examples that Diamond can defend his claim that he has found 'ultimate causes' in history.

Diamond also glosses over the divergence between his hypothesis that a lead in food production and subsequently, as a consequence, in other technologies as well, is the 'ultimate cause' of one civilization's dominance over another, and the inconvenient fact that the first region to develop agriculture, animal husbandry, and writing was the Fertile Crescent, roughly located in what today is Iraq, Syria, and Turkey. None of those countries are dominant powers in today's geo-political scene. He dismisses this anomaly by noting the environmental degradation of the relatively fragile ecology of the Near East due to extensive human exploitation of the area's natural resources, such as the almost complete de-forestation of the region that occurred as its residents cut down trees for timber and to clear land for farming. He declares that, as a consequence, 'with the Greek conquest of all advanced societies from Greece east to India under Alexander the Great in the late fourth century B.C., power finally made its first shift irrevocably westward.'[10] Diamond fails to explain exactly how, if this shift of power was 'irrevocable' and was an inevitable result of human damage to the Near East's ecology, power, as well as the cutting edge of scholarship, shifted back to the Near East during the first six or seven centuries after the fall of Rome. After all, if Alexander's triumph was merely a 'proximate cause' of the waning dominance of southwestern Asian culture, while the 'ultimate cause' was environmental, then it should have been impossible for the region to ever regain its former glory. Nevertheless, many centuries after 'power' had scurried 'irrevocably westward,' the territory ruled by the Muslim caliphate exceeded that of the grandest empires of the ancient Near East. Nor is it obvious that Alexander's triumph over the Persian Empire had anything to do with the ecological state of affairs in the Near East – it seems, by truly historical accounts, to have been primarily due to Alexander's brilliance and tenacity as a general.[11] And was the 'ultimate cause' of Alexander's conquests really some environmental advantage held by Macedon, a late-too-develop and resource-poor backwater of the Greek world?

Diamond Does Not Comprehend the True Character of History

I believe that Diamond's desire to transform the practice of history stems chiefly from the fact that he understands neither the nature of the material from which the historian launches his inquiries, nor what the historian's task is in relation to that material. Diamond has reverted to the view of history held by nineteenth century positivists, who believed that the historian is presented with a collection of 'historical facts,' and that his job is to discover the 'laws' or 'historical forces' that explain those facts.[12]

For example, Diamond declares that, since the 'whole modern world has been shaped by lopsided outcomes [in clashes of different cultures] ... they must

---

[10] Diamond, *Guns, Germs and Steel*, 410.
[11] See Peter Green, *Alexander of Macedon 356–323 B.C.: A Historical Biography* (Berkeley, Los Angeles, Oxford: Univ. of California Press, 1992).
[12] See Collingwood, *Idea of History*, 126–33, for more on the positivist conception of history.

have inexorable explanations, ones more basic than mere details concerning who happened to win some battle or develop some invention on one occasion a few thousand years ago.'[13] Yet he neither attempts to refute the proposal that our most satisfying explanations of those outcomes arise from tracing their emergence to the historical contingencies that render their appearance intelligible, nor does he defend his insistence upon 'inexorable' (i.e., deductive-nomological) explanations of the human past.

Notwithstanding the contention currently common among philosophers of the natural sciences, with which I happen to concur, that all facts are 'theory laden,' there is still a sense in which certain 'objective' aspects of the goings-on that concern the natural scientist *do* provide a 'given' starting point for his investigation. A certain star just *does* produce a certain spectral pattern. There may be disagreement as to what the pattern means, or even as to whether it is significant, but there it is. If some astronomer doubts its factuality, then by following a well-known procedure he can try to observe the 'fact' for himself. If one does not wish to dispute the central tenets of modern chemistry, then one must acknowledge the well-demonstrated finding that compound A and compound B just *do* produce a certain amount of heat when combined. Even though these facts, like any similar result in the natural sciences, depend on the epistemologically prior adoption of a particular theoretical platform for their factuality, nevertheless they appear as 'the given data' to any scientist pursuing a research program constructed atop that base.

But the historian, in erecting his theories, cannot build upon any analogous foundation of uncontroversial facts waiting to be related by abstract, general principles. Instead, he begins his quest for greater comprehension by considering how some subset of the elements of his present world might be read as signs of a past that is categorically beyond the reach of any observations or experiments.

Furthermore, if he is to succeed, he must resist the temptation to interpret the portion of his evidence consisting of any deliberately generated texts according to the intention of its author, a natural and easy, but quite unreliable method of constructing the historical past; the testimony of the humans who acted in or witnessed the episodes he is hoping to illuminate can never be taken at face value. A text purporting to describe a battle 'just as it happened' actually may have been composed to glorify the victor or excuse the loser. A politician's memoirs may have been written with an eye to making him look good to future generations. The inscription on a statue may have been re-inscribed at the behest of a ruler jealous of his illustrious predecessor's accomplishments.[14] The historian always starts with a collection of initially ambiguous and often, on their face, mutually contradictory present artifacts surviving from the past, and it is only by critically and cannily interrogating his witnesses that he can hope to determine what really occurred. The 'facts of history' do not provide the input to his inquiry; quite to the contrary, they are its output, as Collingwood illustrates with the following example: 'The fact that in the second century the legions began to be recruited wholly outside Italy is not immediately given. It is arrived at inferentially by a process of interpreting data

[13]   Diamond, *Guns, Germs and Steel*, 25.
[14]   Egyptologists must deal with this problem regularly.

according to a complicated system of rules and assumptions.'[15] Cassirer reaches the same conclusion: 'For a 'fact' is no longer [– after the work of Bayle –] the beginning of historical knowledge, but in a certain sense its end; it is the 'point toward which' ... not the 'point from which' ... such knowledge proceeds.'[16]

Diamond, quite likely because of his apparent failure to grasp that genuine historical research is an exercise in critical interpretation, often engages in a form of pseudo-theorizing that professional historians have dubbed 'scissors and paste' history. He places unwarranted faith in sources offering support for his own preconceived theories, and assembles his account of the past by snipping out favorable bits of testimony to place in his collage, while discarding anything that does not fit into his design.

For instance, when Diamond tells the story of the infamous QWERTY keyboard, he asserts, 'trials conducted in 1932 with an efficiently laid-out keyboard showed that it would let us double our typing speed and reduce our typing effort by 95 percent.'[17] Those are startling figures; if they were accurate, then the fact that no company employing large numbers of typists, and wishing to double their productivity while at the same time making its employees' jobs less onerous – surely a profitable move! – has not chosen to break with convention and switch to this efficient keyboard layout is astonishing, and suggests that we can get stuck with patently inferior conventions like QWERTY far more readily than was previously suspected.

But we can save our astonishment for another day: It turns out that the study Diamond cites was severely flawed, as it lacked a genuine control group and did not employ random sampling for selecting the participants. That the study was biased in favor of the new, 'efficiently laid-out keyboard' might be thought, by those more cynical than the author of this paper, as having something to do with the fact that it was designed and conducted by none other than August Dvorak, the inventor of the purportedly more efficient keyboard, who, holding the patent to his design, had a large financial stake in proving the superiority of his model. Later, independent studies did not confirm Dvorak's outlandish claims.[18]

Another case where Diamond cherry-picks his evidence so that it backs his preconceptions can be found in his more recent book, *Collapse: How Societies Choose to Fail or Succeed*. There he contends that the Greenland Norse settlements expired primarily because those Scandinavian colonists did not adapt sufficiently to their new environment. One purported piece of evidence with which he supports this claim is that, despite the wealth of fish available at their doorstep, the Norse settlers did not eat them. That they did not consume fish is demonstrated, according to Diamond, by archeologists' failure to find fish bones in the Norse 'middens' (piles of rubbish).

---

[15] Collingwood, *Idea of History*, 133.
[16] Ernst Cassirer, *The Philosophy of the Enlightenment* (Princeton: Princeton Univ. Press, 1951), 205.
[17] Diamond, *Guns, Germs and Steel*, 248.
[18] See Stan J. Liebowitz and Stephen E. Margolis, 'Typing Errors,' *Reason Magazine* (June, 1996): 29–35; and Stan J. Liebowitz and Stephen E. Margolis, *Winners, Losers, & Microsoft* (Oakland: Independent Institute, 1999).

But research, which although fairly recent still was available well before the publication of *Collapse*, appears to falsify Diamond's conjecture:

> As a result of 80 years of excavations in Greenland, The Danish National Museum possesses a large collection of bones from burials in churchyards in the old Norse colonies. Stable-isotope analysis of selected parts of this bone material has enabled us to determine which kind of food each individual has eaten – or more precisely: the balance between terrestrial and marine diet.... At the same time, we have ^{14}C dated the bones by the AMS technique.... We cannot claim to have solved the enigma of the disappearance of the Norsemen from Greenland, but we can at least exclude some hypotheses. The isotope analysis indicates that the Norsemen changed their dietary habits. The diet of the first settlers consisted of 80% agricultural products and 20% food from the surrounding sea. But seafood played an increasing role, such that the pattern was completely turned around towards the end of the period – from the 1300's the Greenland Norse had 50-80% of their diet from the marine food chain. In simplified terms: they started out as farmers but ended up as hunters/fishers. Some archeologists have claimed that the Greenland Norsemen succumbed because they – being culturally inflexible – either could not or would not adapt to changing conditions and therefore came to a catastrophic end, triggered by deteriorating climate. This hypothesis may now be refuted.[19]

How, then, can the absence of fish bones in the middens be explained? Fairly easily, it seems: 'For example, the absence of fishbone in the middens does not prove that the Norse did not eat fish. Not only will fishbone rapidly decay in a midden, more likely they never got there in the first place – fishbone is a food source highly appreciated by, e.g., birds, dogs and pigs.'[20]

Others who have researched this question in depth tend to agree with Arneborg and her co-authors: 'Kirsten Seaver, an independent scholar based in Palo Alto and author of *The Frozen Echo: Greenland and the Exploration of North America* (Stanford), a book Diamond himself recommends in his endnotes, is also skeptical of Diamond's argument. "To say that they did not eat fish was ridiculous," she says.'[21]

Yet another instance of Diamond selectively choosing his sources is detailed by Peiser, who critiques Diamond's diagnosis of the collapse of the civilization that built the famous stone heads on Easter Island.[22] Peiser writes:

> It is generally agreed that Rapa Nui's oral traditions are untrustworthy and of relatively late origin; they are extremely contradictory and historically unreliable.... In spite of this widely-held consensus among researchers, Diamond insists that these highly questionable

[19] J. Arneborg, J. Heinemeier, N. Lynnerup, H. L. Nielsen, N. Rud and Á. E. Sveinbjörnsdóttir, 'C-14 Dating and the Disappearance of Norsemen from Greenland,' *Europhysics News*, 33, no. 3 (2002); http://www.europhysicsnews.com/full/15/article1/article1.html, downloaded on October 28, 2005.

[20] Arneborg et al., 'C-14 dating.'

[21] Christopher Shea, 'Big Picture Guy: Does Megaselling Scientist-Historian Jared Diamond Get the Whole World Right?' *Boston Globe* (January 16, 2005); http://www.boston.com/news/globe/ideas/articles/2005/01/16/big_picture_guy?pg=full, downloaded on October 28, 2005.

[22] Jared Diamond, *Collapse: How Societies Choose to Fail or Succeed* (New York: Viking Press, 2005), 79–119.

records are reliable. In his view, 'those traditions contain much evidently reliable information about life on Easter in the century or so before European arrival.' Without his confidence in the reliance on mythology and concocted folklore, Diamond would lack any evidence for pre-European civil wars, cannibalism and societal collapse.[23]

Peiser also suspects that Diamond has failed to grasp the critical attitude central to historical research: 'In many ways, Diamond's methodological approach suffers from a manifest lack of scientific scrutiny. Instead of carefully weighing up and critically assessing the quality, authenticity and reliability of the data he employs to support his arguments, he consistently selects only the data and interpretations that seem to confirm his conviction that Easter Island self-destructed.'

Despite not being a professional historian, I was able to find the above examples of Diamond's naïve use of historical sources without expending too much effort. I think it likely that scholars who are intimate with the various historical episodes with which he hopes to illustrate the relevance of his theories could locate many more. But that is not the only way in which he misunderstands the character of history; another is his acceptance of a significant division between 'human history' and an earlier time, before the invention of writing, called 'pre-history.'[24] Collingwood debunked that notion many decades ago:

> A consequence of the error which regards history as contained ready-made in its sources is the distinction between history and prehistory. From the point of view of this distinction, history is coterminous with written sources, and prehistory with the lack of such sources. It is thought that a reasonably complete and accurate narrative can only be constructed where we possess written documents out of which to construct it, and that where we have none we can only put together a loose assemblage of vague and ill-founded guesses. This is wholly untrue: written sources have no such monopoly of trustworthiness or informativeness as is here implied, and there are very few types of problems which cannot be solved on the strength of unwritten evidence.[25]

This failure to comprehend what distinguishes an historical inquiry from other modes of theorizing is manifest on the very first page of *Guns, Germs, and Steel*. Diamond introduces his project with a question Yali, a New Guinean whom the author met while undertaking biological research on the island, asked him: Why is it that Europeans have so much more 'stuff' than New Guineans? Diamond laments that most professional historians 'are no longer even asking the question.'[26] He never pauses to consider whether or not Yali's query is the proper sort of question for historians to address. If the defining job of history is to increase our understanding of unique episodes from the past by revealing them as intelligible sequels to the particular circumstances of time and place that preceded them – the task assigned to it by Collingwood and Oakeshott, among others – then historians

[23] Benny Peiser, 'From Genocide to Ecocide: The Rape of Rapa Nui,' *Energy and Environment*, 16, nos. 3 & 4 (2005), 535.
[24] Diamond, *Guns, Germs and Steel*, 49.
[25] Collingwood, *Idea of History*, 372.
[26] Diamond, *Guns, Germs and Steel*, 15.

who respect the inherent boundaries of their subject will naturally ignore questions such as 'Why are Europeans generally wealthier than New Guineans?'

Diamond apparently denigrates historical inquiry, when understood as the science of the particular, because it does not mimic the natural sciences by attempting to discover universal laws. To do so implies that there is little or no value in simply determining what specific events compose humanity's past. Setting aside, for the moment, the question of whether it is even feasible to formulate 'laws of history,' a question that we will address below, I suggest that the effort to discover the historical past is worthwhile in its own right, even if there is another discipline that *could* discover 'historical' laws. To learn what really occurred in the past is to understand how we came to be where we are today. The knowledge gained through historical inquiry enables us to see how the myriad decisions and actions of our predecessors, the ideas they held, the ideals to which they aspired, the gods they worshipped, and the demons they feared, all combined to create the world in which we currently find ourselves.

Oakeshott argued against the contention that the only scientifically respectable approach to the human past is to seek out 'historical laws' as follows:

> [The] alleged task is to discern [an historical event's] 'true' character by coming to understand it as an example of the operation of a 'law of history' or a 'law of historical change.' In order to perform this task [the historian] must equip himself with such a 'law' or 'laws.' And he is said to do this in a procedure of examining (and perhaps comparing) a number of such occurrences and situations and coming to perceive them as structures composed of regularities. But this, also, is clearly a mistake: no such conclusion could issue from such a procedure. What this 'historian' needs and what he must devise for himself is a collection of systematically related abstract concepts ... in terms of which to formulate 'laws.' How he may set about this enterprise we need not enquire.... But what is certain is that they cannot be laws of 'history' or 'historical change' because they do not and cannot relate to the circumstantially reported situations he designs to explain, but only to model-situations abstracted from them in terms of these 'laws.' In short, the distinction between such a model-situation (explicated in terms of regularities) and a circumstantially reported situation is not a difference of truth and error; it is an unresolvable categorical distinction.[27]

Ludwig von Mises makes much the same point: 'The notion of a law of historical change is self-contradictory. History is a sequence of phenomena that are characterized by their singularity. Those features which an event has in common with other events are not historical.'[28]

The critique of 'historical laws' offered by Oakeshott and Mises does not entail that it is *a priori* impossible to detect interesting and general patterns in humanity's past; rather, it contends that even if the search for such patterns should prove to be fruitful, it would not render otiose the investigation of the unique and unrepeatable aspects of the past, much as a general science of street patterns, if one were

---

[27] Oakeshott, *On History* (Oxford: Basil Blackwell, 1983), 81–2. Herafter: *OH*.
[28] Ludwig von Mises, *Theory and History* (1957; reprint, Auburn, Alabama: Ludwig von Mises Institute, 1985), 212.

developed, would not make the detailed knowledge of particular neighborhoods superfluous.

The list of errors presented above supports my contention that Diamond does not really grasp the nature of historical inquiry, and that his attempt to replace what he has misunderstood with his own brand of 'scientific history' is badly misguided. Nevertheless, I still think his work deserves our serious attention, because it quite usefully has described a number of common patterns in human affairs. The economist Tony Lawson calls such patterns 'demi-regs,' by which he means 'a partial event regularity which *prima facie* indicates the occasional, but less than universal, actualization of a mechanism or tendency, over a definite region of time-space.'[29] Diamond's grandiose claims about what he has achieved ignore the contingent and transient nature of all such regularities in the social world. As Lawson notes,

> in the social realm, indeed, there will usually be a potentially very large number of countervailing factors [to any particular cause] acting at any one time and/or sporadically over time, and possibly each with varying strength... [And] the mechanisms or processes which are being identified are themselves likely to be unstable to a degree over time and space... Indeed, given the fact of the dependence of social mechanisms upon inherently transformative human agency, where human beings *choose* their courses of action (and so could always have acted otherwise), strict constancy seems a quite unlikely eventuality.'[30]

The above casts a curious light on what seems to have been one of the chief motivations behind Diamond's recent work, namely, his desire to discredit racial explanations of the course of history. If he had comprehended the true character of historical explanation, he would have realized that he was battling a chimera. Race can no more substitute for genuine historical understanding than can geography. How could it possibly explain the concrete particularities of history, when the past presents us with Germans as different as Johann Goethe and Adolf Hitler, Jews as dissimilar as Karl Marx and Ludwig von Mises, Irishmen as far apart as James Joyce and Gerry Adams, Chinese as divergent as Lao Tsu and Mao Tse Tung, blacks like George Washington Carver and Idi Amin, and so on.

Conclusion

Mises categorized the type of history Diamond proposes as 'environmentalism.' He said of it, 'The truth contained in environmentalism is the cognition that every individual lives at a definite epoch in a definite geographical space and acts under the conditions determined by this environment.' But, he goes on to note the flaw inherent in all attempts to regard the environment as the 'ultimate cause' of historical events: 'The environment determines the situation but not the response. To the same situation different modes of reacting are thinkable and feasible. Which one the actors choose depends on their individuality.'[31]

---

[29] Tony Lawson, *Economics and Reality* (London and New York: Routledge Press, 1997), 204.
[30] Lawson, *Economics and Reality*, 218–9.
[31] Mises, *Theory and History*, 326.

Diamond, I believe, has discovered some very interesting 'demi-regularities' in the human past. But he has not realized that, quite apart from the search for such demi-regs, there is a different and quite legitimate discipline called history that explains some unique going-on by way of those antecedent events that make its actualization more intelligible, and that forms the sequential narrative relating them by critically analyzing artifacts from the past that have survived into the historian's present.

While Diamond's book is filled with valuable insights, it is not, as he would like to believe, the first step in the reformation of history along more 'scientific' lines, but only another interesting vantage point from which to contemplate humanity's past.

III

Currents in Philosophy

8

Timothy Fuller

The Relation of Philosophy to Conservatism in the Thought of Michael Oakeshott

I

David Hume begins his essay 'Of the Original Contract,' observing that 'no party, in the present age, can well support itself, without a philosophical or speculative system of principles, annexed to its political or practical one; we accordingly find, that each of the factions, into which this nation is divided, has reared up a fabric of the former kind, in order to protect and cover the scheme of actions which it pursues.'[1] Specifically, Hume tells us, one party traces the basis of government to the Deity, the other to the People in a kind of original contract. Hume does not quarrel with this development, allowing to each party a certain kind of insight. But neither of these views is philosophical. Rather these speculations are, as we would now say, ideological. That is, each party takes its relevant, but partial insight to be sufficient. Neither view exemplifies philosophy. In his essay, 'Conduct and Ideology in Politics,' Oakeshott says this:

> for many of us politics have become an activity in which we often believe ourselves to be unable to make decisions until we have found the answer to such questions as: What is liberty? What is justice? What is Democracy? or Socialism? or Liberalism? or Communism? etc. That is to say, we find ourselves equipped with a supply of words, most of them abstract nouns, and we want to discover their meaning.... It sometimes happens that even political parties are divided & inhibited from action because of a doubt about what one of these words means, or a dispute about its meaning. And alternatively, we feel well equipped and ready to make decisions when we are clear and confident about the meanings of these words.

In short, our politics have become what we call 'ideological politics'.[2]

---

[1]   David Hume, *Essays Moral, Political, Literary, edited and with a Foreword, Notes, and Glossary*, ed. and with a foreword, notes, and glossary by Eugene F. Miller; with an apparatus of variant readings from the 1889 edition by T.H. Green and T.H. Grose (Indianapolis: Liberty Fund 1987), 465.
[2]   Oakeshott, 'Conduct and Ideology in Politics,' in *What is History? and other essays*, ed. Luke

For Hume and Oakeshott, philosophy requires one to consider these partisan positions and disputes about abstract nouns philosophically, and thus to understand what element of insight we may find, while recognizing what each leaves out in order to make their positions or definitions coherent to themselves and, by concealing ambiguity and abridgement, to give the appearance of authority in political debate.

The assumption of the sufficiency of a partial insight deprives the speculations of politicians and intellectuals of philosophical status. For Hume, to give allegiance to a party is to abandon philosophy. As a practical matter, the compromise or moderation of these speculative antagonisms, a compromise between parties or the acceptance of a loose range of definitional meanings, though they may be politically efficacious, do not constitute a philosophical understanding. Philosophy is neither about partisanship nor about compromise. The philosopher recognizes the prevailing political terrain for what it is and must be, but does not intrude to offer policy alternatives. Philosophic reflection might or might not soften partisanship for the sake of stability and the retention of openness to the life of the mind, but what happens will reflect suspension of inquiry and a decision to limit debate.

Philosophy, when considering politics, is not in the business of seeking power but of understanding what is going on. Were the politicians to pursue philosophy they would sacrifice their effectiveness for action, as they are always ready to point out if pressed. The philosopher's critical examination does not seek to overthrow the prevailing order, nor to justify it as if it were in need of a foundation other than that emergent from the choices in contingent circumstances that a set of human beings have made through time and found to work, or not work, for them, in their own terms.

Thus no regime can claim finality in the face of the insuperable temporality and mortality of human things. On the other hand, achieving stability and decency is possible, and the sobriety of the philosopher constrains his desire for more than the human condition permits. Should one call this 'conservative'? Needless to say this is not necessarily the meaning of 'conservatism' in the contemporary Anglo-American world. In debates this is usually and loosely referred to as political realism, although such realism does not end the debates over what is really the case, and those who call themselves realists regularly offend the others who naturally think they know what is real.

It would be better, perhaps, to call what Hume and Oakeshott present philosophic sobriety. For they recognize, as did Socrates before them, that human claims to know do not amount to much, and that the beginning of wisdom is in knowing that we do not know. It is my contention that Oakeshott follows in Hume's footsteps in his understanding of political philosophy. The real object of Hume's critique of the original contract, however, is not those who, as a practical matter, place their faith in the people and advocate political authority by consent. His sharpest criticism is

---

O'Sullivan (Exeter: Imprint, 2004), 245.

reserved for those who have elevated the idea of the original contract into a grand philosophical scheme: 'They assert,' Hume tells us, 'not only that government in its earliest infancy arose from consent or rather the voluntary acquiescence of the people; but also, that, even at present, when it has attained full maturity, it rests on no other foundation.'[3]

Hume is criticizing the Lockean tradition and the idea that politics has an independently identifiable rational foundation. But he is also noticing the revolutionary character of such thinking. Anticipating Kant, and long before Marx, Hume could see that this type of political philosophy encouraged the proposition that philosophers should change the world in accordance with an abstract idea of how it ought to be. These thinkers, Hume asserts, can find nothing in the observable world corresponding to their abstract ideas. What we do observe are the habits of keeping promises and submitting to laws which emanate from acknowledged authority, all of which is the cumulative result of long periods of trial and error in which those habits were doubtful and intermittent, a difficult achievement to say the least, the end not the beginning of a long, arduous development:

> No compact or agreement, it is evident, was expressly formed for general submission; an idea far beyond the comprehension of savages: Each exertion of authority in the chieftain must have been particular, and called forth by the present exigencies of the case: The sensible utility, resulting from his interposition, made these exertions become daily and more frequent; and their frequency gradually produced an habitual, and, if you please to call it so, a voluntary, and therefore precarious acquiescence, in the people.[4]

The breaking of these civil habits through revolution is perilous. Speaking of the so-called Glorious Revolution of 1689, Hume says:

> Let not the establishment at the Revolution deceive us, or make us so much in love with its philosophical origin to government, as to imagine all others monstrous and irregular. Even that event was far from corresponding to these refined ideas. It was only the succession, and that only in the regal part of the government, which was then changed.[5]

There was no popular consent, but only acquiescence to a change perpetrated by a few hundred individuals. Oakeshott's inaugural address at The London School of Economics in 1951, 'Political Education,' and his essay from the early 1960s on 'Political Discourse,' are modern versions of Hume's argument. 'Political Discourse' Oakeshott remarks, 'has, then, for a very long time been distinguished on account of the variety of special vocabularies of belief in which it is conducted ... In this manner they impose conditions upon political deliberation and discourse, and upon the kinds of choice to be made in response to emergent situations.'[6] And, he continues,

---

[3]   Hume, *Essays*, Miller ed., 469.
[4]   Hume, *Essays*, Miller ed., 468.
[5]   Hume, *Essays*, Miller ed., 472.
[6]   Oakeshott, *Rationalism in Politics and other essays, new and expanded edition*, ed. Timothy Fuller, (Indianapolis: Liberty Press, 1991), 76. Hereafter: *RIP*.

'this craving for demonstrative political argument may make us discontented with ordinary political discourse which, because it is not demonstrative, we may be tempted to regard as a species of unreason' (*RIP*, 95). And,

> so far from a political ideology being the quasi-divine parent of political activity, it turns out to be its earthly stepchild. Instead of an independently premeditated scheme of ends to be pursued, it is a system of ideas abstracted from the manner in which people have been accustomed to go about the business of attending to the arrangements of their societies. (*RIP*, 51)

Hume does not intend to 'exclude the consent of the people from being one just foundation of government where it has place. It is surely the best and most sacred of any. I only pretend,' he goes on,

> that it has very seldom had place in any degree, and never almost in its full extent. And that therefore some other foundation of government must also be admitted.... Reason, history, and experience shew us, that all political societies have had an origin much less accurate and regular; and were one to choose a period of time, when the people's consent was the least regarded in public transactions, it would be precisely on the establishment of a new government.'[7]

In short, political authority based on consent is an achievement emerging from a long process of accommodation, representing not the origin of political authority but rather the gradual transformation of the relationship of authority from command and obedience to acknowledgment and consent. The revolutionary implication of contract theory lurks in the insistence that existing regimes must be continually re-formed to conform to the shape some imagine they would have if they had originated in a pure contract in which all residual alternative forms of human relationship are also transformed. One need think only of the question of the family today to see this.

Contract theory is thus a sophisticated argument criticizing the past and present in terms of a model for an imagined and desired future, an argument such as Rousseau launched in his 'Discourse on the Origins of Inequality.' It is philosophizing in order to change, not only, or even principally, to understand and explain. Such a 'philosophy' naturally allies itself to party movements attuned to the preferred alterations; and, it is, therefore, a higher form of partisanship, the carrying on of politics by other means, seeking to lend gravity to a party program.

But in criticizing abstraction and thus political radicalism, Hume by no means abandons the radicalism of philosophy. He understands perfectly well that philosophy as such calls into question all conventions and habituations, if only by naming them as conventional and habitual. Philosophy cannot avoid politics because philosophy can have powerful political implications, as is evident in his time. From the Platonic Socrates we learned that radical questioning opens the way to the quest for the best regime altogether, the search for political knowledge

---

[7]   Hume, *Essays*, Miller ed., 474.

transcending mere political opinion. But Hume is content to warn of the disruption philosophy can cause, especially when it is perverted by becoming ideological and partisan, and the quest for the best regime is itself subject to this perversion. Hume's skepticism dictates that neither longing for the heavenly city, nor longing for the end of history, is fulfilled or achieved in the philosophical understanding of politics. When Socrates says at the end of the ninth book of the *Republic* that, having caught sight of the heavenly city, one could order one's life in accordance with the heavenly city, he means to show us that this comes after liberation from the illusion that politics can take us there.

For, Hume argues, 'though an appeal to general opinion may justly, in the speculative sciences of metaphysics, natural philosophy, or astronomy, be deemed unfair and inconclusive, yet in all questions with regard to morals, as well as criticism, there is really no other standard, by which any controversy can ever be decided.' There can be no moral authority in opinions that run far from the 'general practice of mankind.' Hume thus draws, a 'conservative' lesson from his philosophic radicalism in his concluding comment on Plato's *Crito*:

> The only passage I meet with in antiquity, where the obligation of obedience to government is ascribed to a promise, is in PLATO'S *Crito*: where Socrates refuses to escape from prison, because he had tacitly promised to obey the laws. Thus he builds a tory consequence of passive obedience, on a whig foundation of the original contract. New discoveries are not to be expected in these matters. If scarce any man, till very lately, ever imagined that government was founded on compact, it is certain, that it cannot, in general, have any such foundation. [8]

What then is political activity? Is it the interminable effort to make our ideals and aspirations cohere with the contingent circumstances in which as historical and mortal beings, saturated with temporality, we live and die? Must we forever live at this intersection in which the actuality of things continually outstrips our comprehension and control? If meaning is to be found, must we look for it elsewhere than in politics? I think this is the lesson from both Hume and Oakeshott.

They are political skeptics: It is only in our latter day political world – suffused by the ideological deformation of philosophy, and which, at the same time, has lost confidence in the ancient pursuit of the divine, eternal things – that they are called conservative. To be conservative in this sense is accused of being itself an ideology. To argue this way is ultimately to deny the possibility of philosophy in the classic sense.

Hume and Oakeshott do not live and die by the prevailing sentiments and longings, the political rages, of their time and place. But neither are they reactionaries who long for an imagined past which is, after all, over and done with. Their philosophical reflections are entirely clear and un-deluded as to the dominant political terrain of their times. Philosophically, they think beyond the confines of their time without believing they can leap out of their time into some other. If, as Oakeshott famously argued, the task of politics is to keep the ship afloat, the other

---

[8]   Hume, *Essays*, Miller ed., 486–7.

tasks of life belong to other modes of living, beyond the comprehension of politics. Politics gains importance because it is intrusive and unavoidable, an intractable feature of human existence; and it is interminable because it must try to make the temporal manageable. Yet because politics is the very emblem of temporality, it cannot extricate itself from temporality's endlessness. Politics must attend to the arrangements of sets of people whom chance and choice have brought together through time. Oakeshott, quoting F. H. Bradley, found politics 'a necessary evil.' Politics cannot get to the end of its task and terminate itself.

Oakeshott held that practical life, unavoidable and ever-present, is nevertheless not the foundation of other activities such as philosophic reflection, historical study, scientific research, or poetic expression, and the question of religion he left in ambiguity. These are not, for him, peculiar ways to carry on the struggles of practical life by eccentric means; they are revelations of the multidimensional character of human experience in which play counters work, enjoyment moderates ambition, conversation restrains debate, and contemplative delight releases us from the deadliness of doing. Oakeshott of course acknowledged his conservative disposition, but he thought of himself as a philosopher. His interest in policy debates was modest, and he was as capable of criticizing a conservative who mixes politics with philosophy as he was a liberal or a radical. The thinkers he admired were those relative few whom he thought honored the distinction between studying and explaining on the one hand, and asserting and prescribing on the other. For him, philosophy seeks to identify and understand the assumptions that people make in order to make sense of the world for themselves, and to justify the conclusions they reach. Philosophy, he said, expresses itself in the indicative mood; to philosophize is to disengage, not to intervene. To consider politics philosophically is to describe the necessary character of politics in its endless efforts to preserve and to change; it is not to prescribe courses of action.

In revealing the character of politics, philosophers have done what, as philosophers, they can do. They derive from their philosophical understanding no authority to direct politics because, to act politically, they must, like everyone else, accept uncritically some presupposition, for purposes of action, thus leaving philosophy behind; they cannot, as the saying goes, unite theory and practice. Those who seek this unification may use philosophic ideas to lend support to their political dispositions, but they are using them in an unphilosophic way. Oakeshott, in being consistent, does not quite tell individuals not to do this, but rather tries to identify what they are doing and to elicit recognition of what they are doing. To make the point clear: Oakeshott does not think that it is possible to unify theory and practice. Whatever anyone thinks or claims he is doing, he is not doing that because it cannot be done.

This is not a conservative argument in the usual sense. That is, it is not a prudential argument that it would be better for us to be cautious, nor is it an argument that what is older is better than what is newer. Even if there was an antiquarian or romantic streak in Oakeshott as some allege, there is nothing antiquarian or romantic in Oakeshott's arguments. He is speaking about what he thinks we can and cannot do regardless of felt urgency or attractiveness.

Oakeshott is speaking also, as did Hume, of how political parties are moved by different attitudes and outlooks while all being subject to the limitations of politics. Political activity receives all of these alternatives and constrains them by its own logic. Radicals will be radicals; reactionaries will be reactionaries, but what they will not do is transcend or supersede the interminability of politics, nor the complications that beset their ideas in action. Of course, they can cause enormous wreckage in the effort to do what cannot be done, and in the twentieth century, needless to say, they did so repeatedly. Nor is there reason to think that this will fail to be repeated in the twenty-first century, on the contrary, continuations are evident. There can only be better and worse regimes, and there can be a wide range of ways to be better or worse. This will, of course, suggest inquiry into the principles for judging better and worse. Whatever those principles may be, they must acknowledge diverse practical arrangements. Even if there are universal principles, as I think, the local circumstances of regimes cannot be disregarded. Practical judgments of what is possible for local regimes are inevitable and unavoidable.

II

For Oakeshott, the local cannot be replaced by the universal, the abstract cannot control the concrete, even though the idea of the universal is central to thinking about politics in our time. Oakeshott's understanding of the character of politics thus needs further explication. I propose to do this by considering another of Oakeshott's famous remarks: that politics is the 'pursuit of intimations.' I want to explore this in some detail because to understand it is essential to grasping the relation between his philosophical understanding of politics and what is usually identified as his conservatism.

When Oakeshott said that 'this is the best of all possible worlds, and everything in it is a necessary evil,' he thereby contradicted the prevailing wisdom in intellectual circles. His view runs athwart much academic opinion – conservative, liberal, and radical alike.

His criticism was directed less at specific beliefs, programs, or actions, and more at what he thought to be a pervasive and mistaken modern understanding of the function of reason in practical life. He thought that virtually all the current political stances, wherever they might be located on the Left/Right spectrum, were infected in some measure by rationalism and ideology. None of them could command the allegiance of the philosopher as Oakeshott understood the philosopher. The central passage from his inaugural address in which he seeks to describe the actuality of political activity is this:

> In politics, then, every enterprise is a consequential enterprise, the pursuit, not of a dream, or of a general principle, but of an intimation. What we have to do with is something less imposing than logical implications or necessary consequences: but if the intimations of a tradition of behaviour are less dignified or more elusive than these, they are not on that account less important. Of course, there is no piece of mistake-proof apparatus by means of which we can elicit the intimation most worth while pursuing; and not only do we often make gross errors of judgment in this matter, but also the total effect of a

desire satisfied is so little to be forecast, that our activity of amendment is often found to lead us where we would not go. Moreover, the whole enterprise is liable at any moment to be perverted by the incursion of an approximation to empiricism in the pursuit of power. These are features which can never be eliminated; they belong to the character of political activity. (*RIP*, 57)

Oakeshott intended to put activism, utopianism, policy science, and a certain sort of pietism in their place by demonstrating that their voices in politics promote an illusory understanding of what politics actually is. He did not expect that his critique would silence these voices, nor did he intend to legislate about what voices might express themselves there; to do so would be to expect too much from philosophic understanding, and would betray philosophy by turning it into a political, rather than an explanatory, engagement. In a sense, the philosophic critique is indifferent to the presence or absence of those voices since, once philosophic understanding has been achieved, the philosopher's interest in such goings-on is satisfied. The description of the prevailing political terrain, and the critique of misplaced pretensions within that context, were as far as one could go philosophically. He cast his skeptical eye on his own political predilections as well as those of others.

Oakeshott also thought that modern politics has long been constituted in a dialectic between those who are skeptical of the power of governments to reconstruct and perfect social life, and those with faith in our power to do exactly that. Thus, rationalism will not disappear, but if its pretensions are prey to disillusionment, they can be restrained from extremism by the continuing presence of the skeptical voice. Nonetheless, his description of political activity as the 'pursuit of intimations,' which has been attacked as vague traditionalism, mysticism, or romanticism remains a central summary expression of his thinking. The accusations of vagueness, mysticism, and romanticism, are ways of asserting that he lacked, 'concreteness in his political philosophy,' or that he could not deal with the modern world. Yet to understand what he meant by 'the pursuit of intimations,' which he thought to be the opposite of these things, is essential to understanding the precise meaning of Oakeshott's position on the character of political activity, and the degree of concreteness Oakeshott achieved. As he said, in response to his critics, the phrase 'pursuit of intimations' is intended neither 'as a description of the motives of politicians nor of what they believe themselves to be doing, but of what they actually succeed in doing' (*RIP*, 67). He intended to make a statement, as he put it, in the indicative mood, not to propose another world.

What, then, did he mean by the 'pursuit of intimations'? Let us consider the salient points of the passage cited, and place then in the context of his philosophy of the practical life. Oakeshott used the term 'intimations' in contrast to the terms 'dreams', 'general principles', 'logical implications', and 'necessary consequence'. Dreams and general principles naturally figure constantly in politics. Oakeshott was questioning the adequacy of such terms, philosophically speaking, not their presence. Accurate description notices and accepts their presence.

He knew as well as anyone that dreams of possibilities not yet realized obviously are catalysts of political action. And general principles, such as, for instance, the principles expressed in natural law theories, constitutions or Declarations of Independence, are central features of political life. He did not think they unambiguously tell us what, in specific cases, to do, and they are appealed to in defense of contradictory interpretations of our rights and duties. Oakeshott thought that natural laws are descriptive of the forms in which we think about moral duties, but he did not think we could deduce from them legal obligations. Between the expression of moral duty and the statement of legal obligation there must intervene judgment and decision, presumably emanating from an authority acknowledged to be entrusted with this responsibility.

He thought that most of the common terms of political discourse are irreducibly ambiguous in their meaning. We might all agree that *salus populi suprema lex*, but does *salus* mean survival or does it go on to guarantee a certain standard of living? And who exactly do we include in *populi*? Does the term 'democracy' imply a procedure for preventing tyranny by limiting the power of governments, or does it mean a plebiscitary legitimation of the unlimited use of that power?

Oakeshott was pointing to the unavoidability in politics of appraisal, judgment, and decision. Political actors continually characterize their states of affairs, and devise what they hope are appropriate responses. If they could deduce logical implications from their situations, they could leap over the familiar, apparently ineluctable, constraints in politics. They would simply know what is to be done instead of having to try a course of action in a condition of uncertainty.

In politics, freedom does not mean being able to devise courses of action unconstrained by previous actions. Yet previous actions do not determine us either, if by that is meant that there is a necessary path, direction, or pattern in our circumstances that cannot but work itself out. The task is to understand better what we already understand: a complex state of affairs susceptible to differing accounts, requiring judgment as to what within it is a resource and what a hindrance, what is desirable and what is undesirable, what is appropriate or not. Wherever the possibilities of conversation or argument are not suppressed, this complexity cannot fail to show itself. We can discover no unarguable path to travel from where we have been to where we imagine we may be going. Yet neither is there an infinite number of paths available to us. There are only those that we can discern emerging from the context we have, and we must decide the relative merits or appropriateness of the alternatives. What is imaginable to us depends on what we are prepared to recognize in the context of what we have already experienced. This actuality coexists with, but is not transformed by, the rhetoric of certainty that also appears. It is part of the reality of politics that we must discriminate among the claims to know according to what seems possible to know.

If we could show that there are logically necessary consequences that follow from our situation, we might in principle transcend the need of argument and persuasion. We would then not be imaginative agents of plausible but uncertain courses of action, but conduits through whom the necessary course of action expresses itself. 'Human activity,' Oakeshott says,

> with whatever it may be concerned, enjoys a circumscribed range of movement. The limits which define this range are historic, that is to say, they are themselves the

product of human activity. Generally speaking, there are no 'natural' limits as distinct from historic limits: those which we ascribe to 'human nature', for example, are not less historic than those which we immediately recognize as springing from conditions determined by human activity. Even what a man may do with his physical strength is determined by the historic devices and inventions of men, and no community has been without such devices. Being historic, they are not absolute, but on any occasion they are not on that account any the less limits. They may be wide or narrow, they are never absent. The flight of imagination, the poet's power over words and images, the scientist's hypotheses, the philosopher's engagements and disengagements and the practical man's projects and enterprises are all of them exploitations of what is given or intimated in the condition of the world he inhabits.... So it is with our political activity.... The politician always has a certain field of vision and a certain range of opportunity; what he is able to contemplate, to desire or to attempt is subject to the historic limits of his situation. And in order to understand his activity it is necessary first to consider the field within which he moves, the choices that are available to him and the enterprises he is able to entertain. Indeed, until we have understood this, any other judgement we may make about his activity – judgements of approval or disapproval for example – are liable to lack force and relevance.[9]

The 'pursuit of intimations' captures an element in many familiar experiences: imagining possibilities; desiring to try something new; believing that a course of action is necessary or unavoidable; wanting to correct what are believed to be past errors; defending current practices against arguments that they are mistaken or inadequate; reconciling the pressure of the new with affection for the old; extricating oneself from a too constraining situation; trying to settle disputes in the hope of tranquility or orderliness; extrapolating trends from what we understand ourselves to have been doing; responding to what others insist is important; deciding how important an issue is; considering what is appropriate, tasteful, morally acceptable, or simply possible given our resources as we now understand them; translating ideals into something we might actually do; discovering what changes reformers really might undertake; determining what terms like 'solidarity', 'community', 'rights', 'social justice', 'welfare', or 'new world order' mean in terms of policies we might actually adopt. These engagements are all embedded in contexts.

Oakeshott was prone to say, the pursuit of perfection as the crow flies is a delusion. It is all very well for me to say that what I want is to be happy. But eventually I must specify what would make me happy: 'I can not want to be happy,' Oakeshott once remarked, 'what I want is to idle in Avignon or hear Caruso sing.'[10] His point was that the desire to be happy has to turn into something intelligible to do in the practical realm. The abstraction of desire in practical life cannot ultimately escape from the limits imposed by the actually available resources of the practical life. For Oakeshott, then, to examine politics philosophically is to recollect that no direction is logically implicated – there are only intimations. Such recollection may inhibit the politician who equips himself for practical action by forgetting this in

[9]   Oakeshott, *The Politics of Faith and the Politics of Scepticism*, ed. Timothy Fuller (New Haven: Yale Univ. Press, 1996), 116–7. Hereafter: *FS*.
[10] Oakeshott, *On Human Conduct* (Oxford: Clarendon Press, 1975), 53. Hereafter: *OHC*.

discovering a felt necessity. What such a 'necessity' is, of course, is the intimation
to pursue at that point, but the politician may feel he needs something grander,
a cause, or crisis, to grease the skids of persuasion (and he may well be right).
What the philosopher risks forgetting is not this, but that for him to transcend the
practical life is not to subdue or command it:

> From the standpoint of practical experience there can be no more dangerous disease
> than the love and pursuit of truth in those who do not understand, or have forgotten,
> that a man's first business is to live. And life, we have seen, can be conducted only at
> the expense of an arrest in experience. The practical consciousness knows well enough
> what is inimical to its existence, and often has the wisdom to avoid it. *Pereat veritas,
> fiat vita.* It is not the clear sighted, not those who are fashioned for thought and the
> ardours of thought, who can lead the world. Great achievements are accomplished in
> the mental fog of practical experience. What is farthest from our needs is that kings
> should be philosophers. The victims of thought, those who are intent upon what is
> unlimitedly satisfactory in experience, are self-confessed betrayers life, and must pursue
> their way without the encouragement of the practical consciousness, which is secure
> in the knowledge that philosophical thought can make no relevant contribution to the
> coherence of its world of experience.[11]

Oakeshott's skepticism, then, did not exclude accurate description of what goes
on in the world. It denied the power to transform the practical life into something
else. Oakeshott established that the common acceptance of the primacy of the
practical life, and hence of politics was, philosophically speaking, mistaken. It is
easy, he admitted, to see why we are receptive to the claims of practicality upon
us: We are born into mortality and must, from birth, start to learn how to make
our way in the midst of what is both hospitable and inhospitable to our presence.
Practical activity requires us to undertake alteration and preservation, and we
experience the 'necessity of which no man can relieve himself' (*EM*, 256). The
world, understood practically, is familiar and ever present, it is where we pass
our lives. Its necessity does not, however, constitute its comprehensiveness, and
its necessity is a 'necessary evil': There are strong 'prejudices and preconceptions
of the larger part of mankind, who find it impossible to entertain the idea that
this practical world, within which they are confined as if in a prison, is other than
the universe itself' (*EM*, 249). In extricating himself from conventional thinking,
Oakeshott sought what he called a philosophy of practical experience, as opposed
to a 'practical philosophy'. He dismissed practical philosophy because it is not an
effort to understand politics philosophically, but rather an undertaking to defend a
political position by, first, transposing the terms of argument into abstract concepts;
and then, secondly, appealing to those concepts as the ground for the practical
conclusions one wants to defend. To declare, for example, that all history is the
story of class struggle, and then to search for evidence to support this contention
with a view to identifying the historically relevant class or classes, is to give up the
desire for comprehensive understanding in favor of an abridgement that supports

[11] Oakeshott, *Experience and Its Modes* (Cambridge: Cambridge Univ. Press, 1933), 320–1. Hereafter:
     EM.

various practical political engagements. That this engagement is wrapped in the trappings of theoretical language, which give the appearance of transcending the limitations of the pursuit of intimations, is either a disguise or a self-deception.

To elaborate a philosophy of practical experience, by contrast, is to try to understand the distinguishing features of practical engagement that will attend every specific practical undertaking whatever. Here, Oakeshott undoubtedly had in mind such achievements as Aristotle's recognition, in the *Nicomachean Ethics*, that a theoretical account of the practical moral life insightfully describes, but offers no relief from, the necessity to act in contingent circumstances, through specific conduct, arrived at by making judgments within a way of life, and not by deductions from abstract principles. There was for Oakeshott, as for Aristotle, no way for a theoretical account of what goes on in practical conduct to eliminate the complex difficulties of moral decisions. In response to the objection that, by rejecting general principles, he provided no standards for detecting incoherencies or deciding on reforms, Oakeshott replied,

> Do you want to be told that in politics there is, what certainly exists nowhere else, a mistake-proof manner of deciding what should be done? How does a scientist, with the current conditions of physics before him, decide upon a direction of profitable advance? What considerations passed through the minds of medieval builders when they detected the inappropriateness of building in stone as if they were building in wood? How does a critic arrive at the judgment that a picture is incoherent, that the artist's treatment of some passages is inconsistent with his treatment of others? (*RIP*, 69)

Practical activity thus has a character of an identifiable sort. The ends pursued there exemplify practical engagement, but do not transform it. A theoretical account is an attempt at saying faithfully, in different words, what is going on. For Oakeshott a philosophical understanding of politics is categorically distinct from theorizing a justification for political ends or goals.

Because practical life is constituted in promoting and preventing change in our existence, it cannot change once and for all. If it could, it would cease to be what it is, and become something altogether different. Claims that we could work through the 'necessary evils' of politics to end the necessity of politics, misunderstand what is actually going on. Practical life is driven by the desire to make coherent and satisfactory what is incoherent and unsatisfactory. Oakeshott thought he had accounted for why the practical desire for coherence must remain unfulfilled. In *Experience and its Modes* he argues along the following lines (to paraphrase):

> In practical life, what seems to offer coherence is what is taken to be true. In practical conduct we always, implicitly or explicitly, consider the degree to which we have achieved coherence. Every human being is, in principle, an agent of opinion. Opinions are significant since they are assessments of coherence or incoherence in our lives. The existing state of affairs at every moment exposes possibilities of something 'to be' which is 'not yet' and each moment of coherence is precarious, an incipient incoherence. There is no point at which it ceases to be possible to think of a 'to be' which is 'not yet'. The 'to be' which is 'not yet' expresses a possible alteration of 'what is' and thus defeats the hope of having already achieved coherence. There are no gaps in consciousness, but

always a contiguity – a touching – of what has been, what is, and what we imagine may
come to be: "The 'to be' of practice is never a world merely discrepant from 'what is'; it
is always and everywhere considered, not merely a 'not yet' or a 'not here', but in some
sense, more coherent than 'what is' " (Cf. *EM*, 261, *passim*).

Thus the 'to be' can become 'what ought to be' – we can find value in it. What
we take as practical facts are unstable for they are what 'is', now, as opposed to
what may have been yesterday, and what might be tomorrow. In practical activity,
what is the case now could be otherwise, and possibilities for being otherwise are
always with us. We look for what is satisfactory, which always involves trying to
find what we think coherent. The consequences of specific, practical undertakings
cannot suffice. Success, no less than failure, in the gaining of specific ends excites
appraisal and assessment, leading on to other 'not yets' that we think either ought
or ought not to be. 'Truth is sought in what is other than what is given' (*EM*,
265).

So long as the future is an essential element in practical appraisal, coherence
has to elude us; we are never without unrealized ideas. The completeness we may
hope to enjoy is always attended by not yet integrated possibilities. There is no
independent body of things we might fix in a conclusive arrangement. Alterability
is inexhaustible. Thus, if, as we stated earlier, freedom does not mean liberation
from what we have been, it does mean acting towards what we think will make for
coherence as a response to what we have been. 'Freedom,' Oakeshott concluded, is
to be understood as 'an idea which has relevance in the practical world of activity
and nowhere else' (*EM*, 267 n. 1). As Oakeshott saw it, freedom is realized in
attaining practical truth in the sense of attaining coherence, of harmonizing the
disharmonies of life. To attain what we think true because in it we find coherence
involves reconciling conflicting opinions in the practical life. Individuals are
agents of the pursuit of coherence, differentiating themselves from each other as
they define themselves in the context of each other's presence. But if we think the
momentary attainment of coherence is discovering our *telos*, we are mistaken. The
restlessness of the human spirit cannot be content; coherence is evanescent. 'The
practical world,' Oakeshott remarks,

> because it is a world of activity and change, is a world of oppositions to be balanced
> (because they cannot be unified), of contradictions which (because they cannot be
> resolved) must be coordinated. The practical self and its interests can never give way
> before the interests of 'others'; the relationships into which it enters are external to itself;
> and, since in practical experience the practical self is the very embodiment of reality, its
> dissolution is a contradiction and inconceivable. (*EM*, 270)

To the extent we find coherence we think ourselves free, unless and until we find
the coherence we have attained turning into unlooked for constraint. When this
happens, we find ourselves cast once more into necessity:

> If a man thinks to set himself free, in any save a vague and metaphorical sense, by the
> study of science or of history or by the pursuit of philosophy he is grossly mistaken. The
> only truth that makes a man free is practical truth, the possession of a coherent world

of practical ideas. Indeed, practical truth and freedom seem to me inseparable; wherever the one is, the other will be found also. (*EM*, 268)

Practical life undertakes to manage what is never fully under control. Will and desire cannot be purged from a world in which self-awareness and diversity of opinions can at most temporarily be suppressed. There is always more that could be said than has been said, and those who may say it. The stability of coherence is the friendly enemy of the restlessness of freedom. In conjunction, they make for the discordant concord of practical life.

9

Roy Tseng

Conservatism, Romanticism, and the Understanding of Modernity

Introduction

'To be conservative,' says Oakeshott, 'is to prefer the familiar to the unknown, to prefer the tried to the untried, fact to mystery, the actual to the possible, the limited to the unbounded, the near to the distant, the sufficient to the superabundant, the convenient to the perfect, present laughter to utopian bliss.'[1] In contrast to a form of political ideology, Oakeshott's concept of conservatism is more likely to entail a certain disposition of human activity; and thus unlike those who depreciate conservatism as an anti-modern tendency toward anti-individualism, the conservative disposition unveiled by Oakeshott actually provides an important approach to understanding the intricate and complex meanings of modernity in terms of the 'morality of the individual'. By examining the relation of 'philosophical conservatism' to modernity through this lens, I intend to clarify some debated issues in Oakeshott studies, mainly regarding the places of Romanticism and liberalism in the map of Oakeshott's thought.

Firstly, following Isaiah Berlin and Charles Taylor, it is my view that Western moral outlooks still operate in the wake of two 'large-scale cultural upheavals,' which are by nature in conflict with each other, i.e. the Enlightenment and the Counter-Enlightenment or Romanticism.[2] Although Oakeshott rarely mentions the terms 'Counter-Enlightenment' or 'Romanticism', his notion of the self owes much to this well known debate and his famous criticism of Rationalism is reminiscent of Berlin's and Taylor's reflections on the Enlightenment. Moreover, Oakeshott's 'historical enquiry' into the character of a modern state identified as *universitas* and *societas* contains a wider horizon that can accommodate being read in terms of Berlin's and Taylor's understandings of modernity in terms of the Enlightenment

---

[1]   Oakeshott, *Rationalism in Politics and other essays, new and expanded edition*, ed. Timothy Fuller (Indianapolis: Liberty Press, 1991), 408. Hereafter: *RIP*.

[2]   Charles Taylor, *Sources of the Self: The Making of Modern Identity* (Cambridge: Cambridge Univ. Press, 1989), 393; Isaiah Berlin, *Conversation with Isaiah Berlin*, ed. Ramin Jahanbegloo (London: Peter Halban, 1992); Berlin, *The Roots of Romanticism* (Princeton: Princeton Univ. Press, 1999); Berlin, *Three Critics of the Enlightenment: Vico, Hamann, Herder*, ed. Henry Hardy (London: Pimlico, 2000).

and the Counter-Enlightenment. Although Oakeshott's work constitutes a momentous challenge to the Enlightenment, that must not be translated into a total rejection of modernity, inasmuch as the Enlightenment just represents one single facet of modernity. In short, it is my contention that to evaluate the achievement of modernity in general and the import of Oakeshott's thought in particular, Romanticism is an indispensable source.

Secondly, if Berlin is correct in saying that the result of Romanticism 'is liberalism, toleration, decency and the appreciation of the imperfection of life, some degree of rational self-understanding,'[3] it appears that for Berlin, as for Oakeshott, the tension between the Enlightenment and Romanticism would operate less drastically in the sphere of politics than in the notion of the self. This explains to some degree why Berlin's and Oakeshott's inclinations to conservative/romanticist thought in recognizing the imperfection of the human condition should bring forth political liberalism of some sort. Yet, from the standpoint I am taking, the fact that Oakeshott advocates individualistic values gives us no sufficient reason to consider him a liberal unless his connection with romanticist expressivism (or expressionism)[4] can be better appreciated. For Oakeshott's philosophical reconstruction of the self is so different from the mainstream liberalism that the point is not whether he is a devotee of liberty, but whether his love of liberty has the same quality as the liberal's, whether of the deontological or utilitarian variety. Due to the conflict between the Enlightenment and the Counter-Enlightenment, two emphatically distinctive ideas of the self emerge in modern times: the epistemic self and the expressivist self. Consequently the most crucial and yet less recognized groupings of liberalism are 'rationalistic liberalism' and 'romanticist liberalism'. While it is widely claimed that the replacement of rationalistic liberalism with civic republicanism has to do with the fact that the liberal was more sensitive to the severe change of social and political conditions in modern history, I shall argue conversely that one of the main failures of liberalism is owing to its incapability of making sense of another distinctively modern issue; that is, the issue of self-identity. In short, the expressivist self rooted in Romanticism could be treated as Oakeshott's answer to the difficulty of living in a modern world, as well as his antidote to rationalistic liberalism.

The Counter-Enlightenment

It is a commonplace opinion that the conservative disposition at stake should have serious quarrels with many currents of thought in our times, such as logical positivism and analytical philosophy, deontological and utilitarian liberalisms, rational choice and the empiricist-based social sciences, inasmuch as they fall short of a serious historical consciousness in understanding the human condition and in pursuing human knowledge. Because such mistakes arise from the fact that modern intellectuality has for a long time been colored by the Cartesian anxiety,

---

[3]   Berlin, *The Roots of Romanticism*, 147.
[4]   The term 'expressionism' was coined by Berlin, whereas Taylor uses the cognate and synonymous term 'expressivism'.

obsessed with moral foundations, and eager for scientific certainty, Oakeshott embarks on a long-term critique of Rationalism. This critique seeks to expose the incoherency of several modern projects or dispositions, among which we find the indiscriminate pursuit of universal knowledge, the sovereignty of technique, and the supremacy of the scientific voice diminishing the autonomy of history (and of poetry). It can therefore be inferred that Oakeshott's 'Rationalism' in actuality spells out the Enlightenment project, and so his attacks on Rationalism unveil his bid to transcend the Enlightenment positions in terms of *philosophisme*, formalism, and scientism.[5]

It follows that the conservative disposition, among other things, is of special significance in Oakeshott's historiography, for that which 'history' contains is nothing but 'the familiar, the tried and the actual' which would help us grasp the comprehensiveness and complexity of human performances and utterances under particular circumstances. And, as is well known, there are two viewpoints that are seemingly indispensable for grasping Oakeshott's reading of history. First, a proper understanding of a complex historic alloy is to be reached by identifying the poles, which protects the identity of the manner of thinking concerned. Thus, Oakeshott maintains that modern European reflection on the character of a state can be realized in terms of two categorically distinctive ideas, *societas* and *universitas*. Second, Oakeshott essentially believes that there is an 'unresolved tension' between these two opposite modes of human association, so that we are not surprised by hybrids, such as the modern state at times appearing, historically, to be '*a societas cum universitate.*'[6] In short, Oakeshott's philosophical understanding of politics does not lead him to outline a utopia dismissive of the historical context of ideas, and his skepticism prevents him from systemizing historical ideas into a unified concept.

It is noticeable that in understanding the modern experience of governing and being governed Oakeshott has altered his terminology from time to time, but the references basically remain the same. Although unlike his earlier works Oakeshott deliberately claims in *On Human Conduct* that he is writing a 'history' about the matter concerned (*OHC*, 199, 323–6), whether Oakeshott's analysis is historical enough in the sense of having given us a unity of ideas as comprehensive and detailed as he expected from historiography is contestable.[7] Regarding this debate, my view is that the 'pastness' of Rationalism discovered by Oakeshott, no less than the pastness of *universitas* and *societas*, is not a historical past, nor is it a practical past;[8] but rather, that it can only be a 'quasi-philosophical past' on the account that

[5]   See Roy Tseng, *The Sceptical Idealist: Michael Oakeshott as a Critic of the Enlightenment* (Exeter: Imprint Academic, 2003).

[6]   Oakeshott, *On Human Conduct* (Oxford: Clarendon Press, 1975), 200–1. Hereafter: *OHC*.

[7]   David Boucher, 'Politics in a Different Mode: An Appreciation of Michael Oakeshott,' *History of Political Thought*, 12 (1991): 722–3, 728.

[8]   Some writers, however, believe that Oakeshott traces the emergence of Rationalism as a historical genesis. See, for example, Paul Franco, *The Political Philosophy of Michael Oakeshott* (New Haven: Yale Univ. Press, 1990), 111, 125, 250 n. 12; cf. Terry Nardin, *The Philosophy of Michael Oakeshott* (Univ. Park: Penn State Press, 2001), 141 n. 1. T. W. Smith, by contrast, argues that it is a practical past that is at the heart of Oakeshott's interpretation of the history of political ideas. See his 'Michael Oakeshott on History, Practice and Political Theory,' *History*

some abridgements are inescapably made in order to accommodate Oakeshott's own philosophical reflections.[9] As a result, to avoid misunderstandings that might result from Oakeshott's criticisms on the Enlightenment positions through his usage of Rationalism, we shall pay careful attention to his qualified statements on Rationalism.

On the one hand, although analyzing the logic of Rationalism is his main concern, the moral situation it has caused is never far from his mind. He is quite aware that the formalistic tendency in ethics is firmly predicated on *philosophisme*, or alternatively foundationalism, meaning that philosophy should be a master discipline that lays foundations for the natural sciences and authorizes the validity of any other knowledge in terms of an objective scientific criterion.[10] In other words, since the Enlightenment positions constitute a whole package in favor of philosophy *par excellence*,[11] what is required in the first place is a critique of the foundationalist notion of philosophy itself. For this reason, Oakeshott's appreciation of Rationalism is chiefly from a philosophical perspective. And it is precisely at this philosophical level that Oakeshott's definition of Rationalism reflects Berlin's comprehension of the propositions of the Enlightenment and the idea of universal reason it presumes.[12] Moreover, Rationalism so understood is not dissimilar to what Taylor diagnoses using the term 'Naturalism'. Because Oakeshott would not deny that the common feature of this family eventually consists in 'the ambition to model the study of man on the natural sciences,' a family of ideas in which the Enlightenment plays a decisive part.[13] Both Taylor and Oakeshott realize that a

of Political Thought, 17 (1996): 609–14.

[9]   Tseng, *Sceptical Idealist*, 137–8, 171, 179, 186 n. 190, 205. Even Oakeshott himself later acknowledges that he may have stretched certain historical events to make his point in the third essay of *On Human Conduct*. See Oakeshott, 'On Misunderstanding Human Conduct: A Reply to My Critics,' *Political Theory*, 4 (1976): 359–60. By way of contrast, when dealing with the political thoughts of the Greeks, the Romans and the Medievals in his LSE *Lectures* I think Oakeshott has really come to meet his own criterion as to what makes possible genuine historical knowledge. See Oakeshott, *Lectures in the History of Political Thought* (Exeter: Imprint Academic, 2006). Hereafter: *LHPT*.

[10] Richard Rorty, *Philosophy and the Mirror of Nature* (Oxford: Basil Blackwell, 1982).

[11] 'The essence of Rationalism,' says Oakeshott, 'is their combination' (*RIP*, 10).

[12] According to Berlin, the propositions of the Enlightenment are (1) that 'all genuine questions can be answered,' (2) that all the answers to these questions 'are knowable,' and (3) that the answers proposed 'are compatible with one another' under a universal system (*The Roots of Romanticism*, 21–2). In a very similar way, Oakeshott writes that the Rationalist's activity 'is activity in search of a certain, conclusive answer to a question, and consequently the question must be formulated in such a way that it admits of such an answer' (*RIP*, 103); that Rationalism is identical with a form of 'intellectual equalitarianism' (*RIP*, 6, 105) in the sense that the Rationalist takes the view that the attempt to discover a perfect solution will lead different people to the same conclusions and issue in the same form of activity. Furthermore, what lies at the heart of Berlin's definition is nothing but *philosophisme*, i.e. the 'perfectly reasonable hope' that 'there is no reason why such answers, which after all have produced triumphant results in the worlds of physics and chemistry, should not equally apply to the much more troubled fields of politics, ethics, and aesthetics' (*The Roots of Romanticism*, 24, 22).

[13] Charles Taylor, *Human Agency and Language*, vol. 1 of *Philosophical Papers Vol. 1* (Cambridge: Cambridge Univ. Press, 1985), 1. It should be remembered that Taylor's usage of Naturalism is broader than the radical Enlightenment (*Aufklarer*) appearing in the works of Diderot, Holbach, Condorcet, Voltaire, Hume, and so forth. But Taylor believes that the radical Enlightenment has largely enforced modern Naturalism by looking at the world 'as a neutral domain, which

vital upshot of *philosophisme* is scientism, namely, an identification of knowledge proper with knowledge acquired by scientific method.

On the other hand, just because by 'Rationalism' Oakeshott is concerned with the 'most remarkable intellectual fashion of post-Renaissance Europe' (*RIP*, 5), he seems to have accepted Alasdair MacIntyre's assumption of a single, distinguishable Enlightenment Project so as to make clearer the moral predicament of modern society.[14] That is to say, since Oakeshott's philosophical concern has penetrated into his study of Rationalism, the Rationalism in question wears the property of what Oakeshott would call an 'ideal type'.[15] No matter whether Oakeshott's ideal type is applicable to MacIntyre's, Berlin's, or Taylor's cases, that does not affect the fact that for these thinkers 'at bottom, the mistake of the Enlightenment project is the failure to see that rationality is as such an abstract capacity.'[16] That said, an observable philosophical attitude toward the study of modern ideas has shown itself to be alarmed by the moral crisis that the Enlightenment has carried into the modern world; and thus, attentions are directed, not to the diversity of the Enlightenment thinkers, but to the conceptions of the person and of human reason that the mainstream modern philosophers have encouraged the ordinary people to believe (*RIP*, 107).[17]

With these qualifications, it seems safe to say that Oakeshott's double-sided interpretation of a great historical event now appears to have become an influential approach to appreciating modernity, where the two conflicting boundaries are recognized as the Enlightenment and the Counter-Enlightenment or Romanticism. Berlin, for instance, writes, 'we are children of both worlds' in question, and 'we oscillate between the two.'[18] More recently, when discussing contemporary moral visions Taylor has arrived at the similar conclusion by articulating that 'these two big and many-sided cultural transformations, the Enlightenment and Romanticism with its accompanying expressive conception of man, have made us what we are;' that these two forms of life are 'partly defined in contrast to each other.'[19] In what follows, I shall show that the features of *universitas* and *societas* that Oakeshott takes in are more than mere political institutions and values. In point of fact, they

---

we have to understand in order to master it, and whose causal relations we have to make use of in order to produce the greatest amount of happiness' (*Sources of the Self*, 321).

[14] Alasdair MacIntyre, *After Virtue: A Study in Moral Theory*, 2d ed. (London: Duckworth, 1985), 36–78.

[15] In discussing medieval government, for example, Oakeshott uses two ideal types of monarchy: 'absolute monarchical rule' and 'conditional monarchical rule'; and here, by ideal type he means the 'direction in which medieval belief about monarchy found itself pulled' (*LHPT*, 269).

[16] Charles Larmore, *The Morals of Modernity* (Cambridge: Cambridge Univ. Press, 1996), 49.

[17] At this point, it is notable that Berlin also remarks that the Enlightenment 'was certainly not, as is sometimes maintained, a kind of uniform movement of which all the members believed approximately the same thing;' and yet in summing up the propositions of the Enlightenment it is only sufficient to look for 'what is common to all these thinkers' (*The Roots of Romanticism*, 24, 25). Charles Taylor has a similar consideration, too. According to Taylor, the study of past philosophical ideas are of importance because 'philosophers helped articulate the change [of our moral situation]; and no doubt this articulation added force and impetus to it' (*Sources of the Self*, 285).

[18] Berlin, *The Roots of Romanticism*, 141.

[19] Taylor, *Sources of the Self*, 393, 424–5.

convey a perspective for understanding modernity in terms of the Enlightenment and the Counter-Enlightenment, too.

I have mentioned that there are a number of analogous expressions Oakeshott uses to analyze the modern history of political thought. To illustrate: *Societas* is taken to mean an identifiable association in which the tie that joins the agents is loyalty to one another, i.e. observing the customs of legality, whereas *universitas* stands for a corporation aggregate recognized as persons in respect of some identified common purpose, or acknowledged public interest (*OHC*, 201–6). On reading this, it does seem clear that these forms of human relationship would bear simultaneously different notions of morality, namely, the 'morality of the individual' and the 'morality of the anti-individual'.[20] However, it becomes even less clear while we turn to ask: What exactly does the 'morality of the individual' mean?

Some writers have come to equate the 'morality of the individual' with *societas* and the 'morality of the anti-individual' with *universitas*, simply in order to support their view that Oakeshott's theory of civil association is to endorse a cluster of liberal values;[21] indeed, the recent scholarship has tried to show that Oakeshott's political philosophy can be treated as a restatement of liberalism.[22] And yet, it seems to me that the 'morality of the individual' rests first and foremost on the political or institutional dimension of individualism and goes beyond scrutiny on the issue of the self.[23] To borrow a phrase from Will Kymlicka, they 'center not on the liberal idea of the self and its interests, but on the 'individualistic' way that liberals seek to promote those interests politically.'[24] In a word, the prominent ambition to liberalize Oakeshott's political thought is largely referring to the 'advocatory issues' and leaves the 'ontological issues' untouched.[25]

I shall return to examine Oakeshott's conception of the self and its relation to Romanticism later. For now, I must establish (1) that Oakeshott's discussion of *universitas* and *societas* does imply two distinguishable ideas of the self, i.e. the epistemic self and the expressivist self; (2) that while both the epistemic self and the expressivist self may result in the advocacy of individualistic values, the

---

[20] See, for example, 'The Masses in Representative Democracy'(*RIP*, 363–83), and, 'On the Character of a Modern European State' (*OHC*, part. 3).

[21] Franco, *The Political Philosophy of Michael Oakeshott*, 152–6.

[22] See, for example, Paul Franco, *The Political Philosophy of Michael Oakeshott*; and 'Michael Oakeshott as a Liberal Theorist,' *Political Theory*, 18 (1990): 411–35; John Gray, *Liberalisms: Essays in Political Philosophy* (London: Routledge, 1989), 199–217; Wendell, J. Coats, Jr., 'Michael Oakeshott as A Liberal Theorist,' *Canadian Journal of Political Science*, 18 (1985): 773–87; D. A. Lloyd Thomas, 'Review of *On Human Conduct*,' *Mind*, 86 (1977): 454; Noel O'Sullivan, 'In the Perspective of Western Thought,' in *The Achievement of Michael Oakeshott*, ed. J. Norman (London: Duckworth, 1993), 106; D. J. Manning, 'The Philosophical Foundations of Liberal Ideology,' *Journal of Political Ideologies*, 2 (1997): 137–58.

[23] Insofar as I agree with Nardin's remark that 'to read Oakeshott narrowly as a conservative critic of the welfare state or liberal defender of individualism and pluralism,' is 'to misunderstand, and seriously to underrate, his contribution to philosophy' (*The Philosophy of Michael Oakeshott*, 235, cf. 225–6).

[24] Will Kymlicka, *Liberalism, Community and Culture* (Oxford: Clarendon Press, 1989), 74.

[25] Charles Taylor, 'The Cross-Purposes: The Liberal-Communitarian Debate,' chap. 10 in *Philosophical Arguments* (Cambridge: Harvard Univ. Press, 1995).

self that fits into *societas* can only be the expressivist self; and (3) that in view of the fact that the notions of the self can be traced back to the Enlightenment and the Counter-Enlightenment correspondingly, the 'unsolved tension' between *universitas* and *societas* actually indicates Oakeshott's realization of the deepest moral conflict underlying the modern world, viz. the Enlightenment *cum* the Counter-Enlightenment.

First of all, it should be remembered that in addition to *universitas* and *societas*, there is another set of ideas more closely associated with the issue of the self that Oakeshott used in his earlier work, namely, 'rationalism in politics' and its opponent, 'conservatism in politics'. The thrust underscoring *Rationalism in Politics*, as I understand it, is to repudiate 'rationalism in politics' as a misguided move to set up a philosophical foundation ensuring our practical certainty, which is based on an epistemic self initiated by the Cartesian-Lockean theory of mind, holding a trans-historical attitude toward our moral and political life, and leading to the universal application of abstract moral and political rules (*RIP*, 99–131). By way of contrast, the sort of individual Oakeshott prefers is not simply one that is fond of individualistic values, but it also must be a non-Cartesian-Lockean self, in order that morality and politics can be seen as ways of living in which the expressivist self is engaged, a rhetorical form of reasoning through the 'pursuit of intimations' of a moral and political tradition.[26]

As a matter of fact, in *On Human Conduct*, Oakeshott's final statement on political theory, Oakeshott also takes both the 'ontological issues' and the 'advocatory issues' into account. When explicating the character of moral practice suitable for *societas* Oakeshott obviously returns to the theme of *Rationalism in Politics* by remarking that moral life involves a manner of living, not a set of principles; that general principles, of course, may be elicited from a moral tradition, 'but (like other languages) it is not the creation of grammarians, it is made by speakers;' and consequently that the moral self 'has a 'history', but no 'nature', [an agent] is what in conduct he becomes' (*OHC*, 79, 41). All this affirms that Oakeshott's theory of civil association or *societas* is more than a defense of individualistic politics; it is also a far-reaching reconstruction of the notion of self. Far-reaching because, as we shall see, in *On Human Conduct* a brand new idea of self-enactment is supplemented to deal with the problem of self-identity. The latter Oakeshott proposes that there are two distinctive aspects of moral conduct understood in terms of self-disclosure (which remains to ensure the existence of a more durable, historic moral discourse) and self-enactment.

No matter how important the idea of self-enactment can be, it is apparent that there are two criteria that Oakeshott employs to categorize modern political thought, namely, the 'ontological issues' in relation to the understanding of the moral self and the way of philosophizing presumed, and the 'advocatory issues' in relation to the weight of social and political values maintained. Based on this view, we may now approach the second point mentioned above. The 'ontological issues' really matter for several reasons. First, while at the level of 'advocatory

---

[26] For a fuller account on this view, see Tseng, *The Sceptical Idealist*, 164–79.

issues' liberalism and socialism are possible to tell apart in the sense that for the liberal the ultimate principle in politics is the idea that 'value is individual', and for the socialist, the notion of 'common good', the conventional liberal nevertheless shares in common with the socialist the Rationalistic characteristics of being abstract, perfect and trans-historical in their understanding of the moral self. Thus, Oakeshott claims that 'the modern European political consciousness is a polarized consciousness' in terms of *universitas* and *societas*, and 'all the other tensions (such as those indicated in the words 'right' or 'left' or in the alignments of political parties) are insignificant compared to this' (*OHC*, 320).

But further, that which turns the liberal self into an epistemic self, as indicated, has everything to do with what one presumes is the purpose of philosophizing; it goes without saying that the formalistic attributes of the liberal self are bound with *philosophisme*. Thus, in *Morality and Politics in Modern Europe: The Harvard Lectures*[27] despite cherishing individualistic values Oakeshott severely accuses the 'political theory of individualism' as it appears in the works of Locke, Kant, Bentham, and Mill of a Rationalistic attempt to pursue some 'unnecessary hypotheses,' whether it be natural right theory, categorical imperatives, or utilitarianism (*MPME*, 83-4). More to the point, in *The Politics of Faith and the Politics of Scepticism*[28] Oakeshott concedes that these styles of politics both are stepchildren of the 'enlargement of power' which marks the beginning of modern times; and that some aspects of Locke's, Bentham's and Paine's thoughts contain the elements of skeptical politics in favor of rule of law. One of the main failures of modern skeptical politics, Oakeshott soon points out, was its alliance with something like Locke's natural right theory which led Europe in establishing government 'on a firm foundation' in the name of justice, truth or certainty. For this reason, Oakeshott criticizes Locke for being 'a political sceptic who inadvertently imposed the idioms of faith upon the sceptical understanding of government' (*FS*, 82–3).

This shows that the moral self Oakeshott tries to figure out cannot be an epistemic self struck in the Cartesian allegory of certainty; but rather, that it must be an expressivist self capable of narrating stories and disclosing the meanings of moral language. For, even though the epistemic self and the expressive self both welcome individualistic values, the former coheres more closely with the Enlightenment from which Oakeshott has no hesitance in turning away. It thus comes as no surprise that in *On Human Conduct* Oakeshott remains with the view that liberalism as an individualistic way of understanding politics stands obliquely in between the extremes of *societas* and *universitas*. Oakeshott maintains this assertion because the self that corresponds to the moral character of *societas* actually corresponds more closely with the Counter-Enlightenment.

To say that the notions of the self and the way of philosophizing presumed are requisite to make sense Oakeshott's study of *universitas* and *societas*, is therefore equivalent to say that Oakeshott's interpretation of the character of a modern

[27] Oakeshott, *Morality and Politics in Modern Europe: The Harvard Lectures*, ed. Timothy Fuller (New Haven: Yale Univ. Press, 1993). Hereafter: *MPME*.
[28] Oakeshott, *The Politics of Faith and the Politics of Scepticism*, ed. Timothy Fuller (New Haven: Yale Univ. Press, 1996). Hereafter: *FS*.

state entails an approach to perceiving modernity in terms of the Enlightenment and the Counter-Enlightenment. As a result, it may not be going too far to infer that the 'unsolved tension' between *universitas* and *societas* could be imagined as Oakeshott's realization of the profound moral conflict in the modern world, that is, the conflict between the Enlightenment and the Counter-Enlightenment. Thus, Oakeshott's criticisms of the Enlightenment positions do not signify a total rejection of modernity. For Oakeshott, as for Berlin and Taylor, the Enlightenment just symbolizes one explicit facet of modernity, and anyone who tries to evaluate the achievement of modernity completely should take seriously the implicit forces of the Counter-Enlightenment.

The Expressivist Self

What has been said, of course, does not mean that Oakeshott is opposed to liberalism; instead, a crucial interest in this paper is to examine Oakeshott's liberal thought with regard to the romanticist expressivism. In asking whether Oakeshott is a liberal, I am not simply looking for the individualistic values he promotes, but searching for the notion of self that he adopts to justify the individualistic style of politics understood as the rule of law. In this part of the study, I shall argue that the expressivist self is, in fact, immanent in Oakeshott's conservative disposition which acknowledges the imperfection of the human condition; that Oakeshott's conservative disposition in selfhood, so to speak, is morally more sensitive to the historical conditions of modernity than the rationalistic liberal idea of the self in that it accounts for a distinctively modern issue recognized as self-identity.

To start with, it should be kept in mind that Oakeshott's treatment of the self is under two postulates in relation to his conservative disposition toward the imperfection of the human condition. The first is the 'formal postulate' of a free will to act, and this is expressed in *Experience and Its Modes*[29] and some passages of *On Human Conduct*; the second is the 'substantial postulate' maintaining the historicity of human action, and this is presented in *Rationalism in Politics* and other places in *On Human Conduct*. So far as the first postulate is concerned, Oakeshott makes his point in *Experience and Its Modes* that human practice in terms of morality and politics is an accomplishment of human freedom. More precisely, as Oakeshott later supplements in *On Human Conduct*, in practice every individual is free to make a response to a contingent situation (deliberation), to diminish the hazards of his action (persuasion), and to make his action more intelligible (explanation), and all this is carried out on his own, not in the sense of doing, saying, and thinking in isolation from others, but in the sense that whatever input others may have, the 'buck stops', so to speak, with oneself. By age 40, every man is responsible for his own countenance, as Camus might have said (*OHC*, 36–51).

It is clear that Oakeshott's intention is to dissolve the abstract mental self of the *philosophe's* dreams, in order to return the individual to the practical world in which his freedom can work for its own sake. However, according to the theory of

---

[29] Oakeshott, *Experience and Its Modes* (Cambridge: Cambridge Univ. Press, 1933). Hereafter: *EM*.

modality established in *Experience and Its Modes*, Oakeshott also insists that what makes practice self-consistent (i.e., its resting on a group of more-or-less coherent presuppositions) mean that it is conditional and abstract at the same time. For a mode's explicit character as a mode actually and continuously conflicts with its implicit character as experience, and more crucially, this self-contradiction (and thus conditionality and abstractness) cannot be removed without stamping out the mode itself. As for practice, this suggests that our practical experience produces a specific 'permanent dissatisfaction' in the sense that its explicit feature as the will to alter or maintain 'existence' contradicts its implicit feature of being present experience (*EM*, 304–5). In other words, the will to change or maintain must presuppose the world of 'what is' and the world of 'what ought to be' and in practice they are waiting to be reduced to one, however, the two worlds in question can never be finally reconciled (unless in and through religion as the completion of practical experience) without putting an end to practice itself. Insofar as our practical life, as it were, must be transient and contingent, the satisfactions of countless desires come and go. But there is no final way out of the discrepancy between the two worlds presumed in practice as every practical action is an exercise of the free will, which is a necessary condition of human agency (*EM*, 303–4).

In Oakeshott's mind, then, the human condition is imperfect on the ground that life is full of strivings, desires and dissatisfactions, and yet philosophical reasoning is limited in being able to help work things out for the ordinary man, if it can do anything at all besides confounding the poor chap. Here, it is notable that Oakeshott's understanding of the human condition seems to demonstrate a certain romanticist outlook. As Berlin indicates, there is 'the notion that there are many values, and that they are incompatible; the whole notion of plurality, of inexhaustibility, of the imperfection of all human answers and arrangements; the notion that no single answer which claims to be perfect and true, whether in art or in life, can in principle be perfect or true – all this we owe to the romantics.'[30]

What is more, the imperfection of the human condition by definition echoes Oakeshott's conservative disposition which prefers 'the limited to the unbounded, the near to the distant, the sufficient to the superabundant, the convenient to the perfect.' Yet, one cannot deny that 'to prefer' is not to be self-isolated, to be self-abandoned, but 'to conserve' something proper, 'to act' on some reliable grounds. So, by seeing the human condition from a conservative point of view, Oakeshott is putting forward the second postulate that makes human practice more comprehensible to us, i.e. the view that the human mind must be historically conditioned. In other words, the conservative disposition also leads Oakeshott to grant that we must appreciate the historicity of human action, meaning that human activity involves a tradition of convenient manners, rather than a set of perfect principles.

Now, it has become clearer why Oakeshott should accommodate the expressivist self in *societas*. Given that in practice we are always exercising a free will to act in accordance with a tradition of manners, considerations, observations and customs,

---

[30] Berlin, *The Roots of Romanticism*, 146.

moral engagement is parallel to human language rather than to the application of principle. Accordingly, Oakeshott claims that moral language 'is not the creation of grammarians, it is made by speakers;' that the moral self 'has a 'history', but no 'nature', he is what in conduct he becomes' (*OHC*, 79, 41). In this place, I would like to add that Oakeshott's insistence that every moral discourse is an historic achievement emerging as a ritual of utterances and responses in which agents are colloquially related to one another in the idiom of a familiar moral language resonates with Herder's philosophy of language to a great degree. Once again, it is to Berlin and Taylor's credit that the importance of Herder, one of the pioneers of Romanticism, has been made apparent to the English-speaking world. For the purpose of this paper, nevertheless, it is just adequate for me to reveal three crucial ideas concerning Herder's theory of language, which may help shed light on Oakeshott's moral thinking in respect of its romanticist heritage, namely, expressivism, context-dependence, and pluralism.

First, Herder's theory of language was established on the precondition that a pursuit of philosophical perfection in terms of abstract reason held by the *philosophe* in his times had become harmful for the 'healthy understanding' of human beings.[31] To eliminate this blunder, Herder thus came to terms with the relation of language to humanity. Herder's theory of language, as Berlin puts it, can be well labeled as 'expressionism', because it initiated the romanticist doctrine that 'one of the fundamental functions of human beings was to express, to speak, and therefore that whatever a man did expressed his full nature; and if it did not express his full nature, it was because he maimed himself, or restrained himself, or laid some kind of leash upon his energies.'[32]

Taylor goes even further to argue that before Herder the western philosophy of language was dominated by the instrumental theory or the designative theory appearing in the works of Hobbes, Locke, and Condillac, which claimed that language was a tool to represent the world, as what it is, to us. By way of contrast, Herder's expressivist theory changed all this drastically. Human language, as Herder understood it, was by nature a human activity involving our 'reflection', the ability to conduct one's self-interpretation. On Herder's view, then, when a speaker spoke a language he actually engaged in a conversation by means of which his feelings were expressed, his relationships to others were recognized, and the values he pursued could be better conveyed.[33] To conclude, in the course of rethinking the task of philosophy Herder actually shifted our understanding of the human condition, i.e. the orientation of 'philosophical anthropology',[34] from an epistemic standpoint to an expressivist view. As Herder remarked in his famous

---

[31]   Johann Gottfried von Herder, 'How Philosophy Can Become More Universal and Useful for the Benefit of the People,' in *Philosophical Writings*, trans. and ed. Michael N. Forster (Cambridge: Cambridge Univ. Press, 2003), 3–29.

[32]   Berlin, *The Roots of Romanticism*, 58.

[33]   Charles Taylor, *Human Agency and Language*, part 3, and *Philosophical Arguments*, chaps. 4–6.

[34]   Here, a sentence from Herder's essay 'How Philosophy Can Become More Universal and Useful for the Benefit of the People' is worth quoting: 'Philosophy is reduced to anthropology, modified according to the [different] types of the people' (*Philosophical Writings*, 26 n. 54).

essay, *Treatise on the Origin of Language* (1772),[35] self-expression was inescapable because human beings were at the same time creatures of freely active language-users and creatures of society.[36]

The expressivist self as Oakeshott renders it is, then, as Taylor has called it, a dialogical self, able to perform an utterance, an idiom of certain sorts in the 'conversation of mankind'; that is to say, for Oakeshott to be a participant in human discourse one is likewise required to learn how to use language in a conversational manner rather than argumentatively. 'Conversation' and 'argument' become emblems of distinct philosophical styles, as well as moral characters. Timothy Fuller has, therefore, argued, 'Oakeshott was an individualist, but not an abstract individualist. Individuality is a self-understanding composed in responding to others in a certain tradition of behavior. We understand ourselves to be individuals because we are self-conscious within a context of innumerable self-conscious agents.'[37] Seen from this view, Oakeshott's affirmation of the importance of tradition in our understanding of practical affairs is a position that is closer to that of the post-Herderian classical hermeneutics in the nineteenth century when the writers such as Schleiermacher, Droysen, and Dilthey claimed that 'the awareness of one's own history and of that of mankind as a whole is an indispensable condition for a rich and fulfilled life.'[38] In this respect, the 'expressive conception of man' also seems to have had impacts on other contemporary communitarian thinkers than Taylor. Just like the way in which Taylor dissolves the 'disengaged reason,'[39] Michael Sandel's critique on the 'disencumbered self,'[40] and MacIntyre's repudiation of the 'emotivist self'[41] can all be seen as attempts to revitalize the Herderian expressivist self.

Secondly, it follows from expressivism that human thought must be context-dependent. Herder writes that language is 'a vehicle of human thoughts and the content of all wisdoms and cognitions,' and similarly, 'we cannot think without thoughts, and learn to think through words, … language sets limits and an outline for the whole of human cognition.'[42] It may be not too much of a stretch to claim that Herder's view is similar to Wittgenstein's notion of a language game purporting to maintain that the meanings of language consist in its usages and thus when we use a language we are conducting certain forms of life embedded in the very linguistic context. This, of course, does not mean that Herder belittles human reason; instead, it means only that a significant aspect of Herder's enterprise is to reconcile the sharp contrast between reason and tradition as defined by the Enlightenment thinkers. Human reason, properly understood, is precisely the ability to express

[35] Herder, *Philosophical Writings*, 65–164.
[36] Herder, *Philosophical Writings*, 127, 139.
[37] Timothy Fuller, Introduction to *FS*, 10.
[38] Josef Bleicher, *Contemporary Hermeneutics: Hermeneutics as Method, Philosophy and Critique* (London: Routledge and Kegan Paul, 1980), 9.
[39] See Taylor, *The Sources of the Self*, esp. chap. 8.
[40] See Michael Sandel, *Liberalism and the Limits of Justice*, 2d edition (Cambridge: Cambridge Univ. Press, 1998).
[41] See MacIntyre, *After Virtue: A Study in Moral Theory*, esp. chaps. 2–3.
[42] Herder, *Fragments on Recent German Literature*, in *Philosophical Writings*, 48, 49.

oneself as one wishes by means of language. In some sense, then, Herder's idea of linguistic context goes perfectly with Hegel's *Sittlichkeit*, implying that ethical principles are specific to a certain community, and thus that human reason and freedom can only be completely achieved within a concrete context.

It is no surprise that Oakeshott and contemporary communitarians all intensely share with Herder and Hegel the romanticist view that human thought must be context-dependent; and this is why their thoughts wear the outlook of philosophical conservatism; that is, they happily grant the historicity of human action. However, so far as the notion of the self is concerned, neither Oakeshott nor contemporary communitarians have ever proposed an entire reaction against modern individualism. Quite to the contrary, it is their contention that the expressivist self should take the place of the epistemic self if the value of individuality is to be reconstructed and preserved without stepping into the trap of universal reason; that human agency can be truly performed and well empowered only if we take seriously our own manners of thinking. In summation, I think Terry Nardin is correct in saying that Oakeshott is likely to hold a form of 'hermeneutical scepticism that follows the conclusion that all identifications and therefore all things are context-dependent.'[43]

The third romanticist character of Oakeshott's ethical thinking has to do with pluralism. That Herder's theory of language accommodates the point of pluralism is not difficult to grasp. For, according to Herder, the differences between languages are the differences of their usages, i.e. the differences of cultural forms. Even within a certain cultural form, language always keeps developing over time. In other words, Herder clearly detects the problems of cultural distinction and historical alternation through his study of languages and cultures. And based on this detecting, together with the notions of expressivism and context-dependence, Herder therefore cannot but concede that pluralism has emerged as an historic condition of modern society. In the context of Herder, as it might be expected, pluralism at least embraces two levels of meanings. In one, it presents the cross-cultural differences with which various language speakers are confronted; and it is in this sense of 'cultural pluralism' that Herder sets out to criticize the abstract spirit of *philosophisme* more deeply by finding fault with the European-centric myth embedded in the Enlightenment project.[44] In another, it denotes what may be better called 'value pluralism' which, as I have followed Berlin to remark, means 'that there are many values, and that they are incompatible.' Here, it is pluralism in the second sense that I wish to take into consideration.

---

[43] Nardin, *The Philosophy of Michael Oakeshott*, 29.

[44] Along with his critique of the idea of philosophical perfection predicated on a form of universal reason, Herder notices that the formation of 'modern spirit' has the best to do with the mechanical world-view supported by the advance of modern natural sciences (*This Too a Philosophy of History for the Formation of Humanity*, in *Philosophical Writings*, 315, 318). In other words, Herder believes that the reason why his contemporaries intend to dismiss cultural distinction and historical alteration lies in the fact that 'our century has marked the name *Philosophy!*' (*Philosophical Writings*, 279, cf. 308, 310). Thus, the attack on the 'abstracted spirit' of *philosophisme* also leads Herder to take issues with the European-centric ideology. For instance, Herder writes that: 'In Europe there is supposed now to be more *virtue* than there ever was in the whole world? And why? Because it has more *enlightenment* in it. I believe that just for that reason there must be *less*' (*Philosophical Writings*, 332).

This is mainly because, unlike Berlin and Taylor, Oakeshott rarely goes about the problem of cross-cultural dialogue; it is certain that due to his stricter skepticism Oakeshott is far less optimistic about what Berlin takes for granted – a list of 'basic human rights', or what Taylor refers to as the 'highest human good' in favor of human dignity.[45] Yet it is unquestionable that Oakeshott also regards value pluralism as a distinguishable condition of modernity, and this inference can be attained from several angles of Oakeshott's thought that we have disclosed. For one thing, the phrase *'a societas cum universitate'* acclaimed by Oakeshott can be related to the polarity/synthesis of Enlightenment *cum* the Counter-Enlightenment. Besides, Oakeshott's assertion that ethical life involves moral discourses in which 'permanent dissatisfaction' is unavoidable dismisses at once the idea of *philosophia perennis* that takes human values into a unified system. Additionally, Oakeshott's theory of modality that claims that reasoning appropriate to a mode of understanding should not be applied to any others without being self-deconstructed has prevented the conversation of mankind from being dominated by one voice. In short, what unites Oakeshott's ideas is the 'idea of difference.'[46]

So far, I have indicated how Oakeshott's moral thinking echoes Herder's philosophy of language. And yet, it must be recollected that modern thinkers often have had a more self-conscious awareness of the problem of self-identity. That is, the recent reconstruction of the expressivist self seems to have gone some way to fulfilling this lacuna in Herder's theory of language: If human thought must be context-dependent, if social values must be plural, how could an expressive self identify him- or herself as a self from the multitude of experiences, values and desires in a contingent situation? In other words, do we lose, as some maintain, any idea of the self at all? Is there a discernible 'thing' there at all, or is 'self' itself a fluidity of converging accidents?

In the case of Oakeshott, the answers go to the ideas of self-disclosure and self-enactment. Self-disclosure, as Oakeshott defines it, is 'the intercourse of agents, each concerned with procuring imagined and wished-for satisfactions (which need not be self-gratifications) and seeking them in the response of another or other selves;' whereas self-enactment is 'conduct in respect of the sentiments or motives in which actions are chosen or performed' (*OHC*, 70, 74). Synthetically, it may be said that moral conduct is not only the behavior of agents engaging in transactions with one another in the recognition of the authority of considerations to be subscribed to in choosing satisfactions, it is also the behavior of an agent enacting himself in terms of the motives in which he permits himself to act. So, it is not inappropriate to remark that self-disclosure as it is understood is compatible with that which Sandel calls the 'inter-subjective form of self-understanding,' whereas self-enactment is the 'intra-subjective form of self-understanding.'[47]

---

[45] See, for example, Berlin, *Conversation with Isaiah Berlin*, 37–40; Taylor, *Sources of the Self*, 4, 11, 14; Taylor, *Philosophy and Human Agency*, 232; and Taylor, *Philosophical Arguments*, 35, 53, 56. In an essay titled 'Human Rights: The Legal Culture,' Taylor writes that: 'Every moral system has a conception of what we might call human dignity, ... of the quality which, in man, compels us to treat him with respect, or ... a conception that defines what it is to have respect for human beings.' Quoted in Ruth Abbey, *Charles Taylor* (Princeton: Princeton Univ. Press, 2000), 22.

[46]   Nardin, *Philosophy of Michael Oakeshott*, 230–1.

[47] Sandel, *Liberalism and the Limits of Justice*, 62–3.

At this point, it can be noted that while the idea of self-disclosure with regard to inter-subjective moral relationships restates at large the formal and substantial postulates that we have discussed, it is the idea of self-enactment that proposes a fresh implication to enhance Oakeshott's theory of human agency. Put clearly, because of its inter-subjective character, self-disclosure is 'immersed in contingency, it is interminable and it is liable to frustration, disappointment and defeat' (*OHC*, 73). This is what often happens to a speaker when he expresses himself in a conversation. And yet, in order to escape 'the transience of life by finding eternity in each moment,'[48] Oakeshott now claims that the agent should at the same time have some kind of 'inner deliberation' to accomplish its self-identity, i.e. to enact a self. Thus Oakeshott argues that self-enactment 'is never separable from the deadly engagement of agents disclosing themselves in responding to their contingent situations and achieving their passing satisfactions or suffering their transitory disappointments. And the enacted self is itself a fugitive; not a generic unity but a dramatic identity without benefit of a model of self-perfection' (*OHC*, 84).

John Gray once said that contemporary liberal philosophy 'proceeds as if the Enlightenment project had not failed, or could be salvaged in some restricted form.'[49] And it seems to me that this is partly because it is widely believed that from early modernity, through the Enlightenment to contemporary times, liberalism has always realistically accepted the irresistible tendency of history leading to modernity. In other words, since styles of politics are the product of thought about the conditions of political life, the sweeping victory of liberalism from the nineteenth century onwards is due to the fact that it takes seriously the tremendous change of the modern situation. For example, Mill's principle of neutrality can be understood as a response to the circumstance of modern mass society. Constant's distinction between ancient freedom and modern freedom consists in a response to the scale of modern politics and the possibilities of agency that that generates.[50] It is plain that the idea of human agency that mainstream liberalism generates is based on thoroughly appreciating the principles of justice in the terms that modern epistemology commands human knowledge to be. Modern liberalism, for all its faults, has the strength that comes from being one-sided – it is clear, unambiguous, and without necessitating polemic, facilitates it, by having a side to take.

However, there is a crucial dimension of modernity simply missing in this common sense defense of liberalism and the epistemic self it presumes, the dimension pointing exactly to the difficulty of living in a plural society where the issue of self-identity is at stake. According to Taylor, self-identity is a distinctively modern issue, because the senses of the self have now been achieved from three main aspects of moral engagement exercised in modern history. In addition to Descartes' disengaged reason – 'with its associated ideals of self-responsible

---

[48] Glenn Worthington, *Religious and Poetic Experience in the Thought of Michael Oakeshott* (Exeter: Imprint Academic, 2005), 71.

[49] John Gray, *Liberalism*, 2d ed. (Buckingham: Open Univ. Press, 1995), 86.

[50] Jeremy Waldron, 'Virtue *en Masse*,' in *Debating Democratic Discontent: Essays on American Politics, Law, and Public Philosophy*, ed. Anita L. Allen and Milton C. Regan, Jr. (Oxford: Oxford Univ. Press, 1998), 32–9.

freedom and dignity – of self-exploration, and of personal commitment'[51] which largely influenced the formulation of liberalism from the very beginning, the sources of the modern self are derived equally from the affirmation of ordinary life and the expressive conception of man. The affirmation of ordinary life, provoked by Rationalized Christianity and the various theories of moral sentiments, is introduced by Taylor to 'designate those aspects of human life concerned with production and reproduction, that is, labor, the making of things needed for life, and our life as sexual beings including marriage and the family.' In short, it implies the sense of 'inner depths' which cannot be explained by the epistemic self.[52]

Although with the coming of the radical Enlightenment and the Counter-Enlightenment Western people seem to have sensed themselves to have departed from the orbits, say, of Descartes' metaphysics and Deism, the human goods arising from the affirmation of ordinary life and by expressivism have already penetrated into the making of modern identity. Insofar as familiar examples of life goods include freedom, reason, religious piety, benevolence, authenticity, poetic creation, etc., the limit of abstract liberalism is not that it neglects the plurality of individualistic values, but that it is in full support of the Cartesian disengaged instrumental mode of life incapable of making sense of our moral life by evaluating the life goods with which we are confronted in our everyday life. Liberalism, in other words, turns out to be a theory in the worst sense – a tendentious half-truth that claims to trump all counter evidence arising from the shabby, disheveled experience of being alive and self-aware. It is true that Taylor also welcomes a cluster of liberal/individualist values,[53] but he would surely suggest that the expressivist mode of life is the more suitable answer to the historical conditions of modern society. The reason why modern individuals are frequently lost in moral space, Taylor would agree with Oakeshott at this point, is not because they lack principles, but because they cannot escape from 'the transience of life by finding eternity in each moment;' that is, they are unable to enact a self for themselves.

Conclusion

It seems clear from the above discussion that Oakeshott, Berlin and Taylor, the three important contemporary thinkers, all still have beliefs in modernity and all give us some hints about how to get rid of modern malaises; in a sense, they are all philosophically conservative. None of them attempt to dissolve the idea of the self, or the 'subject', as post-structuralism or post-modernism might like to do; nor are they reluctant to conserve something significant in modern history, that is, the idea of self-expression and the individualistic values related to it.

Nevertheless, as for the historical conditions of modernity, Oakeshott and Berlin are more pessimistic about the inner tension between the Enlightenment and the Counter-Enlightenment than Taylor appears to be; and politically Oakeshott is

---

[51]   Taylor, *Sources of the Self*, 211.
[52]   Taylor, *Sources of the Self*, 211.
[53]   For this part of discussion, see Abbey, *Charles Taylor*, 125–6, 145–6, 148.

allied with Berlin under the idea of rule of law, whereas Taylor would rather like to embrace some kind of republicanism. Even Berlin and Oakeshott have somewhat different attitudes toward pluralism and defend liberal values from quite different philosophical angles. To do justice to the differences between Oakeshott, Berlin and Taylor, I think the attention must be drawn to their diverse notions of philosophy with regard to the modern traditions of conservative thinking.[54] This is the place where the significance of Oakeshott's skepticism will be made clear. But lacking space, I will leave that topic by for another day.

---

[54] As for this issue, it is my contention that the three discernible traditions of conservative thinking that Oakeshott, Berlin and Taylor seem to have adopted in that order are Humean, Herderian, and Hegelian.

10

Leslie Marsh

Ryle and Oakeshott on the 'Knowing-How/Knowing-That' Distinction

The *Social* Nature of Rationality

Politics make a call upon knowledge. Consequently, it is not irrelevant to inquire into the kind of knowledge which is involved.[1]   – Oakeshott

Gilbert Ryle's 'Knowing How/Knowing That' distinction (KH/KT) gave crisp articulation to a long-standing epistemological concern that Michael Oakeshott had: that is, what is the epistemic status of the area that comprises our waking lives, the domain of practical reasoning, of which political practice, on Oakeshott's account, is but one aspect.[2] This concern is set against a much broader purview: that of the nature of rationality, or more accurately the *social* nature of rationality.

Though Ryle's KH/KT distinction has been taken to be primarily an epistemological distinction, it is as much a claim about the operations of the mind. Ryle's *The Concept of Mind*[3] was a work in philosophical psychology; and though Oakeshott could not be considered a philosopher of mind, his work is replete with concerns about the bipartite relationship of mind to world and of the bipartite relationship of theorizing to action. Oakeshott's concern with the KH/KT distinction is coextensive with a concern with 'unconsidered actions,' supposedly 'irrational' conduct; and reflective consciousness, the latter supposedly the spring of rational conduct. On Oakeshott's account the former is not *irrational* (where tradition is the only reliable resource, *its disregard is irrational*); the latter is illusory and hardly *rational*. The contrast is a spurious one; all there ever is, is a

---

[1] Oakeshott, *Rationalism in Politics and other essays, new and expanded edition,* ed. Timothy Fuller (Indianapolis: Liberty Press, 1991), 45. Hereafter: *RIP*.

[2] Ryle's 'Knowing How, Knowing That' essay was first published in the *Proceedings of the Aristotelian Society,* New Series, 45 (1944 – 45): 1–16. The terms 'rationalism' and 'knowledge of' and 'knowledge about' make an appearance some thirty years earlier than the celebrated formulations of *Rationalism in Politics* in Oakeshott, *Experience and Its Modes* (Cambridge: Cambridge Univ. Press, 1933), 23, 25, 53, 318. Hereafter: *EM*. The original essay 'Rationalism in Politics' appeared in the *Cambridge Journal,* 1 (1947–8): 81–98, 145–57.

[3] Gilbert Ryle, *The Concept of Mind* (1949; reprint, Harmondsworth: Penguin, 1990).

socially embedded intelligence – 'intelligibility is contextual' – to use what might be considered an Oakeshottian slogan. This said, Oakeshott does not subscribe to the Marx-Mannheim line (and their intellectual heirs comprising the sociology of knowledge movement) that human conduct can merely be explained as being subject to "false consciousness" or a distortive *mis*cognition.

Oakeshott rejects the prevailing Cartesian orthodoxy across cognitive science, the philosophy of mind, epistemology and metaphysics: an orthodoxy that has systematically overlooked not only the location of thinkers in their physical environments, but has also overlooked the interactions amongst thinkers in the ambient socio-cultural soup:

> You do not first have a mind, which acquires a filling of ideas and then makes a distinction between true and false, right and wrong, reasonable and unreasonable, and then, as a third step, causes activity. Properly speaking the mind has no existence apart from, or in advance of, these distinctions. These and other distinctions are not acquisitions; they are constitutive of the mind. The whole notion of the mind as an apparatus for thinking is I believe an error and it is the error at the root of this particular view of the nature of 'rationality.' (*RIP*, 109–13)

For Oakeshott, a tradition or practice implies the social situatedness of the self and the rejection of focal individualism, the idea that human drives and behavioral characteristics are socially and historically invariant: individuals draw their self-understanding and their conceptions of the good, their 'constitutive' ends, from what is conceptually to hand in historically specific societies or civilizations. Society is in some sense antecedent to the individuals that compose it. Mind does not merely respond to a *given* world; mind is *enacted*[4] through a particularized history of socio-environmental coupling: perception is an *act* of interpretation and the generation of meaning, a self that is embedded and has coherence in a matrix of practices and traditions. Situatedness, for Oakeshott, is captured in the following:

(i) Manners of behavior that are meaningless when separated from their context (*RIP*, 63);

(ii) 'Politics may be said to be the activity of responding to conditions of things *already* recognized to be the product of choices' (*RIP*, 70, italics added);

(iii) 'Human self-understanding is inseparable from learning to participate in what is called a 'culture'' (*VL*, 16–7)[5];

(iv) 'Selves are not rational abstractions, they are historic personalities, they are among the components of [the] world of human achievements' (*VL*, 41).

------

[4] The terms 'enacted' or 'enactive,' coined by Francisco J. Varela, Evan Thompson & Eleanor Rosch, *The Embodied Mind: Cognitive Science and Human Experience* (1991; reprint, Cambridge, MA: MIT Press, 2000), here implies sense-making, embodiment, emergence, and experience. Enacted in this sense is not co-extensive with Oakeshott's term 'self-enactment.' Oakeshott, *On Human Conduct* (Oxford: Clarendon Press, 1990), 70–8, *passim*. Hereafter: *OHC*.

[5] Oakeshott, *The Voice of Liberal Learning*, ed. Timothy Fuller (Indianapolis: Liberty Fund, 2001), 57. Hereafter: *VL*.

Therefore, knowledge and cognition only exists against a background fabric of cultural possibility, a *preexisting*, complex web of linguistic, technological, social, political and institutional constraints – a social ecosystem if you like.[6] There is nothing external to a tradition in terms of which it can be appraised: an artless conduct is 'as impossible as an utterance in no language in particular' (*OHC*, 86; *RIP*, 14). And again 'Volition cannot carry us beyond thought, because there is no beyond' (*EM*, 26). A tradition fixes and applies its own internal criteria, methods, distinctions and standards of cogent argument, its own immanent standard of epistemic weight regarding its methodological, conceptual and empirical problems. Only from within a tradition-based politics can a tradition can be interrogated and applied. In Oakeshott's terminology, it is to 'pursue its intimations' or enter into a 'flow of sympathy' (*RIP*, 57, 59, 60, 61, 129, 131) where there is no 'changeless centre … everything is temporary but nothing is arbitrary' (*RIP*, 61). This means that one is always dealing with a reflective tradition, *not* an inert pattern of habitual behavior:

(i) 'A human art is never fixed and finished; it has to be used and it is continuously modified in use' (*VL*, 13);

(ii) 'A human being is a "history" and he makes this history for himself out of his responses to the vicissitudes he encounters' (*VL*, 9; cf. *VL*, 63, passim);

(iii) 'Practices are not stable compositions' (*OHC*, 100).

Later in *On Human Conduct* Oakeshott talks of a 'practice' not as the outcome of a performance (*OHC*, 56) but as emerging and continuously invented: 'an instrument to be played upon, not a tune to be played' (*OHC*, 58; cf. *OHC*, 91). In language reminiscent of *Rationalism in Politics* he writes: An agent's understanding of a practice he or she is engaged in, 'is not that of knowing the rules but of knowing how to speak it … ' (*OHC*, 91; and cf. *OHC*, 26, where the theorist's understanding is contrasted with the agent's).

Tradition (or culture) is of such complexity, a complexity generated by infinitely fine-grained constantly shifting local and ephemeral variables, that as a guide to action, social knowledge (KH) cannot be reduced, abridged, or restated propositionally (KT) without remainder. Oakeshott's conception of the KH/KT distinction manifests itself in two ways, the former I believe, morphed into the latter:

(i) *Modality*: Oakeshott's idea that science, history, practice and aesthetics are domains constitutive of their own criteria of objectivity and standards appropriate to their own subject matter. Any attempt at cross- or trans-modal thinking is bound to be a corrupting exercise.

---

[6]   Elsewhere I have examined the relativistic implications of Oakeshott's social constructivism. See Leslie Marsh, 'Constructivism and Relativism in Oakeshott,' in *The Intellectual Legacy of Michael Oakeshott*, ed. Corey Abel and Timothy Fuller (Exeter: Imprint Academic, 2005), 238–62.

(ii) *Political skepticism*: the idea that politics has no intrinsic purpose or end; liberal society should properly be conceived as a civil association not an enterprise association. Social complexity will always defeat the calculation of efficient means ('scientific' politics) to clearly conceived, large-scale political ends. Aims are only incompletely accomplished and unforeseen side-effects always cause results to be markedly different from intentions.[7]

KH and KT: Three Permutations

I will return to Oakeshott in the next section with a critical evaluation of his deployment of the KH/KT distinction once I have presented the standard lines of argument for and against the KH/KT distinction. There has been a resurgence of interest in the KH/KT distinction[8]: for the purposes at hand I can only examine the broad outlines of KH/KT.

KH and KT Are Sui Generis: Ryle

Ryle expounds what he takes to be the implications of the Cartesian project: I reconstruct Ryle's critique as follows:

(i) Ryle rejects the idea that it seems that all intelligent performance involves 'conscious' thought, which typically involves the observance of rules, the consideration of propositions and the application of criteria. Were this the case, to do something would always be to do two things – to first *think* about rules, propositions and criteria, and *then* to put into practice what they enjoin.

---

[7]   This is not an argument against all attempts at social change or improvement. For a Burkean, change is inevitable and desirable. As Burke said in *Reflections on the Revolution in France*, 'a state without the means of some change is a state without the means of its conservation.' I am loath to use the term 'conservative' as it is a term that carries too many often incompatible connotations in Anglo-American philosophy (let alone in the public mind): there are self-avowed conservatives who are rationalists; the corollary is that not all anti-rationalists can be classed as conservative.

[8]   Ian Rumfitt, 'Savoir Faire,' *Journal of Philosophy*, 100, no. 3 (2003): 158-66; Maxwell R. Bennett and Peter Michael Stephan Hacker, *Philosophical Foundations of Neuroscience* (Oxford: Blackwell, 2003); Paul Snowdon, 'Knowing How and Knowing That: A Distinction Reconsidered,' *Proceedings of the Aristotelian Society*, 104, no. 1 (2004): 1–29; Tobias Rosefeldt, 'Is Knowing-How Simply a Case of Knowing-That?' *Philosophical Investigations*, 27, no. 4 (2004): 370–9; John Quay, 'Knowing How and Knowing That: A Tale of Two Ontologies,' in Andrew Brookes, ed. *Conference Papers of the International Outdoor Education Research Conference: Connections and Disconnections* (Bendigo: Latrobe University, 2004), at http://www.latrobe.edu.au/oent/OE_conference_2004/papers/quay.pdf; John Williams, 'Know-How,' *SMU Humanities & Social Sciences Working Papers Series*, Paper No. 4 (2004); Paul Duguid, 'The Art of Knowing: Social and Tacit Dimensions of Knowledge and the Limits of the Community of Practice,' *The Information Society*, 21, no. 2 (2005): 109–18; Jonathan Schaffer, 'Knowing the Answer,' *Philosophy and Phenomenological Research*, 75, no. 2 (2007): 383–403; Peter Markie, 'Knowing How Is Not Knowing That,' *Southwestern Philosophical Review*, 22, no.1 (2006): 17–24; Charles Wallis, 'Consciousness, Context, and Know-How,' *Synthese*, 160 (2008): 123–53; Wallis, 'The Proper Role of Know-How in Epistemology,' (unpublished MS); John N. Williams, 'Propositional Knowledge And Know-How,' *Synthese*, 165 (2008): 107–25; John Bengson, Marc A. Moffett & Jennifer C. Wright, 'The Folk On Knowing How,' *Philosophical Studies*, 142 (2009): 387–401.

(ii) This gives the impression that the mind is a storehouse of representations – the 'intellectualist legend.'[9]

(iii) The combination of the assumptions that theorizing is the pre-eminent activity of minds and that it is a private operation,[10] amounts to the postulation of a shadowy additional metaphysical entity – the dogma of the 'ghost in the machine.'[11]

(iv) This has the further consequence in that it requires the positing of a 'central theatre,'[12] some central place in the brain where something like an 'I' or the self[13] attends to and witnesses consciousness.

(v) The positing of some central authority or homunculus gives rise to 'Ryle's regress': an observing self must necessarily contain another observing self, and so on *ad infinitum*.[14]

(vi) Tempted by our language, a folk anatomy posits the mind as an object made of an immaterial substance (because predications of substance are not meaningful for a collection of dispositions). Thus Descartes allocates concepts to logical types to which they do not belong – hence the 'category mistake.'[15]

Ryle's corrective is summarized as follows:

(i) Ascription of intelligence *is to describe behavior*, not to name an entity.

(ii) Intelligent conduct of serial operations does not entail that the agent is throughout the progress of the operation conscious both with what he has completed and with what remains to do. The careful driver does not plan for all possible contingencies. His readiness to cope would reveal itself were an emergency to arise but it is latently there even when nothing critical is happening.[16]

(iii) Misunderstanding is a by-product of KH – *mistakes are exercises of competences.*

KH As A Species of KT

Stanley and Williamson have led recent discussion of the KH/KT discussion.[17]

---

[9]   Ryle, *Concept*, 31.
[10] Ryle, *Concept*, 28.
[11] Ryle, *Concept*, 55. Though not named, Ryle is clearly alluding to Collingwood as a proponent of this error.
[12] Ryle, *Concept*, 149, 152–3, 211.
[13] Ryle, *Concept*, 178–88.
[14] Ryle, *Concept*, 31–2, 156, 157.
[15] Ryle, *Concept*, 49.
[16] Ryle, *Concept*, 47.
[17] Jason Stanley and Timothy Williamson, 'Knowing How,' *The Journal of Philosophy*, 98, no. 7 (2001): 411–44. Their ostensibly reductive position has a progenitor in Donald. G. Brown 'Knowing How and Knowing That, What,' in Ryle: *A Collection of Critical Essays*, eds. Oscar

Stanley and Williamson deny that they are offering a reductive analysis: 'To ascribe knowledge-how to a person is to ascribe to her knowledge of a proposition, where the proposition in question contains a way of doing something. It is simply irrelevant whether the modes of presentation of these propositions can be reductively analyzed in terms that do not invoke knowledge-how.' On a standard approach to reducibility, a KH statement ('KH1') is reducible to a KT statement ('KT1') if and only if (if) KH1 can be translated into KT1 in such a way that the translation preserves truth-value, predicate-structure and theoremhood. Whether or not Stanley and Williamson accept in full the above characterization of reduction in the case of KH statements, it is clear that they operate with notions of predicate structure and translation. In the first place, what could a 'reductivist analysis' be if it did not involve a type of reformulation or translation? Secondly, only within a predicate structure can 'terms' (predicates) be invoked. To preserve predicate structure is not necessarily to preserve specific predicates. Stanley and Williamson's claim is that it is 'simply irrelevant' to a reductivist analysis of know-how whether 'know how' and its variants and derivatives are eliminated from the translation. Irrelevant, that is, to whether we can ascribe to an agent the knowledge of a proposition, 'where the proposition in question contains a way of doing something.' So 'know how' and its variants and derivatives need not be eliminated.

'Proposition' needs elucidation here. A proposition may be (a) that which is capable of being true or false, (b) the linguistic meaning of a sentence, (c) the content of what is said, or (d) the content of a certain psychological state.[18] Stanley and Williamson appear to have at least (d) in mind: for KH the relevant psychological state includes a complex set of dispositions.

The response to the concern that on a [Quinean] theory one proposition would have the same sense as another because they have identical truth conditions, I think needs amendment.[19] Quine rejects the notion of sense or meaning in his purely extensional theory of reference. (I do not find this theory plausible but that is another matter.) Quine operates not with senses or meanings but with truth-values: If 'KH1' and 'KT1' have the same truth-value such that whenever one is replaced in a sentence, X, the truth-value of X is not altered by the substitution, then 'KH1' and 'KT1' are logically equivalent. 'KH1' and 'KT1' are intersubstitutable *salva veritate* in Quine's Leibnizian phrase. (Quine offers ways of expanding this account to cover singular terms and predicates.)

The question, I suppose, is whether we can get by with just logical equivalence. Quine recognizes the widespread occurrence of intensional (i.e. non-extensional) sentences in ordinary language. 'X heated Y' and 'Energy was transferred from X to Y as a result of a difference in temperature' are not exceptionlessly intersubstitutable *salva veritate*. This is paradigmatically so in the case of propositional attitudes. 'Mary

---

Wood and George Pitcher (New York: Anchor Books, 1970), 213–48.

[18] Pascal Engel, *La Norme du vrai, philosophie de la logique* (Paris: Gallimard, 1989), revised English translation Pascal Engel and Miriam Kochan, *The Norm of Truth, An Introduction to the Philosophy of Logic* (Toronto: Univ. of Toronto Press, 1991), 15–6.

[19] Thanks to Joel Parthemore and Corey Abel for pressing me on this issue and to Geoff Thomas for an ongoing discussion.

believes that X heated Y' may be true while it is just false that 'Mary believes that energy was transferred from X to Y as a result of a difference in temperature' if Mary has no idea of the relation of heat to energy. The epistemological states reported by the two sentences are quite different since Mary could not even in principle self-attribute the second sentence in any list of her propositional attitudes.

Quine's response is very roughly that this kind of extensional failure simply reflects the inadequacy of a non-naturalized epistemology, an epistemology continuous with natural science. Mary's propositional attitude is plainly non-naturalized in this respect. But if extensional failure occurs, how are we to characterize it positively? Whatever Mary's epistemological shortcomings from a Quinean perspective, there is presumably something that she believes of which a purely extensional theory of reference does not offer a satisfactory account. A different way of handling Mary's propositional attitude is by appeal to concepts: Mary has a concept of heat and a concept of heating. Mary's concepts of heat and heating are different from those of current physics. She uses 'heat' and 'heating' in different 'senses' – which embody different concepts – from those of physics, as the claim would standardly be expressed.

A complication here is introduced by the Fregean dispute over psychologism. Frege is adamant that sense ('Sinn') is not merely mental or psychologically individual: senses are 'public property'.[20] Frege is right in this matter but for our purposes the need to recognize 'sense', however precisely construed, in addition to extension is the main point. There is place and use for both theories of reference. That is to say that the two sentences in our example, 'Mary believes that X heated Y' and 'Mary believes that energy was transferred from X to Y as a result of a difference in temperature', are logically equivalent extensionally but not intensionally. Both vocabularies are necessary, depending on context.

Noë points out that 'Stanley and Williamson do not question that if you do something, then you can do it; what they deny is that if you do something, you *know how* to do it.' Noë further points out that Stanley and Williamson 'think that the scope of such non-intellectual abilities is much more limited than has been thought.'[21] Their target is Ryle's identification of KH with the possession of abilities. Stanley and Williamson think it is just not the case that to *know how* to do something is to have an ability: to have KH is, on their account, to have a certain kind of intellectual, propositional knowledge. Their aim is to criticize the idea that there is a 'fundamental distinction' between KH and KT. My considered view is that Stanley and Williamson are *not* reductionists: they do not reduce KH to KT. Rather, they analyze KH in such a way that it falls within KT. They alter KH's class-inclusion; it is not a distinct class of knowledge but comes within KT. Their exercise is one of reclassification. This is what allows them to say that their analysis does not require them to translate KH claims and ascriptions into different, non-KH-referring terms.

---

[20] Hilary Putnam, 'The Meaning of 'Meaning',' in *Mind, Language and Reality* (Cambridge: Cambridge Univ. Press, 1975), 218.

[21] Alva Noë, 'Against Intellectualism,' *Analysis*, 65, no. 4 (2005): 279.

The Agnostic View

Katherine Hawley's position might be termed an agnostic position; one should not prejudge whether one form of knowledge is a sub-type of the other.[22] Even though they share structural features it remains open whether or not these structures are realized in different ways.

Hawley presents an account of KH in light of the standard epistemological condition for knowledge – justified true belief. Hawley's concern is that just as the justified true belief view was shown to be inadequate,[23] that even KT should not be accidentally true, so too should KH be understood in terms of successful action. Hawley makes the good, if somewhat obvious point, that the *sine qua non* of KH is practicality, about 'how to do stuff,' so some notion of success must be factored into KH. Of course success cannot amount to KH unless intentional action is involved. But success is not a necessary condition for KH since in many instances we know how to do things that we have never actually attempted. Even skills that are honed through a great deal of experience are liable to failure – Hawley's example of the expert baker who from time to time will produce duds. So KH just like KT requires warrant as well as success. As Hawley says: 'It is common in human affairs to define competence in terms of competent performers: to be a competent performer is to succeed under circumstances under which a competent performer would succeed.'

Hawley suggests that there is no unique task or range of tasks that is always invoked when we ask, for example, whether someone knows how to drive. Rather, different tasks are salient in different conversational contexts. It seems clear that context does play some such role as in the case of manual and automatic driving in the U.K. and in the U.S. Second, we often rely on a (perhaps inarticulable) default notion of 'normal' or 'ordinary' circumstances. Failure to perform in abnormal circumstances for that task doesn't usually count against someone's possessing KH. Recall Ryle's idea that *mistakes are exercises of competences*. Third, the default presumption that normal circumstances are in question may be overridden: actual, present circumstances may be more salient, or unusual circumstances may be explicitly invoked, as when someone claims to know how to find her way home blindfolded. It is possible to know how to perform one of the tasks in a family, without knowing how to perform other tasks in that family.

Oakeshott on KH/KT: A Critique

Oakeshott's brief but sympathetic review[24] of *The Concept of Mind* endorses Ryle's

---

[22] Katherine Hawley, 'Success and Knowledge-How,' *American Philosophical Quarterly*, 40, no. 1 (2003): 19–31.

[23] Edmund L. Gettier, 'Is Justified True Belief Knowledge?' *Analysis*, 23, no. 5 (1963): 121–3.

[24] Oakeshott, 'Body and Mind,' in *Spectator*, 184, 6th January (1950): 20–2. *Prima facie*, Ryle and Oakeshott are unlikely philosophical bedfellows. The former was the ultimate ('analytical') philosophical insider (Waynflete Professor of Metaphysical Philosophy at Oxford and editor of *Mind*); the latter an historian, never holding a position in a philosophy department. Yet despite these differences, they are kindred spirits. Stylistically they both wrote with an accessible and elegant non-technical style, laced with wit and erudition, with minimal references and addressing current issues obliquely. Philosophically, both were positively anti-systematic and

overall critique of the Cartesian legacy. In particular it supports Ryle's assault on sense datum theory, not surprisingly since this theory was Oakeshott's target in chapter 2 of *Experience and Its Modes*. What is odd is that, given the crucial similarity of Ryle's KH/KT distinction to Oakeshott's own account of the relation of practical to theoretical knowledge in the essays of *Rationalism in Politics*, Oakeshott makes no mention of Ryle's distinction in the review or indeed even in *Rationalism in Politics*.[25] In any event, let us begin with a schematic reconstruction of Oakeshott's attack on the Cartesian myth, noting the many places where he identifies key features of that myth. Oakeshott's criticisms include, among much else, these 'Rylean' points:

(i) the 'unencumbered intellect' as something that posits (*RIP*, 11, 111, 120)

(ii) the mind as *tabula rasa* (*VL*, 57)

(iii) the mind conceived as an engine, an independent instrument (*RIP*, 106, 109–13)

(iv) the idea of the mind or intelligence as the cause of bodily activities ... giving rise to the notion of Reason hypostatized, an attenuated rationality (*RIP*, 105, 113)

And, like Ryle, he affirms that:

(v) a man's mind cannot be separated from its contents and its activities (*RIP*, 14, 106,)[26]

---

deflationist in that they sought to dissolve what they saw as metaphysical portentousness. Both had an appreciation of Heidegger; unlikely as it sounds, Ryle's critical notice warmly welcomed *Sein und Zeit*, in *Mind*, 38, no. 151 (1929): 355–70. Perhaps their greatest bond was that they shared that most belligerent of critics – Ernest Gellner. Ryle in passing over reviewing Gellner's *Words and Things* in *Mind* sparked a *cause célèbre*, beautifully documented in Ved Mehta's *Fly and the Fly-Bottle* (Middlesex: Pelican, 1963). Gellner characterized so-called 'ordinary language' philosophy as being inherently socially conservative, and given his predilection for ideas with practical application, he was profoundly at odds with Oakeshott's unworldly 'neo-Burkean romanticism.'

[25] It must be remembered that though *The Concept of Mind* appeared two years after Oakeshott's 'Rationalism in Politics' Ryle's KH/KT distinction predated Oakeshott by eleven years (see notes 3 & 4). According to Robert Grant, Oakeshott only ever communicated with two 'official' philosophers, one of which was Ryle: See Grant, *Oakeshott* (London: Claridge Press, 1990), 14; and Grant, *The Politics of Sex and Other Essays* (Basingstoke: MacMillan, 2000), 26. Oakeshott warmly introduced Ryle, who delivered the annual London School of Economics (LSE) August Comte Memorial Lecture on 26 April, 1962 entitled *A Rational Animal* (Oakeshott, London School of Economics and Political Science, box 1/3 untitled 1953–1975c, undated). John D. Mabbott who read the proofs for *On Human Conduct* had, years earlier, been the first to recognize Oakeshott's KH/KT connection with Ryle in his review of *Rationalism in Politics*, in *Mind*, 72, no. 288 (1963): 609–11. Mabbott crossed paths not just with Oakeshott but with Ryle, as a member of Ryle's 'Wee Teas,' philosophical tea parties. See Oscar Wood and George Pitcher, eds., *Ryle: A Collection of Critical Essays* (New York: Anchor Books, 1970), 6.

[26] Though Oakeshott does not offer an extended discussion of 'mind' as 'embodied' and would have treated contemporary neurosciences' contributions to understanding human conduct with cautious interest, he does endorse a non-Cartesian approach that has now become an influential force in philosophical neuroscience. See Oakeshott, *Lectures in the History of Political Thought*, eds. Terry Nardin and Luke O'Sullivan (Exeter: Imprint Academic, 2006), 42. Hereafter: *LHPT*. This is consistent with his understanding of conduct in his essay titled 'Rational Conduct'

(vi) to learn KT entails extant knowledge and understanding (*RIP*, 17); the corollary being that extant knowledge cannot be merely deleted

The cumulative upshot of (i)–(vi) is that:

(vii) KT cannot be self-complete (*RIP*, 17)

Just as Ryle held that KH does not involve two operations of mind (or in Oakeshott's words 'dualism of technique and practice') so too does Oakeshott: The artist 'writes only about the technique of his art … not because he is ignorant of what may be called the aesthetical element, or thinks it unimportant, but because what he has to say about *that* he has *said already*' in the work of art (*RIP*, 14, the last italics added).

Elsewhere Oakeshott makes the same point by invoking the example of the cyclist (*VL*, 48). This notion is later expanded by Oakeshott from an ability to the much broader notion of conduct: 'Understanding exercised by an agent in conduct is not itself a theoretical understanding of conduct' (*OHC*, 89). That is to say, practical understanding is exhibited in the performance of actions, not in the formulation of theorems. Just as Oakeshott writes of the will as 'intelligence in doing' (*OHC*, 39, and *passim*) he conceived doing as itself a kind of understanding; an exhibition of the agent's awareness of the world, and not something causally (or otherwise) related to such an understanding.

Having identified reflective consciousness as a postulate of conduct, Oakeshott is concerned that he will be tarnished with the intellectualist brush (*OHC*, 88–9)[27]: this because he draws the distinction between reflective consciousness and 'goings-on.' For Ryle the 'intellectualist legend'[28] amounts to Cartesian computationalism; the idea being that mind is merely a storehouse of representations that are processed in anticipation of thinking or acting intelligently. Oakeshott too rejects the notion of mind as a storehouse or repository of knowledge: 'What we are aware of is not a number of items of knowledge available for use, but having powers of specific kinds' (*VL*, 45). Ryle criticizes the 'storehouse' view as mere applications of considered truths,[29] echoed in Oakeshott as mere knowledge of technique.

For Oakeshott both KT and KH are *always* involved in any actual activity (KH is found across other modes, namely science[30]); the two sorts are distinguishable but *inseparable* (*RIP*, 12). KT is most akin to what Oakeshott calls 'technical', KH to 'practical'. The former can be formulated in rules; the latter, by contrast, exists only

---

where he describes all conduct, including the practice of scientific enquiry, as 'activities of *desiring*' (*RIP*, 124–30, italics added) which one might term, to use recent terminology, 'situated' knowledge and cognition.

[27]   Corey Abel has pointed out that Oakeshott anticipates this concern in his earlier work; cf. *EM*, 37, where he also denies his view suffers from 'intellectualism.'

[28]   Ryle, *Concept*, 31.

[29]   Ryle, *Concept*, 27.

[30]   Oakeshott cites Polanyi on this topic, *RIP*, 13. William T. Scott, 'Tacit Knowing and the Concept of Mind,' *Philosophical Quarterly*, 21, no. 82 (1971): 22–35, makes the connection between Ryle and Polanyi.

in use, is not reflective and cannot be formulated in rules. Furthermore, there is *no* knowledge that is not KH (*RIP*, 13–4).

These excerpts I take to be Oakeshott's definitive statement on the matter despite his implying an epistemic gap between KH and KT in 1965:

> A rule like proposition … is often called a 'principle' … advanced in order to explain what is going on in any performance; they supply what may be called its 'underlying rationale.' And consequently, as I understand them, they are never components of the knowledge which constitutes the performance. They belong to a separate performance of their own – the performance of explaining a performance (*VL*, 47–51; cf. *OHC*, 89).

It is perhaps because of this ambiguity that some mistake Oakeshott to be arguing, via the KH/KT distinction, for the primacy of practice (KH). Again, the following seems to be suggesting the primacy of KH:

> Doing *anything* depends upon and exhibits knowing *how* to do it; and though part (but never the whole) of knowing how to do it can subsequently be reduced to knowledge in the form of propositions (and possibly to ends, rules and principles), these propositions are neither the spring of the activity nor are they in any direct sense regulative of the activity (*RIP*, 110).

There is, nonetheless, ample textual support that Oakeshott did not subscribe to the primacy of KH, notably in his rejection of Pragmatism (*EM*, 318, 247, 248; chapter 5). In support of the canonical formulation, that KH and KT are *sui generis*, Oakeshott writes:

> Nowhere, and pre-eminently not in political activity, can technical knowledge be separated from practical knowledge, and nowhere can they be considered identical with one another or able to take the place of one another (*RIP*, 14).[31]

Will the Real Rationalist Please Stand Up?

Though there is nothing unsound in the logic of Oakeshott's anti-Cartesian argument, Oakeshott infers a great deal more than his argument admits: I am of the view that Oakeshott has underplayed certain key elements of Ryle's critique of Cartesianism and overplayed the secondary issues.

Oakeshott thinks that Descartes' incorrigibility (infallibility) is the key flaw in the Cartesian system and that had Descartes placed more emphasis on his skepticism, the problem of incorrigibility could be ameliorated. Oakeshott hones in on Cartesian incorrigibility via three inextricable aspects of what he calls Rationalism:

   (i) 'Never to take anything for true without my knowing it to be such, that is, carefully to avoid haste, thus securing some solid ground which is entirely within my purview … as a man who walks alone and in darkness' (*RIP*, 21)[32];

---

[31] Cf. *VL*, 53: 'Information and judgment can both be communicated and acquired, but not separately.'

[32] *Discours de la Méthode, II* : 'de ne reçevoir jamais aucune chose pour vraie que je ne la connusse

(ii) The rules for their application are mechanical and universal;

(iii) Knowledge does not admit of grades – it is an all or nothing deal.

I cannot see that had Descartes placed more emphasis on his skepticism, the problem of incorrigibility could be ameliorated. For Descartes, skepticism is inextricably linked to the notion of incorrigibility. On the contrary, Descartes' systematic skepticism generates the greatest modern philosophical puzzle of all, dualism. Oakeshott himself concedes that the hypostatization of Reason derives from the Cartesian 'supposition that a man's mind can be separated from its contents and its activities' (*RIP*, 105–6).

Though the progenitors of a Rationalistic style of thinking were, for Oakeshott, Bacon and Descartes, he does not wish to lay our predicament solely at their door: 'Descartes never became a Cartesian' (*RIP*, 19–22, 34).[33] Rationalism, on Oakeshott's account, is the bastardized offspring[34] of an exaggerated Baconian optimism and a neglected Cartesian skepticism.

Oakeshott overlooks a critical difference in methodology between Descartes and Bacon. Descartes began with intuitive principles – 'clear and distinct' ideas of which the *Cogito* was a star example. These principles operated as premises in a standard deductive method of reasoning; the movement of inference was downwards from axiomatic premises to a logically guaranteed conclusion. Bacon on the other hand, began with empirical observations – data of observation – that were used inductively to adduce higher axioms; the movement of inference was upwards from data of observation to tentative generalizations. Taken *together* Descartes and Bacon set the ground for the modern scientific method. Now it cannot be that Oakeshott rejects this notion of scientific method. Oakeshott says as much:

> The influence of the genuine natural scientist is not necessarily on the side of Rationalism … they are mistaken when they think the rationalist and the scientific points of view coincide (*RIP*, 34–5, 52).

What Oakeshott has to be rejecting is the perpetrator of *scientism*, if by scientism we mean a dilettantish engagement with science and/or its misapplication. This clearly pulls apart the mistaken view that as an anti-naturalist, Oakeshott is committed to the rejection of scientific method *per se*, which of course is nonsense since Oakeshott

---

évidemment être telle, c'est-à-dire d'éviter soigneusement la précipitation et la prévention, de bâtir dans un fonds qui est tout à moi … comme un homme qui marche seul et dans les ténèbres.'

[33] Ryle too, was restrained. Insofar as dualism was concerned 'No-one could think that Descartes invented this mistake. The point was that he put nice firm edges and labels onto it so that it was, a doctrine or dogma …' Ryle in conversation with Bryan Magee in *Modern British Philosophy* (Oxford: Oxford Univ. Press, 1986), 140.

[34] Cf. Ryle: 'Whether this Faculty of Practical Reason is to be thought of as the brother-officer of Theoretical Reason or its sergeant major is a question … ' in *A Rational Animal* (London: The Athlone Press, 1962), 6. This is the published version of Ryle's LSE lecture that Oakeshott introduced.

sought to preserve the integrity of science as a form of experience.[35]

Oakeshott's KH/KT distinction in *Rationalism in Politics* was intended to highlight what he saw as an unsustainable *a priorism* as the only guide to action. But later in *On Human Conduct*, Oakeshott seems to be cautioning the reader that *a posteriori* propositions are also to be avoided since they also fall into the realm of the calculated or reflected upon, again removed from the unreflective conditions of conduct (*OHC*, 89). If this is right, then who can escape being labeled a rationalist? Is the rationalist to be identified with *a priori* propositions and/or *a posteriori* propositions?

What perhaps links the two views – the two rejections – is that Oakeshott is operating with a highly specialized notion of KH. This is an empirical notion; KH is *practically* acquired. So it is not *a priori*: nobody knows *a priori* how to run a country, to interpret a tradition, or to write a novel. Equally KH yields only rules of thumb, prescriptions that hold good only for the most part. I know how to bake a cake or ride a bicycle; but, in instructing someone else in how to do it, I could produce general guidelines but not exceptionless rules. The 'incomparable Mr. Newton' could probably have given useful tips to a beginning scientist, but nothing like an elaborate and comprehensive methodology. There is a contrast with Descartes in both cases.

(i) Descartes believes in the existence of *a priori* knowledge on the basis of innate ideas;

(ii) Descartes does not settle for mere rules of thumb drawn out *a posteriori*. As a result of his own (undoubtedly brilliant) mathematical and scientific discoveries, he delivers his *Regulae* – Rules for the Direction of the Mind. We need not settle for rules of thumb, for considerations that are generally to be taken into account, or anything so vague and imprecise. The *Regulae* are a handbook for scientific discovery adduced *a posteriori* from Descartes' reflective experience as a scientist. Descartes can deliver precise and reliable KH, *a posteriori* knowledge delivered in the form of step-by-step, exceptionless and comprehensive rules (cf. Oakeshott's 'rule specification') in dealing with any analytical or experimental problem. That is the concept of the *Regulae*.

One can surely reject either or both views – *a priori* innate ideas and *a posteriori* cast-iron methodological rules – and hence keep clear of entanglement in rationalism. In the current context, one would just have to avoid these extreme Cartesian views. These views represent the kind of rationalism Oakeshott has in mind: that

---

[35] Oakeshott's treatment of science in part 2 of *Experience and Its Modes* denies that there is an absolute distinction between, for example, observation and experiment (among many other things). Also, he explicitly denies scientific knowledge is adequately defined as 'inductive' knowledge (*EM*, 185–6, 202–6); what he sees instead is a world of mathematical (statistical) generalities. For more on Oakeshott and science see Byron Kaldis' 'Oakeshott on Science as a Mode of Experience' and Corey Abel's 'Oakeshottian Modes at the Crossroads of the Evolution Debates,' both to be found in *Zygon: Journal of Science and Religion*, 44, no. 1 (2009): 169–96 & 197–222.

is, KT is sufficient for KH. This is, as I have already indicated, and as Oakeshott knew, a caricature of Cartesian rationalism. It might not appear too far removed from the Plato of the *Republic*, however, for whom acquaintance with the Forms automatically produces efficiency of relevant action. But then, acquaintance with the Forms is not a type of KT.

Ryle and Oakeshott: A Discontinuity

Many take Oakeshott's *ignoratio elenchi* to be roughly coextensive with Ryle's 'category mistake.'[36] The term, *ignoratio elenchi*, derived through Latin from a fallacy identified in Aristotle's *On Sophistical Refutations*, but Oakeshott employs it specifically in the context of his doctrine of modality.[37] Any cross- or trans-modal thinking is that most fatal of all errors – irrelevance or *ignoratio elenchi* (*EM*, 5). This theme of irrelevance later morphs into the KH/KT distinction, which as we have seen takes the view that KH should not be subservient or reducible to KT. Ryle's idea of a 'category mistake', also derives from Aristotle, this time from the *Categories*. The key idea is that all objects are classifiable into categories – e.g. substance or thing, time, place, and position. It is a category mistake if an object in one category is described in terms applicable only to another category. For example, we can ask of a substance how much it weighs, but to ask this about time would be absurd: a category mistake. Rylean category mistakes assume a fairly commonsense, uncontroversial ontology. In the *Concept of Mind* Ryle argues that dualism – the distinction or separation of mind and body – involves a category mistake or set of such mistakes. Though Oakeshott endorses Ryle's anti-dualist critique, his deployment of the notion of an '*ignoratio elenchi*' diverges somewhat from Ryle's use of 'category mistakes.'

Ignoratio elenchi, like 'category mistake,' is a logical rather than an epistemological term. It refers to any process of argument that fails to establish its relevant conclusion; or any counter-argument that fails to establish the negation of the proposition attacked. Ignorance would often lie behind these failures, of course, which brings in epistemology through the backdoor. Now we can note two points. First, a 'category mistake' need not involve any process of argument. A single proposition ('Green quadrilaterals dream furiously,' which contains a number of such mistakes) can exemplify a category mistake. Secondly, Oakeshott's application of the term *ignoratio elenchi* is contestable, not in the sense that he understands anything different by the term from Aristotle, but in the sense that it is only because he holds particular views that he regards certain arguments as failing to establish a relevant conclusion. For example: 'The state is a human artifact ... the proper goal of state action is to promote equality of distribution.' Because he understands the nature of politics in a particular way, Oakeshott regards any view about the

---

[36]   Terry Nardin, *The Philosophy of Oakeshott* (Univ. Park: Penn State Press, 2001), 42; Roy Tseng, *The Sceptical Idealist* (Exeter: Imprint Academic, 2003), 112; Kenneth B. McIntyre, *The Limits of Political Theory* (Exeter: Imprint Academic, 2004), 55; Suvi Soininen, *From A 'Necessary Evil' to the Art of Contingency* (Exeter: Imprint Academic, 2005), 36; Robert Grant, *Oakeshott* (London: Claridge Press, 1990), 41.

[37]   Ryle, *Concept*, 17–8.

promotion of a social ideal as misplaced in political argument. So an argument which concludes that the state should promote equality of distribution involves a misunderstanding of the nature of politics in civil association (according to Oakeshott), and such a conclusion *would always be an irrelevant answer to the question of what the state as* civitas *should do.* But of course it is a matter of opinion and dispute whether Oakeshott is right about the nature of politics, and hence whether the conclusion that the state should promote a social ideal really would involve *ignoratio elenchi.*[38] Rylean 'category mistakes' do not presuppose a distinctively unusual – modal – view of the world and experience of the kind we encounter in Oakeshott.

It should be noted that Oakeshott does not use the idea of *ignoratio elenchi* with technical precision. I take *ignoratio elenchi* to be the mistake of proving a conclusion other than the one we are required to prove. So in historical explanation for example, to try to show that one event caused another would be a case of *ignoratio elenchi* because the concept of cause is irrelevant to historical explanation (on Oakeshott's view). In this sense a single proposition, 'Russia's defeat in the Crimean War caused the emancipation from serfdom in 1861' would be an example of *ignoratio elenchi* to the extent that, regardless of any specific debate, this is not the kind of conclusion any historian could be required to prove. From Oakeshott's viewpoint it would also be a Rylean category mistake because causation is logically impossible between 'historical' events in Oakeshott's sense of the term.

In the context of a specific debate, one might hold that a single proposition could not constitute *ignoratio elenchi* because one would also need a question that one is required to answer but does not answer. In my wider sense a single proposition could constitute *ignoratio elenchi* if it offers a kind of answer that is irrelevant to the kind of inquiry one is engaged in. This seems pretty close to Oakeshott's *'confusion des genres.'* Even there, I concede, there are two items: the kind of proposition and the kind of inquiry.[39]

To further clarify the differences between Oakeshott's *'ignoratio elenchi'* and Ryle's 'category mistake', we can ask, for example, if 'Water is really H_2O' is a single-statement; and, is it a category mistake? To confuse what practical agents drink and what chemists measure is an offense in Oakeshott's system. Similarly, other claims like 'All art is a sub-conscious effort to defend class values' would appear to be cross-modal.[40] My response is this. In 'Water is H_2O,' the 'is' is the 'is' of identity; in 'All art is a sub-conscious effort to defend class values,' the 'is' is the 'is' of predication. I cannot see that the proposition about art involves any logical mistake whatever its empirical validity. It would involve *ignoratio elenchi* in a debate about the literary merits of Dickens' Martin Chuzzlewit but surely in a debate about cultural history it could be true. 'Water is H_2O' would involve

[38] Walter B. Gallie, 'Essentially Contested Concepts,' *Proceedings of the Aristotelian Society*, New Series, 56 (1955–1956): 167–198

[39] In my introduction to a symposium on Oakeshott on religion, science, and politics ('Reflecting on Michael Oakeshott'), I set out five problems with Oakeshott's modal conception: *Zygon: Journal of Science and Religion*, 44, no. 1 (2009): 47–51.

[40] Thanks to Corey Abel for pressing hard on this issue.

ignoratio elenchi in a discussion about the aesthetic properties of water but in a scientific context, it is true and appropriate. In other words, Oakeshott's *'ignoratio elenchi'* separates modal areas of logic, whereas Ryle's categories belong to a simple, commonsense ontology.

The case of mind/body is difficult to take up generically because we do not know what the identities are. If mind/body are identical and we use an extensional language, then anything true of the mind is true of the body and no category mistake or *ignoratio elenchi* would be involved in running together statements about mind and statements about body. If, on the other hand, Cartesian dualism is the proper analysis of the relation of mind and body then there is a massive category mistake in asking or answering questions about mind that are appropriate only to body, and vice versa. Here, we would need a disputation between Ryle, Descartes, Aristotle, and Churchland before we could decide where illogic lies.

Tradition or Practice as an Extended Cognitive System

It has recently been said that the fault-line dividing orthodox Cartesian representationalism and anti-Cartesianism turns on the KT/KH distinction,[41] between defenders of the symbolic paradigm constructed of discrete and repeatable units, and defenders of the spontaneous, intuitive, tacit, dynamic, practical paradigm. Indeed KH is taken by some as the 'very essence of *creative* cognition.'[42] It should not therefore be surprising that Oakeshott speaks to what is termed the situated movement in cognitive science; a loose and internally fluid philosophical and empirical coalition, bound by a non-Cartesian sensibility that emphasizes autonomy, sense-making, embodiment, emergence, and experience.[43] The situated movement challenges the prevailing Cartesian orthodoxy across the philosophy of mind, epistemology and metaphysics, a stance that has systematically overlooked not only the location of thinkers in their physical environments, but also the interactions amongst thinkers in the ambient social soup.

So how specifically might Oakeshott's KH/HT writing be interpreted from a situated perspective? We know that the Oakeshottian agent is enmeshed in a matrix of traditions and practices. Traditions and practices are the *fundamentum* and the *residua* of practical reasoning. We also know that whatever a tradition or a practice is, by definition, it cannot reside solely within an individual – there is no direct brain-to-brain/mind-to-mind memetic transmission – continuity can only be mediated albeit imperfectly through a web of social artifacts.[44] This social view of mind is self-evidently externalist: externalism being the thesis that an individual's environment has *some* causal determinant on the content of the

[41] Daniel Hutto, 'Knowing What? Radical Versus Conservative Enactivism,' *Phenomenology and the Cognitive Sciences*, 4, no. 4 (2005): 389–405.
[42] Varela, Thompson, and Rosch, *The Embodied Mind*, 148. Steven Pinker, *The Blank Slate: The Modern Denial of Human Nature* (London: Penguin, 2002), 292, has the terms 'Utopian Vision' and 'Tragic Vision' as coextensive with KT and KH respectively.
[43] First pointed out by Keith Sutherland, 'Rationalism in Politics and Cognitive Science,' in Abel and Fuller, *Intellectual Legacy*, 263–80.
[44] Stephen Turner, *Brains/Practices/Relativism: Social Theory After Cognitive Science* (Chicago: Univ. of Chicago Press, 2003), 3, 11.

individual mind.[45] To be sure, the mark of advanced cognition *depends* upon our ability to diffuse propositional and practical knowledge or wisdom (KH) through external epistemic and cognitive structures, offloading the epistemic burden with a reciprocal and cybernetic 'enactive' relation between our conceptual creativity and the environment, to intimate, regulate and inform concepts and action. And that is why the Rationalist who seductively holds out a timeless and universal hypostatized Reason ('uncontaminated "rational" principles,' *OHC*, 81) that only requires perfunctory *technical* implementation across all epistemic domains – is bound to be defeated by the inherent complexity of traditions and practices.[46]

The perpetual feedforward and feedback complexity that is characteristic of the *embedded enactive* mind undermines the stark polarities of methodological individualism and social holism, which respectively generate the idealized pernicious fictions of the 'unencumbered' self and the anthropomorphic society.[47]

Oakeshott is certainly not rejecting the notion of individuality, freedom, autonomy or self-determination (*OHC*, 36–7). He only maintains that freedom is a profoundly incoherent notion if not set against a background fabric of possibility: the Oakeshottian agent still forms a core part of a wider epistemic system, one in which the individual still serves as *a locus of cognition and autonomy* within a wider system. It is in this sense, tradition and practice function as a kind of *extra-neural spreading of epistemic credit*.

For Oakeshott all intentional phenomena are saturated with background experience, which is itself irreducibly intentional.

> Mind is made up of perceptions, recognitions, thoughts of all kinds; of emotions, sentiments, affections, deliberations and purposes, and of actions which are responses to what is understood to be going on. It is the author not only of the intelligible world in which a human being lives but also of his self-conscious relationship to that world, a self-consciousness which may rise to the condition of a self-understanding (*VL*, 4, 25).

The term 'goings-on' which Oakeshott coins in *On Human Conduct* denotes intentionality (and understanding) that emerges from the infinite richness of experience, a kind of pattern recognition ability, rather than an explicit inferential capacity.[48] Though there may be discursive thought in response to a situation (a

---

[45] Internalism or individualism being the defining characteristic of Cartesianism.

[46] It should be noted that advocates of large-scale social planning need not be epistemological rationalists; and in opposing their projects the conservative may simply object to means/ end or 'instrumental' rationality as applied systematically and globally to politics. It is in opposition to this kind of rationalism that typically the conservative is anti-rationalist. The anti-rationalist faces the objection that if consequences of large scale social planning are thus unpredictable, the logic of the argument is that we *never* know what we are inaugurating, whether it be a piecemeal or incremental approach. For this reason a conservative, even in a piecemeal approach, believes we should still be *cautious*.

[47] *OHC*, 24: 'An alleged totality of human relationships. ' See also, *OHC*, 88.

[48] The relevance of connectionist models to social theory has been pointed out by Stephen Turner, 'Tradition and Cognitive Science: Oakeshott's Undoing of the Kantian Mind, *Philosophy of the Social Sciences*, 33, no. 1 (March 2003): 53–76; see also, Turner, *Brains/Practices/Relativism*. On connectionism and social theory see also Leslie Marsh, 'Hayek: Cognitive Scientist *Avante La Lettre*,' in *The Social Science of Hayek's 'The Sensory Order'* (*Advances In Austrian Economics* series), ed. William N. Butos (Bingley, UK: Emerald, 2010).

situation understood or misunderstood), there is only one thing – intelligence:

> Wherever there is action or utterance there is an intelligent agent responding to an understood (or misunderstood) situation meaning to achieve an imagined and wished-for outcome, and this cannot be 'reduced' to a psychological process or 'structure', however gross the misunderstanding, however lunatic the imagination, however fanciful the wish, and whatever its similarity to the actions and utterances of others. (*OHC*, 23)

Concluding Remarks

A history of thought is a history of men thinking, not a 'history' of abstract, disembodied 'ideas' (*LHPT*, 42).

A more succinct and pointed statement of Oakeshott's non-Cartesian credentials cannot be found. Oakeshott rejects the Cartesian bifurcation of the person into brain and body, apparent in the *still* prevailing methodological supposition that cognition can be studied independently of any consideration of the body and the physical and ambient social environment. Oakeshott's emphasis on the notion of embodiment implies a goal driven and purposeful engagement with the world. The situated mind is *enacted* through a particularized history of socio-environmental coupling: perception is an *act* of interpretation and the generation of meaning, a kind of know how. Political philosophers would do well to see the broader relevance of Oakeshott's epistemological concerns; situated cognitive science[49] should now add Oakeshott to the roster of theorists that include titans such as Heidegger, the later Wittgenstein, Merleau-Ponty and Hayek.

---

[49] Wallis, 'Consciousness, Context, and Know-How'. Wallis' work is notable for putting forward a positive account of what a unified account of KH-KT might look like from a cognitive science perspective.

11

Richard Flathman

Conversation, Conversion and Conservation: Oakeshott, Arendt and a Little Bit of Cavell

Both Oakeshott and Arendt identify and theorize a number of possible and desirable, impossible and undesirable, relationships *inter homines*. Particularly in the case of Oakeshott, but also significantly in Arendt, much of their thinking concerning human relationships is presented in the course of their reflections concerning formal and informal education. To my knowledge, Cavell has written very little directly concerning education, but his notion of conversion and conservation through conversation has strong affinities with the thinking of Oakeshott and Arendt. Engaging these thinkers on these topics (particularly the first two thinkers) may shed light both on their thinking and on important issues in political and related bodies of theory.

I

Famously, Arendt places great emphasis on the distinction between human beings in the merely biological sense of *homo sapiens* and human beings in the sense of agents capable of thought and action.[1] Paired with this is her distinction between human beings as denizens of the *earth*, and human beings who learn to live in the *world* by learning to speak and otherwise to act.

For Oakeshott, all those of us who are not mentally or otherwise deeply defective begin to learn immediately after birth and continue to do so throughout our lives. Much of what we have come to believe is erroneous and needs to be corrected, but from our earliest days learning is always correcting previously held

---

[1] Arguably the deepest version of these distinctions is one that she took from Kant and developed as the difference between human beings that are no more than 'whats' and those that become 'whos'. This last differentiation is presented in her early article 'What is Existenz Philosophy?' This is essay is now available in Jerome Kohl, ed. *Arendt: Essays In Understanding, 1930–1954* (New York: Harcourt Brace & Company, 1994). The distinction is repeated in various versions in her later works.

beliefs[2] or adding new beliefs to those previously acquired.[3] As with Arendt, our earliest learning takes place in the family or some analogue thereto, continues in the neighborhood, on the playground, in churches and workplaces, and takes increasingly organized and directed forms in school.

Learning is at once acquiring language and using language to acquire various further abilities and beliefs. Oakeshott distinguishes between language as a stock of tools that is used to learn and do other things, and as a capital that is 'something known and enjoyed only in use.' Thinking of schooling (in particular but not exclusively university schooling), he writes,

> Education I will take to be the process of learning, in circumstances of direction and restraint, how to recognize and make something of ourselves. Unavoidably, it is a two-fold process in which we enjoy an initiation into what for want of a better word I will call a 'civilization', and in doing so discover our own talents and aptitudes in relation to that civilization and begin to cultivate and to use them.'[4]

'Some people,' he continues, 'think of a civilization as a stock of things like books, pictures, musical instruments' etc.,

> in short, as the results of mankind having impressed itself upon a 'natural' world. But this is an unduly restricted (indeed, an exceedingly primitive) understanding of that 'second nature' ... which is the context or our activity. The world into which we are initiated is composed, rather, of a stock of emotions, beliefs, images, ideas, manners of thinking, languages, skills, practices and manners of activity out of which 'things' are generated. And consequently it is appropriate to think of it not as a stock but as a capital: that is, something known and enjoyed only in use.... This capital has been accumulated over hundreds of years. And in use it earns an interest, part of which is consumed in a current manner of living and part reinvested. (*RIP*, 187)

We have, then, the possibility, through informal and formal education, of conservation of the inheritance bequeathed by our civilization and conversion of persons from bare creatures of nature into feeling, perceiving, thinking, making and otherwise acting human beings. As will shortly appear, much – and much the best – of both this conservation and conversion occurs through that distinctive form of interaction that is conversation or some close analogue thereto.

Although Arendt takes these views to conclusions, particularly political conclusions, that Oakeshott would not accept, there are important respects in which her views run parallel to those just discussed. Following Aristotle, she holds

---

[2]   Oakeshott, *The Voice of Liberal Learning: Michael Oakeshott on Education*, ed. Timothy Fuller (New Haven: Yale Univ. Press, 1989), 59. Hereafter: *VLL*.

[3]   In *Experience and Its Modes*, Oakeshott uses a figure from Plato's *Theaetetus* to make this point: 'Thinking, according to the analogy of the *Theaetetus*, is a process of catching not wild birds ... but tame birds already in the cage of the mind' (Cambridge: Univ. of Cambridge Press, 1933), 19. Hereafter: *EM*.

[4]   Oakeshott, 'The Study of 'Politics' in a University,' in *Rationalism in Politics and other essays, new and expanded edition*, ed. Timothy Fuller (Indianapolis: Liberty Fund, 1991), 187. Hereafter: *RIP*.

that the ability to use language, and especially to use it to make moral and political judgments, is what distinguishes human beings from all other known creatures. And in her sparse but important reflections concerning education she insists that the first task of parents, schools, and teachers is to acquaint those 'newcomers' with the way the world has been and is.

> For education belongs among the most elementary and necessary activities of human society, which [echoing Oakeshott] never remains as it is but continuously renews itself through birth, through the arrival of new human beings. These newcomers, moreover, are not finished but in a state of becoming. Thus the child, the subject of education, has for the educator a double aspect: he is a new human being and he is becoming a human being. This double aspect is by no means self-evident and it does not apply to animal forms of life; it corresponds to a double relationship, the relationship to the world on the one hand and to life on the other.[5]

In respect to life and its development, the child differs little if at all from other animals. 'But the child is new only in relation to a world that was there before him, that will continue after his death, and in which he is to spend his life.'[6]

Here we have one of the basic, the most fundamental, modes of human relationship, that is (generically) teacher/learner, educator/educatee. It is in and through this relationship that newcomers to the world or to a civilization begin to acquire (or not, because education often fails) the language(s), images, ideas, beliefs, skills and criteria of judgment that make it possible (or fail to do so) for them to enter more or less successfully into the great diversity of further relationships that characterize every society and polity known to us.

Both thinkers are intensely aware of the fact that education often fails. Arendt writes of the 'crisis' of education (especially in the United States); Oakeshott does not use this melodramatic terminology, but his several essays concerning education are replete with expressions of regret and disapproval concerning the educational practices that were current or emergent as he wrote. And both attempt to identify conditions that must be satisfied for education at its various levels and in its several venues to achieve the civilizing (Oakeshott) and humanity-engendering (Arendt) objectives appropriate to it. Neither is a 'professional educator,' and neither presents detailed proposals for curricula, school organization, teaching and testing methods, or the like. There are, however, significant commonalities in their understandings of the circumstances and arrangements that are, and that are not, conducive to effective education.

The clearest difference between them concerns education at the university level. At least in respect to the United States, Arendt regards it as primarily pre-professional or otherwise oriented to career success, whereas Oakeshott argues that it must be 'liberal,' must provide an 'interim' between the primarily preparatory studies of family and pre-university schooling on the one hand and life after formal

---

[5] Hannah Arendt, 'The Crisis in Education,' in *Between Past And Future* (New York: Penguin Books, 1993), 185.

[6] Arendt, *Between Past And Future*, 185.

education has ended on the other. He recognizes and does not disdain polytechnics and other post-high school training, but views these as providing students with the 'tools' necessary to a trade, whether it be business, carpentry, tool and die making, medicine, or 'politics.'[7] In the university, teachers 'impart' an appreciation, a conversibility, in the 'languages' (understood as capital not as stock) of history, the sciences and the arts, and philosophy. (To the limited extent that university education can prepare students for participation in politics, it does so by helping them to understand the history, that is the languages, institutions, and practices of 'notable' politically organized societies.) To repeat, he does not specify curricula, but he holds that substantial additions to and subtractions from traditional curricula should be made sparingly and only after students (dons, professors and other scholars) have established substantial bodies of understanding and practice concerning the proposed subject matters.

These differences, however, coexist with important areas of agreement between the two thinkers. Although famous for her view that full humanization and freedom are possible only by participation in the public/political realm, Arendt insisted on the vital importance of a sphere of privacy, a sphere of thinking and acting shielded from the 'harsh light' of the public realm. Although presented at intervals throughout her writings, nowhere is this theme as strongly developed as in her thinking about education. Education begins in the family, which, along with seeing to the child's biological needs, must protect the child from the world that it is not yet ready to enter. 'The responsibility for the development of the child turns in a certain sense against the world: the child requires special protection and care so that nothing destructive may happen to him from the world.'[8]

The four walls within which private family life is lived 'constitute a shield' against the world and specifically against the public aspect of the world. They enclose a secure place, without which no living thing can thrive. This 'holds good not only for the life of childhood but for human life in general,' but it is especially important for the child who is not yet ready to cope with the world.[9] Much the same *should* be the case with the next stage in the development of the child, that is, the school. One of the two great mistakes made by educators in the United States is to treat the school as a kind of public space – an ersatz one – in which the students, largely unsupervised, compete with one another for the kind of recognition that citizens quite properly seek in the public/political realm of the *polis* or polity. The consequence is that the weaker among them are either tyrannized by the stronger or they are all subjected to the worst kind of tyranny, the tyranny of the majority.

The second mistake, which goes hand in hand with and compounds the first, is to largely eliminate the authority – and hence the responsibility – of teachers and principals. Properly, the chief task of the former is to acquaint – impart to, as

---

[7]   I put 'politics' in scare quotes because, as we see below, in *On Human Conduct* and elsewhere he reserves the term politics very narrowly. See Oakeshott, *On Human Conduct* (Oxford: Clarendon Press, 1975). Hereafter: *OHC.*

[8]   Arendt, *Between Past and Future,* 186. She adds, 'the world, too, needs protection to keep it from being overrun and destroyed by the onslaught of the new that bursts upon it with each new generation.'

[9]   Arendt, *Between Past and Future,* 186.

Oakeshott would say – their students with the world as it has been and is. But since it is believed that students learn only by doing, the classroom is turned into a kind of playground in which students study (or not) as they see fit, and, if they study, study only what presently interests them. It is the dual responsibility of teachers and principals both to control and direct the students and to shield them from the larger society. But because direction and control are regarded as infringements on the freedoms of the students, and because the lines separating the school from the larger society have been blurred if not erased, these responsibilities are either denied or ineffectively performed.

This brings us to the question of what, on Arendt's view, teachers should teach their students. Her answer will come as no surprise to those familiar with her essay 'What is Authority?'[10] 'It seems to me,' she writes, 'that conservatism, in the sense of conservation, is of the essence of the educational activity, whose task is always to cherish and protect something – the child against the world, the world against the child, the new against the old, the old against the new. Even the comprehensive responsibility for the world that is thereby assumed implies, of course, a conservative attitude.'[11]

She immediately warns against two misunderstandings of this view. The first is that her argument concerning authority also holds for political relations among adults. In this domain 'we act among and with adults and equals.' Contrary to Plato and a whole tradition that treats political authority as properly grounded in superior knowledge and wisdom, authority in the sense that parents and educators should have authority over their children and students has no proper place there. The second is that 'conservation' and 'conservatism' do not mean merely preserving the status quo. The 'world, in gross and in detail, is irrevocably delivered up to the ruin of time unless human beings are determined to intervene, to alter, to create what is new.' Hamlet's words, 'The time is out of joint' have always been true and 'they have perhaps acquired a more persuasive validity than before.'[12]

As regards parents and especially teachers, she then makes a distinction between their authority and their 'qualifications.' The authority of teachers over their students derives from the state, which requires school attendance and licenses teachers to teach. (This is a distinction central to Oakeshott's theory of authority and it can be identified as a distinction between being *an* authority on a subject matter or activity and being *in* authority by virtue of holding an office invested with authority.) But they must be qualified to teach, which means that they must have a command of whatever subject matter they teach their students.

Generically, the subject matter they should teach is how the world has been and is, which, again generically, is to teach the elements of what Arendt calls a tradition and that Oakeshott sometimes also calls a tradition, sometimes the elements constituting a civilization. And it is in these respects that the crisis in education is deepened. It does so for three closely related reasons, each of which compounds the difficulties created by the other two. The first is that those licensed to teach

---

[10] Arendt, *Between Past and Future*, chapter 3.
[11] Arendt, *Between Past and Future*, 192.
[12] Arendt, *Between Past and Future*, 192.

are not adequately trained in any of the elements of the tradition (or traditions) that they are to pass onto their students. Under the influence of professional educationists, teachers are taught how to teach, not what to teach.[13] The second, already discussed, is that authority itself is regarded as an improper thing, as an infringement on the freedom or autonomy of students. And the third is that almost no one, including educators, believes that there is a tradition or traditions that are worth sustaining and passing on to new generations.

In regard to the last she writes: 'The crisis of authority in education is most closely connected with the crisis of tradition, that is with the crisis of our attitude toward the realm of the past.'[14] In the pre-modern 'Roman-Christian' era, it was taken for granted that the past provides the model for the present and hence that 'to educate, in the words of Polybius, was simply "to let you see that you are altogether worthy of your ancestors".'[15] By contrast, 'modern man could find no clearer expression for his dissatisfaction with the world, for his disgust with things as they are, than by his refusal to assume, in respect to his children, responsibility for all this,' that is responsibility to educate them in the way the world has been and is. 'It is as though parents [and teachers] daily said: "In this world even we are not securely at home; how to move about in it, what to know, what skills to master, are mysteries to us too. You must try to make out as best you can; in any case you are not entitled to call us to account. We are innocent, we wash our hands of you".'[16]

II

One of the most basic modes of relations *inter hominess*, then, is that of learner to teacher. And this relationship commonly exists in both desirable and undesirable forms. What are some of the other relationships that can and do develop among persons who have been provided not only with language but with a stock and in some cases a capital? And what role do and do not, should and should not, conservation, conversion and conversation play in them?

Both Oakeshott and Arendt locate these further relationships on what deserves to be regarded as a hierarchy moving from the least to the most desirable. As could be expected from those of her views already discussed, for Arendt, the bottom of this hierarchy is occupied by 'relationships,' which border on and often in fact become a kind of non-relationship or the negation of relationships. Because all human beings share certain constant and incessantly renewed bodily needs, they

---

[13] 'Under the influence of modern psychology and the tenets of pragmatism, pedagogy has developed into a science of teaching in general in such a way as to be wholly emancipated from the actual material to be taught. A teacher, so it was thought, is a man who can simply teach anything; his training is in teaching, not in the mastery of any particular subject.... This in turn means not only that the students are actually left to their own resources but that the most legitimate source of the teacher's authority as the person who, turn it whatever way one will, still knows more and can do more than oneself is no longer effective.' Arendt, *Between Past and Future*, 182.

[14] Arendt, *Between Past and Future*, 193.

[15] Arendt, *Between Past and Future*, 194.

[16] Arendt, *Between Past and Future*, 191.

necessarily relate to one another in the course of their efforts to satisfy those needs. And persons who relate to one another exclusively in this way, those she calls *animal laborans*, may share a language and the stock of beliefs and abilities necessary to need-satisfying labor; but because they are the same in all of the respects that matter to them they have little use for language and such communication as occurs among them consists largely of the endless repetition of 'stock phrases,' of *clichés* and mimicries. And when, or to the extent that, they fail to receive recognition as anything more than laborers struggling to satisfy their bodily needs they experience that worst of all human conditions, namely 'loneliness.' (She distinguishes sharply between loneliness and solitude, a distinction to which I return below.) Insofar as they communicate with one another about anything beyond their bodily needs, their communications most often consist in mutual mimicries or expressions of resentment against those who do not share their condition.

It is important to emphasize that the bottom of the relationship hierarchy is not defined or occupied exclusively by those in material poverty or those commonly referred to as the 'masses.' In a world dominated by what Arendt famously called the 'social,' there are many persons who are materially well off, even affluent, and who nevertheless live lives dominated by the concerns of the body and who relate to one another primarily through interactions instrumental to those concerns. Along with their quest for ever more material goods, pursuing that form of 'consumption' called 'entertainment' becomes their passion and they value everything, including the objects of high culture, exclusively for its 'use' in satisfying their needs and desires.[17]

Because the goods and services they seek are used up as quickly as they are used there is little conservation. And because they and their relationships with one another remain locked in the diurnal succession of needs and desires that immediately beget further needs and desires there is little if any conversion. Finally, while there is much chatter (as Emerson called it), such 'conversation' as occurs consists primarily of expressions of resentment against those who they believe are doing better than they in the endless attempt to satisfy their needs and their desires.

For Oakeshott, the comparable place at the bottom of the relationship hierarchy is occupied by those he calls the 'individual *manqué* ' and the 'anti-individual.' On his reading of 'modernity' or modern Europe (which he dates from roughly the fifteenth century forward), the distinctive character of modern societies has been the emergence of a strongly favorable evaluation of individuality. With the gradual breakup of societies governed by communal norms (there are of course vestiges of such societies or sub-societies) there developed a belief, highly valued, in the freedom of individual persons, and a disposition to enjoy that freedom through self-concern and self-assertion. This disposition achieved its most developed form in what he calls the moralities of 'self-disclosure' and especially the morality of 'self-enacting individuality.' Persons devoted to and living by the principles and rules of these moralities, in particular the latter, exemplify the highest achievements of modernity; their characteristics concern us below.

---

[17] On this theme, see Arendt, 'The Crisis in Culture,' *Between Past and Future*, chapter 6.

The development of this individuality-oriented mentality, disposition or sentiment, and the norms and conventions that inform it, however, produced a reaction on the part of those who found its demands too great to meet or even to endure, a reaction that eventuated in the emergence of characters closely akin to those just discussed in respect to Arendt. 'The familiar warmth of communal relationships was being dissipated for all alike, and [*sic*] an emancipation which excited some and depressed and discomforted others. In short, the circumstances of modern Europe bred, not a single character, but two obliquely opposed characters, that of the individual and that of the individual *manqué*; and in one idiom or another they have been with us ever since those times' (*OHC*, 275).

In ways strongly reminiscent of Arendt, Oakeshott does not mince words in describing this latter character and his/her yet more degenerate fellow the 'anti-individual.' The individual *manqué* is 'disposed to prefer substantive satisfactions to the adventure and risk of self-enactment' (*OHC*, 276). 'Already outmaneuvered in the rough field of prudential conduct, he now suffered defeat in his own character. What had been no more than an inability to hold his own in belief and conduct became a radical self-distrust; what had been the discomfort of ill success turned into the misery of guilt.... And hidden in his character was a small seed of resentment' (*OHC*, 277).

In the paragraphs that follow these passages Oakeshott expands upon the political consequences of the emergence of characters of this description. More important for immediate purposes is how the combination of the prevalence of such characters and governments that purported to service them led to the germination of that seed of resentment and the growth of the 'anti-individual'. 'From the character of the individual *manqué*,' this combination 'evoked the character of the determined 'anti-individual', one intolerant not only of superiority but of difference, disposed to allow in all others only a replica of himself, and united with his fellows in a revulsion from distinctness.' He craved a '*solidarité commune* in which there was no distinction of persons and from which no one was exempt;' a politically organized society that was 'a therapeutic corporation devoted to remedying the so-called self-alienation' that he had been taught and had learned to feel (*OHC*, 278–9).

As with Arendt, Oakeshott is clear that he is not describing a 'class' phenomenon in a Marxist or any other socio-economic sense. Neither the individual *manqué* nor the anti-individual are to be identified as the

> poor (although wealth affords some superficial protection); they are not the peasantry of Europe who (until recently) mostly escaped it; nor are they exactly those whom others have identified as the 'proletariat' because the ingredient of spiritual indigence is not less important ... than the absence of possessions; ... And if they were to be identified ... as the 'masses', then it must be understood that what is being referred to is not their numbers but their incapacity to sustain an individual life and their longing for the shelter of a community. (*OHC*, 275–6)[18]

---

[18]   On these points see also Oakeshott, 'The Masses in Representative Democracy' (*RIP*, 363–83). Readers of Tocqueville, J. S. Mill and especially Nietzsche will recognize the close affinities between important elements of their thinking and the views of Arendt and Oakeshott.

It is clear that the above comments concerning Arendt apply directly to this aspect of Oakeshott's thinking. Once again, the only thing that is conserved by such relationships as there are among these 'characters' is the 'tradition' of seeking the satisfaction of needs and desires.

Because they continue to live as they learned to do in their earliest days, if they undergo any conversion, it is the conversion from narrow self-seeking to *ressentiment* against those different from the herd of which they are part. And as with those at the bottom of Arendt's relationship ladder, nothing worthy of the name of conversation has any place in their lives.

The passages just reviewed do not make agreeable reading. It is undeniable that there are persons and relationships among persons that have the characteristics that Oakeshott and Arendt describe. Arendt, however, has virtually nothing to say about how and why such characters and relationships develop and continue and she shows little sign of wanting to ameliorate them. And while both she and Oakeshott are of course fully entitled to imagine and advance higher ideals for human being and conduct (I personally find much to admire in Oakeshott's ideal of self-enacting individuality, very little to admire in Arendt's ideal of action in concert in a *polis* or other politically organized society), it is one thing to present and recommend such an ideal, a very different thing to treat those who do not find it attractive as therefore sub-human or otherwise to be disdained. As Nietzsche said of his ideal of self-overcoming free-spiritedness, 'My ideal is *mine*.... You can go to hell.'[19]

III

Both Oakeshott and Arendt identify and theorize a great variety of further types of relationships and as these ascend the hierarchy of relationships the ideas of conservation, conversion and conversation play a progressively richer and more complex role in their thinking.

A large number of these relationships, probably a preponderance of them numerically speaking, concern material goods and things. Of course many of these 'transactional relationships' (as Oakeshott often calls them) concern goods and other objects that meet bodily needs. Adam forms ('discloses' himself as having, as Oakeshott says), a desire or a felt need for a good or service that Baker discloses himself as having the wherewithal to satisfy; if Adam has something (money or some other exchangeable good) that Baker desires, a transaction may take place between them.

Both Oakeshott and Arendt recognize the prevalence and the importance of such transactions (how could they not!) but both of them view engaging in them as a necessary but rather dreary business. As Arendt emphasizes concerning bodily needs and desires, the satisfactions sought, though recurrent, are themselves typically fleeting, and because success in achieving them so often depends on the uncertain responses of others, this form of transaction, in Oakeshott's redolent description,

---

[19] Friedrich Nietzsche, *The Will To Power*, trans. and ed. Walter Kaufmann (New York: Vintage Books, 1967), § 349.

'is a hazardous adventure; it is immersed in contingency, it is interminable, and it is liable to frustration, disappointment and defeat.... "Don Juan lui même n'achève pa sa liste" ' (*OHC*, 73).

Relationships of this generic kind, however, can and often do take on a more lasting and more estimable quality. For Oakeshott they do so if and to the extent that they are understood to be conducted as a part of a 'morality,' what he calls the morality of self-disclosure. (There are numerous such moralities and they are embedded in and vary with the great variety of traditions.) The satisfactions sought, substantively speaking as it were, are fluctuating and evanescent, but the 'practice' of pursuing them is a continuing form of activity that – when well conducted – is governed by rules and conventions that are more general and stable than the substantial satisfactions sought. The rules and conventions are 'adverbial' in character; that is, they do not tell agents what they need or desire but rather tell them how and how not to act in pursuing whatever needs and desires they may experience or form. Their 'formality' can abate somewhat the contingency and hazardousness that would otherwise pervade transactional relationships.

These rules and conventions must be learned and must be interpreted when applied to particular contingent circumstances. They constitute a capital that accrues interest as it is used, not a stock that is used up in use. And they change, albeit usually slowly, as they are used. They form an important part of traditions that are at once conserved and adapted as they are passed on (imparted) from generation to generation and extended to reach into new, more encompassing domains of conduct. Once having learned their basic features, agents may converse about them as they apply and interpret them in the course of conducting their relationships. This is not likely to be conversation in its most distinctive and valuable forms (to be discussed below), but it may prepare those who participate in it for less immediately purposive or instrumental conversations, conversations that are not concerned, or not concerned exclusively, with needs and desires.

As Arendt theorizes them, durability and stability in relationships concerning needs and desires develops primarily when they are among those she identifies as *Homo faber*, that is as persons who make the earth into a world by building and creating the lasting material objects that make it possible for human beings to know where they are, to know their way about, and that allow them to orient their conduct toward one another and toward the world that they share. These objects range from the humble tables and chairs of the amateur carpenter to the architectural creations that organize much of human activity, to the elaborate machines of heavy industry, and to the sleek and powerful ocean liners and airplanes of the shipyard and giant airplane manufacturing plant. Their highest, most estimable and most humanizing forms are those produced by artists; by architects, sculptors, poets, composers, and creators of the institutions within the organizing settings of which much human activity takes place.

Homo faber, literally man the maker but also man the creator, makes tools that can be used again and again to make many things; and with those tools, which include hammers and chisels, paint brushes and palettes, drawing boards and tape measures, pens, pencils and composition paper, computers and centrifuges, he makes tables and chairs, drawings and paintings, blueprints and buildings, poems and symphonies, nuclear reactors and space ships.

As with Oakeshott's rules and conventions, the making and basic uses of these tools has to be learned and once they have been learned they must be adapted to the task of particular makings. The tools and the skills necessary to using them are handed on to newcomers, adapted to meet new makings, and new tools are invented. They too are a capital, not a stock.

As with Oakeshott's partners to transactional relationships, conversation may occur among those who make and use the products and creations of craftsmen, builders and artists. To the extent that they do so, conversations concerning them may help to preserve the capital they create and use, and they may convert participants in them to new skills and help them to create works of art and other makings never before seen.

Because these conversations have an instrumental, a purposive, quality, they help participants in them to sustain and augment a world; but, with one important exception they do not otherwise have a humanizing effect.

The exception is conversation concerning what can be called the aesthetic qualities of the objects made and used and it involves the development of the capacity (of those who are 'gifted' with it) for what Arendt, following Kant, calls 'judgment' or 'taste.'

Even the humblest of useful objects have a shape or form and 'cannot help being either beautiful, ugly, or something in between.' Again, 'Everything that is, must appear, and nothing can appear without a shape of its own; hence there is in fact no thing that does not in some way transcend its functional use, and its transcendence, its beauty or ugliness, is identical with appearing publicly and being seen.'[20] In judging objects, attention is directed away from their use or function and focuses instead on their beauty or ugliness. It requires a capacity to do so that cannot be taught – that can develop only in use – but it can develop through conversation with others about the aesthetic qualities of this or that object. Indeed, with rare exceptions, it develops only through such conversations.

Arendt's treatment of this process of conversion anticipates her more widely discussed view of how, in politics, persons come to 'act in concert' and create a 'web of relations,' a *sensus communis* and a 'solidarity' with one another. Persons with the inborn capacity for aesthetic judgment give expression to their assessment of objects (and actions), others become aware of those expressions and repeat or express their own, often differing assessments. Out of these interactions – these story-tellings as Arendt often says – there may emerge shared beliefs and evaluations which create a bond among the participants, thus providing a basis on which they are able to 'empower' one another to 'act in concert' in new ways. As these shared beliefs and evaluations accumulate and circulate, there may develop a common sense, a web of more or less lasting relationships, and possibly a sense of solidarity.

---

[20] Arendt, *The Human Condition* (Garden City, NY: Anchor Books, 1959), 152.

Thus even relationships that are primarily instrumental and functional in their basic character may provide a starting point for quite different relationships that humanize as well as create and sustain a world that all of the participants inhabit. It must of course be emphasized that such relationships do not rise to the heights of the humanization and freedom that can only occur in politics, but it would not be incorrect to say that, for Arendt, they are a necessary condition of the latter.

With this last thought (and comparable thoughts of Oakeshott) in mind, it might be said that there is a somewhat troubling quality or tendency to Oakeshott's and Arendt's treatments of the kinds of relationship discussed in this section. Although not as disdainful or dismissive of them as of the relationships among *animal laborens* and individuals *manqué* and anti-individuals, there is a certain supercilious quality to both of their discussions. This is of course primarily because they both have a conception of higher forms of relationship by comparison with which those just discussed are judged to be inferior. But one can judge, for oneself and perhaps for others of like mind, type of relationship 'A' to be inferior to type of relationship 'B' and yet appreciate that for many human beings relationships of type 'A' are what, in William James's well-known phrase, 'makes their lives significant.'[21] For many the 'little things of life,' having bread on the table, a roof over one's head and the like, are what matters most to them. And for others, the zest of athletic, entrepreneurial, artistic, and other competitions is what gives their life its savor and makes it worth living. For yet others, private relationships in families, among friends, colleagues, and avocational associates are what matter most.

Arendt clearly values such relationships, but she does so primarily because they are necessary conditions of the higher forms that are, for her, possible only in politics. Oakeshott does not accept this among her views, but it is clear that for him a life consisting exclusively of 'transactional relationships' is an impoverished life. This is an example of what James calls 'A Certain Blindness' common among human beings.[22]

IV

It is now time to examine the notion of conversation more directly, that is not as an adjunct to or companion of activities and relationships that are primarily devoted to some other purpose or objective, but as a form of relationship or interaction that is to be sought and valued for its own sake. Oakeshott has such a conception and Cavell does so as well. The distinction between conversation for its own sake and conversation for some other purpose is not as clear in Arendt, but she does think of the former or something close to it as intrinsic and hence necessary to the activities, that is political activities, that she values most highly. I begin with Arendt.

In discussing aesthetic judgment we saw that the beauty or ugliness of objects is a matter of how they appear to and are judged by this or that person. The exchange

---

[21] William James, 'What Makes a Life Significant,' in *The Writings of William James*, ed. John J. McDermott (Chicago: Univ. of Chicago Press, 1977).
[22] James, 'On a Certain Blindness in Human Beings,' in McDermott, ed., *Writings*.

of these judgments leads to 'enlarged thinking' on the part of those who tell and perhaps more particularly those who hear the stories of the former.

In its generic form, this view is at the center of what are arguably Arendt's most general theoretical positions (call them her ontological positions or her ontological/epistemological positions). Human experience is in the realm of appearances, not of some reality independent of how it appears to any assignable agent. Better, with some specialized exceptions, she collapses the appearance/reality distinction. 'In politics, more than anywhere else, we have no possibility of distinguishing between being and appearance. In the realm of human affairs, being and appearance are indeed one and the same.'[23] The bringing of these appearances together, finding or making meaningful relations among them, is what leads not only to the enlarged thinking that she discusses in her theory of judgment, but what she calls 'understanding.'

This bringing together can be done by the individual person thinking in solitude (not his loneliness[24]) as in the famous cases of Cato and Socrates.[25] It is more often done in what Arendt sometimes calls 'dialogue,' sometimes 'discourse,' and sometimes conversation among two or more persons. Of course she is famous for her high estimation of the role of such discourse in politics, but her admiration for it extends to domains that, on her distinctions, must be regarded as private. The clearest case is its role in friendship. In her essay on Lessing in *Men In Dark Times*, after emphasizing the political importance that the Greeks accorded to friendship, she goes on to praise it highly in personal relationships. She writes: 'the world is not humane just because it is made by human beings, and it does not become humane just because the human voice sounds in it, but only when it has become the object of discourse. However much we are affected by the things of the world … they become human for us only when we can discuss them with our fellows…. We humanize what is going on in the world and in ourselves only by speaking of it, and in the course of speaking of it we learn to be human.'[26]

In *The Human Condition*, she distinguishes between speech and 'mere talk' (the latter is presumably what she thought takes place among the *animal laborans* of the earth), arguing that the former but not the latter is 'revelatory' in nature:

Without the accompaniment of speech … action would not only lose its revelatory character, but, and by the same token, it would lose its subject … not acting men but performing robots would achieve what, humanly speaking, would remain incomprehensible. Speechless action would no longer be action because there would no longer be an actor, and the actor … is possible only if he is at the same time the speaker of words.[27]

---

[23] Arendt, *On Revolution* (New York: The Viking Press, 1963), 93–4.
[24] On this distinction, see among many other places, Arendt, *Human Condition*, 54, 67.
[25] On Cato, see Arendt, *Human Condition*, 297; and cf. Arendt, 'Some Questions of Moral Philosophy,' in *Responsibility And Judgment*, ed. Kohl, (New York: Schocken Books, 2003), 99.
[26] Arendt, *Men in Dark Times* (Middlesex, UK: Harmondsworth, 1955), 32.
[27] Arendt, *Men in Dark Times*, 158. The distinction between speech and mere talk is on page 160. This theme also connects with, and informs, her view that violence is mute, a view that she develops in several places, perhaps most notably in her discussion of Billy Budd in *On Revolution*, 78–9.

Owing to its 'revealatory' character, speech exchanged in discourse or dialogue leads not to truth (as distinct from truthfulness) – which is the enemy both of politics and friendship – but to 'meaning' and 'understanding.' 'Understanding precedes and succeeds knowledge. Preliminary understanding, which is at the basis of all knowledge, and true understanding, which transcends it, have this in common: They make knowledge meaningful.'[28] Again, the 'Greeks learned to *understand* – not to understand one another as individual persons, but to look upon the same world from another's standpoint, to see the same in very different and opposing aspects.'[29]

Although perhaps already implied, it is important to emphasize that when Arendt writes of dialogue, she is not thinking of dialectic in a Platonic, Hegelian or Marxist sense. The validity of judgments, whether of the beauty or ugliness of an object or the quality of a speech or other action, is not and cannot be demonstrated. It 'never has the validity of cognitive or scientific propositions, which are not judgments properly speaking.' The making and exchanging of judgments is a 'persuasive activity' that 'appeals to the 'community sense'.'[30] This view is closely analogous to Oakeshott's and Cavell's understanding of conversation.

V

Arendt's most developed, certainly her most intensive thoughts on human relationships concern relationships among individuals thought of and thinking of themselves as citizens of a *polis* or republic, that is as participants in the activities of certain types of politically organized societies. Persons with this self-identification interact with one another as individuals participating in the production of a common, potentially an agreed upon, orientation or disposition that they mutually regard as being of common concern. This is a formal objective or concern; it does not specify a substantive objective or purpose on which agreement has coalesced. Rather, the objective is to find ways in which to act together to generate what Arendt calls (idiosyncratically) 'power.' We can say that this is an end in itself, but we can also say that its end, or rather the good that it produces, is humanization and freedom. Whether acting in concert also produces other more material goods is a question about which Arendt is intriguingly silent.

The term 'conversation' figures only rarely in Arendt's discussions, and her emphasis on the agonal character of political relationships might be regarded as reason for avoiding it in interpreting of her thought. As we will see with Cavell, however, conversation is often stimulated and sustained ('stirred' as he often puts it) by deep disagreements between the parties, and if we keep in mind what Arendt says about friendship, discourse, dialogue, story-telling, persuasion and

---

[28] Arendt, 'Understanding And Politics,' in Kohl, *Arendt*, 311.

[29] Arendt, *Beyond Past and Future*, 51. Arendt recognizes that there are questions about which Truth can be known; that is, Truth independent of the standpoint of any individual, independent of how it appears to this or that person. This is the domain of logic. But logic and its Truths are the enemies of both politics and friendship.

[30] Arendt, *Lectures On Kant's Political Philosophy*, ed., with an interpretive essay by Ronald Beiner (Chicago: Univ. of Chicago Press, 1982), 72.

(most generally) speech from a variety of standpoints or perspectives, it is no great stretch to think of those acting in concert as in conversation with one another. And just as formal and informal education can lead to both conservation and conversion, so can the teaching and learning that go on in conversational relations among citizens.

The question whether Oakeshott's conception of conversation allows of agonal relationships among conversational partners is more difficult. I postpone that and related questions concerning his conception and return to it after a brief discussion of Cavell.

Throughout his works, and most forcefully in his recent *Cities of Words*[31] Stanley Cavell has promoted a view that he calls Moral Perfectionism without perfection. He distinguishes this view from various other moral outlooks and theories, most especially on the ground that its concerns are with the quality of lives more than with the rightness or wrongness of actions, policies and the like, but also from other versions of perfectionism that posit and seek to promote a condition that itself defines and, if attained, would constitute human perfection.

His theory works with a notion of the 'doubled self,' the self already 'attained' or arrived at and a possible further, not yet attained self.[32] The attained self develops through interactions with other persons, with language, with social and political relationships and with other elements that constitute the 'ordinary.'

Although necessary to becoming capable of meaningful, understandable, thinking, patterns of conduct and relationships with others, these interactions often produce states of confusion and uncertainty, of disappointment with and aversion toward self and others.

These experiences may give rise to the thought of a further self that has greater self-clarity and more satisfactory relationships with others. As with all perfectionist theories, each variation

> provides [for] a position from which the present state of human existence can be judged and a future state achieved, or else the present position judged to be better than the cost of changing it. The very conception of a divided self and a doubled world, providing a perspective of judgment upon the world as it is, measured against the world as it may be, tends to express disappointment with the world as it is, as the scene of human activity and prospects, and perhaps to lodge the demand or desire for a reform or transfiguration of the world.[33]

It is at this juncture, however, that Cavell's 'moral perfectionism' parts company with other perfectionists (call them 'ultimate perfectionists') such as Plato, aspects of Aristotle's thinking, and more recent thinkers such as Shaw, Murdock, and Raz. The latter (ultimate perfectionists) specify in general and in some cases universal

---

[31] Stanley Cavell, *Cities of Words* (Cambridge: The Belknap Press of Harvard Univ., 2004).
[32] Although perhaps reminiscent of Arendt's distinction between individuals that as yet are no more than *homo sapiens* and must become human, and Oakeshott's view that we are born with the capacity to become human but must learn how to do so, Cavell configures and deploys this distinction in ways distinctive from the other two thinkers.
[33] Cavell, *Cities*, 2.

terms the shape and character that the future self should have and in some cases the path that leads to it. They do not converse with us, they *instruct* us, sometimes in considerable and substantive detail, concerning the qualities of character and life that future selves and lives, selves and lives that are the best, must have.

By contrast, Cavell and those he follows (above all Emerson) refuse to offer a universal or even a general specification of the as yet unattained self. The attained self emerges – if or to the extent that it does so – out of or through conversations that take place among attained selves. To the limited extent that it is appropriate to identify in affirmative terms the aim or purpose of these conversations, it is to achieve great self- and mutual clarity and understanding; it is 'to lead the soul, imprisoned and distorted by confusion and darkness, into the freedom of the day.'[34] The substantive content of these understandings is left open, left to emerge out of the conversations. 'I do not ... regard the perfectionism I ... follow out as requiring an imagination of some ultimate human perfection. Emersonian perfectionism ... specifically sets itself against any idea of ultimate perfection.'[35]

In what, then, does and does not conversation consist? A first point here is that it does not consist in doing without, in entirely leaving behind, the attained self. While often a source or, better, a locus, of confusion and disappointment, the already attained self and the ordinary self out of which it develops and in which it largely resides, is the source or repository of the criteria that distinguish clarity from confusion, the desirable from the undesirable, that which is worth conserving and that which it would be better to change. Cavell's well-known Wittgensteinian view that our criteria always disappoint us (hence a skepticism) but that we cannot do without them (hence a skepticism tempered by 'acknowledgements') is at work throughout his perfectionist reflections. There is the possibility of conversion, but it must always take place in company with conservation.

Second, conversation has the usual meaning of exchanging thoughts and words with and among others, but it is more than 'familiar discourse or talk' (OED). Perhaps reminding us of Arendt's notion of 'mere talk,' Cavellian conversation is an achievement, an overcoming (as Nietzsche would say) of the opacity of self and other but (as Nietzsche would also say) never a final, now-and-for-all-time overcoming.

Third, conversation is to be distinguished from a variety of other familiar modes of communication. It is obviously incompatible with pious preaching, intimidation by force or violence, bribery, and the like. It is also importantly different from argumentation.

Cavell has harsh words for those who, having arrived at a belief or conclusion, enter into 'conversation' with the objective of arguing others into accepting their view. Something like Arendtian (and Oakeshottian) persuasion to shared understandings may go on, but understanding emerges out of, in the course of, the conversations.

Fourthly and important in relation to tendencies currently prominent in political theory, conversation should be distinguished from debate and deliberation.

[34] Cavell, *Cities*, 4.
[35] Cavell, *Cities*, 3.

Deliberation aims to achieve a result, a decision that brings closure to itself. As Hobbes parses the term, to deliberate is to 'de-liberate' oneself and other participants in the relationship, to take away from oneself and them a liberty that they otherwise would have. This includes the liberty to continue, at least for now, to debate the question or issue that is (was) the subject of the debate.

There is no book of etiquette that will tell you how to converse. But there are certain general and affirmative guidelines to conducting it. One of these is that 'Conversation ... means my speaking for others and my being spoken for by others, not alone in speaking to and being spoken to by others.'[36] In passages closely akin to Arendt's account of judgment leading to a *sensus communis*, Cavell says that speaking for, as well as to, requires 'mutual responsiveness;' it requires 'that you have sufficiently appreciated the situation from the other's point of view, and ... have articulated [in your own {not a 'hollow'} voice] the ground of your conviction.'[37] In order to converse with others you must acknowledge 'the awful ... awesome truth that the acknowledgement of others, of ineluctable separation, is the condition of human happiness.'[38] The most common form of refusing this truth, perhaps, is 'indifference' to others, but preaching, threatening, arguing and debating with others is also speaking to, not for, others.

These remarks also signal other respects in which Cavell is close to Arendt (and to Oakeshott), but also points on which he disagrees with her (and him). Conversation, he holds, is something that cannot be 'accomplished alone.'[39] This agrees not only with ordinary understandings of conversation but with the views of Arendt and Oakeshott that it is a form of relationship that ordinarily involves two or more persons. Moreover, Cavell agrees with the other two thinkers in his view that genuine conversation, conversation at its best, is not merely with others but with those special others that are one's true friends. 'The other to whom I can use the words I discover in which to express myself is the Friend – a figure that may occur as the goal of the journey but also as its instigation and accompaniment. Any moral outlook ... will accord weight to the value of friendship. But only perfectionism, as I understand it, places so absolute a value on this relationship.'[40]

Carrying this further, if we regard the relationships that Cavell has studied and theorized in several 'remarriage comedies' and plays as especially strong examples of friendship, he argues that conversation between them is exclusive in a very strong sense. He speaks of 'the inevitable feature of classical remarriage comedy in which the pair becomes incomprehensible to (most of) the rest of the world' and generalizes this by saying 'this may be taken as the essential risk perfectionism runs, since at the same time it fully recognizes the moral demand for making itself intelligible – but first, in the case of our couples, to each other.'[41] It is important to recognize that Cavell rejects both Montaigne's view that we can have no more

---

[36] Cavell, *Cities*, 51.
[37] Cavell, *Cities*, 235.
[38] Cavell, *Cities*, 381.
[39] Cavell, *Cities*, 27.
[40] Cavell, *Cities*, 27.
[41] Cavell, *Cities*, 153.

than one genuine friend and Aristotle's argument that friendship is possible only between equals, that is (for Aristotle) between men who are or eligible to become citizens. Nevertheless, his insistence that conversation among friends shuts out the rest of the world (recall that draped blanket in *Adam's Rib*) substantially confines, as compared with Arendt and Oakeshott, the domain in which conversation as he primarily understands and theorizes it can have its converting and conserving effects.

One final comparison before turning to Oakeshott: Cavell's view that conversation is something that one cannot do alone seems to reject the possibility of that conversation between me and myself that Arendt finds in Cato and sometimes in Socrates and that Oakeshott thinks of as philosophizing. This is unfortunate because we know of many instances in which conversation with oneself (and perhaps an imagined partner such as God or the gods) has been a major impetus to conversion. It also seems odd given Cavell's positing of a doubled self, a postulate that is essential to the notion of conversation or dialogue with(in) oneself and often goes together with that notion.

VI

In a related essay, while finding much to appreciate in Cavell's theory, I have raised some questions and offered some objections to it. Rather than rehearsing them here I return to Oakeshott and his identification and theorization of conversational relationships at what he regards as its highest level.

Although most fully developed in his essay 'The Voice of Poetry in the Conversation of Mankind' (*RIP*, 488–541), the notion of conversation is prominent in numerous of Oakeshott's writings both before and after the original 1959 publication of that paper. In 'A Place Of Learning' he says that a 'culture' is 'a continuity of feelings, perceptions, ideas' and the like 'pulling in different directions, often critical of one another and contingently related, ... so as to compose not a doctrine, but what I shall call a conversational encounter' (*VLL*, 28). Elaborating on this notion he writes that 'we may think of [the components of a culture] ... as voices, each the expression of a distinct and conditional understanding of the world and a distinct idiom of human self-understanding' and that these 'voices could only be joined ... in a conversation – an endless unrehearsed intellectual adventure in which, in imagination, we enter into a variety of modes of understanding the world and ourselves and are not disconcerted by the differences or dismayed by the inconclusiveness of it all' (*VLL*, 38–9).

In 'The Idea of A University' (*VLL*, 95–104), Oakeshott writes that we begin to learn to converse in school, and develop conversability especially in our university days, in which the 'pursuit of learning is not a race in which the competitors jockey for the best place, it is not even an argument or a symposium; it is a conversation.' In this 'conversation',

> each study [appears] as a voice whose tone is neither tyrannous nor plangent, but humble and conversable. A conversation does not need a chairman, it has no predetermined course, we do not ask what it is 'for,' and we do not judge its excellence by its

conclusion; it has no conclusion, but is always put by for another day. Its integration is not superimposed but springs from the quality of the voices which speak, and its value lies in the relics it leaves behind in the minds of those who participate. (*VLL*, 98)[42]

As we have seen, something akin to conversation may take place in transactional engagements conducted in a practice of moral disclosure. On Oakeshott's view, however, conversations in such settings are usually purposive; participants in them are seeking some substantive satisfaction and what they say to one another has the aim of improving their chances of obtaining it. As with Arendt, in conversation in its most distinctive and most valuable forms in participating in it we learn not particular truths or obtain bits of information but rather develop the capacity for judgment.

Conversation that nurtures the capacity for judgment involves mutual 'acknowledgment and accommodation.' In 'The Study of Politics in A University,' Oakeshott says that the 'civilizations' with which he is most intimately familiar may be regarded as involving

> a conversation being carried on between a variety of human activities, each speaking with a voice, or in a language of its own; the activities (for example) represented in moral and political endeavour, religious faith, philosophic reflection, artistic competition and historical or scientific inquiry and explanation. And I call the manifold which these different manners of thinking and speaking compose, a conversation, because the relations between them [as in Arendt and Cavell] are not those of assertion and denial but the conversational relationships of acknowledgment and accommodation. (*RIP*, 187).

Oakeshott returns again to this theme in perhaps unexpected places, such as when he considers (in the essay of the same name) 'The Political Economy of Freedom'. In that essay, he notes that in the political interactions of a civilization of the sort he has in mind, there is 'a conversation in which past, present and future each has a voice; and though one or other of them may on occasion properly prevail, none permanently dominates' (*RIP*, 388). It involves, and produces and sustains, complex and fluctuating combinations of conservation and conversion.

The ability to engage in conversation requires that one has learned one or more of these languages. It also requires the development of a certain sensibility and disposition; a sensitivity to the differences between, on the one hand, instructing, arguing, asserting and denial; and, on the other, the pleasures of an undirected exchange of views; a disposition to respect and appreciate those differences by acknowledging and accommodating the views of others. Learning the languages begins at birth, continues throughout life, and is intensified among those who have the good fortune of receiving a liberal education. The sensibility and disposition develop (when they do so) in the course of participation in the moralities of self-disclosure and self-enactment that are in place in the civilizations and their traditions with which one has become familiar.

---

[42] Admittedly, this is an idealized conception of the university.

Oakeshott's thinking about conversation has its most striking expression in his essay 'The Voice of Poetry in the Conversation of Mankind,' which he wrote and published in 1959, well before most of the essays just reviewed. Here are a couple of the main passages:

> In a conversation the participants are not engaged in an inquiry or a debate: there is no 'truth' to be discovered, no proposition to be proved, no conclusion sought. They are not concerned to inform, to persuade, or to refute one another and therefore the cogency of their utterances does not depend upon their all speaking in the same idiom. (*RIP* 489)

There may be passages of argument or demonstration, but these are interruptions in the conversational flow. 'Thoughts of different species take wing and play around one another, responding to each other's movements and provoking one another to fresh exertions. Nobody asks where they have come from or on what authority they are present; nobody cares what will come of them when they have played their part' (*RIP*, 489–90).

A conversation is 'an unrehearsed intellectual adventure.... Properly speaking, it is impossible in the absence of a diversity of voices: in it different universes of discourse meet, acknowledge each other and enjoy an oblique relationship which neither requires nor forecasts their being assimilated to one another' (*RIP*, 490).

Conversation, we may say, is always playful but never frivolous.

VII

Some combination of conservation of that which has been and is, and conversion to new understandings, values, and practices is vital to a decent politics, to a politics that merits the more or less continuing acceptance by those whose lives are lived within it. Among the many important strengths of the thinking of Oakeshott and Arendt is that they make clear why this is the case and identify and theorize familiar types of relationship in which both conservation and conversion are created and sustained.

I have complained that both thinkers undervalue relationships other than those that they value most highly, relationships that may also contribute to a combination of conservation and conversion; but both of them do recognize many such further forms of interaction and interchange and they undervalue them primarily by comparison with high ideals that they know are achieved only intermittently and never more than in part. Oakeshott is certainly aware that much of what goes on in the societies he theorizes occurs in relationships of competition, of truck and barter, of threat and promise, of gain and loss. And he is persuasive concerning ways in which these forms of relationship can acquire a value that goes beyond the substantive outcomes sought by participants in such transactions. Arendt is more given to lament the prevalence of purely or primarily instrumental thinking and interacting, less willing to acknowledge ways in which they sometimes transcend their immediate, narrow purposes. On the other hand, she places great emphasis on the ways in which our lives are dependent on the efforts of human beings who are makers and creators of our 'world;' and, she values highly the relationships that develop among them and between them and those whose lives are enriched by their efforts and accomplishments.

Of course the forms of interaction just mentioned hardly constitute the entirety of human 'relationships,' including many that, hopefully rare occasions apart, have little to be said for them. Violence, coercion, intimidation, bribery, suppression, oppression, maliciously inflicted suffering, snobbery, disrespect, and the like have been prominent features of human affairs from time immemorial; in many places they have been and are not only prominent but pervasive. It might be objected that in focusing on conservation and conversion, especially as initiated and sustained through teaching/learning and the arts of discourse and conversation, Oakeshott, Arendt and Cavell (and the author of this essay) show themselves to be blind to these 'realities' and hence to be poor guides to our thinking. This focus, the objection might continue, inflects their thinking with a preciosity, an intellectualism, perhaps a minority-privileging elitism.

As indicated, I think there is some validity to this objection, especially in regard to Arendt's thinking about *animal laborens* and perhaps what might be called the bourgeoisie, and Oakeshott's disdain for the individual *manqué* and the anti-individual. But the objection can easily be overstated, can readily be shown to overlook or underestimate major features of the work of both thinkers. Arendt, after all, is among the best of the students/theorists of totalitarianism. Oakeshott has had less to say, or at least to say directly, about such matters, but it can be argued (as I have recently argued), that the restraint or diminution of the place of violence and oppression is a major objective of his thinking.[43] Cavell has perhaps had yet less to say about such matters, but to mention only one striking example he does recognize the continuing presence of 'scoundrels' who are 'touched with the satanic, with an intolerance precisely for membership, for reciprocity in the intelligible, or any other, realm.'[44]

Coming at this issue from another direction, if we follow these thinkers in stressing the differences between discourse and conversation on the one hand, and dogmatism, deliberation, incontrovertible demonstration and other modes of exchange we may see that conversation as they understand it is the least privileging among these types of interaction. It is open to all prepared to enter into it, and it is open-ended in being without a substantive goal or desired outcome. It encourages people to be responsive to one another, to speak for as well as to one another. In respect to the cruder forms of interaction, it encourages tolerance, acceptance where possible and celebration of difference where appropriate.[45] In this regard we might say that, by being civil, it seeks to, or might have the effect of, civilizing the uncivil.

---

[43] See Richard Flathman, *Pluralism and Liberal Democracy* (Baltimore: The Johns Hopkins Univ. Press, 2005), especially chapter 5. In chapter 3 of the same work I respond to some related criticisms of Arendt.

[44] Cavell, *Conditions Handsome And Unhandsome* (Chicago: Univ. of Chicago Press, 1990), xxxiv. He is not, he goes on to say, 'as keen as others seem to be to let the worth of moral theory depend on its being able to (re)convince a convinced scoundrel' (*Conditions*, xxxvii). Cf. *Cities*, esp. 207.

[45] I do not develop this theme here, but it is worth underlining that each of these theorists promotes a robust moral and political pluralism.

A further objection might be that the emphasis on conversation is idle, self-indulgent, even parasitic. After all, there are questions that must be answered, issues that must be resolved, decisions that must be taken and implemented. Politics must lead to governance, as must the conduct of a business, a university, even avocational associations. To go on and on with insistently open-ended, adamantly non-instrumental talk simply will not do jobs that must get done. Very few human activities can be conducted in the manner of a Quaker meeting.

The thinkers engaged here could hardly be said to be unaware of these necessities. Oakeshott has a developed theory of 'ruling' in politically organized societies and he is explicit that education requires direction and control. It is a familiar question about Arendt's highest ideal conception of politics whether it has any place for such a thing as ruling, but her emphasis on authority in the Roman and American republics and in education makes it clear that she understands the importance of ruling – and of course she has plenty to say about what goes on under the name of ruling in nineteenth and twentieth century societies. Cavell is not primarily a political theorist, but he has developed thoughts about the conditions necessary to sustaining a sufficient range and intensity of consent to governmental authority to maintain a political society with what he calls a 'good enough' justice.

This last point is perhaps the most important one in this connection. Governments are expected to govern, as are CEO's, university and foundation presidents, and the like. But they cannot do so, or do so effectively, without substantial acceptance and support from those they govern. How is this achieved and maintained? The first answer to this question is of course that very often it is not. There is not enough responsiveness and accommodation, not enough speaking for as well as to, among the members of the polity or other associations to sustain acceptance of and support for policies and decisions that have wide and deep effects.

I opined that conversation can have a civilizing effect, perhaps can have this effect better than any other mode or manner of human relationship. If or to the extent that this is true, societies replete with genuine conversation among their members will be those in which the possibility of effective governance will be at its greatest.

Once again, however, there is another way of thinking about this question. Even if we agree that ruling, governance, is necessary (which I do, but ruefully), it is not a pleasant business.

As the words themselves all but tell us, it involves some people telling other people what they must and must not do. In this perspective, what the theorists engaged here help us to realize is that conversation, along with being a source of support for governance, is an alternative to it, even a distraction from incessant concern with it. The imaginative flight of ideas and words that Oakeshott loves, the narratives and story-telling that Arendt adores, the soul-liberating conversations that are Cavell's enthusiasm and excitement can take us away, even if only at intervals, from the often dreary business of deciding and concluding.

In these respects we would do well to follow the lead given us by these thinkers.

12

Jeff Rabin

Richard Rorty, Michael Oakeshott and the Impossibility of Liberalism Without Tradition

The difference between a search for foundations and an attempt at redescription is emblematic of the difference between the culture of Liberalism and other forms of cultural life. For in its ideal form, the culture of Liberalism would be one which was enlightened, secular through and through. It would be one in which no trace of divinity would be left over, either in the form of a divinized world or a divinized self. Such a culture would have no room for the notion that there are non-human forces to which human beings should be responsible. It would drop, or drastically reinterpret, not only the idea of holiness but those of 'devotion to truth' and of 'fulfillment of the deepest needs of the spirit.' The process of de-divination would, ideally, culminate in our no longer being able to see any use for the notion that finite, mortal, contingently existing human beings might derive the meanings of their lives from anything except other finite, contingently existing human beings. In such a culture, warnings of 'relativism,' queries whether social institutions had become increasingly 'rational' in modern times and doubts whether the aims of Liberal society were 'objective moral values' would seem merely quaint.

— Richard Rorty[1]

Rorty et les Philosophes

Richard Rorty to this day is the leading English speaking *philosophe* in political philosophy. By calling Rorty a latter day *philosophe*, I mean that Rorty shares much in common with the French *philosophes* of the eighteenth century such as Diderot, Voltaire, Helvetius, and d'Alembert. Like them, Rorty has attracted great popular attention, becoming one of today's most fashionable (and popular) proponents of 'postmodernism.' Moreover, Rorty displays the same curious self-confidence and optimism in his method and results that the *philosophes* enjoyed in their work. He does so by applying his rather eccentric understanding of philosophy and

---

[1] Richard Rorty, *Contingency, irony, solidarity* (Cambridge: Cambridge Univ. Press, 1989), 45.

knowledge to any and everything that his post-modern gaze should alight upon. Freudian psychoanalysis, sociology, philosophy, literature and literary theory, art, intellectual history, and what is of most concern in this paper, political philosophy, all bear his 'post-modern' examination.

I will argue that the comparison with the eighteenth century *philosophes* goes further. This is insofar as Rorty, like them, is also a thorough-going 'Rationalist' in thought, word, and deed, even if the postmodernism he employs is itself born out of an anti-rationalist, anti-enlightenment critique. For just as the *philosophes* wished to rebuild and reclassify all the world's knowledge anew as the encyclopedists endeavored to do, Rorty also wishes to rethink and re-erect all of the world's knowledge along firm anti-foundational, post-modern lines, self-contradictory as this endeavor would seem to be.

Moreover, residing in Rorty's Pollyanna-like hope for a post-foundational Liberal utopia (a place safe for poets and revolutionaries whose purpose is none other than to provide the framework for Mill's 'experiments in living'), lies the same emancipatory, humanist dream of personal autonomy, and freedom from the shackles of history, tradition, nature and contingency, that so illuminates the writings of the *philosophes*. In following this goal, Rorty has thus become for some a visionary 'prophet' of post-modernism, while for others, a traitor to the cause of proper philosophy.[2]

And while originally, the focus of Rorty's attention was the more traditional concerns of epistemology and metaphysics, in recent years Rorty has shifted his attention to literature and political philosophy, especially the debate between the Liberals and the Communitarians. With this change, many have noted, Rorty himself included, that he has exhibited a decided similarity of philosophical outlook and political philosophy to that of Michael Oakeshott.

Both Rorty and Oakeshott are 'anti-foundationalists,' eschew universalism for a 'relativist' 'historicism,' found their argument upon a critique of enlightenment rationalism, and can loosely be called 'liberals.' Moreover, they are both a peculiar kind of 'liberal.' This is so insofar as they, unlike the deontological liberals such as Kant, Rawls, or Nozick, deny that the historic body of practices characteristic of liberal western practice can be philosophically justified as the best form of political practice independently or prior to practice.[3]

There is nothing extreme in this last point. It would seem also to be the position of Walzer, Taylor, Hegel, Wittgenstein, and many others. But, Rorty's identification

---

[2] See David L. Hall, *Richard Rorty, Prophet and Poet of the New Pragmatism* (Albany, NY: State Univ. of New York Press, 1994); and, Charles Taylor, 'Rorty in the Epistemological Tradition;' Tom Sorrell, 'The World From Its Own Point of View;' Donald Davidson, 'A Coherence Theory of Truth;' all in *Reading Rorty: Critical Responses to Philosophy and the Mirror of Nature (And Beyond)*, ed. Alan R. Malachowski (Oxford: Blackwell, 1990).

[3] Brian Barry, for example, professes in his work, 'to believe in the possibility of putting forward a universally valid case in favor of liberal egalitarian principles.' This makes cogent his ambition to start' from the premise that Burke percipiently attacked as fundamental: the denial of the authority of prescription. Once we ask for some justification of social and political institutions that can be presented for the approval of each person's reason, we are launched on a journey that must, I contend, proceed along the lines of this book.' Barry, *Justice as Impartiality* (Oxford: Clarendon Press, 1995), 6.

of Oakeshott as a fellow 'post-modern bourgeois liberal' as well as his adoption of Oakeshott's conception of 'conversation' for how philosophy and political discourse ought to understand and conduct themselves, have done much to popularize Oakeshott, and have led some to equate the two theorists.

Doing so, however, would be a mistake and a grave one at that. For though on the surface there are great similarities between these two thinkers, their differences are greater. Though Rorty and Oakeshott somewhat agree on the content and practice of philosophy, the consequences for political practice that they derive from their anti-foundationalism differ. Whereas Rorty passionately believes in the possibility (and desirability) of establishing a post-foundational, liberal utopia that has much in common with the humanist emancipatory ideal, Oakeshott's skeptical conservatism mitigates against the possibility and desirability of bringing about such a cosmopolitan, and, ultimately, I would suggest, 'rationalist' eventuality. Instead, Oakeshott's understanding of politics as 'the pursuit of intimations' and his critique of 'rationalism in politics' undercuts such grandiose plans of liberal emancipation, suggesting that they are not only impractical but pernicious.[4]

Whereas Rorty ultimately understands philosophy as merely another genre of 'edifying literature,' and literature itself as an instrumental tool of socialization and persuasion for the achievement of a cosmopolitan liberal utopia, philosophy and education for Oakeshott both retain a task and a self-contained purpose that for Rorty they must renounce. In the end, Rorty becomes an exemplar of what Oakeshott has identified so clearly in his post-war essays (post-enlightenment protests notwithstanding): the rationalist in politics and the *philosophe* in philosophy.[5]

For 'Rationalism' and the project of Enlightenment, have other aspects too, and are not simply identified with 'giving reasons,' as Rorty seems to characterize them. 'Rationalism' and the 'project of the Enlightenment' are associated with a liberationist ideal of a person, and with an overpowering belief in the efficacy of ideas to change society for the better through the self-conscious pursuit of 'rational ideals' (according to a peculiarly western model of the good society and ideal of the good individual). On all these counts, I submit, Rorty is alike guilty.

The Argument

The argument of this paper is as follows: *I take it (this will not be argued) that any political philosophy which promotes rationalist principles with which to regulate our polities must give reasons as to why the norms it espouses are normative.*

If a political philosophy fails to give such reasons, it cannot be normative political philosophy, but must therefore be something else, say of a piece with political polemic – this, ultimately, being my conclusion with regard to the 'political philosophizing' of Richard Rorty. This is different from the other political theorists – Rawls, *et al* – who do give reasons, though reasons I find but argue

---

[4]   John Gray, *Enlightenment's Wake* (London: Routledge, 1995), 146.

]5]   For my discussion of what a *philosophe* is, I draw upon Oakeshott's essay, 'The New Bentham' in *Rationalism in Politics and other essays, new and expanded edition,* ed. Timothy Fuller (Indianapolis: Liberty Press, 1991), 132-50. Hereafter: *RIP.*

elsewhere to be ultimately wanting. In Rorty's case, as Rorty expressly gives no reasons why we should pursue the norms he espouses, Rorty's contribution to the Liberal-Communitarian debate cannot therefore be considered political philosophy; for he cannot maintain both that philosophy can give no such reasons, and that nonetheless an ideal of a Liberal Utopia (where cruelty and humiliation are minimized, and ideals of persons as poets and revolutionaries are maximized) should merit our most serious theoretical and practical attention.[6]

To the end of achieving Rorty's (perhaps) laudable, though definitely impractical ideal of a Liberal utopia that has at its center the humanist emancipatory ideal, a description of which I will provide shortly, Rorty goes on to detail methods and strategies by which we can realize such a utopia in practice. According to Rorty, for example, the writing, reading, and promulgation of imaginative and other 'edifying literature' (such as that which we generally consider to be philosophy) can sensitize us to and make us aware of the myriad ways in which we can knowingly and unknowingly inflict cruelty upon and humiliate others through our private pursuits of self-perfection and the defects of our social institutions.

Indeed, it would not be too much to say that like Marx and his treatment of Hegel, Rorty stands the contemporary practice of political philosophy on its head, but in a very different way. Instead of providing us with norms of practical conduct justified by philosophical demonstration, which if we accept the argument, it is then incumbent upon us to implement, Rorty only provides us the methods for achieving his liberal utopia, but does not provide the reasons for the superiority of his liberal ideal.

How can we explain this rather odd contradiction: Rorty on the one hand presents us with Liberal, poetic norms which we are to follow, and on the other hand, does not provide us with reasons for embracing these norms. Rorty does not however see any difficulty.

Rorty does not believe he has to justify his norms, as his post-modernism absolves him of all such responsibility. As John Gray has noted, Rorty's 'post-modernism – like most post-modernism – is the modernist humanist project without its foundationalist matrix.'[7] As such, Rorty has no reasons for why we should work towards establishing a world in which there is less cruelty and humiliation and more poets and revolutionaries. Neither has he any need to give any, either. What Rorty claims to be doing, like Hegel, is articulating the norms inherent in our current political practice – what Rorty calls 'Liberalism.' However, when we unpack what Rorty considers liberalism to be, and the ideal of a person that this presupposes, we find only truisms, banalities, and platitudes that do not accurately reflect (if such a thing could be accurately reflected) something so nebulous and protean as 'the Liberalism of the rich North Atlantic democracies.'[8]

---

[6] It is not my intention to say that political theory must produce norms, or that something without norms cannot be political theory. It is only that if a political theory promotes, suggests or proffers norms of practical conduct, it must give reasons why.

[7] Gray, *Enlightenment's Wake*, 146.

[8] This 'liberalism of the rich north Atlantic democracies' of which Rorty speaks is a very different kind of liberalism, and presupposes a different ideal of a person than that espoused by deontological liberals who argue for the primacy of right on the basis of egalitarian ideals,

Moreover, we shall find that these truisms, banalities, and platitudes have the character of the self-conscious pursuit of ideals that Oakeshott so rails against in the essays of *Rationalism in Politics,* and in practice have the effect of undermining the morality of custom and habit upon which such ideals depend.

What are these truisms, banalities, and platitudes? I believe they are caught up with Rorty's philosophical *Weltanschauung,* that is, the American pragmatism that Rorty is so steeped in, which indeed goes so far as to provide a reason, anti-foundational protests notwithstanding, for his ideal liberal utopia.

Whereas for the pragmatist a 'true' belief is a belief that 'is good for us to believe,' Rorty's reason (or at least shadow of a reason) for why we should adopt his liberal utopia is that such a utopia will be 'good for us to live in,' because it is one in which there will be 'less cruelty and humiliation,' and more poets and revolutionaries, of which it is always better to have less and more respectively. A Liberal simply is the kind of person who, says Rorty (employing Judith Shklar's definition), understands that the infliction of cruelty and humiliation upon others is the worst thing that we do. The best kind of person simply is, for Rorty, a poet or a revolutionary.

I think there is something else going on here too. There is a terrible instability in Rorty, such that for reasons that Rorty himself gives, it would seem as if anyone would be permitted to pursue any political program he or she desired, liberal or theocratic. There is nothing to constrain one in the absence of any foundations (or what for Rorty amounts to the same thing, reasons) that establish the superiority of liberal practice to any other social practice.

Oakeshott does not face this problem. For according to Oakeshott, in the absence of such reasons, we must fall on the traditions and practices that constitute our ethical patrimony. If there are moral ambivalences and ambiguities to resolve in these traditions and practices, we must use these traditions and practices as best we may, knowing that no tradition or practice is incapable of change and refinement in the face of present and future eventualities.

Returning to Rorty, unless we suppose such a pragmatist view of the good society and an ideal of a person from whence it is derived, and that it is 'good' for us to live in such a society, it is my contention that Rorty's views on political philosophy can only be a recipe for *anomie* and conflict as is presently the case in certain regions of the Middle East and Sub Saharan Africa. This is because there is nothing, no legitimate arguments that may be made, to constrain anyone from pursuing any sort of utopia or any ideal of a person whatsoever, regardless of an ideal's palatability or effects upon others. This would of course contradict Rorty's belief that he has no need to provide such reasons, yet I think they are here nonetheless.

---

an ideal of a person, and an hypothetical choice situation which they regard as capable of generating valid and effective norms. It is, however, a kind of liberalism, and a kind of ideal of the person every bit if not more controversial and substantive than their own. In a comparison between a society in which the pursuit of justice is pre-eminent, and another where the existence of cruelty and humiliation is minimized and the presence of poets and revolutionaries maximized, there will surely be overlap, but they will certainly not be identical.

Rorty's denial of the possibility of giving an account of our traditions, norms, and beliefs, a denial that far outstrips Oakeshott's recognition of the contingency and mutability of all political arrangements, allows us to see why Oakeshott's account of politics is superior to Rorty's. I believe there is a serious evasion in Rorty. Rorty either refuses to acknowledge, or very awkwardly attempts to overcome a crucial distinction between acting upon norms that will not admit of the possibility of justification, whose consequences (beneficial of or otherwise) are only relevant to the actor, and acting on the basis of norms where the consequences of so acting involve others to a highly significant degree. The result of this equivocation in Rorty is the advocacy of what we might term the 'blue-print' theory of politics – the politics of having a 'blue-print' of what society and the individuals who compose it should be like. It is also the attempt to implement this 'blue-print' upon society and the people who compose it, regardless of their present constitution or the character of their social practices.[9] This is precisely the difference that Oakeshott highlights between 'rationalism in politics', underwritten as it is by the morality of the self-conscious pursuit of ideals, and truly rational conduct, depending as it does on the morality of custom, habit and tradition.

Now Rorty may not be the sort of rationalist who believes in the efficacy of instrumental reason to provide us with reasons for the imperative norms with which we should regulate our social practices. Still, Enlightenment Rationalism has other aspects: an overwhelming belief in the power of ideas to change the world in which we live for the better through the self-conscious pursuit of rationalist ideals. And if this is true of rationalism, Rorty, therefore, becomes every bit the 'Rationalist' that he is so at pains to identify others as, and to personally overcome in his own philosophizing.

Rorty & the Idea of 'Philosophy'

To understand Rorty's peculiar amalgam of Anglo-American political philosophy and continental post-modernism, it will prove wise to go back to some of his earliest work in the theory of knowledge and language. In *The Linguistic Turn* and *Philosophy and the Mirror of Nature*, Rorty issued what amounted to a polemical broadside at how philosophy presently conducted itself within the environs of the academy.[10]

In these early works, Rorty pleaded for a radical revision of philosophic practice. Therein, he denied that Philosophy – with an uppercase 'P' – had any privileged access to a non-empirical world 'out there' which it could employ to judge the truthfulness of lesser forms of inquiry. Philosophy, Rorty maintained (even if it hardly ever did) could no longer claim for itself the mantle of a 'master discipline,' dictating the terms in which subsidiary and subservient forms of intellectual inquiry should regard themselves.

[9]   More conventionally, such a theory of politics is utopian, as indeed Rorty calls his theory of politics utopian.
[10] Rorty, *Philosophy and the Mirror of Nature* (Princeton: Princeton Univ. Press, 1979).

Rorty argued for this (really rather less than radical thesis) by relentlessly attacking the doctrine of 'the given' in the theory of knowledge, residual Cartesian mind/body dualism present in philosophy of mind, and the scientific paradigm of hypothesis and verification for how philosophy should conduct itself.

As Rorty boldly stated, his aim was therefore nothing less than

> to undermine the reader's confidence in 'the mind' as something about which one should have a 'philosophical' view, in 'knowledge' as something about which there ought to be a 'theory' and which has 'foundations', and in 'philosophy' as it has been conceived since Kant.[11]

The history of philosophy, Rorty argued, has above all been dominated by the mistaken conviction that the mind was a mirror in which was found reflected the reality 'out there.' Accompanying this error was the further mistaken idea that the task of philosophy was to judge the accuracy of the reflection so presented.

This mistaken understanding of mind as a mirror of nature, Rorty contends, has its roots in ancient Greek ocular metaphors. It is variously taken up, embellished, and modified by the tradition of western reflection on thinking, reaching its apotheosis in the 'Enlightenment Rationalism' of the seventeenth and eighteenth centuries. In addition, it has now become all but inexorably woven into how we think of the world and ourselves. It is an understanding, however, that we must wean ourselves from, because it is wrong, Rorty contends, and to continue to follow it is to further immerse ourselves in a faulty metaphysic.

In support of this bold thesis, Rorty marshals an impressive variety of names in Anglo-American thought, among them James, Pierce, Dewey, Ryle, Kuhn, Davidson, Sellars, and Quine. Rorty uses each of these thinkers for a different purpose: Ryle to undermine our belief in the mind as a Cartesian 'ghost in the machine 'of our body; Davidson to provide a non-correspondence account of language and meaning; Kuhn for his historicist understanding of the practice of science and, by implication, other forms of inquiry, as a series of intermittent 'paradigm shifts'; Sellars for the language of ethics and morality; and Quine, for blurring the distinction between the necessary and the contingent, and for his understanding of knowledge as 'a web of belief' constantly adjusting and re-weaving itself to absorb new 'facts' according to old 'beliefs,' or as he puts it, to 'confront the tribunal of experience as a whole,' and for his showing the search for foundations to be a misguided endeavor.[12]

---

[11] Rorty, *Philosophy and the Mirror of Nature*, 7.
[12] For Rorty, this new conception of philosophy, and human progress, as one language-game supplanting another, and truth as 'the outcome of free un-coerced discussion,' has great practical consequences. As each succeeding language game employs a different vocabulary and grammar than the one it succeeds, it is not always straightforwardly possible for one language game to interact with another on the same terms. This has the practical advantage of not requiring Rorty to substantively engage with theorists who he claims do not speak his language. By putting such theorists aside when thinking about our public culture, indeed calling them 'mad' – Rorty reintroduces them in the private sphere – Rorty neatly side-steps all those who would, like Foucault, Derrida, Schmidt, or Heidegger, disagree with him.

James, Dewey, and Pierce are drawn upon for the peculiarly American philosophy of pragmatism, which equates truthfulness with utility, true beliefs being those beliefs which when acted upon hold out the greatest possibility for our continued success as persons and as a species.

As Rorty puts it, the Pragmatists

> view truth as, in William James's phrase, what is good for us to believe. So they do not need an account of a relation between beliefs and objects called 'correspondence,' nor an account of human cognitive abilities which ensures that our species is capable of entering into that relation. They see the gap between truth and justification not as something to be bridged by isolating a natural and trans-cultural sort of rationality which can be used to criticize certain cultures and praise others, but simply as the gap between the actual good and the possible better. From a pragmatist point of view, to say that what is rational for us now to believe may not be true, is simply to say that somebody may come up with a better idea.... For pragmatists, the desire for objectivity is not the desire to escape the limitations of one's community, but simply the desire for as much inter-subjective agreement as possible, the desire to extend the reference of 'us' as far as we can.[13]

In place of the mistaken conception of philosophy of the mind as a mirror of nature, Rorty suggests a turn towards something like a post-foundational hermeneuticism. This is an approach concerned only with charting the changes and shifts of language games that we use to describe the world, our place within it, and ourselves.

If epistemology is a constraint against knowledge, as Rorty suggests, then hermeneutics, for Rorty, is what is left when this 'constraint' is unfulfilled. To leave such a constraint unfulfilled, Rorty argues is to abandon the problematic Rationalism of the Enlightenment for, say, a holist pragmatism of practice: to adopt a neutral monist conception of mind, and make a turn towards behaviorism.

Truth, therefore, for Rorty, following James, Dewey, and Quine is that which 'works,' and 'what is best for us to believe,' rather than that which corresponds with ultimate reality; and philosophy (with a lower case 'p') is no longer considered a master arbiter of knowledge and culture. Philosophy should, therefore, says Rorty, employing Oakeshott's famous metaphor, usher the 'conversation of mankind' along, and not be concerned with achieving once and for all deductive proof of an insensible and eternal world 'out there,' which it can then employ to judge the truthfulness of other forms of scientific and cultural practice.

Language, for Rorty is a contingent matter, with no meta-language available in which to arbitrate between the various language games that we employ. Philosophical inquiry is, in Oakeshott's terminology, a 'conversation' within which we continuously interpret and reinterpret the relation of ourselves to our environment. I say 'something like hermeneutics' because Rorty is careful to distinguish his sense of hermeneutics from that of say Gadamer, or Habermas, who Rorty suggests, maintain much of 'the epistemic paradigm.' Rorty, in effect,

---

[13]   Rorty, *Objectivity, Relativism, and Truth*, vol. 1 of *Philosophical Papers* (Cambridge and New York: Cambridge Univ. Press, 1991), 22, italics added; quoted in Roger Scruton, *Modern Philosophy: Introduction and Survey* (London: Sinclair-Stevenson, 1996) from which I derive my account of Pragmatism.

wants to shift the self-understanding of philosophers from seekers of unchanging, realist essences of things, to that of historicist and nominalist literary critics. In so doing he shifts from epistemology to hermeneutics, where the reality-appearance distinction is considered an obsolescent relic of an outdated vocabulary, the idea of mind a contingent irrelevance, and philosophy merely a genre of imaginative literature.

What concern is this (if any) to political philosophy? First, according to Rorty, if his critique of philosophy has merit – for if it were true it could not be true in a strict sense – a corollary of it is that to philosophically justify the superiority of liberal practices as against illiberal ones is neither necessary, nor profitable, nor even possible. In recent years, however, Rorty has shifted his energies away from his earlier concerns of epistemology and metaphysics towards drawing out the consequences of his anti-foundationalism for political thought and practice.[14]

Rorty's Contribution to Political Philosophy:
The Liberal-Communitarian Debate

Rorty's contribution to the debate is twofold. First, he gives a rather idiosyncratic reading of the debate through the lenses of his critique of foundational epistemology and metaphysics. Second, he offers an account of a political theory that he believes both meets the challenge of anti-foundationalism, and paves the way towards establishing liberal cosmopolitan utopias.

According to Rorty, the contemporary debate in political philosophy is a three-cornered hat, between 'Kantians,' 'Hegelians,' and a subset of the Hegelians, the 'post-modern bourgeois Liberals.' Theorists such as the early Rawls and Dworkin, who found their political philosophy on ahistoric, universal criteria and make the distinction between morality and *phronesis* as Kant did, Rorty calls the 'Kantians'.

The *post-modern bourgeois liberal Hegelians* are those such as Michael Oakeshott and John Dewey, and in Rorty's latest writing, John Rawls. They are those who wish to preserve the institutions of contemporary political practice, but to do so on non-Kantian, prudential foundations. Rorty calls these theorists 'bourgeois' because he believes those who would defend the institutions and practices of liberalism without Kantian-like foundations, would have no quarrel with those inspired by Marx, who would understand the institutions and practices that constitute them as characteristic of a particular bourgeois time and bourgeois place.[15]

What Rorty means by post-modernism he borrows from Jean François Lyotard, who defines post-modernism as the 'distrust of meta-narratives.'[16] For the 'Hegelians' who are not 'post-modern bourgeois Liberals,' Rorty cites Alasdair MacIntyre and Roberto Unger. They, like the 'post-modern bourgeois Liberals,'

---

[14] As I earlier remarked, differences in understandings of agency, and foundations, do not always equal differences in politics. The links between these are much less strong than often supposed.

[15] See also what Wittgenstein understood as 'bourgeois philosophy': philosophy that sought foundations by which to justify the superiority of current social and political practice over other forms of practice.

[16] Jean François Lyotard, *The Post-modern Condition: A Report on Knowledge* (Minneapolis: Univ. of Minnesota Press, 1993).

reject the Kantian attempts to found correct political practice upon universal, ahistoricist criteria of morality. Unlike them (and mistakenly according to Rorty) the 'post-modern bourgeois Liberals' wish to abandon Liberalism because of its failure to secure philosophically impregnable foundations.

To this end, Rorty provides the following classificatory schema:

Table 1.   Rorty's Taxonomy of Political Philosophy

	Kantians: Those who believe in an essential nature of the self upon which the morality/*phronesis* distinction can be made and correct political practice grounded. They are 'ahistoricist,' 'universalist,' and 'metaphysicians' who employ 'unembedded' or 'emotivist' conceptions of the self.	**Hegelians:** Those who believe in a self without foundations upon which a morality/*phronesis* distinction may be made, and correct political practice be grounded. They are 'historicist,' 'relativist,' and employ 'embedded,' 'situated' conceptions of the self.
Liberals: Those either in favor of, or who attempt to justify the continuance of 'bourgeois,' 'liberal' practices, and the bourgeois selves that these presuppose.	**Liberal Kantians:** Early Rawls, Dworkin, and Kant.	**Post-modern Bourgeois Liberals:** Those who believe that foundations may not be found for liberalism, but think that we should continue to engage and to promulgate these practices none the less: Rorty, Dewey, later Rawls, Oakeshott.
Illiberals: Those who would wish to reject bourgeois political practice and bourgeois selves.		**Illiberal Hegelians:** Those who believe that as foundations cannot be found for Liberalism, we should reject Liberalism outright: Unger, MacIntyre, perhaps Sandel.

A number of criticisms can be made in relation to Rorty's taxonomy: one principal problem is that Rorty's anti-foundational obsession has, to a very large degree, infected his understanding of the contemporary debate.

Rorty's anti-foundational obsession is such that he overlooks common ground between theorists and likewise exaggerates differences; he seems to think that nothing much distinguishes them, other than their method of justification, which is both untrue and deceptive. The effect is to caricature these theorists, almost to the point that they are unrecognizable and to neglect important differences in politics and principles that they do hold.

For, according to Rorty, there would seem to be really rather little that distinguishes John Dewey, the American social democrat of the New Deal, from the conservative Oakeshott, the trenchant critic of the postwar welfare state. Similarly, Rorty makes bedfellows of MacIntyre and the early Unger, two fundamentally different theorists: the former a Thomist, the latter certainly not.

A further difficulty that Rorty presents us with is in ascertaining who (if anyone) could be correctly placed into the Kantian category other than Kant himself. On the matter of Rawls, who is regarded as being the paradigm Kantian in today's debate, Rorty equivocates. Ultimately, Rorty grants Rawls a place among the post-modern bourgeois liberals in the light of the essays Rawls wrote after *A Theory of Justice;* Rorty avers he had originally 'misread' Rawls.

Perhaps what is most important about the Kantian category, however, is that it is the category that best identifies the respective emphasis or disposition that the theorists of deontological liberalism maintain, even if they do not themselves subscribe to Kantian foundations. In this case, even if it is an empty set – or a set that only contains Kant, as I believe it must – it still helps us to distinguish the disposition of the early Rawls, which I call the Kantian disposition, from that of an Oakeshott or a Rorty.

In terms of the Hegelians, it is not so clear that Hegel would or could meet the criteria for inclusion in this category. For what in Hegel is *Geist* other than a non-contingent, progressively actualized manifestation of the necessary in history?

All that said, in terms of the Liberal-Communitarian debate specifically, Rorty has some interesting observations and suggestions about the debate, most of which he makes in his paper 'The Priority of Democracy to Philosophy.'

Rorty says of the communitarians that they are wrong in supposing that liberalism, or contemporary bourgeois political practice is incapable of surviving the loss of belief in the foundations in which it is traditionally justified. As Rorty puts it, the communitarians 'often speak as though political institutions were no better than their philosophical foundations.' Rorty, by contrast, contends that even if the project of justifying deontological liberalism in the manner of Kant is impossible – providing a universal and trans-historical criterion for just political practice denuded of any partial conception of the good – we may still believe in and engage in the institutions and practices that are present within this liberal theory.

This is to go against the thesis made famous by Horkheimer and Adorno in *The Dialectic of Enlightenment* that once we no longer believe in the worth of the manner of philosophy in which liberal practice has been traditionally justified, we will no longer continue to be able to engage in these practices either. As Horkheimer and Adorno put it, this view dictates 'every specific theoretic view succumbs to the destructive criticism that it is only a belief – until even the very notions of spirit, of truth, and, indeed, enlightenment itself become animistic magic.'[17]

As to the sustainability of our current political practices in the absence of secure or even believed philosophical foundations, Rorty notes in passing that the decline in the widespread belief in God experienced in the twentieth century did not, as Dostoevsky prophesied it would, result in absolute license or concupiscence.

In light of this, Rorty goes on to say of the communitarians that they are furthermore wrong in supposing that the political institutions and practices of society require philosophic justification. As Rorty has it, echoing Oakeshott: it is not only impossible to give such a philosophic justification independent of social practice; it is also undesirable. In any event, such a view of philosophy has the relation between practice and philosophy backwards. For Rorty, on occasion (as for Hegel and Oakeshott always) 'the owl of Minerva flies at dusk'. The task of philosophy is to 'apprehend one's moment in time.'

Last, Rorty argues that justifying a political system simply by means of the practices and beliefs current in the public culture is not to simply 'beg the question,' as many contend, but has an important therapeutic or explanatory purpose. To do more than simply 'beg the question' is, I would submit, to go beyond what philosophy is capable of doing. The communitarians, Rorty argues, would do better to criticize the sorts of individuals that coexist in liberal polities, as MacIntyre has it, 'the therapist,' 'the aesthete,' and 'the manager,' and not the foundations on which liberalism is justified.[18]

Liberal Political Philosophy & Rorty

Liberal political philosophers have a felt need to provide reasons for the norms that they wish to effect in our social practices. Rorty suggests that this need arises, as it did for the earlier proponents of 'Enlightenment Rationalism' who sought to underwrite their liberal, egalitarian principles with a new authority based on reason, in replacement for the theological authority that they regarded as having under-girded pre-Enlightenment thought and practice. Today, however, in this 'Post-Enlightenment Age,' we must abandon such a misguided search for 'foundations' in terms of natural law, substantive conceptions of the good, or what is rationally acceptable to all who are reasonable. The old *querelle*, it turns out, was simply a *malentendue*.

For Rorty, to discover or invent norms of conduct which would be acceptable to all who are reasonable – the avowed object of endeavor of the contemporary social

[17] Max Horkheimer and Theodor W. Adorno, *Dialectic of Enlightenment*, trans. John Cumming (New York: Herder and Herder, 1972), quoted in Rorty, *Contingency, irony, solidarity*, 57.

[18] Rorty believes, as with philosophy, that the debate should actually be put on its head. He supposes – what is most probably the case – that the description of the person that underlies Rawlsian liberalism is best understood as a re-description in another idiom of the account of politics present in the work, and not the foundation for the politics. If such is the case (and it is not at all clear that it is), such descriptions of the person are unnecessary, because they add nothing to the account.

contract tradition – would only make sense if the self was bifurcated between a contingent and a necessary part: the contingent part a product of our socialization, the necessary part our sharing in the faculty of reason. This is, however, a distinction that Rorty will not recognize. Indeed, such an endeavor to find foundations is not truly suited for a liberal society. For, according to Rorty (echoing Mill) 'A Liberal society is one which is content to call 'true' whatever the upshot of such encounters [of free speech in the public realm] turns out to be.'[19]

Since there is no independent standard of morality that we may turn to independent of local practice, Rorty's official point about selfhood and community is that there is, therefore, no essential, intrinsic nature of selfhood or community, no self or community prefigured in the womb of time or space, nor any essential nature that can serve as an independent standard for what is good or right.

The self for Rorty, as for Hume, is simply is a center-less concatenation of beliefs and desires with nothing that stands above or behind it. To give an impression of the extreme degree that Rorty officially believes this to be so, I quote him at length:

> The crucial move in this reinterpretation [of philosophy and political philosophy that Rorty wishes to effect] is to think of the moral self, the embodiment of rationality, not as one of Rawls's original choosers [sic], somebody who can distinguish her self from her talents and interests and views about the good, but as a network of beliefs, desires and emotions with nothing behind it – no substrate behind the attributes. For purposes of moral and political deliberation and conversation, a person just is that network, as for purposes of ballistics she is a point mass, or for purposes of chemistry a linkage of molecules. She is a network that is constantly re-weaving itself in the usual Quinean manner – that is to say, not by reference to general criteria (e.g. 'rules of meaning' or 'moral principles') but in the hit-or-miss way in which cells readjust themselves to meet the pressures of the environment. On a Quinean view, rational behavior is just adaptive behavior of a sort which roughly parallels the behavior, in similar circumstances, of the other members of some relevant community. For some purposes this adaptive behavior is aptly described as 'learning' or 'computing' or 'redistribution of charges in neural tissue,' and for others 'deliberation' and 'choice'. None of these vocabularies is privileged over against another.[20]

Though there is no intrinsic nature to be brought out, i.e. one is socialized 'all the way down,' Rorty is concerned to make clear that the task remains for the self to effect its own creation out of the *mores* of the various communities that it has been socialized into. One creates oneself out of the resources conferred on one by one's socialization in the use, refinement and modification of one's 'final vocabulary.'

As Rorty describes it:

> All human beings carry about a set of words which they employ to justify their actions, their beliefs, and their lives. These are the words in which we formulate praise of our friends and contempt for our enemies, our long-term projects, our deepest self-doubts

---

[19]   Rorty, *Contingency, irony, solidarity*, 53.
[20]   Rorty, *Contingency, irony, solidarity*, 73.

and our highest hopes. They are the words in which we tell, sometimes prospectively and sometimes retrospectively, the story of our lives. I shall call these words a person's 'final vocabulary.'

It is 'final' in the sense that if doubt is cast on the worth of these words, their user 'has no non-circular argumentative recourse. Those words are as far as he can go with language; beyond them there is only helpless passivity or a resort to force.'

A person's 'final vocabulary,' Rorty has it, is made up, of both 'thin,' 'flexible,' and 'ubiquitous' words like 'truth' and 'justice,' or more 'parochial,' 'rigid' terms like 'church,' 'kindness,' or 'progressive.' These latter terms do most of the work: the more general a term for Rorty, the less its force. An individual may treat one's final vocabulary either as an ironist concerned to carry on the conversation of selfhood describing and re-describing themselves and their surroundings in a continuous narrative that only ends in death (as Alasdair MacIntyre would have it) or as a metaphysician attempting to discover the unchanging essence of selfhood or community.

There is no prize for guessing with which account Rorty's sympathies lie. Unlike the metaphysician, the ironist is someone who always entertains doubts about his final vocabulary and knows that anything can be made to look better or worse through re-description. And, unlike the metaphysician, the ironist does not believe that these final doubts may ever be dissolved by getting at the 'truth' that lies at the 'bottom' of 'selfhood' or 'community.' As Rorty writes:

> I call people of this sort 'ironists' because their realization that anything can be made to look good or bad by being re-described, and their renunciation of the attempt to formulate criteria of choice between final vocabularies, puts them in the position which Sartre called 'meta-stable': never quite able to take themselves seriously because always aware that the terms in which they describe them are subject to change, always aware of the contingency and fragility of their final vocabularies, and thus of their selves.[21]

The key for Rorty in his positive political philosophizing – not simply his analysis of the debate, or of current political practice, both of which I submit are lacking, but his project for bringing about a cosmopolitan liberal utopia – is to keep the truth of the ironist's quest for self-perfection in the private sphere, while encasing this private pursuit of self-perfection in a framework of public, metaphysical-like liberalism. This is in other words, to make liberalism strictly political by not resorting to Kantian or Kantian-like foundations or any comparable apparatus in principle acceptable to all as reasonable. As Rorty writes in *Contingency, irony and solidarity*: 'This book tries to show how things look if we drop the demand for a theory which unifies the public and private, and are content to treat the demands for self-creation and of human solidarity as equally valid, yet forever incommensurable.'[22]

---

[21] Rorty, *Contingency, irony, solidarity*, 74.
[22] Rorty, *Contingency, irony, solidarity*, xv.

On how this is to be done, Rorty is depressingly vague. But by so radically cleaving the political sphere from the private sphere, and dropping the demand found in Kant and the early Rawls, for example, that the rationale used to justify the political and private spheres be commensurable, Rorty believes he has managed what was once thought impossible: to encase the private pursuit of self-perfection within a sphere of a system of neutral public right without reliance on a metaphysical conception of the self. This allows Rorty to say that:

> Ironist theorists like Hegel, Nietzsche, Derrida, and Foucault seem to me invaluable in our attempt to form a private self-image, but pretty much useless when it comes to politics.[23]

And further, that

> Authors such as Marx, Mill, Dewey, Habermas and Rawls are fellow citizens rather than exemplars. They are engaged in a shared social effort – the effort to make our institutions and practices more just and less cruel. We shall only think of these writers as opposed if we think that a more comprehensive philosophical outlook would let us hold self-creation and justice, private perfection and human solidarity in a single vision.[24]

Although Rorty does not believe his Liberal utopia may ever be philosophically justified as superior to any other form of political practice (that would be to fall into the errors of the metaphysicians whom he is so eager to castigate) he nevertheless believes it may be established. We may establish this cosmopolitan, liberal utopia, where the private goal of the ironist – self-perfection – is hived off from public, political liberalism, by establishing liberal solidarity among diverse people who share nothing essential.

Rorty argues that solidarity between individuals who form communities has traditionally been justified through recourse to something common that they all share. In the extreme case, this community is the whole of humanity. Kant's Kingdom of Ends is justified by the belief that all those who share in the faculty of rationality, including angels and devils, are by virtue of this faculty deserving of the equal dignity and respect that one as a rational being would demand for oneself.[25]

As an awkward example, Rorty cites the case of the Jews during the Second World War. He suggests that why more Jews in Denmark proportionately were saved from extermination than in Belgium was because they shared commonalties that are more parochial with the Danes. Rorty's assertion, which is far from uncontroversial – it is perhaps even fatuous – is that one is more likely to feel

---

[23] Rorty, *Contingency, irony, solidarity*, 83.
[24] Rorty, *Contingency, irony, solidarity*, iv.
[25] Similarly, in communities which are less than universal, solidarity, Rorty maintains, has been justified by something that all the members of the community are thought to hold in common, i.e. they share a common language, common cultural heritage, religion, or history. The strength of solidarity for Rorty, just as in the motive force of the words that compose one's final vocabulary, is inversely proportional to the parochiality of the commonality putatively shared.

solidarity with someone else the more parochially they are associated with you. A baker, by this argument, would have more in common with (and therefore a greater chance of extending solidarity to) a proximate baker than a far away candlestick maker.

Solidarity is therefore achieved not through the discovery of what makes us universally the same, such as our use of reason, as Rorty contends no such thing may be found. Rather, solidarity is created through imagining and becoming acquainted with the suffering of others. Rorty's supposition is that if we deny that humans share something by nature by which we can ground liberal practices, we can still engage in liberal practices by instilling liberal solidarity. This is to say, for Rorty, that those who are presently understood as outside of 'we' may be brought into the category of 'we' and out of the category 'them' or 'other' by extending the boundaries of solidarity into a *focus imaginarius*.

Rorty goes on to argue (borrowing from the feminists of care such as Bayer) that Kant, in so privileging moral obligation to fellow rational beings, and denigrating feelings of compassion, pity, or fellowship for particular people or groups of people as somehow less than fully moral, has prevented us from seeing how particular moral obligations and particular feelings of solidarity can be made in the absence of secure foundations. Rorty, in effect, wants to continually expand 'we Liberals,' as far as possible so that they eventually include the whole race, so that all may then share in this liberal, ironic utopia. As Rorty puts it:

> We see no reason why either recent social and political developments or recent philosophical thought should deter us from our attempts to build a cosmopolitan world society – one which embodies the same sort of utopia which the Christian, Enlightenment, and Marxist meta-narratives of emancipation ended.[26]

Philosophy, therefore, should no longer understand itself as a tribunal of reason, but rather as instrumentally crucial in the service of fostering liberal solidarity among individuals who share nothing otherwise essential. Likewise, literature itself should no longer be considered an autonomous discourse of artful expression. Rather it should come into the service of fostering liberal solidarity among disparate people by imaginatively describing and re-describing others who we do not understand as 'we' so that we may sympathize with them, see 'them' as fellow comrades in the goal of achieving liberal solidarity, gradually bringing them into membership in our liberal utopia. This, along with what we have hitherto understood as philosophy, should only be understood as branches of edifying discourse. This is discourse that is meant to make us believe not because of the soundness of its arguments, but rather because of the skill of its rhetoric.

How is normative political theory to be done if no essential element of the self is available to serve as a foundation upon which reasons for following norms may be justified? Rorty's answer is, in fact, that there is no important difficulty here, real or imagined. Reasons for acting in conformance to particular norms are not required. 'Rational performances' – those performances that are based on justified norms

---

[26] Rorty, *Objectivity, Relativism, and Truth*, 209, italics added.

– are not the only kind of acceptable performances. As Rorty has it, approvingly quoting Berlin (who is himself approvingly quoting Schumpeter):

> 'To realize the relative validity of one's convictions and yet stand for them unflinchingly, is what distinguishes a civilized man from a barbarian.' To demand more than this is perhaps a deep and incurable metaphysical need; but to allow it to determine one's practice is a symptom of an equally deep, and more dangerous, moral and political immaturity.[27]

This is to go directly against the famous thesis of Horkheimer and Adorno in *Dialectic of Enlightenment*, which Rorty suggests, with some justification, riddles the whole of the Liberal-Communitarian debate: that once we no longer believe in the philosophy with which liberal practice has been traditionally justified, we will no longer be able to engage in liberal practice.

This anti-enlightenment view of Rorty's, that we may nevertheless pursue norms of conduct in our practical lives even when we understand them to be contingent, relative, and unjustified, is the other key to understanding Rorty. Prove it incorrect and there is not a lot farther we can take Rorty. That is not quite my intention though; for I believe there is a great deal of truth to Rorty's contention, though I think its consequences are not what Rorty supposes them to be.

It is easy, for example, to imagine a whole menagerie of practices that we engage in, the norms of which will not admit of the possibility of rational justification. But the Rationalist, for Rorty, is one who believes that a norm without rational justification is not an acceptable norm of practical conduct. While this may be true or not true of the Rationalist, I do not see if it is true, that the consequences of rejecting this assumption of the Rationalist are as Rorty supposes them to be. There is a whole host of things that we stand for, act upon, and believe, for which no rational reasons can be given.

Moreover, I would like to say, and this is where Rorty gets it most wrong, that as the consequences of actions differ by degree, so does the degree of justification which norms for actions require, and it is this difference of degree that Rorty ignores by treating all norms as if they were the same.

An example: Each evening I lay outside my door a saucer of milk for the neighborhood felines to have a drink. Though I have never seen a cat drink from the saucer, the saucer is most often empty by morning, and I assume that cats drink the milk. For all I know, however, the tooth fairy may have helped herself to it. Though I may not be justified in my belief that cats come by my door at night to sate their thirst, nothing much is affected by my leaving milk outside my door, whether or not these cats do in fact exist, much less drink from my saucer. I do not in fact require much in the way of justification for the beliefs that I act upon, as the practical consequences of my actions for me are private and for others negligible. The world remains – however I do or do not act, justify or do not justify my actions – pretty much the same: neither much the better nor worse for it.

---

[27] Rorty, *Contingency, irony, solidarity*, 46. Originally from Isaiah Berlin, *Four Essays on Liberty* (Oxford: Oxford Univ. Press, 1969), 172.

In the case of the norms with which we are to regulate society, however, the matter is very much different. In a case such as this, if the norms for actions are to be understood as anything more than brute subjectivist utterance, we do in fact require reasons, indeed very good reasons for conforming to them. What I am saying is: Rorty sees no difference between the continued worship of a God whose existence, much less whose demands, may not be justified, and the proselytizing of a religion that cannot be justified. The difference is crucial and it is that which divides 'rational conduct' from 'rationalism in politics'.

It is as if Rorty sees no difference between the following three cases. In the first case, an elderly man continues to believe in God, and regularly attends church though he has no proof of God's existence. He consoles himself with the thought that such a proof is in principle possible and may soon be provided. In another case, someone else who has all his life regularly attended church continues to do so, though he believes that proof for the existence of God is in principal impossible. If you should ask him why he continues to go, he might say something to the effect that he has regularly attended church all his life and is not about to stop now, but that is about it. In the last case, a young man does not believe in God, does not believe that it is in principle possible to find a proof for the existence of God, but does in fact preach of this God and his demands to all and sundry, and argues that everyone like him should also attend church to do as he believes God demands. In this case, the young man persuades, even forces, everyone he can to live by the religion he has no rational reasons for believing in.

The difference between these cases is a function of the consequences of the actions undertaken on the basis of beliefs, regardless of the possibility of their justification in the absence or presence of 'philosophical foundations,' 'justifications,' or 'reasons.' In the first two cases, nothing much hangs on whether one does or does not attend church, having or not having justified reasons for doing so. The matter is here a strictly private affair, confined to the private life of one man. The last case is very different, however. What is at stake here is nothing less than the legitimacy of enforcing a particular substantive conception of the good, in the absence of legitimate reasons for it, upon others. What looks like moral and political latitudinarianism turns out to be its opposite.

This fatal instability, whose severity is a function of the magnitude of the action, is the point where the 'hidden spring' of Rorty's pragmatism comes in, a 'hidden spring' that Rorty can use to protect himself from such particularly illiberal consequences. In the first two cases, as I tried to show, not a whole lot rides on the consequences of the man's continuing to worship a God that he no longer believes in, whether or not proof for the existence of God is in principle possible. However, when it comes to the associational principles of a polity, there are few cases in which 'getting it right' is more pressing, and it is only reasonable that in this public sphere we demand reasons – very good ones in fact – for the pursuance of norms that will affect us. In addition, this is where Oakeshott's idea of 'rationalism in politics' comes in.

For while it may be that a civilized man should stand unflinchingly for his convictions, though he knows them to be relative, it is not at all clear why these relative values ought to be in fact liberal or even quasi-liberal values. One can, by

Rorty's argument, just as well imagine a civilized Nazi explaining that though he knows that the racialist convictions of his National Socialism are relatively valid, historically and locally contingent, he still unflinchingly stands for them, and he is therefore permitted – just as you may oppose – to persuade, cajole, and in extreme cases force others to act on the basis of these same beliefs. Rorty might object that he only means 'civilized discourse' (as he would), thus excluding the use of force, but I fail to see how he can make this distinction between persuasion and force. Obviously, this is not what Rorty intends; but Rorty's political and moral theory is, I submit, directly vulnerable to just such an objection.

Rorty's Response

How in fact does Rorty counter this at first glance fatal vulnerability, whose importance is magnified by the magnitude of the consequences of the activity – in this case the norms by which a society is to act and believe? Rorty has a trump card.

Rorty's trump card is his belief that we ought to aim to achieve a society where cruelty and humiliation are minimized, and the presence of poets and revolutionaries is maximized. This is because these are (essentially) bad and good things in and of themselves respectively. These are the ultimate, and I would argue for Rorty, universal, non-relative values, upon which he hangs a consequential theory of politics that lie at the heart of his conception of agency and society. Cruelty is included because that is the worst thing we can do to each other; humiliation, because the feature that for Rorty essentially (and I choose this word carefully) separates humans from animals is our ability to be humiliated. You may be cruel to a dog, Rorty suggests, you cannot humiliate him.

Of course, this runs counter to Rorty's alleged anti-foundationalism; yet a close reading of such works as *Contingency, irony, and solidarity* and others shows numerous places where he speaks as if he were employing such essentialist assumptions, anti-foundational protests notwithstanding. If Rorty were as radically relativistic and 'pragmatic' as he wants to be, we would offer only a recipe for anarchy. Any civilized person (or barbarian) could legitimately stand unflinchingly for their convictions, aware of their relative validity, and impose these norms upon others. We would in effect be returned to a kind of Hobbesian state of nature where the will to power reigned, and everyone had the opportunity and legitimacy to compel others to hold to their personal theory of the good life and the good society. The self cannot, however, simply be the center-less concatenation of beliefs and desires, of the kind that Rorty tells us he actually considers it to be if he is to be insulated from just such an objection.

Now officially, Rorty cannot claim this to be the case. According to Rorty the self is a pure concatenation of contingent beliefs and desires with no essential foundation that lies above or below it that we can employ to judge the rightness of particular kinds of actions or beliefs independent of their local and contingent practice. That Rorty does not actually believe the subject to be of this wholly contingent character he shows throughout the text. Indeed, he goes much further, ascribing all sorts of things to his conception of the self that fly in the face of his alleged anti-foundationalism. The ability to inflict and suffer humiliation and the romantic goal of self-creation are just a few examples.

As Rorty has such non-relative, dare I say universalist reasons (though he does not give them) he in fact becomes just the proponent of Enlightenment Rationalism that he believes he overcomes with his Postmodernism. He promotes an emancipatory Enlightenment ideal of a liberal egalitarian society with the same sort of unjustifiable Enlightenment reasons that Rorty accuses Enlightenment philosophy of having produced.

How Rorty Is Himself a Rationalist

There are many criticisms that may be made of Rorty's dream of establishing a cosmopolitan liberal utopia of negative freedom safe for 'poets and revolutionaries' to conduct their positive freedom of personal 'experiments in living.' One can point out difficulties in his understanding of the self, which is at once without a center and also a center of self-creation. Or, one might note that if the self can engage in its own act of self-creation, it probably also has the capacities to imaginatively place itself within the hypothetical thought experiment of Rawls's original position. Therefore, it might have reasons for acting upon liberal, egalitarian norms. One could also point out the problems that inherently reside in so strictly drawing a distinction between the practice of public, political liberal pragmatism, and the goal of private romantic self-perfection. Finally, one can ask whether, if there is no such thing in the debate as the realist metaphysician (as I have tried to show elsewhere that there really is not) Rorty's idealist, post-metaphysical conception of political philosophy is a suitable alternative.[28]

There is also room to criticize Rorty's denigration of philosophy as merely another branch of edifying discourse, with no power to determine what is good and right, and his characterization of imaginative literature as an instrumental tool of socialization and persuasion, not as an expression of delight and artful imagination.

Indeed, we can also note the inadequacy of Rorty's understanding of liberalism, which so effortlessly conflates the variety and miscellany of practices of France, Britain, America, Canada, and so forth into something so nebulous and protean as 'the Liberalism of the rich north Atlantic democracies.' In addition, Rorty omits entirely from view such important facets of Liberalism as the rule of law, justice as fairness or impartiality, distributive justice, desert, the judiciary, political authority, rights and obligations. (All of these, Oakeshott discusses in his account of civil association in *On Human Conduct*.) As Bernstein writes, Rorty 'simply speaks globally about 'Liberal democracy' without ever unpacking what it involves or doing justice to the enormous historical controversy about what Liberalism is or ought to be.'[29]

---

[28] The problem for Rorty is not just that his imagined opponents appear no-where in the debate, but that the alternative he presents seems similarly farfetched.

[29] Richard Bernstein, quoted in Paul Franco, *The Political Philosophy of Michael Oakeshott* (London: Yale University Press, 1990).

Such criticisms all have merit, but I believe they can all be subsumed within, or at least be seen to pale beside a larger one. Rorty, far from being a critic of the 'Enlightenment Project' as he claims, in fact embodies this project. Having so self-consciously shed a particular foundational aspect of Enlightenment Rationalism, an aspect which indeed, as I have tried to show elsewhere, is hardly present in contemporary political philosophy, Rorty is completely blind to other more significant aspects of Enlightenment political thought insofar as Rorty has one model in mind for how the world should be reformed.

Earlier I called this 'the blue-print' conception of politics, but it is symptomatic of any such utopian politics. Rorty's Pollyanna-like dream of a cosmopolitan liberal utopia is the same dream, or nearly the same dream, of a cosmopolitan liberal utopia that animates Kant's ethical and political writing that is the very apotheosis of Enlightenment Rationalism.

Unlike Rorty, however, Kant, Rawls, and Hegel all attempt to justify their ideals: Kant fashions his ideal of a world cosmopolitan liberal order on a transcendental idea of a subject of experience whose rationality was such that it demanded the equal care and respect for all other rational beings similarly constituted. Rawls supports his liberalism with a conception of an ideal choice situation within which agents decide on fair principles of justice. Even Hegel, Kant's greatest critic, grounds his conception of the self (a more hylomorphic, embedded conception of the self than Kant's) in the idea of *Geist*, and understands the nature of man (and man in political society) as embodying a continual quest for self-realization.

Rorty, of course, dispenses with all this; but he still continues to believe in the possibility of his liberal cosmopolitan utopia being achieved, even in the absence of Kantian, or Kantian-like grounding, and without regard to how society is actually composed. Without such grounding, or relevance to reality, Rorty's hope for a liberal utopia becomes a species of pure ideology, and *Contingency, irony and solidarity*, a work of pure politics and not philosophy.

Rorty would perhaps not disagree with me. However, I would like to go on to suggest that it is not simply that it is practically impossible for Rorty's utopia to become realized, it is also wholly undesirable too, as it is a liberal utopia where people have ceased to believe in truth, where philosophy and literature do not look that much different from propaganda used for the successful socialization (or shall we say brainwashing?) of its subjects. It is a Liberal utopia that instead of dealing with the pluralism of the Humean circumstances of justice, runs roughshod over the great variety of practices that people imbue their world and their selves with, leaving everything plain and homogenous in its wake. Thus Rorty's utopian dream is, I suggest, a post-modern nightmare. Oakeshott harbors no such dreams.

13

Stephen Turner

The Conservative Disposition and the Precautionary Principle

To be conservative is to prefer the familiar to the unknown, to prefer the tried to the untried, fact to mystery, the actual to the possible, the limited to the unbounded, the near to the distant, the sufficient to the superabundant, the convenient to the perfect, present laughter to utopian bliss.

[The disposition] asserts itself characteristically when there is much to be lost, and it will be strongest when this is combined with evident risk of loss.[1]

[T]he precautionary principle requires us to assign the burden of proof to those who want to introduce a new technology, particularly in cases where there is little or no established need or benefit and where the hazards are serious and irreversible. It is up to the perpetrators to prove that the technology is safe 'beyond reasonable doubt'. We cannot expect the precautionary principle by itself to tell us what to do about GM crops or any other new technology. Like a jury, we have to weigh up the evidence, and like a jury we have to come to a decision.[2]

The precautionary principle is a poorly defined idea, but it is generally understood to mean that innovations should be given special scrutiny with respect to risk, and to reject changes that involve not merely risks, which can be calculated, but uncertainties, which cannot. The formulation quoted above tries to specify this further, and whether and how it can be made more precise is a constant issue in the large literature on the subject. The principle of giving special scrutiny to innovation is not, as its critics have tirelessly pointed out, a principle at all, but something else. To use Oakeshott's term, it is a disposition. It is canonized in many legal and treaty contexts, and held to mean either that in the face of any sort of uncertainty about risks of bad consequences (for example, for the environment, but not limited to this sphere) of innovations, we should prevent their implementation until the uncertainties can be resolved. In some forms this becomes a legal demand that the 'burden of proof' in the resolution of uncertainties is the responsibility of

---

[1]   Oakeshott, 'On Being Conservative,' in *Rationalism in Politics and Other Essays* (London: Methuen, 1962), 169. Hereafter: *RP*.

[2]   Mae Wan Ho, 'The Precautionary Principle is Coherent,' *ISIS* (October, 2000); http//www. biotech-info.net/PP.coherenthtml.

the innovator. In its more extreme forms, the standard for asserting that there are uncertainties is itself not susceptible of definition in terms of 'scientific evidence' to the effect that there is a possible risk. To accept the standard of scientific evidence of possible risk is already, on this view, insufficiently precautionary or pro-active in the face of possible risk.

My focus in this essay is not with the details of the debate over the 'principle', or with the question of whether it is coherent. I will note only that the criticisms for the most part also apply to Oakeshott's account of the conservative disposition. My concern, however, is with the political meaning of the principle.

The similarities between Oakeshott's account of the conservative disposition and the precautionary principle are obvious but perhaps superficial. What I will argue is that the similarities are deep, and that the problem of the risks of change, the problem of knowledge about risks, and the attitude one takes toward those risks, especially the question of the appropriate intellectual tools for talking about these risks, is fundamental to Oakeshott's account of the conservative disposition.

This in turn points to some conclusions about the political meaning of some of the prominent events of the political present, particularly the problem of the present meaning of the division between Left and Right. The rise of the precautionary principle is itself a sign of the changed meaning of the division: the principle is embraced both by such figures of the European 'Right' as Jacques Chirac and by the extreme Left. Moreover, I will suggest that much of what passes for Left politics and 'resistance' in the sense of Foucault is more closely connected to the Conservative disposition than might be supposed.

The European side of the European-American divide is also connected to the principle. The precautionary principle has been adopted by the European Community; cost benefit analysis has been enshrined in law by the U. S. Congress. The adoptions are sometimes held to reflect the fundamental difference between American and European values, a difference famously articulated by Habermas and Derrida in the wake of 9/11.[3] They are, however, differences closely connected to not only with the values listed by Habermas and Derrida but also with European social attitudes. The French, for example, are said by survey researchers to be especially fearful about the future. Thus the academic puzzle of the present meaning of a fifty-year-old text is not entirely academic.

Left, Right and Risk

If a discussion of the differences between the United States and Europe had been conducted before 1848, it would unhesitatingly have associated the preferences pointed to by the precautionary principle as evidence of aristocratic reaction, and understood European conservatism as its expression. It is one of the many ironies of present political discourse that the obsessive concern with the preservation of privilege is today a preoccupation of the Left. The dramatic events of early 2006, in which French workers and students forced the French government to

---

[3]   Giovanna Borradori, *Philosophy in a Time of Terror: Dialogues with Jürgen Habermas and Jacques Derrida* (Chicago: Univ. of Chicago Press, 2003).

back down on a revision of labor law designed to facilitate the employment of young people, illustrates both this irony and the puzzle about present political dispositions that it reveals. In the European edition of Jon Stewart's *Daily Show* during the demonstrations against this revision, he addressed this irony by noting the incongruity of professed anarchists demonstrating for greater government regulation, in this case of employment.

One might add to this the irony that the suspicion of and hostility to expert knowledge, such as the expert knowledge of the French bureaucracy that led to the employment proposal but especially the expert knowledge that has repeatedly minimized the risk associated with genetic modification of food, is today a staple of left wing thinking. Ségolène Royal, a leader of the French socialists, was quoted as characterizing the demonstrations as a manifestation of the expertise of the people. This is a not a novel idea: it is also a staple of the political writing and indeed academic writing on such topics as genetically modified foods, which also pits the beliefs of the people against science.

To get a sense of the difference from Oakeshott's time, consider the position of John Desmond Bernal, Communist, Soviet admirer, and the leading left wing scientist of the generation of the 30s and 40s, who is cited by Oakeshott. A new biography of Bernal was recently published to the nostalgic applause of old Reds like Eric Hobsbawm.[4] The nostalgia passed over a crucial change in the Left. Hobsbawm did not note Bernal's now politically incorrect identification of Communism with expert rule. Nor did he note that in Bernal's main work, *The Social Functions of Science*,[5] he had praised, as an exemplary case of the application of scientific knowledge to the betterment of mankind, a plan under the Stalinist regime to produce climatic change in the northern hemisphere that would make Russian soil open to agriculture far into the north. Thus the leading Communists of the thirties were *for* climate change; the present day left treats it as the greatest of terrors and definitive evidence of the perfidy and unsustainability of *capitalism*.

In Bernal's time the Left excoriated capitalism for its inability to take advantage of the power of science and technology. Today it excoriates it for doing precisely this. This is a reversal that signifies a fundamental transformation. And the celebration of the defeat of the expertise of the experts by the 'expertise of the people' by the French Left shows that this difference is no blip on the radar.

In what follows I will consider this puzzling set of changes and similarities in terms of Oakeshott's own words, and suggest that they reveal new aspects of both the precautionary principle and the conservative disposition as Oakeshott describes it. Begin with the term 'principle' itself. Although Oakeshott starts his essay with a denial that the attempt to articulate conservatism as a set of principles is doomed to failure, he self-consciously selects the notion of 'disposition' to capture something he takes to be more fundamental than principles. The brunt of the discussion of the conservative disposition involves the problem of knowledge. The conservative will, he says, 'look twice' at the claims made on behalf of an

---

[4]   Eric Hobsbawm, ' "Red Science": A Review of J. D. Bernal, *The Sage of Science*,' *London Review of Books* (March 9, 2006).

[5]   J. D. Bernal, *The Social Function of Science* (Cambridge, MA: MIT Press, 1939).

innovation before accepting them, even when one is satisfied that the benefits of an innovation outweigh its costs.

> [T]here will be other considerations to be taken into the account. Innovating is always an equivocal enterprise, in which gain and loss (even excluding the loss of familiarity) are so closely interwoven that it is exceedingly difficult to forecast the final upshot: there is no such thing as an unqualified improvement ... the role of what is entailed can neither be foreseen nor circumscribed. Thus whenever there is innovation there is the certainty that the change will be greater than intended, that there will be loss as well as gain, and that the gain will not be equally distributed among the people affected; that there is the chance that the benefits derived will be greater than those which were designed; and there is the risk that they will be off-set by changes for the worse. (*RP*, 171–2)

Thus the innovations to be preferred, for Oakeshott, are those which minimize the likelihood of loss, meaning those designed to restore an equilibrium, or that grow organically, are limited rather than large and indefinite, and that the occasion is important: the most favorable being one in which the change is most likely to be limited and 'least likely to be corrupted by undesired and unmanageable consequences' (*RP*, 171).

The similarity between this appeal to the organic and the restoration of equilibrium and the sense of the phrase 'serious and irreversible' in the version of the precautionary principle quoted above is close enough to repay our interest. Oakeshott in this passage and elsewhere in this paper is concerned with the epistemic issues that arise in connection with innovation and their value. He commends suspicion about the value of innovations on the grounds that our knowledge with respect to the likelihood of loss is greater than that of gain, that 'a known good is not so lightly to be surrendered for an unknown better,' and suggests that consequently the burden of proof should be higher for the innovator. As he puts it, 'innovation entails certain loss and possible gain, therefore, the onus of proof, to show that the proposed change may be expected to be on the whole beneficial, rests with the would-be innovator' (*RP*, 172). The term 'whole' is relevant: the fact that changes ramify in their consequences means that it is difficult or impossible to calculate the potential effects of change. In short, we decide in the face of contingency, causal complexity, and unknowability, and when there is equilibrium to be lost.

The natural antagonist to this kind of thinking in Oakeshott's middle years was planning, but by 1956 the star of planning had faded. The antagonist of the precautionary principle today is the Anglo-American model of philosophizing about justice pioneered by John Rawls and dependent on a kind of cost-benefit accounting. For the conventional Anglo-American cost-benefit philosopher of justice, uncertainties and risks are simply variables to be encompassed in the model, and the standard of right action is the standard of action done by an observer who calculates the quantitative values of risks and uncertainties of changes, and also the social consequences, notably for equality. The egalitarian consequences are typically understood to be the central fact to be managed, and managing the consequences through a pro-active policy of redistribution and increase of resources is taken to be the standard for evaluating policy. This kind of philosophy is antithetical to Oakeshott's.

One way into an understanding of the conflict here is through an equivocation in the Anglo-American model of decision-theoretic political thinking. On the one hand, the model seeks to be empirically realistic. Ordinarily its exponents assume the possibility of constructing good models of the consequences of policy decisions, typically on the model of econometrics, in which outcomes can be evaluated against one another both with respect to the quantitative values of various consequences and in terms of the probabilities associated with the predictions. On the other hand, the model seeks to be a normative ideal toward which one should strive and in terms of which we should evaluate actual policies, and when challenged as unrealistic its defenders tend to retreat into this 'normative' meaning.

The difference between the two ways of thinking about these models becomes evident in the face of uncertainties about the models themselves, which can be wrong. They may include the wrong variables, fail to model the underlying causal relations correctly, fail to apply in new circumstances in which different variables emerge as causally relevant, or simply abstract incorrectly, for example by assuming linearity, the normalcy of the population distribution, or the representativeness of the time-slice from which the data on which the model's estimates are based is derived. From the 'empirical' point of view, the models are merely representations of some sort of underlying reality that is not known, and may differ from the model. From the 'normative' standard point of view, these empirical considerations are irrelevant by definition: the right policy is one that an ideal observer would select. We can then use this standard to 'normatively' judge the actual selection of empirical models as well as outcomes.[6]

The normative standard of the ideal observer, indeed the presumption that something akin to omniscience about consequences is part of an appropriate normative standard, is what sets the precautionary principle against this standard Anglo-American style of reasoning and against the model of cost benefit analysis of risks known as risk analysis. The precautionary principle is designed to place a special burden of proof on change, especially the introduction of new technology, on the grounds that the cost-benefit model fails to deal successfully with uncertainties whose scope and character is unknown and unknowable. The similarity to Oakeshott with respect to the problem of knowledge of consequences needs no additional comment. Both are centrally concerned with what Donald Rumsfeld called the unknown unknowns.

The problem of unknown unknowns gives rise to what the Anglo-American model treats as a fatal flaw. The trap that the precautionary principle falls into, from the point of view of the critics, is that even claims about uncertainty or unknown unknowns require evidence that provides some certainty, and consequently the attempt to avoid the calculus of risk either fails or falls into incoherence. The incoherence results from the fact that one cannot be averse to risk or uncertainty as

---

[6] An example of this way of thinking is Phillip Kitcher, *Science, Truth, and Democracy* (New York: Oxford Univ. Press, 2003).

such,[7] because any strategy to reduce risk, such as a novel policy on evaluating risk, produces its own risks. Even the precautionary principle itself, if it is understood as a method of reducing risk by increasing the burden of proof on innovators is a novel policy with its own risks. At best one may balance uncertainties and risks. Thus the precautionary principle is not an alternative, but just another policy that needs to be judged by the standards of rationality of the Anglo-American model.

One is either compelled to calculate by balancing risks against one another, in the manner of risk analysis, or one must supply content to the principle by selecting certain kinds of risks as acceptable. The first alternative collapses into the Anglo-American model; the second alternative collapses into the first if one chooses the content on the basis of some principle of selection which is itself related to risks and benefits which balances different kinds of risks and benefits against one another. To treat the selection of content as something that cannot be done as a matter of principle, a third option is, by the lights of the model, arbitrary, and if so the precautionary principle is not a principle. These considerations mean, in short, that there is no separate principle of 'precaution'. At best it is a procedural idea about burdens of proof, to be assessed as such. But as a procedural idea it begs the question of how decisions are to be made using the procedure. To put it in terms of the quotation above, suppose that a 'jury' decides based on the evidence: how is it supposed to decide other than in terms of risks, benefits, and the calculation of the epistemic weight to be given uncertainties, which is to say the Anglo-American model itself?

The same difficulties would arise for a principle or policy of 'conservatism'. As Cass Sunstein points out, even continuing to do the same thing involves risks, sometimes very large risks. So if the principle is understood as a principle of risk avoidance, it could only be stated coherently without a concealed and arbitrary preference for that which is already done. Alternatively, if it simply is a preference for that which is already done, it has no meaning apart from the specific content that is given by the phrase 'that is already done', and it is useless in the face of the inevitable decisions that must be made in order to continue to do one thing, such as enjoy bird watching, without ceasing to do some other thing, such as polluting the air that the birds breathe.

With this argument we have the germ of a genuine philosophical problem. Do the apparent alternatives to the 'normative' sense of the Anglo-American philosophical model of decision-making, on examination, collapse into this model? Or does the alternative rest on assumptions that are problematic, i.e. for which there are good alternatives? Does the consideration of content provide such an alternative, that is to say, are there non-arbitrary substantive commitments that would lead to the rejection of the model? And how might these commitments relate to what Oakeshott called the 'conservative disposition'?

Oakeshott was aware of the problem of content. Dropping the term 'principle' and inserting the term 'disposition' avoids this problem. As he puts it, it can be applied to anything except the love of fashion, 'that is, wanton delight in change

---

[7] Cf. Cass Sunstein, *Laws of Fear: Beyond the Precautionary Principle* (Cambridge, MA: Cambridge Univ. Press, 2005), 56.

for its own sake' (*RP*, 178). The person disposed to precaution, or alternatively to conservatism, would attempt to (or be disposed to) preserve both, but the disposition would make no pretense of deciding between the two. Oakeshott was also well aware that the preference for the familiar required appropriate occasions of application, as he put it. This reasoning is central to his argument in this essay, which was concerned with the following apparent anomaly: the preference for a certain kind of politics which he considered to be an appropriate application of the conservative disposition for the occasion of politics as practiced and perhaps practiced to an unusual extent by people who were in other realms 'adventurous' (*RP*, 178). What he had in mind was the fact that defense of the rule of law and of the political conception of the state as an umpire was particularly characteristic of those capitalists and commercial innovators who were engaged in the business that Schumpeter described as creative destruction. He was also well aware that it could be shared by the adherents of 'alternative life styles', as the '60s expression had it, such as the Bohemianism that he himself practiced.

The conservative disposition then, like the precautionary principle, is a creature of its occasions of application rather than the kind of overarching moral conception that the technical philosophy of justice purports to be. It can be applied to anything. But the term 'occasion' itself, and the qualification 'important' attached to it are pregnant with implication. One implication might be this: Oakeshott had a concealed idea about content that needs to be uncovered and examined. But there are other possibilities, including the possibility that considerations that follow from the epistemic issues surrounding risk themselves dictate something about content. In any case, there is the charge of arbitrariness to consider. Even if Oakeshott acknowledged, as he did, that the occasions for the application of the disposition are arbitrary in the sense that they do not follow from a principle, they are not necessarily arbitrary as a matter of practical fact. The precautionary principle itself has a similar structure. The version quoted above provides content to the principle by singling out two types of changes to be avoided — those that promise little and those which have irreversible consequences and uncertainty. But this does not follow from the notion of precaution itself, and thus seems arbitrary, especially to the adherents of the Anglo-American model, such as Sunstein.

The Problem of Content

When Oakeshott speaks of the conservative disposition as a preference for the familiar and for the enjoyment of present things, he is implicitly speaking the language that has been such a focus of writing on the problem of risks, from the writings of Mary Douglas and Aaron Wildavsky onward. When he says 'the man of conservative temperament … is not in love with what is dangerous and difficult; he is unadventurous; he has no impulse to sail uncharted waters,' he does this explicitly (*RP*, 172-3). The writings of Douglas and Wildavsky have also been implicitly opposed to the cost-benefit model of thinking about risks, but in their case by pointing out the cultural specificity of attitudes about risk and consequently their irreducibility to some sort of general calculus of risks.

Much of what Douglas and Wildavsky call 'cultural' about risk is easily understood in terms of Oakeshott's language of familiarity. The risk of dying in an automobile accident, for example, is impossibly greater than the risk of suffering ill effects from nuclear power or genetically modified food. What makes these into public obsessions and automobile accidents into the subject of fatalistic acceptance is the fact of familiarity. We accept those risks with which we are familiar with stoicism and even indifference. We have become used to them. And this makes them risks that we are comfortable with.

The precautionary principal and the conservative disposition alike are unconcerned about these risks. When Oakeshott speaks of danger, it is understood within the compass of our scheme of familiarity rather than in the absolute sense envisioned by the cost-benefit model of risk analysis. Critics of risk analysis on the Left have often championed the specific risk aversions of 'the people' as deserving of special consideration regardless of how rational it is from the point of view of cost-benefit risk analysis. Sometimes there is an attempt to have it both ways, to treat the 'irrational' risk perception of the people as representing their values, and then devising expert policies to correspond with these values.

The liberal critics of this kind of thinking, such as Sunstein himself, take a different view. The law (which he is a professor of), he argues, is there not to merely reflect irrational prejudices but to improve on them and correct them as well as reconcile them. And the role of the law in reconciling them is especially important in these cases because popular preferences with respect to risks are characteristically disordered, meaning that they are not transitive. One focus of this literature has been on the valuation of human life, and it is a commonplace that the implicit values attached to human life in compensation for accidents or in the creation of safety measures do not yield consistent values. Consistency of some kind is essential to a rational policy and this is precisely what popular attitudes to risk fail to produce. It is arguments like this that enable one to see the importance of Oakeshott's emphasis on the issue of appropriate occasions for the application of the conservative disposition.

Where Oakeshott differs from the rationalized model is in rejecting the very idea of the possibility of a comprehensive overview of the consequences of innovation. Neither politics nor life can be, for Oakeshott, reduced to a plan, which could then be rationalized and executed to bring about predetermined goals. To be sure, on some occasions it is possible to make and execute plans successfully. But in the larger frameworks of politics and life itself, it is not. The reasons for this are partly epistemic. Our knowledge of the world and especially of the world of consequences of change is extremely limited. There are two primary reasons for this. The first is the predominant fact of contingency of circumstances. Life and political life include much that is incalculable. We simply do not know what might happen that will change the circumstances under which we act. But there is another. We have limited knowledge of the consequences of our actions. As Machiavelli said, one change is a toothing stone for another, by which he meant that changes create the conditions for other changes. Oakeshott made the same point, but emphasized the incalculability of the results of changes and their ramifying character.

The effect of this is to introduce an epistemic bias against change. Change in general involves the unknown; it is an adventure, meaning it is action with danger. With the familiar, the dangers are for the most part known. So even for Oakeshott, a preference for the present and familiar and for the enjoyment of the present is connected with our sense that the promises of the future are almost always partly false, in the sense that the results are not as advertised, and they contain incalculable dangers as well as, incalculable opportunities of an unfamiliar kind. The language of risk and danger is Oakeshott's (e.g., *RP*, 172-3, and *passim*); indeed, this text is full of variations on this language, and it is central to his main problem in the text, to account for the anomaly that the conservative disposition in politics occurs side by side with, and in the same persons as, the 'adventurous' disposition characteristic of capitalistic entrepreneurialism.

This anomaly is what leads Oakeshott to ask when the disposition to be conservative is appropriately applied. Human nature, he says, is not very informative here, for it is 'no steadier than anything else in our acquaintance' (*RP*, 174). But it does lead him to some general considerations; namely that activities which are not instrumental but are enjoyed in themselves, such as friendship are an especially appropriate thing to be conservatively disposed toward (*RP*, 177), and that familiarity of the kind we have with tools which typically do not change rapidly, also bound up with our personal skills in using them, fits with and provides an appropriate occasion for the application of the conservative disposition.

He combined these thoughts in his discussion of conservatism in politics, a discussion that anticipates the themes of *On Human Conduct*.[8] The key precondition for the application of the conservative disposition in politics is 'observation of our current manner of living' and the satisfactions it provides 'combined with,' as he puts it, 'the belief (which from our point of view need be regarded as no more than a hypothesis) that governing is a specific and limited activity, namely the provision and custody of general rules of conduct' (*RP*, 184). This gets us what might be called conservative liberalism. What we conserve are general rules of conduct, which are tool-like and familiar, and which also happen to be the ones that permit us to enjoy the activities we have come to enjoy. This notion of politics allows for a great deal of tolerance toward our special and distinctive enjoyments. The contrast he provides is to a politics of dreams, in which, inevitably, *my* dreams, *my* imagined future enjoyments must be imposed on *you* by the state for me to get them at all (*RP*, 186).

The Conservative Disposition and the Left

The precautionary principle, and even the resistance to changes in the welfare state which have become characteristic of, not only French but European politics more generally in recent years, more strongly resembles Oakeshott's formulation of the conservative disposition than the politics of rational dreams. For the European Left, any alteration in the arrangement of the welfare state, its benefits, its actual practices, is experienced not as opportunity or even as opportunity mixed with risk,

---

[8]   Oakeshott, *On Human Conduct* (Oxford: Clarendon Press, 1975). Hereafter: *OHC*.

but as loss of the familiar. And these societies are increasingly present oriented and concerned with the enjoyment of the present, which is more and more understood as the best of all possible worlds. The European Left has no grand project. It is committed instead to resistance, resistance to what it characterizes as neo-liberalism and the savage inequalities of feral capitalism, and, on a practical and less rhetorical level to the specific rights that are enjoyed by citizens of a pervasive welfare state.

It is they rather than the expert neo-liberal transformers with whom they are in combat who fit Oakeshott's characterization of people who have learned from experience what the good life is and seek first and foremost to enjoy it. Put differently, the European welfare state is today a political tradition. It is no longer merely a program of redistribution, but a form of life that is distinctive, much admired by outsiders, and which has proven to be difficult to emulate, perhaps even more difficult to emulate than liberal democracy itself. Weber famously said that although the rights of man were a rationalist fantasy, we could nevertheless not imagine life without them. Something similar may be said for the European welfare state for those for whom it is the 'familiar' mode of life.

What would Oakeshott have said to this? Perhaps he would simply have accepted it. As I have suggested, the point of his essay was to explain the anomaly that conservatism about political life co-existed with 'adventurousness' in economic life, and with a society that was not static. The present European welfare state attempts to eliminate the adventurousness in economic life, in some respects at least, and is thus in an important sense more fully conservative than its more adventurous alternatives. And although it is hardly the kind of question that one can settle empirically or by adding conceptual distinctions, it does seem plausible, especially in view of the considerations I have been alluding to here, of familiarity, security, and the enjoyment of the present, that these welfare states provide something beyond the material and beyond the legal security of rights to care. Perhaps the security of the welfare state produces some additional unanticipated and difficult to describe human qualities or qualities of joined existence analogous to, or perhaps even a form of, the kinds of relationships of friendship and the like. Or perhaps these states simply show that security itself, once experienced, is impossible to imagine giving up. The fact that French twenty-somethings who move to London to work and are grateful for the opportunity still oppose the idea of dismantling the guarantees that govern French jobs suggests that this is so. In any case, these arrangements have by now become part of these societies in an organic way.

If we put together Oakeshott's acknowledgement of the ideological moment, the partly organic and partly planned character of the modern European welfare state, and the unanticipated present pleasures that might be thought to arise from it, which arise organically, it does seem that this is an appropriate occasion for the application of the conservative disposition. Here there is something to be conserved, something unacknowledged by cost-benefit liberalism. Oakeshott's defense of economic liberalism and economic and political liberalism as forms of life is a nonexclusive form of argument; that is to say, it is able to justify other potentially very different forms of life in addition to the particular forms that Oakeshott concentrates on in this essay. If there is a place for the adventurous in Oakeshott's depiction of market capitalism, there is a place elsewhere for the unadventurous, and satisfactions of security and social equality.

But there is another issue that appears to point in a quite different direction. Even if the present day European welfare state, governed by the precautionary principle, eschewing the adventures of feral capitalism, can be seen to stand on its own as a form of life of its own satisfactions, the politics of these states are perhaps less amenable to this treatment. Albert Venn Dicey predicted that twentieth century politics would be a defective form of liberal politics oscillating between parties of redistribution and parties which would come into power intermittently when redistribution and taxation had gone so far as to cause difficulties that only lighter taxation and less redistribution could resolve.[9] This impoverished kind of politics, as Dicey imagined it, would be centered entirely on the material and was barely a politics at all. Whether this is a fair characterization of the political life of these states as they have developed is an open question that needs to be examined, but it obviously has an element of truth.

Environmental Dystopia

As noted above, Oakeshott distinguished a kind of politics of competing plans in which individuals aspire to impose their dreams on others through politics. This is not only an echo of the language of planning, and thus of the battles of the thirties and forties, it is also curiously similar to the expert-driven politics of the present, though with a peculiar difference. Consider the politics of global warming, which is of a piece with the politics of genetically modified foods, with the difference that one appears to be endorsed by a consensus of scientists and the other rejected. What makes both movements similar to the politics of imposing one's plans on others is that although their visions of the future are dystopian rather than utopian, dreams which are nightmares, they are nevertheless competing visions of the future. Politics thus again becomes a politics of visions of the future in which various rivals attempt to impose their visions on the unwilling through state action.

This is not a politics that lends itself to the politics of give and take, of compromise, of respect for contingency, and of non-fanaticism, that Oakeshott had in mind when he described the role of the state as an umpire. For the welfare state as such, matters are different. The state can still be understood as an umpire who takes on a task of preserving the balance that allows for the preservation of a form of life. This state can muddle along, make errors, make corrections, adjust to contingencies, and subsist on a politics that acknowledges all these things. The politics of environmental dystopia, like the politics of positive rationalism, is absolutist. Knowledge and rationality are on one side; power, obdurateness, irrationality, and evil are on the other.

I need hardly point out how far this kind of politics is from the politics of epistemic humility practiced by Oakeshott in the face of what he recognized as

---

[9]   Albert Venn Dicey, *Lectures on the Relation Between Law & Public Opinion in England During the Nineteenth Century*, 2d ed. (1914; reprint, London: Macmillan and Co., 1962), xxiii–xciv, esp. lxxxi–lxxxviii.

contingency and the complexity of consequences. The politics of dystopia has no place for contingency or complexity. It is the politics of the overwhelming and overriding emergency. It is the politics in which compromise always leads to catastrophe. And it cannot be denied that there is more than an element of this politics in the street politics and even in the parliamentary and congressional politics of those for whom, as Al Gore's book title has it, earth is 'in the balance'. And there is more than a whiff of fanaticism in the obdurate unwillingness of at least some in the religious right to take any account of environmental risk. Moreover, this is our politics of the future to an extent that the planners or for that matter the Communists never dreamt.

What has changed, from Oakeshott's point of view, is the combination of attachments to the salvageable pleasures of this world in the face and fear of its imminent destruction by the practices of the present. The positive program of this politics is *sauve qui peut,* which is ordinarily the politics of not only reaction but of defensive reaction. Today it is a politics of crisis. The question it raises is whether the crisis is genuine. But if it is genuine, it is a crisis that threatens all that we value and is thus an occasion for the conservative disposition. But it is also an occasion where political business as usual may simply not be enough. The conservatively disposed necessarily take a different view of future dystopias than of future utopias. Both may be speculative and demand our epistemic humility, but the prospect of calamity is a prospect of the loss of the present pleasures that the conservative values, that is to say something tangible and familiar, as distinct from the prospective and theoretical benefits of utopia. And although the conservatively disposed have a reluctance to part with normalcy, just as there are occasions for the conservative dispositions and there are occasions for dispensing with what is familiar and this may be such an occasion. The conservative disposition, the precautionary principle and the politics of fearfulness have this in common: for each of them the continued enjoyment of the present and the familiar overrides hypothetical benefits in the future.

The application of the precautionary principle and indeed giving any sort of determinant meaning to it has been a problem in European politics and European law. The incoherence that Sunstein attributes to it appears in this context as well. The initial meaning is to establish a bias against risk, to say that the reality of risk is such and the contingencies of introducing new things is such that merely using what is known to balance benefits and costs or risk is not enough. But turning this into a legal doctrine has been problematic. First there is the problem of evidence. Just as there is questionable evidence of benefits, which is in effect what Oakeshott is trading on in this essay, there are also questions of risks. It is not meaningful to place the entire burden of proof on the innovator to assure us that the risks are minimal. To prove that there are no risks, anticipated or unanticipated, would be to ask for proof of a negative. And as Oakeshott was the first to say, this is an area in which contingency and complexity reign.

The idea of the rule of law itself constrains our application of this principle. For there to be any semblance of legal certainty, decisions about new technologies, for example, need to be made according to standards known in advance and applied equally to different cases. If legal certainty requires factual determinations to attain a degree of certainty, we cannot demand a blank check. And what the courts have decided is to limit the questions that had to be asked of a new technology under the precautionary principle to a relatively short list of specific risks which could addressed by specific kinds of evidence. Setting the standard of proof for risks higher has the effect of reducing the number of decisions to the effect that there is no evidence of risk. Setting it lower is a kind of poor substitute for the epistemic humility and acknowledgment of contingency that Oakeshott makes part of being conservative. And perhaps it is an unsatisfactory one.

There is a more extreme interpretation, which might go as follows. The environmental crisis is sufficiently severe that liberal politics itself is incapable of dealing with it, of producing willingness to act, or of establishing the kind of clarity about our situation that resolute action demands. Because of this, the thing we need to sacrifice that we are familiar with is liberal politics itself. It must be said that there is in the green movement and even more so in the anti-globalization movement a strong strain of antipathy to politics as usual, not only because politics as usual got us into this mess, but because politics is insufficiently rational. Here the green and anti-globalization movement returns to the politics of rationalism in a way that sacrifices the epistemic humility that Oakeshott's conservative disposition includes. Here meet the rationalistic liberalism of Rawls or Sunstein, in which uncertainty is merely another variable to be included in one's rational model of decision making, and the apparently irrational anti-politics of anti globalization and green activism.

Where they differ is in the weight that they give to uncertainties about the calamities that will befall us and to the extent to which they believe that these calamities outweigh all other considerations. But they agree in thinking that our response and its 'rationality' is the test by which we can judge politics, and thus they agree in their sense that politics is not so much a form of life appropriate to its own contingencies and the contingencies of life, but rather an instrumental activity.

Let me close with what appears to be an enormous irony. The end of utopia, a topic that is much discussed and bemoaned on the Left, has radically altered the way in which we can now think of conservatism. In 1956 Communism was still alive, though fatally wounded, and reform of some radical or significantly different kind was still, though by then barely, a meaningful political agenda. The critiques of planning of the previous decade still were theoretical. The actual experience of the failure of Keynesianism and the kind of socialism represented by pre-Thatcher Labour was still in the future. The equilibrium that was eventually achieved by governments that talked Left and governed Right was also far in the future.

In the intervening fifty years, what it meant to be on the Left changed from hoping for a better world and proposing experiments to get there, meaning the plans which Oakeshott discussed that need to be imposed by the state, to resisting the oppression, exclusion, and the disempowerment of long-suffering groups. Resistance, however, typically has had two sides, sides that were uneasily related to one another. One side is frankly utopian or, worse, merely dystopian, such as the anti-capitalism of the self-proclaimed anarchists who oppose world trade, for example. Their anarchism seems to consist in the fact that although they have no intelligible alternative, they resist anyway. But another side to resistance is conservative.

The conservative side to resistance involves resistance to changes that take away the possibility of the living of lives which people already enjoy, and which they do not wish to trade away for an abstract promise of a better life, or indeed to trade away at all. This side is local, episodic, untheoretical, and motivated by nothing so much as a desire to live in the present. One of the staple forms of resistance movements globally has been resistance to dam projects by people who are very poor, who are being offered relocation and compensation, but who refuse to give up what is familiar to them. Often this desire involves the preservation of tariffs and special treatment, and is interest motivated. But tangled up with these interests and supplying a powerful motivation is a sense of danger and loss and an unwillingness to accept the promises of the future that can correctly be described in Oakeshott's terms as dispositionally conservative. They reflect the same preference for the familiar and the understood that Oakeshott and the precautionary principle attempts to articulate. And in doing so, they confound the philosophers who employ the Anglo-American model as much as they do the policy scientists who are attempting to impose 'rational' policies meant to better their lot.

IV

On Being Conservative

14

George Feaver

Being English: The Conservative Witness of Michael Oakeshott

I

Michael Oakeshott was an English-language political essayist of the first rank. This is richly evidenced in his celebrated essay 'On Being Conservative,' a text many agree deserves inclusion in the company of such luminaries of the British conservative disposition as Halifax, Hume, Burke and Coleridge. 'On Being Conservative' originated as a spoken performance presented at the University of Swansea in 1956, six years before its earliest print publication in *Rationalism in Politics* (1962). Half a century on, it still conveys a distinct atmosphere, an invitation to conversation with a philosophically and stylishly unique voice. Commentators have noted this textural feature of Oakeshott's writings, particularly his essays. Paul Franco saw fit to title the opening chapter of his recent summation of Oakeshott's writings for the non-specialist 'The Oakeshottian Voice.' He pointedly prefaced it with Oakeshott's own words: 'Not to detect a man's style is to have missed three-quarters of the meaning of his actions and utterances.'[1]

Yet, if Oakeshott's philosophical voice is stylishly his own, it evokes a broader, pervasively English self-identity. W. H. Greenleaf, in the earliest of what would become a steady stream of books elucidating aspects of Oakeshott's thought, drew express attention to this strong sense of his British cultural self-identity – despite Oakeshott's general predilection to express his ideas indirectly. Greenleaf was impressed by what he saw as Oakeshott's 'deep and genuine patriotism.' And though he cautioned that it would be misleading to depict him simplistically as a nationalist, his writings do display 'a profound sense of the greatness and uniqueness of the British political achievement and way of life generally.'[2] As Oakeshott's reputation grew following his appointment to succeed Harold Laski as Professor of Political Science at the London School of Economics in 1951, others reacted less favorably to this proclivity. They saw in Oakeshott's evident affection for the British way of life the point of view of a Tory dandy, a Little Englander, even a romantic reactionary whose conspicuous hostility to much in contemporary British

---

[1]   Paul Franco, *Michael Oakeshott: An Introduction* (London: Yale Univ. Press, 2004), 1–23.
[2]   Cf. W. H. Greenleaf, *Oakeshott's Philosophical Politics* (London: Longman's, 1966), 84.

political life barely disguised acute dismay over England's lost imperial grandeur. His cultural insularity, they averred, ruled out the possibility that Oakeshott's ideas had anything much to say about broader philosophical concerns.

In the immediate post-war decades, then, admirers and detractors alike regarded Oakeshott as a writer with a stylishly individual yet evidently embedded English self-identity. Little sustained attention has been accorded the character of this self-identity, which is an integral part of Oakeshott's characteristic way of seeing and saying things. He was an accomplished, if unselfconscious rhetorician of Englishness, no small attainment in a political society whose literary history abounds in gifted practitioners of the idiom.

II

Being English or *British*, like *being conservative*, entails something more than a capricious or straightforward 'now and then.' It requires attention to the features of a continuing and settled disposition – to 'a certain limited stock of ideas, images, beliefs, desires, projects, practices, expedients, and so on.' These features link beliefs about being English *then* with the sense of England *now*. Such dispositions are capable of modification, but their present character importantly reveals itself in 'what is already there' – *a kind of groove or rut or channel*, which, as Oakeshott himself says, 'has been excavated by human choices … it establishes itself by a long continued movement which gradually chisels out its own restrictions, each absence of deviation contributing to a balance of dispositions, which in the course of time discloses itself unmistakably.'[3]

It is noteworthy that, many years after crafting this suggestive image, in which a disposition is likened to a groove, rut, or channel, Oakeshott saw fit to take a somewhat different rhetorical tack, in prefacing *On Human Conduct* with the touching passage: 'The themes explored here have been with me nearly as long as I can remember; but I have left the task of putting my thoughts together almost too late and the reader must forgive me if I have consequently gone slowly in order to avoid being flustered. And *when I look back upon the path my footprints make in the snow* I wish that it might have been less rambling.'[4]

These two images, of the rut and the temporary footprint, adjoin considerations of both metaphoric locale and seasonality. Each speaks to an appreciation of the vicissitudes that always attend the 'balance of dispositions' contributing to the shape and texture of a settled character. Thus, in the figurative winter of Oakeshott's advancing old age, the snows have for now blanketed the rut beneath.

---

[3]   Oakeshott, *Morality and Politics in Modern Europe: The Harvard Lectures,* ed. Shirley Robin Letwin (New Haven: Yale Univ. Press, 1993), 30–1. Hereafter: *MPME.*
[4]   Oakeshott, *On Human Conduct* (Oxford: Clarendon Press, 1975), vii–viii, italics added. Hereafter: *OHC.* Many years before, Oakeshott had recourse to similar imagery in his brief but revealing 'Introduction to the Second Edition' of his LSE colleague Reginald Bassett's *The Essentials of Parliamentary Democracy,* 2d ed. (London: Frank Cass, 1964), xxi–xxii, where he says of Bassett, in words that apply to himself as well: 'For him, political history was composed, neither of the sweeping movements beloved of the 'intellectual', nor of the fortunes of 'systems' of government, but of the footprints left by those who engaged in political activity, each a moment of significance to be recognized, reflected upon and interpreted in its context.'

But with the arrival of another spring, the groove reveals itself anew in place below, stable, though never secure against possible modification. There is a not dissimilar balancing of the evanescent and the seemingly ineffaceable in the interlinked passage of the human generations. We are begotten and we beget, in a temporal course of inexorable change and constancy, marked by a sense of origination and place, and so too of being abroad and of coming home.

Being English, then, involves a kind of self-recognition, the discernment of a personal identity in certain enduring features of a 'national character' or culture that reflects the wide historical experience of a very old political society.[5] This character has for long been said to be marked, among other things, by a deeply ingrained patriotism and sense of place, a habitual preference for the practical over the theoretical, an inbred regard for context in advance of generalization, and an abiding love of the English language. The temper of this idiom has, in the broadest sense, been persistently liberal. It is broadly liberal because of the primacy among its attributes of an enduring belief that 'English liberty' is inextricably tied to a perennially restorative morality of individuality. This morality is embedded in a crooked logic, a logic of experiential much more than theoretical knowing; and it reflects a pedigree of habits and *mores* long observed to be peculiarly English – flourishing, waning, and flourishing anew, like the recurrent seasons. It is a morality deeply rooted in the ancient common law legal claims of constitutional rule, on one hand, and of private property on the other. And, so far from being much constrained by an equally coeval sense of bonds of locale and community interest, this bedrock British love of liberty and shared celebration of individuality has been ultimately, in some rationally inexplicable sense, an intimated accretion of both public and private considerations. English liberty and individuality, that is, have been substantially nurtured and sustained by a strong British sense of community. Taken together and perceived organically, these self-balancing elements of liberty and tradition have, in the long historical view, provided a healthily consolidating milieu. The British political tradition, in sum, has shown a prodigious capacity relative at least to other European states in modernity, to balance the competing yet overlapping claims of liberty and authority.[6]

The British experience, then as now a cumulative reflection of inattention or inadvertence as much as any conscious design, suggests an arresting instance of

---

[5]   Cf. Peter Mandler, *The English National Character: The History of an Idea from Edmund Burke to Tony Blair* (London: Yale Univ. Press, 2006). Enlightenment values of universality have corroded the idea of national character, but Mandler's account 'also recognizes the conservative view that individuals have characters, and nations have institutions. Some of England's just happen to be extremely old.' David Horspool, 'What Makes an Englishman,' *Daily Telegraph*, December 24, 2006.

[6]   Norman F. Cantor: 'The English achievement is in politics and law; even without a personal commitment to those ideals of liberalism which were largely an English invention, it would have to be admitted that on strictly pragmatic grounds the English must be considered the most successful political society in world history. No other country has had such a remarkable degree of continuity in the history of its political institutions ... the theme that gives value and meaning to the study of English history must in all eras be the ways in which this peculiar island people developed their governmental and legal institutions and ideas.' In Cantor, *The English: A History of Politics and Society to 1760* (London: Allen & Unwin, 1968), 14–5.

the uneven emergence out of an undifferentiated medieval Christendom of the
rudimentary elements now recognized as requisite for the formation of a *bone fide*
modern European state. If America, as has been said, was the first new nation,
parental Albion has as plausible a claim to be regarded as the earliest of the modern
European constitutional states, as well as the most continuous. In consequence,
the preeminently liberal idiom in Englishness, or *'being English,'* may be said, in a
certain sense without paradox, to carry within itself a deeply embedded element
of *'being conservative.'* And here a lengthy quote from Herbert Butterfield seems
apposite:

> One of the paradoxes of history has been the way in which the name of England has
> come to be so closely associated with liberty on the one hand and tradition on the
> other. It seems that freedom amongst Englishmen is not a frisky thing which romps and
> capers in the spirit of April. Rather it sits into the landscape and broods there like the
> trees of autumn, streaked with red dyes, and mellow with the stain of setting suns. If
> in some countries liberty is valued as a recent acquisition – treasured as the reward of a
> battle which was won only yesterday – the British seem to hold it rather as an ancient
> possession, itself a legacy from the past, almost even the product of tradition. The word
> liberty is packed with meanings and implications for us – it comes with all kinds of
> subtle overtones – precisely because it is so ancient a thing and has gathered into itself
> so much history.'[7]

Of course, while stereotypic notions of Englishness are ready to hand in the cultural
and historical imaginings of Briton and non-Briton alike, any attempt to pinpoint
a Procrustean essence of Englishness is bound to end in frustration. The *'being
English'* of Englishness, like *being conservative*, comes down to propensities, or
predilections in thought and conduct over time, or, as Michael Oakeshott ventured
to surmise in 'On Being Conservative,' to a settled disposition.

III

Being English, or *being conservative*, or for that matter, being anything else in the
human estate according to fashionable dogma, entails an engagement to experience
life as a narrative, as a kind of story or collection of stories. In this way of seeing
things, our ultimate transience is inescapably marked by processes of entrance,
passage, and exit. Stripped to essentials, humanness means that we are born to live
and to die in the acting out of a recurrence of narratives, which, whatever might
be the sum of their considerable range of possibilities in detailed variation, are
fated in every discrete instance to be bounded by beginning and end points. And
there does appear to be general psychological acceptance that, to be human, is to
be at once a living narrative and a putative story-teller. In even the most ostensibly
pedestrian of lives, and not only in the vividly imagined life of a Sherlock Holmes,
on this view, the game is always afoot. A not dissimilar point might be inferred

---

[7]   Herbert Butterfield, 'Liberty and Tradition in England,' in his *Liberty in the Modern World*
      (Toronto: Ryerson Press, 1952), 21. See also Butterfield's *The Englishman and His History*
      (Cambridge: Cambridge Univ. Press: 1944).

from Oakeshott's own conception, in *On Human Conduct*, that at least in part, an intelligible performance requires properly to be recognized as an instance of what he calls 'self-enactment.'

Yet, even allowing for an inherence of some conscious capacity for natural narrativity in all human 'goings-on,' considered subjectively, this suggestion is less serviceable when we attempt to apply it – now at a certain remove from pure conceptual subjectivity – to a consideration of exactly what it is to say of an individual that he or she is marked by a recognizable or settled disposition. A more inclusive account of a human performance requires something more. For it is part of a perceived disposition that, while it retains an elusiveness shielding it from degenerating into a mere caricature, it manages to convey a definite and discernible balance of traits and idiosyncrasies. These represent an equipoise or a style that others will spot, in its merest manifestation, as an implicit or 'characteristic' manner of responding to the vagaries and contingencies of emergent experience. That is what it means to 'have' or to 'be' a character; and a fully satisfactory account of character cannot be achieved by concentrating on notions of 'self-enactment' alone. Character entails, as Oakeshott insists, an additional element of 'self-disclosure' – a kind of silhouette '*I*' embedded in a manifold of conduct and discernible more to the scrupulous '*eye*' in propensity, leaning, inclination, or proclivity, than in literal self-enactment.

Conventionally, the idea of a settled disposition or character has been applied to individuals and fictive persons – to Michael Oakeshott as well as to John Bull. Consider the persistence, even in an age otherwise strongly marked by the spirit of 'globalization', of the common practice of stereotyping nation-states (*the* British, French, German, and so on) as if they were human persons incarnate or writ large, their purported predilections in conduct reflecting a shared culture or 'race'. Although decidedly out of intellectual fashion for much of the past half-century because of the sinister successes of virulent forms of nationalism that willfully confused such old metaphoric ideas of culture and race with new genetic categories in the service of pseudo-scientific doctrines of racial superiority and inferiority, such national stereotyping remains still surprisingly robust with deep vernacular roots in pre-Enlightenment European thought.[8]

If notions of disposition and character are habitually deployed to characterize the psychological peculiarities of individuals and collectives, they are also routinely present in considerations of a more traditionally moral nature. What links and binds the discrete self-identity of individual moral agency to the shared

---

[8] 'Of course, we all know that there's no such thing as 'national character'.... So having got that straight, just run through the following thought-experiments. Imagine an Australian man who is shy, riven with self-doubt, and rather effete. Imagine a Japanese woman who is impolite, boorish, and physically messy. Imagine an Irishman who is inarticulate, emotionally frigid, and teetotal. Of course, it is not difficult to imagine such people. But in doing so, we go against the grain of our expectations, where people of those nationalities are concerned. The expectations may be based (more than we realize) on fictions.... But they still have some connection with actual experience, and even crude generalizations drawn from experience must contain some element of truth.' Noel Malcolm, 'What Makes an Englishman,' *Daily Telegraph*, December 24, 2006.

self-recognition of modern political association? In the interstices of the practically overlapping, but conceptually distinct psychological and moral usages, there lies, in the period of the American and French Revolutions, a problem of acute interest to political philosophers coming to terms with an emergent historical hybrid, the so-called 'nation-state.' In France, Rousseau's doctrine of the general will was adduced as evidence in behalf of the revolutionary cause; in America, the example of civic republicanism; while in Britain, Hume and Burke resorted to a defense of tradition, habit, sentiment, and shared community in their own respective attempts to articulate and uphold the characteristic texture of the ancient 'national' liberties long cherished by their fellow countrymen. Kant, in Germany, responded with an elegant deontology designed to separate the spheres of nature and morality, on one hand, and freedom and ethics on the other, thus accommodating the problematic tensions between the rights and the duties of citizenship in a modern state. Hegel subsequently provided a more all-encompassing account still, dialectically differentiating the merest subjectivity of individual freedom from the theoretically distinct and thicker spheres of *Moralitat*, and in turn, *Sittlikeit*.

So, the character of a settled disposition has long been said loosely to reveal itself in the conduct of individual agency but also, at least figuratively, of nation-states. *'Being English'* thus implies an identifiable disposition comprising certain characteristics, found in its completeness, not in any discrete human narrative as such, but in the allegorical narrative of a people *tout ensemble*, itself the reflection in time present of an imagined past of shared moral community constituted in such a fashion that each person or self has been transfigured in the notional person of the state. Each and all, then, are conscious of something other than present time, sharing in a more complete self-recognition than that to be adduced solely from the otherwise inescapably subjective mortality of a fleeting individual passage. In the vicissitudes of the metaphoric lives of nations, and somewhat more tangibly in the parallel enactment of individual human agency, then, are to be found discernments of those necessary features of a human performance identified by Michael Oakeshott: 'self-enactment' and 'self-disclosure.' In the moment of the conjunction of the two, a settled disposition will be found to intimate most fully what amounts to the sense of timeless moments:

> We die with the dying;
> See, they depart, and we go with them.
> We are born with the dead:
> See, they return and bring us with them.
> The moment of the rose and the moment of the yew tree
> Are of equal duration. A people without history
> Is not redeemed from time, for history is a pattern
> Of timeless moments. So, while the light fails
> On a winter's afternoon, in a secluded chapel
> History is now and England.'[9]

[9]   See T. S. Eliot, 'Little Gidding, V,' in *Collected Poems, 1909–1963* (London: Houghton Mifflin Harcourt, 1963).

IV

In a rationalist age of anti-individuals and fabricated nationalisms, not all who style themselves 'individuals', nor all ostensible 'nations', will be equally marked by strongly developed skills of narrativity. But those without them, whether imitation 'individuals' or nations *manqué*, will presumably lack any deeply etched sense of self-recognition.[10] It is said that after the political disaster for the British Conservative Party of the 1945 British General Election, Churchill, as a morale booster, adopted the practice of entertaining his colleagues in the Tory Shadow Cabinet to periodic luncheons at the Savoy Hotel. On one such occasion, as Harold Macmillan recollected in his memoirs, the great man, presented for his inspection with a rather uninspired pudding, grumbled at the waiter in best Churchillian cadence: 'Pray take away this pudding. It has no theme.'[11] Life without narrativity would pose a similarly unhappy plight. Oakeshott himself seems to have had something like this in mind in his own critique of 'empirical activity,' which he took to be an unacceptably simple-minded view of the world understood to be a place where one literally awakened every morning with a totally clean slate, to ponder the question: 'What would I like to do?' The only kind of education appropriate to this way of seeing things, as he suggests dismissively, would be 'an education in lunacy.'[12]

Recently, Galen Strawson has made an interesting argument that is apposite here. While Oakeshott and others dismiss the very notion of completely untrammelled 'empirical activity' – with the clear implication that narrativity, in some form or other, is inescapable – Strawson contends that there is another way to parse experience that embraces narrativity while insisting there is a philosophical alternative to it. Strawson's view is that people tend to think of themselves in one of two quite distinct senses. One of these he terms 'Diachronic'; and he takes it that this way of picturing selfhood is the generally accepted norm. 'Diachronics' regard self-experience as meaningful because they assume it is embedded in continuities of individual conduct that cover long stretches of time. They believe that personal identity entails attributes that have somehow *been there* in the past and *will be there* in the future. In this way, the discrete sense of self, and by extension of nationhood, is transmitted or conserved. Strawson's 'Diachronics' would include Plato, Augustine, Heidegger, Rawls (with the veil of ignorance removed), Sandel, MacIntyre, Graham Greene, and Evelyn Waugh, among others.

Those Strawson labels as 'Episodics' in contrast, such as Montaigne, Aubrey, the Earl of Shaftesbury, Coleridge, Rawls (behind the veil of ignorance!), Rorty[13],

---

[10] I allude here to Oakeshott's well-known indictment of 'The Masses in Representative Democracy' (1961) in Albert Hunold, ed., *Freedom and Serfdom: an Anthology of Western Thought* (Dordrecht, Holland: Reidel), 151–70.

[11] Harold Macmillan, *Winds of Change, 1914–1939* (London: Pan Macmillan, 1966), 29, cited in W. H. Greenleaf, *The British Political Tradition*, vol. 1 (London: Routledge, 1983), 7–8.

[12] Oakeshott, 'Political Education,' in *Rationalism in Politics and other essays new and expanded edition*, ed. Timothy Fuller, (Indianapolis: Liberty Press, 1991), 46–7. Hereafter: *RIP*.

[13] Yet the ostensibly theoretical platforms of understanding of Rawls's *A Theory of Justice* (Cambridge: The Belknap Press, 1971), and Richard Rorty's *Philosophy and the Mirror of Nature* (Princeton, N.J.: Princeton Univ. Press, 1979) presuppose value preferences of a liberal and

Camus, Iris Murdoch and others, see no such continuities. They have instead a belief that in our shared existential predicament of mortality, all is passing, and nothing preserved. In the circumstances, they aver, we ought to just get on with it. 'Episodics' then, believe that it suffices to accept life as a matter of human goings-on that may or may not be subjectively complex, but that there is nothing beyond their occurrence to suggest a clearly discernible pattern. Conduct, for them, might be loosely sequential but there is no need to infer from this, as 'Diachronics' suppose, that it is inherently consequential. And for Strawson, the 'Diachronic' but not the 'Episodic' self has an apparent affinity with narrativity.[14]

This scrutiny of the divergent diachronic and episodic images of self provides a corrective to the uncritical contemporary vogue of regarding narrativity as the final word in philosophical discussions of selfhood. It offers a possible alternative to Oakeshott's own claim that a satisfactory account of performance requires awareness in it of elements of *both* 'self-enactment' and 'self-disclosure.' But Strawson would appear otherwise to complement Oakeshott, since in his episodic and diachronic division, as in Oakeshott's distinction between self-enactment and self-disclosure, the diachronic and self-disclosing features of a human performance, rather than the episodic and self-enacting, are most evidently marked by narrative skills. The ephemeral footprints in the snow that cover the persisting rut or groove below, may be construed as paralleling Strawson's episodic and diachronic forms of self-experience. That said, Oakeshott's account remains arguably superior to Strawson's inasmuch as it moves us beyond a focus on discrete or subjective selfhood *per se*, beckoning our attention past the footprints towards the elaboration of the rut or groove itself. That is where we ought to further pursue our search for answers to the question of just what it means to say of a person or self, or by extension, of a people, that they have recognizable dispositions reflecting a certain character – disclosing themselves in enactment as English,[15] say, or as conservative.

For Strawson's 'episodic', in brief, self-enactment is all that there is; and if that *is* really all that there is, then why not accept the casually resigned recommendation of Peggy Lee, and 'just keep dancing'? But a performance so narrowly construed lacks even the barest rudiments of a settled disposition or character. Maybe that is why Strawson allows that *most of us* are diachronics. Our self-identity is anchored in a personal past reflecting settled beliefs about our place in a common historical past and informing our appreciation of the present and of possible futures. Yet it remains the case, as I understand his argument, that both Strawson's diachronic, who is presumed to have narrativity, and his episodic, who claims to get by without it, are concerned exclusively with matters of self-enactment in agency. And that is where Oakeshott's account, with its insistence on a notional interface between *self-enactment* and *self-disclosure*, offers something that Strawson's separate

---

American democratic nature. See Rawls's later *Political Liberalism* (New York: Columbia Univ. Press, 1993), and Rorty's 'The Priority of Democracy to Philosophy,' in his *Objectivity, Relativism and Truth* (Cambridge: Cambrige Univ. Press, 1989), vol. 1.

[14]   Cf. Galen Strawson, 'Against Narrativity,' *Ratio* 17, no. 4 (December, 2004): 428–52.

[15]   Bearing in mind, as we know from tragic recent 'goings-on,' that simply being born in England, or carrying a British passport, is not necessarily the same as 'being English.'

typologies of human agency as *either* diachronic and episodic does not. Oakeshott's move, while allowing for the celebration of the narrativity in human goings-on that features in *self-disclosure* makes it possible to approach other important, but inherently elusive, features of human performance as well, including such matters as texture, coloration, bent, temperament, and disposition.

Certainly one might think a 'heroic' English life, say that of Winston Churchill, as unthinkable without the strong thread of purpose or direction explicit in narrativity understood as embracing elements of both self-enactment and self-disclosure – though the more heroic, presumably, the more dominant in performance will be the element of self-enactment. And the same might be said, by figurative extension, of the traditional idea of a nation-state in its perceived and self-perceiving progress. Then, the accreted myths, legends and symbols of the nation's story-tellers, believed by high and low, citizen and subject alike to be their common product and shared inheritance, will be supposed to display a particularly marked vibrancy or pace, the reflection of an historic people approaching its zenith. And the same will be thought to apply, though with a necessary modification to the story-line and the place of vibrancy and pace in it, to the perceived and self-perceiving springtime of a nation's figurative ascendancy, as to the eventual autumn of its decline. Of course, this way of seeing things will be most applicable to strong nation-states, with cultures agreed by participant and onlooker to display a rich historicity, that long diachronic tally additional to the episodic costs of war and benefits of peace, of tragedies and triumphs, prudent policy and pure serendipity – all of which, taken together, will be understood to have contributed to lay the ground for a now prized exclusivity of membership in terms of what Oakeshott calls civil association

More conjecturally, there will presumably be more of the episodic than diachronic in the characteristic narratives of federal, as distinct from unitary states; while among the modern constitutional variants of the latter, the mix will be weighted more towards the diachronic than the episodic in both republican and monarchical forms of representative democracy. Finally, in the case of those weak or 'imitation' states that are a prominent feature of the contemporary, United Nations view of the world, an ostensibly diachronic emphasis on inclusivity serves merely as an emblem shielding what sometimes seems in reality to be a merely episodic absence of *bone fide* historical identity, an attempt to substitute for it a largely manufactured communality liable to be heavily indebted to notions similar to those of Oakeshott's enterprise association.

V

Michael Oakeshott's was a scholar's rather than a hero's life, but there was in his loves, friendships, successes, and failures, as in the omnipresence throughout the long days of his flourishing of the intermittent darkness of a century of war, and in war itself, experienced first hand, more than ample opportunity for adventures in self-enactment and narrativity. And in all of this there were elements of episodic agency and of diachronic performance contributing to delineate the character of one who was personally disposed to be and is generally regarded in retrospect as having been in some core sense both English and conservative – a character embracing and reflecting a certain balance of dispositions. Oakeshott's life was a human performance featuring a narrative self-disclosure with a starting point at the twentieth century's beginning in Kent, and an ending point in Devon near century's close; but it was a performance accompanied throughout by a silhouette-like presence or penumbra of Oakeshottian self-enactment.

Certainly, in Oakeshott's case, the propensity liable to reveal itself in self-disclosure seems to have been in formation by the time of his school days at (how perfectly named) St. George's, Harpenden. In particular, one notes the influence upon the youthful scholar's imagination of the school's founder and Headmaster, the Reverend Cecil Grant. 'His power of creating a myth, a legend, was quite remarkable,' Oakeshott would later affectionately recall. 'For a community of so short a duration it was remarkably equipped with heroes, with a past and a relationship to that past – a relationship which sometimes seemed to stretch back to the early Christians.... St. George's was a place surrounded by a thick, firm hedge, and inside this hedge was a world of beckoning activities and interests.'[16] The disposition in question had apparently become more pronounced by the time of Oakeshott's early years at Cambridge, as is illustrated in an early paper on 'The Nature and Meaning of Sociality.' In it, the young Oakeshott earnestly avers 'patriotism is the basis of all morality ... the greatest emotion and intellectual effort of which we are capable. It is a poet's patriotism, perhaps, but for that nonetheless true.... We cannot refuse to acknowledge something real in the impulsive love of country and countryside which plays so great a part in the life of most of us.'[17] And his Englishness seems stylishly secured a decade or so later, albeit more light-heartedly, by his venture in joint authorship, with a Gonville and Caius colleague, G. T. Griffith, of *A Guide to the Classics, or, How to Pick the Derby Winner* (1936).

VI

The British experience is steeped in longstanding traditions of narrativity affectionately celebrating the character of Britons as an intrepid and historic island people destined for greatness. Among its prominent thematic images have been the English countryside and the English country house, the sea, the Crown, the British Empire and Commonwealth, the military, Anglicanism, and the unadorned, practical decency of the common Englishman. These figuratively make a panoramic purview of the British island race from earliest times, without apparent starting point or end. The sociologist Ralf (later Lord) Dahrendorf wrote of the British way of life that, from the standpoint of a 'participant observer' such as himself, 'few things are more bewildering than the extent to which the public debate is preoccupied with yesterday's world.'[18] And it is true that the traditional self-appreciation of Britons features an abiding sense of an immutable past embracing

[16]   Robert Grant, *Thinkers of Our Time: Oakeshott* (London: The Claridge Press, 1990), 'Appendix: Oakeshott on His Schooldays,' 119–20.
[17]   Oakeshott, *Religion, Politics and the Moral Life*, ed. Timothy Fuller (New Haven: Yale Univ. Press, 1993), 60–1. Hereafter: *RPML*.
[18]   Ralf Dahrendorf, *On Britain* (London: BBC Books, 1982), 181.

the historical Boadicea and the half-legendary Arthur, the symbolic St. George and the mythical Robin Hood.

> the people of this land possess,
> Age after age, unaltering agelessness.[19]

The British, since time immemorial, have been an island race whose destiny in consequence has always been linked, literally and metaphorically, with the sea. In his *Crowds and Power* émigré Nobel Laureate Elias Canetti asks his readers to imagine his words as having been written in the inauspicious circumstances of 1940:

> Everyone knows what the *sea* means to an Englishman; what is not sufficiently known is the precise form of the connection between his relationship to the sea and his famous individualism. The Englishman sees himself as a captain on board a ship.... The sea is there to be ruled.... The Englishman's disasters have been experienced at sea and thus the sea has offered him transformation and danger. His life at home is complementary to life at sea: security and monotony are its essential characteristics. Everyone has his place which, except to go to sea, he is not supposed to leave for the sake of any transformation; everyone is as sure of his habits as of his possessions.[20]

In Act 3 of Bernard Shaw's *Heartbreak House*, with the crisis years of the First World War rather than the Second in view, Captain Shotover advised Hector to 'Learn your business as an Englishman:'

> Hector: And what may my business as an Englishman be, pray?
> Captain Shotover: Navigation. Learn it and live; and leave it and be damned.'[21]

Rule Britannia, Britannia rule the waves; the island race, as Shotover and Canetti intimate, has also been an imperial race. The English were the first Britons to learn the habit, at home rather than at sea, in the school of domestic hard knocks as 'governors' in succession to the Normans of an unruly Welsh, Scots, and Irish 'Celtic fringe'. This is a project that never eclipsed so entirely as to have rendered extinct the distinctive cultural myths and symbols of the respective nationalities jointly peopling the British Isles, myths and symbols that have served to sustain romantic as well as more instrumental claims to political devolution, even independence, down to the eve of the three hundredth Anniversary in 2007 of the Act of Union. Abroad, the British would forge a far-flung geopolitical empire rivaling that of Athens and Rome in classical antiquity. And in the wake of its eventual demise, culturally (we take for granted what is arguably the most impressive of British imperial achievements), the British have claims to be the source of what has in

---

[19] William Watson, *Poems*, vol. 2 (London: Foley Press, 1905), 137; cited in R. W. Birchfield, ed., *A Supplement to the* OED, vol. 1 (Oxford: Oxford Univ. Press, 1972), 41.
[20] Elias Canetti, *Crowds and Power* (New York: Continuum, 1960), 159–60.
[21] George Bernard Shaw, *Heartbreak House, A Fantasia in the Russian Manner on English Themes* (1919; reprint, London: Harmondsworth, Penguin Books, 1964), 139.

certain respects become a virtual global hegemony of the English language.

The story-telling skills requisite for a plausible rendering of the 'spirit' of a people are on occasion best displayed by a non-family member inclined to a broadly sympathetic rendering of a tradition's familial strengths and weaknesses. Alexis de Tocqueville's admiration for Britain, combined with acute powers of observation and invention, led him to isolate for emphasis certain enduring features of the British political tradition in a draft notebook compiled during a visit in 1835 to this 'second native land' of his mind. He identified two, intimately combined spirits in England, 'the spirit of association' and 'the spirit of exclusion.' Tocqueville then goes on to sketch in the rudiments of a story-line with which to animate these apparently anomalous spirits:

> On reflection I incline to the view that the spirit of individuality is the basis of the English character. Association is a means suggested by sense and necessity for getting things unattainable by isolated effort. But the spirit of individuality comes in on every side: it recurs in every aspect of things ... one might suggest that it has indirectly helped the development of the other spirit by inspiring every man with greater ambitions and desires than one finds elsewhere. That being so, the need to club together is more generally felt, because the urge to get things is more general and stronger (a clumsy, obscure sentence, but I think the idea is right and needs looking into again).[22]

The British have been a political and a rule-attached more than an artistic people, with a notable pedigree of success in the art of governance tied to an abiding commitment to constitutionalism and legality. As John Stuart Mill once remarked,

> Both in a good and a bad sense, the English are farther from a state of nature than any other modern people. They are, more than any other people, a product of civilization and discipline. England is the country in which social discipline has most succeeded, not so much in conquering, as in suppressing, whatever is liable to conflict with it. The English, more than any other people, not only act but feel according to rule.'[23]

But as an old state with continuously modified cultural and civil traditions symbolized in an 'ancient constitution' traceable to the mediaeval world, there is no question of Britain's having been formed, as political scientists might put it, as a product of 'constitutional design'. Instead one is put in mind of Montaigne's observation that 'the fabric of so great a body holds together by more than a single nail. It holds together even by its antiquity, like old buildings whose foundations have been worn away by age, without cement or mortar, which yet live and support themselves by their own weight.'[24] Or again, as Tocqueville was to muse about the 'spirit' of English legislation:

---

[22] Alexis de Tocqueville, *Journeys to England and Ireland*, trans. George Lawrence, ed. J. P. Meyer (London: Faber and Faber, 1958), 87, 88, *passim*.

[23] John Stuart Mill, *The Subjection of Women* (1869), in Richard Wollheim ed., *John Stuart Mill: Three Essays* (London: Oxford Univ. Press, 1975), 506.

[24] Donald M. Frame, trans., *The Complete Essays of Montaigne* (Stanford, Calif.: Stanford Univ. Press, 1958), 733.

[It] is an incomprehensible mixture of the spirits of innovation and of routine, which perfects the details of laws without noticing their principles; which always goes ahead in a straight line, taking step after step in the direction it happens to be in, without looking to right or left to make connections between the different roads it is following; active and contemplative; sometimes wide awake to notice the slightest abuse, and sometimes sound asleep amid the most monstrous ones; which exhausts its skill in mending, and does not create except, so to say, without knowing it and by chance; the most relentless for improvement and the well-being of society, but the least systematic seeker for these things; the most impatient and the most patient; the most clear-sighted and the blindest; the most powerful in some things, and the weakest and most embarrassed in some others; which keeps [millions of] people under its obedience three thousand leagues away, and does not know how to get out of the smallest administrative difficulty; which excels at taking advantage of the present, but does not know how to foresee the future. Who can find a word to explain all these anomalies?'[25]

One could cite seemingly countless further instances of extraordinary continuities, persisting side by side with the passing novelties of the evanescent here and now, in the historical life of the British people. In human performance, as we have seen, in the case of individuals, as figuratively at least of nations, the balance of dispositions that make up a character displays itself in adventures of self-enactment that, on close scrutiny, will be seen always to be attended by silhouettes of self-disclosure. And, just as context implies a text, there is a kind of equipoise in human performance linking the enduring textual values inherent in disclosure with the more contextual or situational immediacy of enactment. Peter Ackroyd suggests in a recent comprehensive and elegant rehearsal of the lasting features of Englishness that, when all is said and done, its richness of spirit might best be captured in the notion of a ring or circle: 'The English imagination takes the form of a ring or circle,' he writes. 'It is endless because it has no beginning and no end; it moves backwards as well as forwards.'[26]

D. W. Brogan once remarked that 'We British don't take our intellectuals too seriously.'[27] And Tocqueville had noted a related if not quite synonymous point about the English national character, in suggesting that 'Generally speaking, the English seem to me to have great difficulty in getting hold of general and undefined ideas. They judge the facts of today perfectly well, but the tendency of events and their distant consequences escape them.'[28] Walter Bagehot, returning the Frenchman's equivocal compliment with another in kind, was of the view that one substantial historical difference between England and France was that the French were, as he wrote, 'too clever to be practical and not dull enough to be free.' According to Bagehot, 'What we opprobriously call stupidity, though not an enlivening quality in common society, is Nature's favorite resource for preserving steadiness of conduct and consistency of opinion.' And he added, without

---

[25] Tocqueville, *Journeys*, 82–3.
[26] Cf. Peter Ackroyd, *Albion: The Origins of the English Imagination* (London: Chatto and Windus, 2002), xix.
[27] Cited in Raymond Aron, *The Opium of the Intellectuals* (New York: W. W. Norton and Co., 1962) 235.
[28] Tocqueville, *Journeys*, 80.

hesitation, and approvingly, 'in real sound stupidity the English are unrivalled.'[29] This, he concluded, was in fact a cultural strength since, being 'stupid,' Englishmen learned slowly only what they must; they did their duty, contentedly, because they knew of nothing else to do.

In an imagining of the distant British past, one can see how, coeval with the emergence of a bedrock prudential adherence to 'real sound stupidity,' there might have arisen a related trait, a trait evoked in Elias Canetti's imagery of the ship captain cited earlier, centered on the manner in which the British have tended to hold in high regard persons believed to be in possession of time-tested or habitually practiced skills – a regard manifesting itself in a willing deference to those who actually know *how to do things* and to get them done, rather than having merely untried 'theories' about them lacking solid foundation in experience. Instead of being 'stupidity's' ostensible antipode, this related trait might be imagined to have developed alongside it, as a kind of functional complement.

Reflect, for instance, on the evolution of the English word 'cleverness'. Once firmly a term of commendation, it is only in fairly recent British usage that 'clever' has come to convey the slightly pejorative sense of a certain glibness, superficiality or lack of depth. The full etymology of the English word 'clever' is obscure, but there is some apparent relationship with the middle English '*clivers,*' meaning claws, talons, or clutches, in the sense of nimble of claws, sharp to seize. The connection is likely because by the time the word 'clever', already a fixture of local and colloquial use, first became a generally received word in modern English (towards the end of the seventeenth century), it was firmly connected with the use of the hands, and was indeed to remain so, inasmuch as the underlying notion of 'cleverness' is of a kind of adroitness or dexterity signifying, in a word, 'the brain in the hands.' 'Clever', then, entailed the sense of an actual *doer* or a *thing actually done*, just as the etymology of the possibly related word, 'expert' is bound up in its origins with the signification of a person who was actually experienced in, or 'trained by', practice. Here too, of course, there arose a later and typically pejorative usage in which expertise is attached, not to demonstrable experience or actually achieved practice, but to a claim based primarily on theoretical learning.

VII

Much changed in the course of Oakeshott's long life, and has since his death; and a newcomer on the scene might be forgiven a perception that the rut has all but disappeared beneath the autumn leaves and wintry snow of the seasons that have beset Britain in the course of the past half century. But, on a larger view, the insistent rhythm of seasonality has continued in place; and the rut, groove, or channel, further excavated by human choices, with modified contours, remains too. The fashionable fortunes of an exceptionalist, English-dominant national identity, weakened by a fading collective memory of patriotic witness and sacrifice in two world wars, has had to accommodate the spread of a more cosmopolitan, materialist ethos in contemporary, post-imperial British culture. The Lyon's tea

---

[29]   Cited in Melvin J. Lasky, *Utopia and Revolution* (Chicago: Univ. of Chicago Press, 1976), 578–9.

shops of the immediate postwar years have been replaced by the ubiquitous Indian restaurant; James Bond's flash iconic British sport cars, so lovingly lethalized by Q, are nowadays manufactured by the Ford Motor Company[30]; Rolls Royce, the quintessential English icon of the motoring world, is owned by BMW; 'swinging London' has been joined by Londonistan; and lately there have been scholarly claims that what was for long thought to be a harmless oxymoron, the British intellectual, has come to pass.[31] Meanwhile, the happy-go-lucky *Is There a Doctor in the House?* genre of English cinema has given way to *My Favorite Launderette*, *Bend It Like Beckham* – and that recent Bollywood hit, *Bride and Prejudice*. Not to mention politics and public discourse: Who would now doubt, for instance, that Oakeshott's prescient warning about the advance of rationalism in politics has continued apace?

Still, if individuals have biographies and family trees, the same might be said metaphorically, as we have seen, of institutions and ideas, nations and states. George Orwell appreciated this metaphoric notion, writing in the dark days of 1941. Much was changing even as he wrote; and when the war was finally over, more of the England of his critical, but broadly affectionate personal experience, would change too. Yet he was convinced that 'the gentleness, the hypocrisy, the thoughtlessness, the reverence for law and the hatred of uniforms will remain, along with the suet puddings and the misty skies.' Much that was familiar would be lost to evolving circumstance, he ventured; but England would still be England, 'an everlasting animal stretching into the future and the past, and, like all living things, having the power to change out of recognition and yet remain the same.'[32]

VIII

Images of the rut or groove and the seasons are, of course, naturalistic images; and Oakeshott expressly abjures the bedrock of nature in favor of the contingencies of artifice in his account of the traditions requisite for a *bone fide* political society in the Oakeshottian sense. Tradition is itself no adequate foundation; what is required is a certain kind of human conduct that makes room for the intimation of political activity contextualized alongside a presumption of rules of law. Near the end of his 1952 study of *The Politics of Faith and the Politics of Scepticism*, unpublished in his lifetime, Oakeshott had revealingly confessed his belief that there was once a time, especially in British politics, dating roughly from the late seventeenth and early

---

[30]   [This must be a reference to Aston Martin, which was owned by Ford, but which is now owned by a British, American, and Kuwaiti investment consortium; but there is also, as noted, Rolls Royce, owned by BWM; Bentley, owned by Volkswagen; and Jaguar, owned by the Indian group Tata (along with Land Rover). Apropos of this paper, John Sinders, the American investor in Aston Martin had this to say recently: 'I think an essential part of Aston is its English character. Just as I cannot imagine a Ferrari not being Italian or a Peugeot not being French, I cannot imagine an Aston not being English. The essential nature of an Aston-how it's stitched together, how it's hand assembled, how it's designed, how it feels and smells – is English and will remain English.' See: http://www.automobilemag.com/features/news/0706_q_a_aston_martin_future/index.html – Ed.]

[31]   Cf. Stefan Collin, *Absent Minds: Intellectuals in Britain* (London: Oxford Univ. Press, 2006).

[32]   George Orwell, 'England, Your England,' in *Inside the Whale and Other Essays* (London: Penguin, 1957), 63–90.

eighteenth centuries, when a mean between the extremities of faith and skepticism seemed closer than at any other to realization. It was at that juncture that the concrete character of a complex manner of politics seemed momentarily to present itself, and 'enthusiasm was not so much decried as put in its proper place.' And he provides an exquisitely English image to conjure up what he had in mind:

> Faith had knocked up an impressive score, and its innings ended characteristically in hit-wicket. (The scorers, unaware of what had happened, went on chalking up the runs: faith, particularly in France, was believed to have 'a splendid future behind it'.) In the situation, however, it looked as if scepticism would take a mighty revenge. But not at all; the contest was adjourned for tea. And in the conversation that ensued, the political principle of the mean in action made its appearance. Many voices were heard in this conversation, but among the more notable participants were Locke, Berkeley, Shaftesbury, Halifax, Boyle, St. Evremond, Fontenelle and Hume, and there were wits (like de Mandeville) on the circumference who provided the comedy.[33]

They did not compose a political party, or belong to a single nation; their conversation was less original than drawn from the thoughts of others who had gone before; nor was their conversation confined to politics, but ranged over the entire field of human conduct.

In a typescript dated 'September, 1943,' on the final sheet of which is a notation 'Written in Sussex/Waiting for D Day,' in his scrupulously tidy hand, there are recorded Oakeshott's thoughts at the time 'On Peace with Germany.' This topical paper reinforces from an entirely different perspective the impression that Oakeshott's disposition to be conservative was somehow implicitly linked to the good fortune of being English. The Germans, to be certain, in the course of some centuries, had themselves developed certain characteristics. But the first of these Oakeshott describes as self-centeredness 'which, when it reaches the proportion it has reached in the German character, is indistinguishable from self-deception.' Now, the self-deceptive dream of Germanic superiority was accompanied by a sense of inferiority tantamount to a profound insecurity about Germany's place in the world; and the German character, it seemed to him, 'moves always between these two nodal points.' What is menacing in the German character, he concludes, is not its strength, but its instability: 'The German is dangerous because of his uncertain grasp of himself.'[34]

Michael Oakeshott was 'a sceptic, one who would do better if only he knew how;' but he seems never to have been in doubt about who *he* was. His Englishness, and the pervasive sense of a conservative *persona* accompanying it, is never far off in his utterance and prose. It informs his master concept of civilization as a conversation, and there is indeed for him a definite link between the aptness of this metaphoric imagery and his characteristically English view of democracy:

---

[33] Oakeshott, *The Politics of Faith and the Politics of Scepticism*, ed. Timothy Fuller (New Haven and London: Yale Univ. Press, 1996), 122.

[34] Oakeshott: *What is History? and other essays*, ed. with an introduction by Luke O'Sullivan (Thorverton: Imprint Academic, 2004), 161–86. Hereafter: *WH*.

If there is one activity more than another which has benefited from the civilizing touch of conversation, it is politics. That politics is a subject suitable for conversation, only a barbarian would deny. But the view that I want to suggest is that politics is good for nothing else. Moreover, this approximation of politics to conversation is, I think, the gist and meaning of democracy. Democratic politics has been perverted and brought into disrepute by being misidentified with the rule of the people, the government of the majority, the propagation of a dogmatic faith and the pursuit of a manner of living to be imposed equally upon all men. And how it came about may be understood in a brief abridgement of our history; for remarkably enough it was Englishmen (who are otherwise not greatly disposed towards conversation) who first explored the recognition that politics is supremely eligible to be a conversational art.'[35]

'Play up, play up, and play the game' … 'it's not who wins but how you play the game.' Of course, not a few otherwise impeccably English Britons have succumbed to the attraction of Thomas Fuller's contrary-minded admonition, that 'It is a silly game where nobody wins.'[36] A very short list of truants would include, as it happens, Churchill, Orwell, and further back, of course, the inimitable Dr. Johnson.[37] It would certainly include, too, on Oakeshott's own witness, the argumentative author of *Leviathan*, 'the greatest, perhaps the sole, masterpiece of political philosophy written in the English language.' Hobbes was an inimitable expositor of ideas, but 'by disposition he was a fighter, and he knew no tactics save attack.' Yet Oakeshott admonishes him, for 'always to play to win is to take one's standards from one's opponent.' This trait, happily, 'never quite destroyed in him the distinction between beating an opponent and establishing a proposition, and never quite silenced the conversation with himself which is at the heart of philosophical thinking.'[38]

Michael Oakeshott's Englishness is there in his important essay on 'The Rule of Law,' where he invites readers to 'Consider the relationship entailed in playing a game: chess, tennis or cricket,' as it is in his anecdotal consideration in the same paper of the difference between maxims, advices, instructions, pleas, warnings or admonitions and rules properly understood:

> Thus, one of the Comments on Bagshot reads: 'Advice to the poor: in all the emergencies of life act as if you were rich.' Or the solicitor's account I found in my father's papers: 'January 30ᵗʰ 1892. To Advice to let sleeping dogs lie: One guinea.' Or the Duke of Wellington's reply to a correspondent: 'From what you say you seem to have got yourself into a damned difficult situation and you must do your best to get out of it'.'[39]

---

[35] From the essay, 'The Voice of Conversation in the Education of Mankind,' (*WH*, 187–99).

[36] Thomas Fuller, *Gnomologia*, London, 1732, No. 2880, cited in *The Oxford Dictionary of Quotations*, 3d ed. (Oxford: Oxford Univ. Press, 1979), 220.

[37] 'Johnson: Well, we had a good talk. Boswell: Yes Sir; you tossed and gored several persons.' James Boswell's *Life of Johnson*, vol. 2 (c. 1769), 66. Consider too the condemnatory evidence of P. G. Wodehouse's *Chester Forgets Himself*: 'While they were content to peck cautiously at the ball, he never spared himself in his efforts to do it a violent injury.' *Strand Magazine*, no. 401, May, 1924.

[38] Oakeshott, 'Introduction to Leviathan,' in Thomas Hobbes, *Leviathan, or the Matter, Forme and Power of a Commonwealth Ecclesiastical and Civil* (Oxford: Blackwell, 1960), viii, 12.

[39] Oakeshott, 'The Rule of Law,' in *On History and Other Essays* (Oxford: Basil Blackwell, 1983),

His English temper, moreover, is arguably close to the core of his well-known critique of 'rationalism in politics' – his reflections on the circumstances surrounding the emergence of America as a new world civilization being apposite here (Cf. *RIP*, 31–4) – as is his acerbic assessment of the character of 'the rationalist' himself. 'His mind,' Oakeshott avers, 'has no atmosphere, no changes of season and temperature; his intellectual processes, so far as possible, are insulated from all external influence and go on in the void' (*RIP*, 7). Oakeshott's Englishness, it has always seemed to me, is also reflected in perhaps the most frequently cited passage in all his utterances, and arguably the most striking (and most willfully misrepresented) passage to be found anywhere in English-language political writing in the twentieth century, where he says:

> In political activity, then, men sail a boundless and bottomless sea; there is neither harbour for shelter nor floor for anchorage, neither starting-point nor appointed destination. The enterprise is to keep afloat on an even keel; the sea is both friend and enemy; and the seamanship consists in using the resources of a traditional manner of behaviour in order to make a friend of every hostile occasion.' (*RIP*, 60)

His Englishness suffuses, 'On the Character of a Modern European State,' part 3 of *On Human Conduct* as a kind of sub-text, just as it does the texture of 'On Being Conservative.' It is present in the anecdotal evidence of a speech given at a party to mark the publication of a *festschrift* in his honor edited by Bhikhu Parekh and Preston King. Protesting that he was an undistinguished figure, not even a proper scholar, Oakeshott confessed that he had decided in life 'to go *misère*' – which in whist, as Kenneth Minogue explains, 'means that in order to win you must lose all but five tricks. Here in the *Festschrift*, said Oakeshott, was his *misère* hand being quite shattered by winning a trick he never meant to have.'[40]

In the same affectionate cameo, Minogue confides that 'Michael was in large measure the model for [Shirley Letwin's] idea of the gentleman in her book on *The Gentleman in Trollope*.' It was certainly Shirley Letwin's considered conviction that 'a gentleman is a character whose native habitat is England.'[41] Minogue also recollects of Oakeshott that, 'Sometimes jangling coins in his pocket and looking up into the middle distance as he puffed at a cigarette, he would respond to a student making some absolutely banal remark with "oh you think that, do you?" ' It is an evocative and revealing remembrance, with Oakeshott 'looking up into the middle distance' as if lost in thought. We have no way of knowing what he might have seen there. But it is a fair guess that it is to the middle distance we must turn to contemplate the interstices of the human seasons, of birth and rebirth, of growth to fruition, of autumnal leaves and footprints in the snow, each perennially liable to conceal, in its own characteristic manner, the enduring rut or groove beneath. And

125, 128. Hereafter: *OH*.

[40] Kenneth Minogue, 'Michael Oakeshott as a Character,' in Leslie Marsh, ed., *Michael Oakeshott, Philosopher: A Commemoration of the Centenary of Oakeshott's Birth* (London: Michael Oakeshott Association, 2001), 21.

[41] Shirley Robin Letwin, *The Gentleman in Trollope: Individuality and Moral Conduct* (Cambridge, Mass.: Harvard Univ. Press, 1982), 21.

it is a reasonable surmise that it is to the middle distance that we must also journey to capture, however fleetingly, the elusive conjunction of Oakeshott's disposition to be conservative and English, and his idiomatic approach to philosophy and to life.

15

Ferenc Hörcher

A Brief Enchantment: The Role Of Conversation And Poetry In Human Life[†]

Conversation And Poetry As Philosophical Styles And As Autonomous Voices

The most easily noticeable character-trait of Oakeshott's writing is its essay form. On the most superficial level this means that he rejected the academic norms that tried to force on him a certain manner of phrasing his message. He seems to have preserved a detachment – after all, he was and perhaps always wanted to remain an independent thinker, in the best sense of the word, free in his thought as well as in his language. His style was elegant, precise where necessary, but never flat; learned, but never obscure; rooted in the philosophical tradition, but never scientistic or 'professional'.

His stylistic independence led him to reject the distinction that separated the spoken from the written word. Philosophy, the love of wisdom in the ancient Greek sense of the word, has of course always been an oral tradition. Either in the *agora* or in the gardens of the Academy, philosophy was spoken and not written by its heroes. What was all-important was the on-going dialogue between the participants in what was regarded as a never-ending learning process. The Socratic dialogue could preserve this intellectual multi-vocality even in the written form in the best of Plato's works: in them the protagonists talked to each other about the highest matters in a liberal vein, without trying to turn the conventional exercise into a win or lose game.

If Oakeshott were to follow suit, he would have to consider that there are two ways to preserve the original freshness of oral language in writing. You can either keep it conversational, or experiment with one of the conventional literary genres. When your writing is conversational (without necessarily remaining within the

†The first version of this essay was titled 'The Ciceronian Element in Oakeshott's Conception of Conversation,' and was presented to the Third Plenary Meeting of the Michael Oakeshott Association, Colorado College, Colorado Springs, June 8–10, 2006. I am grateful to Corey Abel for encouraging me to write a final version of it, as well as for help in editing it, and to Timothy Fuller, the host of the conference, for the generous grant, which enabled me to participate at the conference.

constraints of the dialogue form) what you want your reader to think is that your linguistic performance has no direct target. It should seem more like a work-in-progress than a finished product, an intellectual exercise and not a strict logical sequence. You are circling around your theme like a cat around the hot porridge. But you do not pounce immediately. You are relaxed, detached, and a bit skeptical about the success of the project. As we shall see, Oakeshott tried to explicate the importance of this way of writing and thinking, and therefore it is not too far-fetched to claim that his own style reflects the merits of this Platonic habit of composition.[1]

On the other hand, literary genres – collected under the term of 'poetry' by Oakeshott – also excel in trying to overcome the distance between the author and the reader so characteristic in the communicational scheme of written language. The illusion awakened by poets is that of the eternal presence: they are with us in our most intimate moments sharing with us their most intimate feelings, whispering in our ears in the most delicate ways. When the poet speaks she does not allow us to think that the word pronounced has been cut away from its speaker: it remains her word, even if the receiver confronts it. All the messages exchanged in a poetic form are personalized by the linguistic performance of the poet, kept alive and particularized, instead of becoming mechanical and neutralized as a result of being parts of an impersonal linguistic system. Poets used to present their works 'live' to a present audience, and therefore each and every word had to be kept vivid and flashy. Poetry was therefore, and remains, a linguistic *tour-de-force*, an *ars* which results in words which in fact never become stabilized or solidified.

Although it would be hard to decide whether the prose style of Michael Oakeshott is nearer to the archetype of conversation or to that of poetry, there is no need to overstrain this distinction. For us it is enough to claim that Oakeshott takes both conversation and poetry seriously as stylistically important alternatives. In what follows, however, we leave the field of stylistics, and we are going to make sense of his often opaque descriptions of conversation and poetry as modes of experience or voices.[2] Moreover it will also be asked what exactly is the function he attributes to these human activities or ways of imagining, and for what particular reason. While explicating this problem, we are going to have a look at his epistemology and theory of human identity. First we deal with his ideas on conversation, and in the second half of the essay we look at Oakeshott's understanding of poetry.

[1]   [See Debra Candreva, 'Oakeshott and Plato: A Philosophical Conversation,' in Corey Abel and Timothy Fuller, eds., *The Intellectual Legacy of Michael Oakeshott* (Exeter: Imprint Academic, 2005), 2–20. – *Ed.*]

[2]   Of the rising number of secondary works that treat Oakeshott's writings on aesthetics, I consulted the following: Elizabeth Campbell Corey, *Michael Oakeshott on Religion, Aesthetics and Politics* (Columbia, MO: Univ. of Missouri Press, 2006); and Glenn Worthington, 'Poetic Experience and the Good Life in the Writings of Michael Oakeshott, *European Journal of Political Theory*, 4, no. 1 (2005): 57–66; the relevant chapters in the following: Paul Franco, *Michael Oakeshott: An Introduction* (New Haven and London: Yale Univ. Press, 2004), 116–33; Efraim Podoksik, *In Defence of Modernity: Vision and Philosophy in Michael Oakeshott* (Exeter: Imprint Academic, 2003), 103–20; as well as the following chapters, all found in: Corey Abel and Timothy Fuller, eds., *The Intellectual Legacy of Michael Oakeshott*: Martin P. Thompson: 'Intimations of Poetry in Practical Life,' 281–92; Robert Grant: 'Oakeshott on the Nature and Place of Aesthetic Experience: A Critique,' 293–305; Wendell John Coats, Jr.: 'Michael Oakeshott and the Poetic Character of Human Activity, 306–15.

In both cases we shall confront similar problems: His main question is whether humans are able to escape the yoke of practical life. Although the vague answers or intimations suggested by him tend to be rather skeptical we will witness that the advantages of conversation and poetry are shockingly similar. Both of them provide momentary relief from the burdens of *praxis*.

The Primary Meaning Of Conversation

From the perspective of professional philosophy, 'conversation' is a loose term. More precisely, it is a term deliberately left loose. In fact, its primary function is to counterbalance the demands that require the philosopher to use a flat and direct language. Whenever a philosopher uses a conversational style, she wants to escape the rigidity so characteristic of the linguistic habits of professional philosophers (including the best ones). It is a rebellion against pedantry, dogmatism, and ideological jargon. What is more, in the Oakeshottian intellectual cosmos, conversational style is meant to oppose what he calls the rationalist way of talking politics so characteristic of the mentality of the twentieth century.

Conversation is first made a central theme in Oakeshott's posthumously published essay entitled *The Voice of Conversation in the Education of Mankind*,[3] and it emerges in the famous essay *The Voice of Poetry in the Conversation of Mankind*.[4] Although the second formulation is much richer and more complex, the earlier essay reflects Oakeshott's original views on conversation.

The earlier essay starts out from a very provocative claim: In the very first sentence 'conversation' is contrasted with 'life': 'People say life's the thing; but I prefer conversation' (*WH*, 187). Although it might seem at first sight as if Oakeshott meant that conversation is a negation of or at least a possible alternative to life, this is not the case. The sense attributed to this rather strong claim is made obvious at a later point: 'All life is necessarily imperfect; it is full of possibilities, but sparing of certainties. The politics of conversation alone recognizes this necessary imperfection' (*WH*, 196). This is the voice of a skeptical philosopher. This voice attributes a lot of hardships and only a few enjoyments to the human condition. But this skeptically realist verdict of the promises of life is pronounced in a very mild tone. Skepticism is mitigated here by self-discipline and urges its readers, too, to detach themselves from the urgencies of daily life.

The skeptical voice speaks in a low key. It is an attitude that allows one to look at the realities of life from a bird's eye perspective. It follows a convention of talk that does not let one pour out one's emotions in an uncontrolled fashion. For it is based on the assumption that life has got a lot of surprises, and therefore one should not let circumstances overcome one's overall mood. Rather, what is needed

---

[3]   In Oakeshott, *What is History? and other essays*, ed. Luke O'Sullivan (Exeter: Imprint Academic, 2004), 187–99. Hereafter: *WH*. According to the 'Introduction' to this volume, it 'appears to have been written soon after the 1939–45 war ended' (*WH*, 15.) However, a footnote (n. 13) claims, that 'It may have been written much earlier,' while the table of contents suggests 'c. 1948.'

[4]   The essay was first published independently in 1959, and republished in *Rationalism in Politics*, in 1962. My citations are from Oakeshott, *Rationalism in Politics and other essays, new and expanded edition*, ed. Timothy Fuller (Indianapolis: Liberty Press, 1991), 488–541. Hereafter: *RIP*.

is a healthy frivolity or playful lightness about the affairs of life that guarantees that one will not be disillusioned in a cruel way by the accidental circumstances of one's life.

Certainly, Oakeshott does not promise that conversation can change anything factual in human life. His claim is, therefore, a more limited, stoical one: humans can find in it an intellectual tool to condition themselves not to be wholly overcome by the very accidents of one's personal life. It helps by offering words to discuss issues in a light and jovial manner with one's conversational partners (a term used to mean a human relationship which resembles that of friendship, although it is less ground-breaking). If one follows what he calls 'the etiquette of conversation' (*WH*, 190), one is performing an act that might prove all important for one's mental hygiene. In an important sense, conversation liberates the human self from the bondages of practical life.

Before proceeding, we need to make a detour to consider the connection between Oakeshott's concepts of conversation and civilization. After that we need to reconstruct the historical roots of these concepts.

Conversation and Civilization

In understanding the conceptual link between these two terms one needs to accept a radical distinction between two standards of human behavior: that of the civilized man as opposed to the barbaric one. The distinction between these forms of human experience lies in their approach to the human predicament. The barbaric man is only concerned to solve practical matters, i.e. matters of survival: On the other hand, the defining feature of a civilized man is that he seeks to find pleasure above and beyond securing the conditions for survival: 'A 'civilized' manner of living is one that accepts the unavoidable conditions of human life and makes the best of them (*WH*, 198). This best is nothing more than exchanging 'intellectual pleasure' (*WH*, 188), and in Oakeshott's view, conversation is a pleasure of this kind.

Civilization is interpreted by Oakeshott as the ability to look beyond the contingencies of practical life. It is a state of human self-awareness that allows for a more relaxed attitude towards the basic necessities of human life. While for the man of practice the contingencies of life are viewed through a lens that tests their use-value, the civilized man does not limit his attention to basic life-conditions and demands the realization of non-utilitarian values in his life.

If we gather the aspects of being civilized from the earlier – and therefore more outspoken – text, what we find is an idealized portrait of the English country gentleman. The civilized man is a hunter who 'participates in the chase merely for the pleasure of the ride: for him it is a hunt without a victim' (*WH*, 187). He is aristocratic, not taking things too seriously because he finds them not only boring but also tawdry. The ideal gentleman pursues absolutely useless activities like conversation in order to strengthen himself against the vicissitudes of life – without directly fighting them.

But Oakeshott is not guilty of snobbery any more than any other intellectuals, and he wants to see in civilization more than the habits and *mores* of the historical British aristocracy and gentry. To be more precise he outlines an ideal of the gentleman, which incorporates the ancient Greco-Roman models of this character type as well. Conversation was originally a luxury of the Greco-Roman country gentleman and this inclination to leisure is now relocated into the British countryside. In what follows I try to substantiate this historical connection between the British nobleman and his antique foreshadows.

Conversation in the European Intellectual Tradition

The term *'conversatio'* comes from the late classical Latin of Seneca.[5] Its original meaning is not more than intimacy, companionship. The French term *'la conversation'* preserved a lot from this original meaning, as it still signifies social relationships. While the earlier meaning of the term referred to social stratification and structure, today it simply signifies oral linguistic activity. Of course, these two strata of the word are interconnected. Human partnership, or society in general, means connection between people, and to 'act out' human relationships what is needed is to speak to the other, to address the other. Or in a reversed order: by talking to one another two partners identify themselves as belonging to the same community, to have something (at least a means of communication, a language, and through it, a culture) in common.

If by way of communicating we create human community, there is no reason to wonder why conversation became so important in the Roman world. In a complex society speech can define social position and distribute social prestige. By talking to someone, you can temporarily be regarded as belonging to the same social stratum. But your manner of speech can just as readily separate you from others. Styles or manners of speaking have been classified in the Roman rhetorical tradition in a detailed fashion for a long time. According to the insight of this convention, public speech was a task of the orator, while private conversation was a right and duty of any adult male (and sometimes female) citizen. In order to use either of these modes of discourse, public or private, you are required to master your language. To achieve this, orators were educated in special educational institutions. But besides the professionals, all citizens became involved in advocating the 'art of conversation'.

It became a fashionable topic in Roman society in Cicero's time – no doubt partly due to Cicero's own influence as the most popular contemporary orator. He discusses this theme in *On Duties*.[6] According to the classification he provides there, oratory belongs to public events (to the courts and the popular assemblies), while conversations are best suited to informal social gatherings, and especially to exchanges among friends. Formality guarantees the rigid rules of oratory, informality the intimacy and effectiveness of private intercourse. Conversation is defined as the form of communication where we do not follow exact rules, though we attend to conventions: 'We must also take the greatest care to show courtesy and consideration toward those with whom we converse.'[7] According to Cicero's

---

[5]   Peter Burke, *The Art of Conversation* (Ithaca: Cornell Univ. Press, 1993), 92.
[6]   Cicero, *De officiis* (*On Duties*), Loeb Classical Library (1913), 1.132–6.
[7]   Cicero, *On Duties*, 1.136.
[8]   Cicero, *On Duties*, 1.134.

bold claim, artful conversation is a kind of Socratic exercise. It 'should be easy and not in the least dogmatic; it should have the spice of wit. And the one who engages in conversation should not debar others from participating in it, as if he were entering upon a private monopoly.'[8]

A talented practitioner of conversation always observes the subject of the conversation, and does not allow 'that his conversation betray some defect in his character.'[9] One should also consider the company participating in the discussion, and take into account how they would receive the words addressed to them. Finally, 'there should be a point at which to close it (the conversation) tactfully.'[10]

These were the guidelines offered by Cicero from his own perspective as a professional orator and public figure. But even more than his concrete discussion of conversation in this and other works and letters, it was his public *persona* that inspired elites in Renaissance Europe to present him as the model conversationalist – and the archetype of a civilized person.

In sixteenth century humanist Italy Ciceronianism came to stand for a manner of behavior which was regarded as representative of the ideal courtier. In the competitive microcosm of Italian city-states, where abrupt changes constantly restructured the social elite, new virtues came to be recognized as opposed to earlier versions of court etiquette. New regimes of what came to be called market exchange required more adaptability, which in turn required unprecedented sociability – you could earn economic benefits by securing honor, which you did by getting into contact easily and elegantly with others, disregarding your and their social status. Social mobility came to be based upon a new etiquette of social behavior, on the concept of civilized conversation.

The new ideal was personified by the most perfect gentleman of the age, the courtier Baldassare Castiglione. During his eventful life this cultured and polite gentleman gathered a treasury of experience as soldier and diplomat all around Italy and contemporary Europe. He was still able to personally represent the traditional values of the Christian knight, but added new tastes to this role. As one of the humanists, he was an advocate of the culture and social manners of the ancients. He was the author of a popular advice book, *Il Cortegiano* (*The Courtier*, 1528), written in dialogue form to instruct fellow courtiers how to achieve worldly success. One of the most important points he keeps emphasizing throughout the discussions of his own protagonists is the art of conversation. Focusing on the recently reinvented ancient art of rhetoric, his point is to show that worldly success requires an openness towards others, which enables one to contact friends and foreigners as well. It was not enough to have a noble birth or to be skilled in the art of war – the courtiers had to confront new challenges, including table manners, courtly behavior and a capacity to impress men and women through one's linguistic proficiency in altogether different social contexts.

Other popular Italian texts of the age that came to be interested in the art of conversation included Giovanni Della Casa's *Galateo* (1558) and Stefano Guazzo's *Civil conversazione* (1574). Taken together with a wave of minor writers, this plethora

---

[9]   Cicero, *On Duties*, 1.134.
[10] Cicero, *On Duties*, 1.135.

of authors, as Peter Burke pointed out, signaled the important changes that took place in public manners and styles of speaking and writing in Renaissance Italy.

The most important aspect of the development is claimed by social historians like Norbert Elias to be steps forward in what came to be called 'civility'. Civility is a concept that is closely bound up with social relations within a political community or society. In the small Italian courts and cities, communities expected their members to exercise very strict regimes of behavior in order to express their conformity to communal values. In the meantime, due to a thriving industry and flourishing long distance commerce, people were coming into contact across much wider geographic areas. Travelers, merchants, warriors, diplomats and adventurers had to learn how to handle different local communities. As a result of the new mobility in Europe, communities had to open up, and social classes were reordered in terms of new expressions of social prestige and status. Arts and crafts, and on a more elevated level, new movements in the fine arts came to be seen as tokens of social prestige and political power. In the newly enriched cities, wealth could not be shown more directly than by the enjoyment of luxury, which brought with it a new tide in the fashion industry. While the mobility of wealth made societies more fluid, new checkpoints were needed to control social order. The way of speaking and orderly behavior became tests of social belonging – in a fully populated urban center one could show one's nobility by way of one's words and gestures much easier than by producing one's assets. Social mobility itself became accelerated – instead of birthrights you had to prove your merits in spirited public and private discussions. All these components of the '*via moderna*' added up to the birth of new standards of social relations, most obviously expressed by the fresh interest in the art of conversation.

The rebirth of Ciceronian norms of civility in Italy had a long-term impact on seventeenth century France and later on eighteenth century Britain. Both of these social arenas contributed to a reformulation of the original matrix in a wider European context. The originality of the French concept of '*civilité*' lay in its aristocratic flavor. The *ancien régime* could for a long time keep its political power, but the social prestige of authors of discourses on conversation and courtesy paved the way for a slow but uncontrollable social unrest, transplanting the court maxims of Versailles into the salons of Enlightened Paris and later on into countryside academies and debating societies.[11] The French preoccupation with the art of conversation played an important part in the birth of an enlightened philosophy that put sociability on the peak of its hierarchy of values.

This gradual change of the intellectual climate and social stratification within the social elite took at least two centuries in France. It was paralleled by a rather dramatic performance on the eighteenth century British scene. While the French kept frequenting their bright salons to tell again and again their little lies, the British attended their dark and smoky clubs and coffee houses, talking politics

---

[11] For the spread of sociability and conversability in the eighteenth century see: Ulrich Im Hof, *Das gesellige Jahrhundert: Gesellschaft und Gesellschaften im Zeitalter der Aufklärung* (München: Verlag C. H. Beck, 1982).

and reading angrily or greedily their newly founded smudgy papers. It was in this context that one has to interpret the effect of Addison and Steele's fashionable media-innovations, called *The Tatler* and *The Spectator*. What these trend-definers achieved was to popularize among the morose and beef-eating Brits a kind of sociability, *à la mode de Paris*, 'the Turn and Polishing of what the French call a *Bel Esprit*, by which they would express a Genius refined by Conversation, Reflection, and the Reading of the most polite Authors.'[12] But no one did more to transform the morose British gentry into the fashionable and sociable dandy of the eighteenth century than the young and cultured Anthony Ashley Cooper, the third Earl of Shaftesbury. Impressed partly by the French moralists, partly by the Ciceronian reminiscences of a patriotic late humanism, Shaftesbury was a key factor in transforming the Roman rhetorical culture into the conversible world of the British novels.

Born into a family where the most famous philosopher of the age was going to be his private instructor, inheriting by his birth right also the political pact which gave the final touch to what came to be called the Glorious Revolution, Shaftesbury became the ideal medium to transform the civic discourse of the late humanists into the artful conversability of the Georgian era. As L. E. Klein very aptly sums up the achievement of Shaftesbury's generation, 'English Whigs constructed a cultural ideology organized around notions of conversation and politeness in order to legitimate the new political and cultural order which emerged then (in 1688) and survived into the nineteenth century.'[13] Shaftesbury himself added to this political ideology the socio-cultural component.

Rebelling against the mechanistic philosophy of the previous generation of scientists and philosophers, including his private tutor, Locke, he produced a thick volume of stylish works to put forward the case for a non-scientific form of philosophizing, which could preserve the freshness of the spoken word. Shaftebury's ideal of conversation and politeness drew the contours of the modern concept of the gentleman. He could make culture fashionable among the social and political elites by convincing his compatriots (and much of Europe), that a society based on the flexible rules of polite conversation is much more comfortable than any other alternatives. Conversation is much better than revolutions, although it is as much or even more alert to social injustice. Through the liberal arts a society brings to life a liberal political order, while preserving elementary discipline badly needed to overcome the threat of anarchy so characteristic of seventeenth century Britain and eighteenth century France. This as it stands is already an educational program based on idealized Platonism and Ciceronian humanism. In what follows therefore we are going to have a look at the inherent classical liberal educational agenda within the ideal of the early modern concept of civilization. It is going to lead directly to Oakeshott's conceptualization of the connections between conversation,

---

[12] Joseph Addison, *The Spectator*, Monday, 3 September 1711, no. 160. From, *The Spectator in three volumes: vol. 1, A New Edition, Reproducing the Original Text Both as First Issued and as Corrected by its Authors, with Introduction, Notes, and Index*, ed. Henry Morley, (London: George Routledge and Sons Ltd., 1891). I used the internet version as downloaded in February 2007 from http://www.gutenberg.org/files/12030/12030-h/12030-h/SV1/Spectator1.html#section160.
[13] Lawrence E. Klein, *Shaftesbury and the Culture of Politeness: Moral Discourse and Cultural Politics in Early Eighteenth-Century England* (Cambridge: Cambridge Univ. Press, 1994), 55.

civilization, and education. But before explaining that let us check if Oakeshott accepts his place in the humanist tradition.

The Discourse Of Politeness In Oakeshott's Account Of Conversation

In the historical overview we tried to show the continuity of mentality which lead from a Ciceronian concept of conversation to the early modern understanding of politeness. The basic claim was that the Renaissance and post-Renaissance mouthpieces of the art of conversation built their own terminology on the Aristotelian-Ciceronian tradition, as interpreted by the modern commentators. Next we compare the language they used with Oakeshott's own vocabulary.

Oakeshott's descriptions of the ideal conversation, as we saw, have overtones which recall the ideal of the British country gentleman as popularized by Addison and the Earl of Shaftesbury. The noble lord famously compared philosophy to good breeding and the philosopher to a kind of moral aristocrat. Himself an amateur philosopher, writing in the polished manner of a Roman moralist, Shaftesbury in fact embodied his own ideal, uniting in his own personality philosophical thought and conversational practice.

His figure is echoed in Oakeshott's account of the amateur and the virtuoso, a concept reshaped in the age of Shaftesbury, derived from the Latin concept of '*virtus*': 'The man of conversation must at least appear to be an amateur. And like piano-playing, conversation is an art which is felt to lack something essential if there is no element of the virtuoso in its practitioners' (*WH*, 188). We have seen Addison's reference to the *Bel Esprit*, and this concept comes to the surface in Oakeshott's account as well: 'A genius for conversation belongs only to those *belésprits* whose touch is light, whose mind is supple and well-stored' (*WH*, 190). It is also characteristically Rococco-like, that in his view the art of conversation 'requires more than the inspiration of the Graces; but it requires less than that of the Muses' (*WH*, 191). Another concept which he shares with the Enlightenment discourse is sympathy, which he – like the Scottish moral philosophers – finds a defining feature of conversational talk. And he goes as far as to admit that conversation is 'at once an exercise in politeness and in tactical humility' (*WH*, 193-4).

If these coincidences are still not convincing, one only needs to recall that Oakeshott presents Michel de Montaigne as his hero for the art of conversation. He calls him the 'emblem of this character,' setting him aside from the 'great talkers of history,' including 'Dr Johnson, Burke, or Coleridge' (*WH*, 193). Now one does not have to argue too long to establish that Montaigne is the conversational philosopher *par excellence*. It is also an undoubted fact that the French essayist represented a link between the ancient moralists and the modern conversationalists. If he happens to be Oakeshott's hero of the modern art of conversation, it proves that the British philosopher still belongs to the very same intellectual tradition as his French counterpart.

Civilization As Educating The Self

Montaigne was not simply a brilliant conversationalist. He is also credited with plumbing the depths of modern subjectivity and offering a reflexive account of the human self. It is not surprising therefore to realize that Oakeshott's own account of conversation also confronts the problem of the self. Readers today can easily overlook the scale and novelty of Oakeshott's effort to give an account of this theme in his 1959 essay on poetry and conversation. One can feel both his courage to reinvent a language to describe the individual and her relationship to her external environment, and also the outmoded and clumsy vocabulary he found to describe the phenomena. But to give a full account of this magisterial effort is not the point here. We only need to concentrate on the fact that Oakeshott, at the zenith of his career, seems to move from the idealist-realism of his youth toward a nominalist position as far as the stability of the self is concerned. In 'The Voice of Poetry in the Conversation of Mankind,' the self is taking its form through imagining an array of images, as opposed to the earlier doctrine of a self created by experiencing the outside world through channels (or as he called them, modes) of experience. To have images requires two things: an actor who imagines (this is going to be called the self) and the images imagined (this is going to be called the not self).[14] But Oakeshott's story is more radical than what is suggested by this simple duality. He questions the existential status of both the self and the not-self. This position is beyond Romantic subjectivism: what he negates is the permanence of the self. As he writes: the self appears as an activity. 'It is not a 'thing' or a 'substance', capable of being active: it is activity' (*RIP*, 496). It is here that references to Ryle's concept of the mind can legitimately come to one's mind.[15] For what is claimed here is that there is nothing more than the activity of imagining and its results, the images, constituting the self and the not-self, respectively. In other words, there is no 'self' that relates to what is outside of it by way of representing it inside of itself, i.e. there is no consciousness and its contents. In Oakeshott's universe there are no things at all, which could be represented by the images: we only have images, which either get together to form a self, or fall apart to form a not-self.

The important thing in this revolutionary description of the self is that it is radically underdetermined by outside mechanisms. It does not exist at all prior to the activity of imagining, which means that the self is created by its own actions. This presents a human personality that is doomed to be free: even its own identity is determined by itself, by its own doings. But if that is the case, and humans are destined to give shape to their selves, it becomes all-important how they form themselves.

To be sure, there are different ways of imagining: these are conventional 'methodologies' to imagine and to handle one's images. As in his earlier work, Oakeshott mentions among these the 'voices' of practice, science, and history. But in 'The Voice of Poetry,' he adds to these philosophy and poetry, not only adding poetry to the list of modes, but also placing philosophy among rather than above and beyond the 'modes' or voices. To become a healthy and all-round personality, balance needs to be kept between these different ways of imagining. So perhaps not surprisingly, Oakeshott reintroduces the concept of conversation

---

[14] There is an obvious logical problem with this distinction. What if the one imagining and the imagined one is the same?

[15] We know that Ryle was perhaps the only professional philosopher who was appreciated by Oakeshott.

to pinpoint the equilibrium state, or to define the civilized balance among these different voices, which have become 'eristic' in the modern world, engaged in a fully institutionalized and well-funded battle for supremacy.

Conversation was earlier defined as a non-partisan form of communication among equal and mutually trustworthy partners. This description led him to a more abstract version of the concept of conversation suitable to refer to the required relationship between the different forms of human imagining. To achieve an equilibrium between the voices – and one has to emphasize the Aristotelian language used by Oakeshott when he talks about conversation, including concepts like the middle position and the mean between extremes – one needs to become indeed civilized. To be civilized means that one is able to see one's own activity skeptically, without becoming a relentless advocate of one's own particular aims and interests. It also means to be able and willing to educate oneself as soon as one realizes that one follows the wrong track.

Education, though, is not simply an individual affair. Although the main point seems to be an alert self-awareness, there is a social component to it. It is mainly in his writings on what he calls liberal education that Oakeshott finds occasion to sum up his views on the European tradition of education. His term of liberal education no doubt points back to the humanist tradition. But one should add to this his appreciation of the institution of a university, which is an (unintended?) invention of Christianity. There are two things Oakeshott keeps emphasizing in his accounts of university education. The first is the fact that a university houses a number of different disciplines none of which can claim superiority over the others. It is a characteristically multidisciplinary system of education where both students and professors can capitalize on the cohabitation of different branches of knowledge, which in many ways converse with one another. That is, the university represents the multiplicity of conventional voices that characterizes the way humans imagine. It is in this sense that one is expected to interpret the claim that 'Education, properly speaking, is an initiation into the skill and partnership of this conversation in which we learn to recognize the voices, to distinguish the proper occasions of utterance, and in which we acquire the intellectual and moral habits appropriate to conversation' (*RIP*, 490–1). This means that in an important sense the subjects we learn during our university years are less important than to learn to see.[16] It is not the subject matter, but the 'manners of the conversation' that we are expected to learn. The basic assumption of the institution is partnership: the university is a 'cooperative enterprise,' where 'a corporate body of scholars' 'live in permanent proximity to one another,' 'a place where a tradition of learning is preserved and extended' (*VL*, 107).

There is a second element that makes a university an exceptionally important place for Oakeshott. It provides the freshman as well as the professor with a relaxed atmosphere where the burden of providing for one's daily needs is removed from one's shoulders. It is an exceptional period in one's life to experience a kind of freedom unparalleled in later life. Basically, it is an 'interval' (*VL*, 114).

What is more, even though students are expected to dive into certain branches

---

[16] Oakeshott, 'The Idea of a University', in *The Voice of Liberal Learning*, ed., with foreword and intro. by Timothy Fuller (Indianapolis: Liberty Fund, 2001), 110. Hereafter: *VL*.

of knowledge and professors to conduct research in certain areas, the approach to these activities is non-utilitarian, and effectiveness does not count in its evaluation. '[N]o clear reason – such as usefulness – can be found to justify its parts' (*VL*, 109). The university provides, therefore, a disinterested and detached atmosphere for its members. Working here one can catch sight of the phenomena of one's research field without the necessity of doing something definite in the next moment, a pressure which is unavoidable in the rush and bustle of one's daily life. Researching and learning at a university means to get acquainted with a determinate field of study through a long and elaborate learning process, but with no directly utilitarian aim, and without giving up the eagerness to learn about anything else one happens to encounter or hear about on the way. This mode of learning is liberal in the precise sense that one is free to wander around on the wide fields of learning without the fear of getting caught trespassing.

Oakeshott's Two Concepts Of Poetry

So far, we have seen that Oakeshott finds liberty to be the common denominator in conversation, civilization, and education. All these forms of imagining and acting provide opportunity for us to liberate ourselves from the dictates of practical life. In fact, freedom is the most important component of what he calls poetry as well. In fact, in his later philosophy, the freedom of poetry becomes an alternative, in a sense, to conversation.

Yet the freedom of poetry means different things in his earlier and in his later thought – even though the two descriptions are not wholly independent from one another. In an early piece, probably written in 1925, *An Essay on the Relations of Philosophy, Poetry and Reality*,[17] poetry is contrasted with philosophy. The analysis tries to convince us that while the form of knowledge characteristic of philosophy focuses on the external features of things, and it therefore cannot give a satisfactory description of the nature of reality, for nothing can be really learnt from the outside; poetry, and more generally the mystic intuition, which includes religion along with poetry, provides humans with a direct contact to reality. The explanation for this difference in the two approaches is of course less than satisfactory. But this is in harmony with the claim itself. For indeed, one cannot logically argue out why philosophically arguing out cannot be fully satisfactory in explaining reality. If one could do so, it would be less a piece of evidence for, but rather a counter-argument against the claim. The interesting point in this text is rather the supposition of the existence of a Reality (with capital R) to be discovered. In the 1959 piece, as we have seen, there does not exist such an outside world, independent from the imagining activity. Consequently, the claim about poetry is not so strong there, either. The defining feature of poetry becomes that it grants 'a release from the deadliness of doing' (*RIP*, 538). In 'The Voice of Poetry,' aesthetic experience or poetry is contrasted with practice, which appears as an obstacle for the individual to fulfill its potential, while poetry is a momentary relief, when humans can enjoy the richness of their own images.

---

[17] Oakeshott (*WH*, 67–115).

In both of these descriptions of poetry Oakeshott starts out from the wisdom of the ancients. He is well aware of the meaning and function of the Greek term 'poiesis' (meaning 'making', an activity by which humans can transform the world around them), from which the concept of poetry is derived. But his concept of poetry is less active and more contemplative than its ancient Greek equivalent. Let us see his reasons for this interpretation of poetry.

Utterance And Voice In Poetry

First we have to give an account of a seemingly technical question. Oakeshott invests huge quantities of energy to point out that the object made by poetry is not simply a sign, which would refer to something outside itself. He calls the use and interpretation of signs 'symbolism'. 'Symbols' are objects with a referential function: they denote more than themselves. As opposed to signs, the words of poetry are just images, with their own enjoyment value regardless of any outside references. This autonomy and self-referentiality of the poetic word is called by him 'metaphorical' language.

Although the circularity of the meaning of the poetic word can be difficult to comprehend, what is meant by the author is perhaps more easily understandable from another angle. Oakeshott is trying to differentiate his position from that of the expressive theories of poetry. He denies the view that poetry would be the expression of an experience, where the poetic word is a tool, an external sign that stands for an internal feeling or for an outside phenomenon. The sort of expressionist theory he wants to deny claims that having experienced something the poet contemplates about her experiences and then presents her findings in a poetic form. Instead of admitting the existence of such a creative procedure, he goes for the unity of the poetic experience: nothing exists outside what is given in the poetic word – it stands for itself, it does not need any warrants for its own poetic existence.

Summing up his views of the nature of the poetic word Oakeshott replaces the traditional analytical tools of content or substance versus form with the expressions of utterance (what is said) and voice (how it is said).[18] The first he identifies with doctrine, the second with activity. In his view, both in science and in practice the two aspects can easily be distinguished. But this is not the case, he claims, in poetry. Here these two aspects are inseparable and intertwined. Nothing exists outside the poetic image itself, it is closed into itself.

Contemplation And Delight In Poetry

With this claim we are reaching the main emphasis of Oakeshott's description of poetry. Once again we have to stress that his account itself has a poetic quality. The most important peculiarity of this type of voice, he claims, is to be seen in its effects: it leads the recipient to contemplation and brings forward a sort of delight

---

[18] Once again Ryle's concepts of 'knowing how' and 'knowing that' comes to one's mind. [See the article by Leslie Marsh in this volume, for a detailed exploration of the relationship of Oakeshott and Ryle's thoughts on practical knowledge. – *Ed.*]

in him that is hard to gain from any other sources. This is one of the points where Oakeshott's theory is the most daring. For, contemplation in the European tradition usually belonged either to religion or to philosophy. In Plato it is the specific privilege of the philosopher that through contemplation he might reach the ideal form of the Good. But Plato is still not clearly separating the act of philosophizing from religious adoration. In Christianity it is the mystic's privilege to contemplate, and this activity might bring the mystic to direct contact with God. As we have seen, the 1925 text discussed poetry under the rubric of mystic intuition, and contemplation is not too far away from the vocabulary used. In *An Essay on the Relations of Philosophy, Poetry and Reality* Oakeshott separates the Greek concept of *theoria* from the Latin concept of contemplation, despite their etymological link. 'Theory' in his early view is kept for philosophy while '*contemplation*' is a poetic act.

Contemplation remains the aim of poetry for the later Oakeshott, even if his general epistemology radically transforms. It is an activity that produces images about which we cannot ask if they are factual or not. When they appear we do not want to ask about their factuality, possibility, or probability. These questions would miss the point of these kinds of images. What matters about them is that they cause delight. They do not have any logical connections to other images, no prehistory or afterlife, no causal relationships whatsoever. They are considered all alone, and their value lies in their particular unity of content and form – of the 'what' is said and the 'how' of saying it.

It is important to add that in his later work Oakeshott explicitly rejects his earlier claim that through contemplation poetry leads us to a higher reality. There is no higher reality directly available any more. He dissociates himself from those writers for whom 'contemplation is the enjoyment of a special and immediate access to 'reality'.' Among these authors he lists, besides Plato, his one time favorite, Spinoza, and Schopenhauer, who 'found in Kontemplation a union of the self with *species rerum*.' He also presents the reasons for his revulsion. He would wish to avoid 'a belief in the pre-eminence of … the categories of 'truth' and 'reality''(*RIP*, 511–2). In other words the later Oakeshott becomes in respect of the existence of an external reality quite nominalist, and therefore his concept of contemplation cannot lead him through an epistemological short cut to reality.

What poetry, through contemplation, leads to therefore is nothing other than delight. This is again an ancient concept, as already Horatius found one of the most important functions of poetry in '*delectare*'. But the meaning of the concept seems to be elevated by Oakeshott. There is nothing of the pleasure principle in it, as it would break the spell of poetry. But there is nothing moral in it either. 'Having an ear ready for the voice of poetry is to be disposed to choose delight rather than pleasure or virtue or knowledge.' But, then, what is this feeling of elevation in connection with delight? Why do we think of poetic imagining as a 'visitation' of a sort, why do we associate it with 'divine inspiration?' Oakeshott's explanation is rather disenchanting: the superior status of poetic imagining is 'testimony only of the unavoidable transience of contemplative activity' (*RIP*, 540).

In other words, he is inclined to think of poetic imagining as intervals within the realm of practical imagining, as 'moments of contemplative activity,' even if there is no *'vita contemplativa'* (*RIP*, 541). That is to say, poetry resonates with the lack of time in human life, the lack of real chances to have free choices. Poetry is nothing more than moments of a 'brief enchantment' (*RIP*, 540). In the final part of 'The Voice of Poetry' we see the metaphors Oakeshott brings forward to describe this special state of grace.

Friendship, Love, Play, And Childhood: Oakeshott's Metaphors Of Practical Poetry

Oakeshott is best known as a conservative philosopher. One can claim that in the core of philosophic conservatism we find dissatisfaction with the time-scale of human life: humans cannot familiarize themselves with the dramatic losses caused by the passing of time. In other words, there is always an element of the elegiac overtone in the conservative voice. At the end of this paper I want to claim that for Oakeshott conversation presents the idyllic moment, while poetry stands for the elegiac in human life.[19]

The literary genre of elegy comes from Greek *'elegeiakos'*. It means more than what we usually associate with it, a nostalgic, melancholic tone. Elegy as a genre originally meant a literary form of mourning or expressing sorrow for that which is irrecoverably past. The inherent skepticism of Oakeshott's tone suggests that he regards the human condition as one for which the ideal is irrevocably lost. Only remnants of this ideal remain, and even these have to be gathered from the ashes by those who still have a taste for it. This search for what is lost is itself the poetic activity. And the findings are not too impressive, but only delightful.

First of all there are the twin relationships between two human beings called love and friendship. The *differentia specifica* of friendship is that the only merit of the friend is that she 'evokes delight,' and '(almost) engages contemplative imagination.' The specificity of love is that it is awakened by the 'uniqueness of a self' (*RIP*, 537). In both cases, we are still in the world of practical imagining, but in both cases, an element of grace is at work: both of these relationships can develop into 'whatever it turns out to be.' The poetic elements of these relationships guarantee that although we have not left the realm of practical activity, they can constitute 'a connection between the voices of poetry and practice' (*RIP*, 538).

The next metaphor for the lost ideal found by poetry is 'moral goodness.' Oakeshott does not mean by this term a Kantian duty, 'virtuous conduct' or 'excellence of character.' Rather it is an activity 'emancipated from place and condition, in which each engagement is independent of what went before and of what may come after' (*RIP*, 538). Through this description moral goodness is again associated with contemplation and delight, ways of imagining which do not

---

[19]   Here I am referring to the concepts of 'idyll' and 'elegy' used by Schiller: 'Either nature and the ideal are an object of sadness if the first is treated as lost and the second as unattained. Or both are an object of joy represented as actual. The first yields the elegy in the narrower sense, and the second the idyll.' From 'On Naive and Sentimental Poetry,' in H. B. Nisbet, ed., *German Aesthetic and Literary Criticism*, in 3 volumes, vol. 1: *Winckelmann, Lessing, Hamann, Herder, Schiller, and Goethe* (Cambridge: Cambridge Univ. Press, 1985), 200.

deal with precedents and causes, and which liberate the mind from the burden of practice.

The themes of friendship, love, and moral goodness represent humans at their best: they are all forms of human flourishing or excellences. But they are indeed rare moments in one's life and not all of us are fortunate enough to share all these images. However, there is a recurring theme in Oakeshott's philosophy of conversation and poetry that is more general and concerns all humans. It is a definite period of life: childhood and children's most characteristic activity – play.

Playfulness is discussed in the context of conversation.[20] Whatever humans do or say to each other, they are expected to do it less than vehemently – passion and seriousness is a part of scientific and practical enterprises but they have nothing to do with conversation. Participants in it regard each other rather like playfellows who owe one another loyalty and affection regardless of the position they hold in the conversation. But play still requires from a good player some sort of seriousness. Conversation, therefore, unfolds in a tension between playfulness and seriousness. To be playful in a conversation means to learn to recognize oneself as one voice among others. In the end, nothing should be taken too seriously, and the self is perhaps the most important thing that should be dealt with playfully. But the rules of the game are all very serious, and following them is a requirement of *fair play*.

The play element turns out to be vital for culture in general – this is an insight made popular in Oakeshott's days by Johan Huizinga, who published his work on *Homo ludens* before the Second World War.[21] Huizinga's point was to show that the anthropological basis of culture is to be found in play, and that there is no high culture and developed civilization where play does not have a role. Consequently the Nazi ideology that waged war against play was a serious threat to civilization. Oakeshott shared Huizinga's concern and extended it to any forms of what he called rationalist politics, i.e. to any totalitarian regimes that wanted to reformulate human nature. Imperfections were necessarily parts of human life, Oakeshott claimed, and playfulness helps humans to accommodate themselves to it. Similarly, if human life is necessarily a life of losses, humans can only survive if they are able to forget themselves – and play is a form of doing so without losing one's dignity and personal identity.

The best conversationalists and players are, of course, the children. By elevating children on top of his value hierarchy Oakeshott drifts to the fringe of the abyss of late romanticism. But his good taste saves him from overstating his case. Childhood is not presented by him as idyllic but as a lost paradise, the recollection of which is full of pains but which still preserves a poetic character for us all: 'Everybody's young days are a dream, a delightful insanity, a miraculous confusion of poetry and practical activity' (*RIP*, 539). It is not so much the enjoyments, as the imperfections of childhood that make it a memorable period of one's life. Linguistic competence is still far from perfect, which helps to save the poetic (i.e. metaphoric) character

---

[20] There is an essay on 'Work and Play' in *WH*, 303–14.
[21] Johan Huizinga, *Homo ludens: Proeve eener bepaling van het spelelement der cultuur*, [*Homo Ludens: A Study in the Play-Elements in Culture*], trans. R. F. C. Hull (1938, reprint; Boston: The Beacon Press, 1955).

of language and the delight of utterance. The language of the child is still poetic, because it is conversable – children are good at taking part in conversation, having an ear to hear the melody of words rather than their strict meanings. They do not take things too seriously; even education is play for them. It is therefore perfectly adequate, and this is the last word by Oakeshott on conversation and poetry, to take their attitude as poetic and conversable, even if its most evident manifestation is truancy: 'Poetry is a sort of truancy, a dream within the dream of life, a wild flower planted among our wheat' (*RIP*, 541).

16

Kenneth B. McIntyre

One Hand Clapping: The Reception of Oakeshott's Work by American Conservatives

Introduction

In the decade and a half since Michael Oakeshott's death, there has been a substantial increase in academic interest in his work. This interest has generated a number of novel and distinctive interpretations of Oakeshott. Among the versions of Oakeshott now extant, there are Oakeshott the Liberal,[1] Oakeshott the Republican,[2] Oakeshott the Modernist,[3] Oakeshott the Postmodernist,[4] Oakeshott the Skeptic,[5] Oakeshott the Historian,[6] and Oakeshott the Idealist.[7] What all of these new readings have in common is their resistance to the facile reduction of Oakeshott's work to the irrationalist or Romantic conservatism of which he was accused by so many of his early readers.[8] However, despite the increasingly subtle and penetrating work of Oakeshott scholars, Oakeshott's reputation in the non-academic world is that of a traditionalist conservative political thinker. In their obituary of him, the *Times* called him a 'pragmatic Thatcherite,' while Perry Anderson included him prominently in his survey of 'the Intransigent Right at the End of the Century,' and Jeffrey Hart claimed that Oakeshott had 'proposed a theory of the state which came down to earth in the practice of Margaret Thatcher.'[9] Oakeshott's actual influence among

[1] Paul Franco, *The Political Philosophy of Michael Oakeshott* (New Haven: Yale Univ. Press, 1990).
[2] David Boucher, 'Oakeshott, Freedom, and Republicanism,' *British Journal of Politics and International Relations* 7, no. 1 (2005): 81–96.
[3] Efraim Podoksik, *In Defense of Modernity: Vision and Philosophy in Michael Oakeshott* (Exeter: Imprint Academic, 2003).
[4] Richard Rorty, 'Postmodernist Bourgeois Liberalism,' in *Objectivity, Relativism, and Truth,* vol. 1 of *Philosophical Papers* (Cambridge: Cambridge Univ. Press, 1991), 197–202.
[5] Stephen Gerencser, *The Skeptic's Oakeshott* (New York: St. Martin's Press, 2000).
[6] Luke O'Sullivan, *Oakeshott on History* (Exeter: Imprint Academic, 2003).
[7] Kenneth B. McIntyre, *The Limits of Political Theory: Oakeshott's Philosophy of Civil Association* (Exeter: Imprint Academic, 2004).
[8] See, for example, Colin Falk, 'Romanticism in Politics,' *New Left Review*, 18 (1963): 60–71; David Spitz, 'A Rationalist *Malgre Lui*: The Perplexities of Being Michael Oakeshott,' *Political Theory*, 4, no. 3 (1976): 335–52; and Hanna Pitkin, 'The Roots of Conservatism: Michael Oakeshott and the Denial of Politics,' *Dissent*, 204 (1973): 496–525.
[9] Perry Anderson, 'The Intransigent Right at the End of the Century,' *London Review of Books*, 14

British conservative politicians and public intellectuals while alive and since his death is a matter of some contention, although a consensus of scholars rejects the notion that his ideas had any profound influence on the Thatcher government.[10] Nevertheless, whatever importance Oakeshott's ideas might have had for conservatives in Great Britain, there is little dispute that his influence on American conservatism has been negligible.[11]

In this paper, I offer a contemporary history of the reception of Oakeshott's work by American conservative public intellectuals.[12] In doing so, I have not attempted to provide a definition of conservatism, but accepted the self-description of the various authors I have surveyed.[13] I concentrate primarily on the work of three writers: the journalist and editor Irving Kristol, the historian Gertrude Himmelfarb, and the literary scholar M. E. Bradford. I focus on these three because, among self-described conservative intellectuals, they are almost alone in either attempting to appropriate Oakeshott's ideas in the context of a discussion of the American political experience or explicitly rejecting the relevance of such an appropriation. Further, they represent two of the more significant strands of conservatism in the United States. Kristol and Himmelfarb are neoconservatives while Bradford was a traditionalist conservative.[14]

I am less concerned with the specific contributions of these thinkers to the scholarship on Oakeshott (and their contributions are minimal at best) than I am with the ways in which these writers use, or decline to use, Oakeshott's writings in furthering their own practical political concerns. The use of Oakeshott by self-described neoconservatives like Irving Kristol and Gertrude Himmelfarb on the

---

(September 24, 1992): 7–11; Jeffrey Hart, 'Michael Oakeshott, *RIP*,' *National Review*, 43 (January 28, 1991): 19.

[10] The notion that Oakeshott was the 'house philosopher' of the Thatcher government has been disputed by several commentators. For example, Timothy Fuller claims that Oakeshott 'never became the guru of Thatcherism as some who lack subtlety have alleged,' in Roy Tseng, *The Sceptical Idealist: Michael Oakeshott as a Critic of the Enlightenment* (Exeter: Imprint Academic, 2003), 3 n. 8. Noel Annan writes that 'it was Hayek and Friedman, rather than Oakeshott, who inspired the new conservatism' in Britain. Annan, *Our Age* (London: Weidenfield and Nicolson, 1990), 394.

[11] Peter Berkowitz writes that 'Oakeshott's work is still not very well known in America … among conservative intellectuals,' in 'Review of *The Politics of Faith and the Politics of Scepticism*,' *First Things*, 72 (April, 1997), 38. Kenneth Minogue notes that Oakeshott is 'regarded with some suspicion by American Neo-conservatives,' in 'Three Conservative Realists,' *Conservative Realism*, ed. Kenneth Minogue (London: Harper Collins, 1996), 156–7.

[12] For an historical account of American conservatism, see Paul Gottfried and Thomas Fleming, *The Conservative Movement* (Boston: Twayne Publishers, 1988); and George H. Nash, *The Conservative Intellectual Movement Since 1945* (New York: Basic Books, 1976).

[13] I accept Elie Kedourie's admonition that 'terms like right and left, whig and tory, conservative and liberal … have no power to explain; rather it is they that call for explanation,' but in this instance I follow another of his suggestions, that 'the historian must be a nominalist.' See Elie Kedourie, *The Crossman Confessions* (London: Mansell Publishing, 1984), 143, 154.

[14] Gottfried and Fleming note that the three strands of American conservatism are libertarian, traditionalist, and neo-liberal anti-communist. The neoconservatives are associated with the last group, but also have affinities with Straussian conservatives. Gottfried, *Conservative Movement*, 1–20, 59–76. For the neoconservatives, see Peter Steinfels, *The Neoconservatives* (New York: Simon and Schuster, 1979). For an account of Strauss's influence on contemporary conservatism, see Anne Norton, *Leo Strauss and the Politics of American Empire* (New Haven: Yale Univ. Press, 2005).

one hand and by traditionalist conservatives like M. E. Bradford on the other manifests two distinct conceptions of the American political experience generally and American conservatism particularly. Kristol's and Himmelfarb's rejection of Oakeshott's relevance to what they understand to be America's exceptional political experience is the result of their conception of the American state as a teleocratic enterprise and their related conception of conservatism as an elucidation and defense of the universal principles which inform the American experience. In contrast, M. E. Bradford's explicit reliance upon Oakeshott's distinction between teleocracy and nomocracy, and his defense of a nomocratic interpretation of American political experience manifest his rejection of the teleocratic views of the neoconservatives and his accord with a more dispositional Oakeshottian conservatism. However, Bradford's work has not been well received by other conservatives and his embrace of Oakeshott has been exceptional even among traditionalist conservatives.

As a way of responding to both the neoconservative critique of Oakeshott's ideas and Bradford's appropriation of them, I will conclude with an account of Oakeshott's comments on the peculiar character of the American political tradition. Despite his generally dubious attitude about American exceptionalism, Oakeshott agreed with Bradford's claim that the form of American constitutionalism is primarily nomocratic. However, he also insisted that American political discourse has always been informed by a rationalist ideology of the kind that manifested itself in the French Revolution. For Oakeshott, the paradox of American politics was that the United States acts like a civil association, but speaks like an enterprise association. If Oakeshott's observations are correct, then his lack of appreciation by the more influential conservative intellectuals in America can be at least partly explained by his refusal to speak in an ideological or teleocratic idiom.

The Neoconservatives – Kristol and Himmelfarb

The reason most commonly given by American conservatives for the rejection of Oakeshott's ideas is that they are inappropriate to the unique character of American politics. This commitment to American exceptionalism is especially evident in the works of neoconservative writers like Irving Kristol and Gertrude Himmelfarb.[15] There are three primary contentions associated with Oakeshott's political thought that these neoconservatives reject. First, they claim that political activity is not inherently traditional. Instead, it is, or ought to be, guided by abstract philosophical principles. Thus, and this is their second criticism, conservatism is, or ought to be, not merely a disposition, but a coherent ideology or creed constructed out of a philosophical understanding of politics. Third, if conservative politics, like all politics, is ideological, then the state must be an inherently teleocratic institution

---

[15] Kristol and Himmelfarb also happen to be husband and wife, a point not necessarily germane to their political principles but relevant because both were introduced to and became friends with Oakeshott during a stay in England in the 1950s. For Kristol on American exceptionalism, see his 'America's Exceptional Conservatism,' in *Neoconservatism: The Autobiography of an Idea* (New York: The Free Press, 1995), 373–86. The emphasis given to the exceptional character of the American polity by neoconservatives is shared by Straussian conservatives, as well. See *Leo Strauss, the Straussians, and the American Regime*, ed. Kenneth Deutsch (New York: Rowman and Littlefield, 1999).

created according to some plan with a definite purpose. According to American neoconservatives, American exceptionalism consists of the fact that the United States is the first state to be guided by a philosophically correct ideology or creed, and conservatism in America consists of the elucidation and promotion of an American politics guided by this ideology.

Irving Kristol is an American journalist and editor who is most widely known as the self-acknowledged 'godfather' of neoconservatism. His wife, Gertrude Himmelfarb, is an American historian who specializes in the history of Victorian Britain, but who is also a respected social and cultural critic. Kristol and Himmelfarb are among the few American conservative intellectuals who are both well acquainted with Oakeshott's political thought and with Oakeshott himself. They met while Kristol was working as the co-editor with Stephen Spender of *Encounter* magazine in London, which Kristol describes as a 'cultural-intellectual-political magazine in Paris to counteract the predominant influence of anti-American and often Communist fellow-traveling magazines in all the democracies.'[16] At the time, Kristol considered himself a liberal social democrat, but was quite impressed with the strength and confidence of conservatism in Great Britain. He writes that English conservatives like Malcolm Muggeridge and Peregrine Worsthorne, whom he also met while working at *Encounter*, 'were ... heirs to a long tradition of conservative politics and conservative thought ..., whereas there was no such tradition in the United States.'[17] However, the encounter with English conservatism did not impress him enough to fundamentally alter his political commitments. Nor did the nomination of Barry Goldwater as the conservative Republican presidential candidate in 1964 make an impression. However, the rise of the counterculture, the protests against the Vietnam War, and the tumultuous events on college campuses during the late 1960s which, for Kristol, culminated in the Democratic nomination of George McGovern for president, convinced Kristol of the need for a return to an older style of liberalism. The neoconservatism that emerged, in Kristol's words, 'accepted the New Deal in principle, and had little affection for the kind of isolationism that then permeated American conservatism.'[18] In fact, for those traditionalist conservatives who rejected Kristol's observation about the lack of an American conservative tradition, Kristol's neoconservatism represented not so much a novel contribution to American conservative political discourse as a rejection of conservatism.[19]

While complimenting Oakeshott's style and reputation, both Himmelfarb, who as a professional academic has been less involved in the world of practical political life, and Kristol have written essays explicitly rejecting Oakeshott's conception

---

[16] Irving Kristol, *Neoconservatism: The Autobiography of an Idea* (New York: The Free Press, 1995), 21. It was revealed later that *Encounter* was funded largely by the CIA. See Kristol's 'Memoirs of a 'Cold Warrior',' and 'My Cold War' in *Neoconservatism* for his reactions to the revelations.

[17] Kristol, *Neoconservatism*, 25.

[18] Kristol, *Neoconservatism*, x.

[19] Russell Kirk's *The Conservative Mind* was an explicit attempt to offer an historical account of American conservatism in a traditionalist idiom. See Gottfried, *Conservative Movement*, 59–76, for the claim that neoconservatism involves a rejection of conservatism.

of conservatism, and their critiques are unsurprisingly quite similar.[20] Ironically, in 1956 as editor of *Encounter*, Kristol had rejected Oakeshott's essay 'On Being Conservative' as 'too abstract and too specifically British.'[21] Forty years later, Kristol elaborated in a more complete way the reasons for this rejection.

First, according to Kristol, Oakeshott's understanding of conservatism is too secular. The true conservative is more intensely tied to the reality of the past, especially the religious past. Kristol claims 'Oakeshott's ideal conservative society is a society without religion.'[22] It is unclear where Kristol locates this particular claim in Oakeshott's text, especially since Oakeshott expressly rejects the notion that it is the mission of philosophy to be engaged in the production of ideal societies. Nonetheless, Kristol's complaint was made earlier in an essay by Himmelfarb in 1975. According to her, Oakeshott is exceptional among self-described conservatives in neither having religious convictions of his own nor respecting the religious faith of others. She writes that Oakeshott has 'something very like an ideological animus against it, a dislike for religion itself, for the very idea of religion, for any idea that has the presumption of truth.'[23] Though there is no textual support cited for Himmelfarb's argument, the critique about Oakeshott's lack of religious sensibility is secondary to the real critique of his conservatism.[24] It is Himmelfarb's judgment that Oakeshott has a fundamental mistrust of any absolute truth claim, and it is this practical skepticism more than his purported religious agnosticism that provokes her disapproval.

Thus, the second and more substantial fault that both Kristol and Himmelfarb find is that Oakeshott is unwilling to offer a systematic program for conservatism. Oakeshott's skepticism about the unmitigated ameliorative possibilities of political activity and his non-prescriptive conception of political philosophy are both rejected

---

[20] Kristol, 'America's Exceptional Conservatism'; and Gertrude Himmelfarb, 'The Conservative Imagination of Michael Oakeshott,' *American Scholar* 44, no. 3 (Summer 1975): 405–20. Himmelfarb has also written a critical appraisal of Oakeshott's philosophy of history. See Himmelfarb, 'Supposing History is a Woman – What Then?' *American Scholar* 53, no. 4 (Autumn 1984): 494–505.

[21] Kristol was one of those who suggested to Oakeshott that he should issue a collection of his essays and was also the editor of Basic Books when it published the American edition of *Rationalism in Politics*, which, according to Kristol, only sold 600 copies. Kristol, 'America's Exceptional Conservatism,' 373. Himmelfarb writes, 'one sometimes suspects that his world is confined to England itself, that it does not even include America.' Himmelfarb, 'The Conservative Imagination of Michael Oakeshott,' 415.

[22] Kristol, 'America's Exceptional Conservatism,' 375.

[23] Himmelfarb, 'The Conservative Imagination of Michael Oakeshott,' 415. For an account of Oakeshott's religious thought and its relation to his conception of the moral life, see Glenn Worthington, *Religious and Poetic Experience in the Thought of Michael Oakeshott* (Exeter: Imprint Academic, 2005). [The reader may also wish to consult Elizabeth Corey, *Michael Oakeshott on Religion, Aesthetics and Politics* (Columbia: Univ. of Missouri Press, 2006), as well as several essays in the present volume for a further reappraisal of Oakeshott's thoughts on religion. – *Ed.*]

[24] Oakeshott writes, 'what makes a conservative disposition in politics intelligible is nothing to do with natural law or a providential order, nothing to do with morals or religion.' His point is not that religion is an unimportant or irrelevant part of a human life, but that it is not necessarily related to a conservative disposition concerning nomocratic government. See Oakeshott, 'On Being Conservative,' in *Rationalism in Politics and other essays, new and expanded edition*, ed. Timothy Fuller (Indianapolis: Liberty Press, 1991), 423–4. Hereafter: *RIP*.

by neoconservatives as incompatible with rational political activity. Himmelfarb writes that 'so long as [Oakeshott] provides us with no means for distinguishing between good and bad, let alone for cultivating a disposition to do good rather than bad, we are obliged to look elsewhere for guidance.'[25] Undoubtedly, Oakeshott would have argued that Himmelfarb should not be consulting philosophers for moral and political instruction. However, neither Kristol nor Himmelfarb directly address Oakeshott's reasons for rejecting what he calls Rationalist or ideological politics. Instead, Himmelfarb complains of Oakeshott's 'tendency to equate ideology with ideas, to be equally suspicious of both, [and] to be impatient with the very exercise of mind,' and compares him unfavorably with Burke who, because he held to a firm set of principles based upon the natural law, predicted the violence and devastation of the French Revolution.[26] It is an intriguing novelty that reveals something of the hold of the aspirations of the social sciences on the public mind that an historian would condemn a political philosopher for not producing accurate predictions. However, it is, in fact, Himmelfarb who is equating ideology with ideas by suggesting that Oakeshott's problem is that he cannot or will not provide a method for separating the good ideologies from the bad.[27]

The final reason for the rejection of Oakeshott by the neoconservatives relates specifically to their claim concerning America's exceptional political experience. Even if Oakeshott's dispositional conservatism is appropriate to some countries, and it is doubtful that Kristol and Himmelfarb would grant even this, it is irrelevant to conservatism in the United States because conservative politics concerns not the rejection of ideology but finding or creating the correct ideology and conserving it, and the United States is the first state to have created the correct one. For Kristol, the United States is an ideological state, like the Soviet Union used to be, and, thus, has a distinctively teleological political life. He writes, 'the United States is a 'creedal' nation,' referring to President Lincoln's claim at Gettysburg that the country was 'dedicated to the proposition that all men are created equal.'[28] As such, instead of enjoying a current manner of living because it is enjoyable, American conservatives must be vigilant in guarding and preserving the *telos* of the American political

---

[25] Himmelfarb, 'The Conservative Imagination of Michael Oakeshott,' 420. This is substantially the same critique of Oakeshott offered by the only Straussian conservatives to have commented upon his work. Harry Jaffa writes in a review of *Rationalism in Politics* that 'he does not … tell us how to evaluate a whole tradition.' Jaffa, 'Review of *Rationalism in Politics*,' *National Review* (October 22, 1963), 361. Walter Berns, reviewing the same work, claims that 'Oakeshott is an opponent of any attempt to gain theoretical clarity concerning the most important things: how we conduct our lives.' Berns, 'Review of *Rationalism in Politics*,' *American Political Science Review*, 57 (1963), 671.

[26] Himmelfarb, 'The Conservative Imagination of Michael Oakeshott,' 420. Bernard Crick notes the American tendency to view Burke as a natural law philosopher, writing that American conservatives 'write as if Burke was a post-Newman member of the Oxford movement.' Crick, 'The Strange Quest for an American Conservatism,' *The Review of Politics*, 17, no. 3 (July, 1955), 372.

[27] Oakeshott once replied to a similar critique by writing that he was not concerned with establishing 'a seminary for training political hedge-preachers in some dim orthodoxy.' Oakeshott quoted in O'Sullivan, *Oakeshott on History*, 2.

[28] Kristol, 'America's Exceptional Conservatism,' 376. In reference to this sort of teleocratic politics, Oakeshott writes, 'if it is boring to have to listen to the dreams of others being recounted, it is insufferable to be forced to reenact them' (*RIP*, 428).

community. One of the most interesting aspects of this neoconservative version of the American political community is that it conceives the US as a teleocratic state that has achieved its *telos*. The neoconservative ideological justification for attempting to make the rest of the world more like America is that, in order for the revolution to remain fulfilled in the United States, it must be accomplished elsewhere. As the completed state among other non-completed states, the United States role is to make the world like itself.[29]

The Traditionalist – Bradford

An exception to this general conservative rejection of Oakeshott's thought can be found in the works of the traditionalist conservative literary critic and historian M. E. Bradford. Unlike Kristol and Himmelfarb who explicitly reject Oakeshott's relevance to American politics, Bradford incorporates Oakeshottian ideas, concepts, and language throughout his work. He makes Oakeshott's distinction between nomocracy and teleocracy the central conceptual apparatus in his critique of the neoconservative and Straussian interpretation of the American political tradition.[30] Bradford uses Oakeshott's ideas to distinguish his own interpretation of the American political experience from what he believes is the radical claim of the neoconservatives and Straussians that the United States is a teleocratic state founded on the abstract idea of equality. Bradford also defends an Oakeshottian conception of conservatism in American politics, claiming specifically that the political traditions of the Southern states of the United States have manifested a distinctly conservative disposition.

Bradford's use of Oakeshott occurs within the context of a larger controversy among American conservative intellectuals concerning the nature of the American political tradition. Bradford's work, like that of his primary intellectual adversary Harry Jaffa, consists not of an academic exercise in making the past intelligible in terms of its independence from present concerns but of the construction of a practical or usable American political past.[31] His work is an attempt to recover

---

[29] Claes Ryn refers to contemporary American neoconservatives as neo-Jacobins who 'regard America as founded on universal principles and assigns to the United States the role of supervising the remaking of the world.' Ryn, 'The Ideology of American Empire,' *Orbis*, 47, no. 3 (Summer, 2003): 384.

[30] George Carey also mentions Oakeshott as an influence on his and Willmoore Kendall's elucidation of the American political tradition. See Carey and Kendall, *Basic Symbols of the American Political Traditions* (Washington, DC: Catholic Univ. Press, 1995).

[31] Bradford writes of his own work 'In a Southern context the fight over the past is … primarily a dispute concerning the choices for the present and future.' Melvin E. Bradford, in *The Reactionary Imperative: Essays Literary and Political* (Peru, IL: S. Sudgen, 1990), 196. See also Bradford, *Original Intentions: On the Making and Ratification of the United States Constitution* (Athens, GA: Univ. Georgia Press, 1993); Bradford, *Founding Fathers: Brief Lives of the Framers of the United States Constitution*, with a foreword by Russell Kirk (Lawrence, KA: Univ. Press of Kansas, 1994); Bradford, *Remembering Who We Are: Observations of a Southern Conservative* (Athens, GA: Univ. of Georgia Press, 1985); Bradford, *A Better Guide than Reason: Studies in the American Revolution*, with an introduction by Jeffrey Hart (La Salle, IL: S. Sugden, 1979). See also Jaffa, 'Equality as Conservative Principle,' in *Keeping the Tablets: Modern American Conservative Thought*, ed. William F. Buckley and Charles Kesler (New York: Harper and Row, 1988), 83–105; and Jaffa, 'Equality, Justice, and the American Revolution: In Reply to Bradford's

hat he believes was the original conservative character of American politics in order to transform contemporary American conservatism.

Bradford first deploys Oakeshottian ideas and terminology to support his interpretation of the American political experience during and after the War of Independence. He claims that the American War of Independence, far from being revolutionary in the French sense of the term, was, in fact, a war of restoration. He rejects the notion that the colonists were intent on creating a completely *novus ordo seclorum*. Instead, he insists that the American colonists 'were prescriptive Whigs who had made a revolution on the model of the Glorious Revolution – in order to continue as they were.'[32] These early American statesmen were traditionalists who understood themselves as heirs to a living political tradition; thus, they did not look favorably on innovation or on the importance of 'foundings'. Bradford writes, 'the inherited politics of their forefathers was for them what the English political philosopher Michael Oakeshott describes as 'a practice', not a set of goals or *telos*.'[33]

Bradford's conclusions about the relevance of Oakeshottian concepts to the experience of the American Revolution also apply to his reading of the United States *Constitution*. Bradford writes of his interpretation of the *Constitution* 'much of its framework (and some of its language) is drawn from the full teaching of the British political philosopher Michael Oakeshott.'[34] Bradford insists that the *Constitution* is properly understood as a document that created the authorized procedures by which the government of the United States operates, not as a set of abstract principles to guide future generations toward a common goal. He claims that the *Constitution* authorizes a 'nomocratic government,' and it is authorized by a political community that is 'characterized not by its objectives but by its mode of operation and devotion to a body of laws which codified that mode.'[35] Thus, the *Constitution* is procedural and not substantive and it is concerned with the creation and custody of a political community composed of individuals with a common concern but without a common goal. Bradford, echoing Oakeshott's description of civil association, writes that the *Constitution* 'organizes and protects a government able to contain our multiplicity without setting out to resolve it.'[36]

Further, Bradford uses Oakeshottian ideas and terminology in order to reject both the centrality of the Declaration of Independence as a founding document and the positive interpretation of the Lincoln legacy in American political life. In

'The Heresy of Equality',' in *Modern Age: The First Twenty-five Years* (Indianapolis: Liberty Press, 1988), 305–17.

[32] Bradford, *Founding Fathers*, xvi. Hannah Arendt also suggests, 'there is very little in form or content of the new revolutionary constitutions which was even new, let alone revolutionary.' Arendt, *On Revolution* (New York: Penguin, 1973), 142–3. Compare with Jaffa's claim that 'the American Revolution represented the most radical break with tradition … that the world had ever seen.' Jaffa, 'Equality as Conservative Principle,' 86.

[33] Bradford, *Remembering Who We Are*, 49. Bradford's conservatism contradicts the claim made by Crick that American conservatives 'reject any doctrine of historical immanence such as is at the heart of both Burke and Hegel's thought.' Crick, 'The Strange Quest,' 373.

[34] Bradford, *Original Intentions*, 106.

[35] Bradford, *Original Intentions*, 104.

[36] Bradford, *Original Intentions*, xxi.

fact, according to Bradford, Lincoln's legacy has been to pervert the nomocratic character of the American republic by claiming, through a tendentious reading of the Declaration of Independence, that the United States is a country founded on a proposition.[37] He asserts that Lincoln 'played the central role in transforming [the Union] into a unitary structure based on a claim to power in its own right, a teleocratic instrument which, in the name of any cause that attracts a following, might easily threaten the liberties of those for whose sake it existed.'[38] So, for Bradford, the American political experience, which emerged from a nomocratic English tradition and was originally itself nomocratic, has, since the Civil War and the triumph of Lincoln's re-definition of the American political community, fallen under the sway of teleocratic ways of thinking. Lincoln's renovation of the American political tradition 'set us off forever to 'trampling out the grapes of wrath'.'[39]

Bradford's purpose in constructing this alternative account of the American past is to recapture and reinvigorate the nomocratic elements of the American tradition, but also to clarify and revivify the tradition of American conservatism. He locates this conservative tradition in the old South whose political community was formed not out of a rebellion against English habits and *mores*, but out of the circumstantial differences between life in England and in the Southern states. Bradford writes that the Southern conservative 'followed not an assertion of propositional truth but rather a pious determination to prefer a given world, a *societas*, which guaranteed his rights as a kind of Englishman or American republican, to a positive political model, a universal teaching on justice and love, liberty and equality, peace and honor.'[40] This commitment to a political life understood in terms of an inheritance to be preserved and enhanced defines the distinctiveness of the Southern political tradition. According to Bradford, Southern conservatives like Patrick Henry, John Taylor, John Randolph, and John Calhoun were the 'vital *nomocratic* force in the

---

[37] This claim is the primary locus of the dispute between Bradford and Jaffa. Jaffa claims that 'the principles of the Declaration are ... presupposed in the *Constitution*.' He also writes, in a passage that confirms Bradford's characterization of Lincoln's teleocratic conception of government, that 'When Jesus asked: 'Who is my mother, and who are my brothers?' ... he transformed the family of pure tradition into one constituted, not by blood, but by faith.... This is exactly what Abraham Lincoln did within the American experience ... he confirmed our community as a sacramental union.' See Jaffa, 'Equality as a Conservative Principle,' 103–4; and Jaffa, 'In Abraham's Bosom,' *National Review* (April 12, 1993), 50.

[38] Bradford is not alone among conservative thinkers in his negative assessment of Lincoln's legacy. Eric Voegelin wrote to Bradford, 'Lincoln's government "of the people, by the people, for the people" is even more a millenarian blasphemy than becomes apparent from your paper. [It is] a transposition of a cosmological formula into a millenarian formula for political action.' See Bradford, *The Reactionary Imperative*, 225; for Voegelin's quote, see Bradford, *A Better Guide than Reason*, 192. Lord Acton, though not a conservative, shared a profound dismay at the fundamental change that the Civil War wrought in the American political system. He wrote to Robert E. Lee, 'I deemed that you were fighting the battles of our liberty, our progress, and our civilization; and I mourn for the stake which was lost at Richmond more deeply than I rejoice over that which was saved at Waterloo.' Quoted in Christopher Clausen, 'Lord Acton and the Lost Cause,' *The American Scholar*, 69, no. 1 (Winter, 2000): 50.

[39] Bradford, *A Better Guide than Reason*, 187.

[40] Bradford, *The Reactionary Imperative*, 121.

nation's public life.'[41] These are the figures to whom Bradford believes that an authentic American conservatism must turn to regain its intellectual coherence. He opposed this Southern traditionalist conservatism to the Puritan millenarianism of the New England states. For Bradford, this opposition between nomocratic and teleocratic tendencies in American politics has defined the American political experience, especially since the end of the Civil War.

Thus, Bradford's work incorporates both Oakeshott's theoretical and historical essays on the distinction between nomocracy and teleocracy and his more discursive essays on the character of rationalism and of conservatism to support his construction of a usable past for American conservatives. However, Bradford, like his fellow traditionalist conservatives, has had little influence on American political discourse in the past twenty-five years, as the conservative movement in America has increasingly relied on the teleocratic language of neoconservatism. Indeed, in a demonstration of the traditionalists' lack of political influence which occurred during the first Reagan administration, Bradford's critical evaluation of the Lincoln legacy in American political life led to a barrage of condemnation from neoconservatives and was at least partially responsible for President Reagan's rejection of his nomination to be chairman of the National Endowment for the Arts.[42]

Oakeshott on America

The divergent reception of Oakeshott's work by Kristol and Himmelfarb on the one hand and Bradford on the other is best understood as a manifestation of a disagreement between the various shadings of American conservatives over the character of the American political experience, with some conservatives, like Kristol and Himmelfarb, holding that the United States is a teleocratic state devoted to the pursuit of a more or less coherent idea of equality, while others, like Bradford, claim that the United States is, or at least was, founded as a nomocratic state committed to procedural constitutionalism. That Oakeshott's influence on conservative political life in the United States has been largely confined to the works of M. E. Bradford might also be taken as evidence that the neoconservative interpretation of the American political tradition is widely accepted, though not necessarily historically or theoretically compelling.

An examination of Oakeshott's scattered comments on American politics reveals that Oakeshott accepted neither the neoconservative version nor the Bradfordian nomocratic version of the American political past unreservedly. Instead, Oakeshott claimed that the United States' political tradition has been informed from the beginning by the kind of rationalist ideology that he dissected in his essays on the

---

[41] In referring to his use of Oakeshottian language in connection with Southern conservatism, Bradford asserts that Oakeshott is 'a thinker I find to be especially valuable in explaining the conduct of Southerners.' Bradford, *The Reactionary Imperative*, 122, 127.
[42] Kristol reportedly spearheaded neoconservative opposition to Bradford on the grounds that his writings about Lincoln were unacceptable. See, for example, Thomas Landess, 'Mel Bradford, Old Indian Fighters, and the NEH,' *LewRockwell.com* (April 23, 2003); http://www.lewrockwell.com/orig4/landess1.html.

subject. Indeed, the neoconservative account of the character of American politics and the exceptionalism of American conservatism is about as good an example of rationalism in politics as can be found. On the other hand, Oakeshott recognized the *Constitution* and the government it created as fundamentally nomocratic institutions. However, contrary to the 'exceptionalist' account of the American 'Founding', Oakeshott rejected the novelty of the American *Constitution* and the government it created insisting instead that they emerged within an individualistic and nomocratic tradition, which predated their creation by several hundred years. Thus, Oakeshott considered the United States to be substantially similar to most other European states. For Oakeshott, the United States is a political community which has oscillated between the poles of teleocracy and nomocracy, but which has also manifested to a higher degree than most an ideological style of politics.

Oakeshott's most extensive observations on the American political experience are found in his essay 'Rationalism in Politics.' In this essay, he offers the early experience of the United States as an exemplary case in the history of political rationalism. According to Oakeshott, the geographical isolation of the colonies from England forced upon an inexperienced people the necessity of ruling themselves. This experience of remoteness supported the notion that the colonists had had to create all that they possessed, which in turn promoted what Oakeshott calls their 'natural and unsophisticated rationalism' (*RIP*, 31). He writes that 'a civilization of pioneers [is] rationalist by circumstance and not by reflection' (*RIP*, 32).

Further, the circumstances surrounding American independence from Britain also encouraged an appeal to rationalist/ideological political ideas. The American War of Independence, as Oakeshott mischievously reminds, was an illegal rebellion against an authorized government. This necessitated a justification that appealed to some principle external to and higher than the British constitution. Thus, according to Oakeshott, the geographical and political circumstances of the colonists combined to convince them 'that the proper organization of a society and the conduct of its affairs were based upon abstract principles [which] were to be discovered in nature by human reason, by a technique of inquiry available alike to all men and requiring no extraordinary intelligence in its use' (*RIP*, 32–3). Fortunately for the colonists, the results of similar inquiries had already been written down in books, and they found their preferred justification and organization in the political writings of John Locke.[43] For Oakeshott, the 'Declaration of Independence' is the preeminent example of this naïve and sentimental ideology. It is 'a characteristic product of the *saeculum rationalisticum*, ... one of the sacred documents of the politics of Rationalism' (*RIP*, 33). Its rationalism lies in the ideological notion expressed in the document that political schemes, plans, and blueprints are understood to be derived from abstract statements of principle and conceived prior to political activity itself. It follows from Oakeshott's elaboration of the incoherent character of rationalist politics that claims that the United States was founded on a proposition are also theoretically and historically confused. He writes, 'the notion of founding a society ... upon a

---

[43] Oakeshott writes that Locke's *Second Treatise on Government* has been misread in both America and France as a 'preface to political activity' instead of what it actually is, which is 'a brilliant abridgment of the political habits of Englishmen' (*RIP*, 53).

'Declaration of the Rights of Man' is a creature of the rationalist brain' (*RIP*, 11).[44]

Nonetheless, the American colonists were heirs to a fundamentally nomocratic English political tradition, and Oakeshott recognizes the American Constitution and the government that it created as manifestations of a nomocratic conception of the state. Over the course of his writings, Oakeshott uses several different terms to emphasize his own variations of the nomocratic theme including *societas*, representative democracy, and 'the rule of law'. He specifically relates these concepts to a skeptical understanding of politics, and in his discussion of the politics of skepticism, he characterizes the United States *Constitution* as 'the most profoundly skeptical constitution of the modern world.'[45] It is a *Constitution* that sanctions a government understood not in terms of substantive purposes but in terms of authorized procedures. Oakeshott asserts, 'although they were not directly concerned to expose or to characterize it, a state understood in terms of *societas* was assumed by those who drew up the American 'Declaration of Independence', by the authors of the Federalist papers (particularly James Madison), and by the framers of the *Constitution*.'[46] Like Bradford, Oakeshott insists on the continuity and congruence of the American political experience with practices and institutions that had already emerged in Europe.

Thus, Oakeshott rejects the exceptionalist claims of American neoconservatives and others relating to the novelty and significance of the *Constitution* and government of the United States. For Oakeshott, the most significant development in the modern world is the emergence of the morality of the modern individual and the practices and institutions associated with nomocratic government, both of which predate American independence from Britain by several centuries. He dates the rise of modern individualism to the fourteenth and fifteenth centuries, and writes that nomocratic government 'appeared first in England, in the Netherlands and in Switzerland, and was later (in various idioms) extended to other parts of Western Europe and the United States of America' (*RIP*, 368). Thus, the American political tradition, insofar as it is nomocratic, is not only not particularly revolutionary, but is in fact derived from and dependent upon an already established tradition of political activity. To borrow a phrase used by Ann

---

[44] In a review of a book by Walter Lippman, Oakeshott writes, 'When Mr. Lippman says that the founders of our free institutions were adherents of the philosophy of natural law, and that 'the free political institutions of the Western world were conceived and established' by men who held certain abstract beliefs, he speaks with the shortened perspective of an American way of thinking in which a manner of conducting affairs is inconceivable without an architect and without a premeditated 'dedication to a proposition'. But the fact is that nobody ever 'founded' these institutions. They are the product of innumerable human choices, over long stretches of time, but not of any human design.' Oakeshott, 'The Customer is Never Wrong,' in *Religion, Politics and the Moral Life* (New Haven: Yale Univ. Press, 1993), 177. Hereafter, *RPML*.

[45] Oakeshott, *The Politics of Faith and the Politics of Skepticism* (New Haven: Yale Univ. Press, 1996), 80. Hereafter, *FS*.

[46] Oakeshott, *On Human Conduct* (Oxford: Clarendon Press, 1975), 244. Hereafter: OHC. Arendt writes, 'the framing of the *Constitution*, falling back on existing charters and agreements, confirmed and legalized an already existing body politic rather than made it anew.... The actors in the American Revolution were spared the effort of "initiating a new order of things" altogether.' Arendt, 'What is Authority,' in *Between Past and Future* (New York: Penguin, 1977), 140.

Richards to describe George H. W. Bush, Oakeshott is suggesting that the United States of America was born on third base and thought it hit a triple. According to Oakeshott, it is this type of historical and practical ignorance that informs claims about American exceptionalism.

Conclusion

In a recent interview, Bruce Frohnen, the editor of the newly published *Encyclopedia of American Conservatism*, relates that an entry on Michael Oakeshott was one of the more divisive questions that the editors had to face, with those opposed to its inclusion claiming that Oakeshott was 'too skeptical, too philosophical, and too English.'[47] Frohnen won the argument and the Oakeshott entry appears in the encyclopedia, but the opposition is suggestive. I imagine that Oakeshott would have readily accepted the second objection because he understood philosophy to be an explanatory not a prescriptive activity, and thus rejected the appropriateness of labeling philosophy and philosophers. He would have at least partially granted the third objection, as well, because, though American political traditions are largely derived from English ones, Americans have had several hundred years to make these traditions their own. He would not have accepted the first, however, because his skepticism about the possibilities of politics informed both his understanding of the character of conservatism and his rejection of the rationalist or ideological politics which he understood to be characteristic of the contemporary age. Thus, in a country in which self-described conservatives proudly proclaim their commitment to an ideological conception of its political life, it might be doubted whether an Oakeshottian conservatism can long persist.

---

[47] 'The Right Book,' online interview with Bruce Frohnen, http://www.nationalreview.com/interrogatory/qa200604200604.asp.

17

Attila K. Molnár

Conservatives' Paradox in Post-Communism

The Master said 'Men all say, "We are wise;" but being driven forward and taken in a net, a trap, or a pitfall, they know not how to escape.'
The Doctrine of the Mean, Confucius

'Conservative' is a rather ambivalent label in Hungary, as maybe in other post-Communist countries today. It was used, around 1990, to refer to hardliner or dogmatic Communists, who insisted uncritically on some radical dogma. More recently it has been used for those who opposed post-Communists and the post-Communist world. Because of our recent past, some people say that there is only a Socialist (or Communist) tradition, therefore conservatives must be Socialist, and the non-socialist political tradition was demolished during the last 40 years. *Mutatis mutandis*, the same can be said about Western mass democracies, as well.

The ambivalent meaning of the term 'Conservative' refers to the problematic relation of Conservatives to the existing world around them. And from this point of view, no difference can be seen between the Conservatives of the West and those of the post-Communist world. In both cases, the problem is their relation to the present and to the recent past that has resulted in the present.

Conservatives are not always or necessarily for the *status quo*. For them the main difficulty is in finding institutions worthy of preservation, institutions that have not been distorted to the point of being no longer worth preserving. Whilst in post-Communist countries totalitarianism made this problem clear, in Western liberal democracies the welfare state, mass society, and mass culture have raised the same question: What do Conservatives want to conserve? Many Conservatives look around the world and do not like what they find. Their complaints about the loss of tradition and authority – to mention only some favorites of Conservatives – express this distaste. But it is not really new; the very founders of Conservative thinking, like Edmund Burke, were not satisfied by their world. One may find the same phenomenon among the German Conservative revolutionaries at the beginning of the twentieth century, or among the Anglo-Saxon Conservatives during the seventies and eighties. These examples show that the critical attitude toward the world is not only common among Conservatives but, with it, they often fall into the sin of rationalism, of seeing the dissatisfying present as a *problem* to be solved.

The double problem of sorting out a tradition's relation to the present while taking either an accepting or a critical stance toward the contemporary world is not a Hungarian post-Communist peculiarity. Nor is conservatism easily confined to merely historical horizons. An idealized past easily throws up abstract ideals. Karl Mannheim, for example, at one time interpreted Conservative thinking as traditionalism, but later mentioned it as a form of utopian mentality.[1] It is simply not true despite Oakeshott's noting the conservative's capacity for delight that Conservatives are generally delighted at what they find.

The concern of this essay is whether Conservatives can be critical of the world around them and not rationalistic or ideological at the same time. Can the criticism of the present and recent past be combined coherently with reverence towards tradition and authority; that is to say, can that criticism resist being transformed into an appeal to abstract principles standing over and against the actual, inherited world in which we live?

Conservatives' criticism of the present is not carried out in a modern Enlightenment style, negating the existing world in the name of a better future. Their criticism is based on tradition, which is not an antiquarian notion in the Conservative mind, but one that refers to ideas of proper and reasonable action, and good order.

I would suggest that we should resuscitate the original normative meaning of tradition: it is not anything at hand, but only what was tried and proved to be good.[2] Tradition answers indirectly to the Aristotelian questions: What should we do? And, what can we do?

No doubt, tradition is selective. As Nietzsche wrote,[3] man cannot live without both memory and oblivion, but both of them are selective. The notion of tradition implies that this selection is not whimsical, but it refers to experience and judgments of the past. It is worth differentiating tradition from heritage. Heritage is what is at hand; it refers to inertia and usage. Heritage might even include some ruins. However, the notion of tradition is normative because it refers to practices that have been probed and tested, explored, and found to be adequate. The authority of tradition arises from this experiential finding of satisfactoriness, and confers a presumption of goodness in what is. The original notion of tradition is normative, because God reveals himself in history; therefore what could survive a long period of time and many tests and trials is probably from God.

The oft-mentioned trial and error learning process of tradition or practical experience presupposes the freedom to make conclusions, decisions, and to form

---

[1] Karl Mannheim, *Ideology and Utopia, An Introduction to the Sociology of Knowledge*, trans. Louis Wirth and Edward Shils (1936; reprint, New York: Harcourt, Brace & World, 1968).

[2] It seems to me that Norman and Ganesh in their recent work try to reinterpret the notion of tradition in a similar way: 'Of course, this is not to say that all tradition is good; that what exists must exist; or that our institutions never require further justification. But it reminds us that change is not reform, and that reform must go with the grain of institutions if it is to have a positive effect.' Jesse Norman and Janan Ganesh, *Compassionate Conservatism: What It Is, Why We Need It* (London: Policy Exchange, 2006), 48.

[3] Friedrich Nietzsche, *Untimely Meditations*, trans. Reginald John Hollingdale (Cambridge: Cambridge Univ. Press, 1983).

interpersonal relations. Lucky countries may learn from their successes, but in the case of a not really lucky country, like Hungary, people may learn from failures as well. But even in this case, tradition needs freedom. The modern form of tyranny, totalitarianism, cannot create political tradition, only meaninglessness. In the past under tyrannical politics some tradition might emerge because pre-modern tyranny did not interfere in everyday life practices. Pre-modern tyranny only creamed off the harvest and took the nicest girls. Only the Enlightened absolutism of the eighteenth century started directly to refashion people's characters and practices in order to construct a new world.[4] Therefore, not simply tyranny as such may demolish tradition, but mainly the modern social tyrannies, because these tend to interfere with the free trial and error learning process in almost every practice.

The more tyrannical politics interfere with everyday practice, the less space is open for meaningful activities in economics, family life, housing, and other areas. Of course, tradition may be initiated by force, chance, speculation, or imagination, but only the free deliberation of several generations can give authority to institutions or to knowledge. The failure of Socialism shows the meaninglessness of forced actions. It collapsed by itself. Today, there is no Socialist tradition, only a dusty heritage.

Beside the threat from totalitarianism, we can learn from Tocqueville's description of democracy that egalitarianism opposes tradition, too. Epistemological egalitarianism (a refusal of intellectual authority and of any kind of epistemological asymmetry) brings about epistemological chaos with political consequences. Tocqueville tells us that democracy coheres with a mental homelessness where everything is opened up to a borderless discussion. Tradition, like authority, is 'aristocratic,' in at least this negative sense – it allows and even welcomes distinction, and to learn its intricacies takes a lot of time and effort. And contrary to egalitarianism, this learning process is based on the recognition of definite significances. Tradition is based on differences: first of all, the difference of master and disciple; secondly, the difference of importance. Tradition teaches us to dare to enhance or highlight something, it teaches us to make a difference between good and bad, important or less important, noble and ignoble, etc. Making a difference is not democratic. Making a difference means pointing to *an* author, to *a* text. In Tocquevillian terms, it means an historiographic principle of explanation in terms of individual deeds, not impersonal social movements or 'forces'.

A World Without Tradition?

It must be asked whether the conservative ideal of non-reflectiveness – whether depicted by Burke,[5] or by Oakeshott in his *On Being Conservative*,[6] reminding us

---

[4]   On this point, which Tocqueville observed contemporaneously, see Zygmunt Bauman, *Legislators and Interpreters: On Modernity, Post-Modernity, And Intellectuals* (Cambridge: Polity Press, 1987).

[5]   'Thousands of great cattle, reposed beneath the shadow of the British oak, chew the cud and are silent.' Edmund Burke, *Reflections on the Revolution in France* (Cambridge: Hackett, 1987), 75.

[6]   'A propensity to use and to enjoy what is available rather than to wish for or to look for something else; to delight in what is present rather than what was or what may be … gratefulness for

of Bagehot's famous remark on the joy and delight of the present state of things – is or is not incoherent with the critical attitude toward contemporary culture and politics. In Burke's case criticism was directed against French and English radicals, while in Oakeshott's case, it was directed against the welfare state and mass society.

'Rationalism' is what Oakeshott called the morality of reflection, and the politics of the book. Perhaps Burke's *Reflection* was itself a step towards rationalism and this or any paper reflecting on tradition simply carries on this original sin – the fall into 'traditionalism'. Talk about tradition is not the same as living in and being embedded in tradition. Talking about tradition is a job dear to a Catholic or an Oakeshottian, but C. S. Lewis' warning should be always kept in mind that 'analytical understanding must always be a basilisk which kills what it sees and only sees by killing.'[7] Although Conservatives are eager to refuse ideologies and, because of that, most of them prefer the term 'Conservative' to the label 'Conservatism',[8] the pursuit of political identity, self-definition, and mobilization after World War II tends to create canons, dogmas. Are the contemporary Conservatives modern ideologues who accept some Conservative principles, but would like to refashion them in terms of rationalistic ideals to pursue 'perfection as the crow flies'? Or is the rationalization of Conservative thinking more or less necessary in a world without tradition and authority?

Rationalism, that is, ideology and dogma-making is not rare among today's Conservatives, maybe, partly, because of the intellectual origin and education of many of them. But, on the other hand, it seems to me that they have to face up to rationalization as a more or less necessary result of the intellectualization of and reflection on tradition. The modernists and the heirs of the French Enlightenment forced them consciously to argue for tradition. As Burke wrote: 'It has been the misfortune ... of this age that everything is to be discussed.'[9] In order to defend tradition people had to reflect on it, which resulted in some dogmatization of tradition. Moderns forced tradition-bound people to give reasons for their prejudices and institutions, to argue for them. This was a victory not over Conservatives, but over conservative habits.[10] And it seems to me that there is no return to Adam's prelapsarian, innocent world. Any effort toward a reflective return to the unconscious and non-reflective way of thinking and acting seems to be 'writing on water'.

Because tradition is a key idea for Conservatives, the assumption of the evaporation of tradition undermines Conservative thinking itself. But besides the

---

what is available, and consequently the acknowledgment of a gift or an inheritance from the past ... What is esteemed is the present.' Oakeshott, *Rationalism in Politics and other essays, new and expanded edition,* ed. Timothy Fuller (Indianapolis: Liberty Press, 1991), 408. Hereafter: *RIP.*

[7]   C. S. Lewis, *The Abolition of Man* (Oxford: Oxford Univ. Press, 1943), ch. 3.
[8]   Samuel P. Huntington, 'Conservatism As An Ideology,' *American Political Science Review,* 51 (June 1957): 454–73.
[9]   Burke, *Reflections,* 80.
[10] James Kalb, 'The Tyranny of Liberalism,' *Modern Age,* 42 (Summer 2000), 239–53.

inevitable creep of rationalism, can one see other answers among Conservatives concerning tradition and the existing world?

One common answer is that tradition is any knowledge and institutions at hand. While this notion of tradition is far from radicalism, it may not bring about conflict or debates, because it is not critical of the contemporary world. If one accepts that tradition is simply 'what is,' he will accommodate himself to the status quo,[11] whatever it is, as Voltaire's Pangloss did in his *Candide*.[12] This domesticated, uncritical interpretation of the tradition is not rare and is welcomed by moderns. The engines of progress will eventually transform the better future into the worser past; Pangloss will be reincarnated as Hegel.

At this point, the question can be raised: are tradition and authority substantial categories or do these refer to a certain mode of knowledge and action? Do the notions of tradition and authority refer to some substance, commonly called good life or good order? Or may anyone have authority; may tradition emerge anywhere and with any content?

What I am suggesting is that the content of tradition is not a chance occurrence, even if it has emerged by chances. What was handed over has some worth because it has survived. On the other hand, if any knowledge and institution may be tradition, what differentiates tradition from fashion? This interpretation would wash away the cultural and political differentiations between the Conservatives and moderns or post-moderns.

A second, rather common answer to the question of Conservatives' relationship to the contemporary world in light of their appreciation of the past is a nostalgia or melancholy because of the disappearance of the old good world of tradition. As Burke wrote characteristically:

> The age of chivalry is gone. That of sophisters, economists; and calculators has succeeded; and the glory of Europe is extinguished forever. Never, never more shall we behold that generous loyalty to rank and sex, that proud submission, that dignified obedience, that subordination of the heart which kept alive, even in servitude itself, the spirit of an exalted freedom. The unbought grace of life, the cheap defense of nations, the nurse of manly sentiment and heroic enterprise, is gone.[13]

While this habit is not alien to us, we have to see clearly, that it assumes that the tradition is already gone and is irrelevant in contemporary life. It is defeatist: So,

---

[11] 'To recognize reason as the rose in the cross of the present, and to find delight in it, is a rational insight which implies reconciliation with reality.' Georg Wilhelm Friedrich Hegel, *Philosophy of Right*, trans. Samuel Waters Dyde (Kitchener, Ontario: Batoche Books, 2001), 19.

[12] 'Well, my dear Pangloss,' said Candide to him, 'when You were hanged, dissected, whipped, and tugging at the oar, did you continue to think that everything in this world happens for the best?'/'I have always abided by my first opinion,' answered Pangloss; 'for, after all, I am a philosopher, and it would not become me to retract my sentiments; especially as Leibniz could not be in the wrong: and that preestablished harmony is the finest thing in the world, as well as a plenum and the materia subtilis.' Voltaire, 'Voltaire, *Candide*, in *The Works of Voltaire*, vol. 1, trans. William F. Fleming (New York, E.R. DuMont, 1901), 199.

[13] Burke, *Reflections*, 66.

finally, we lost. With this assumption, Conservatives' task is only to slow down inevitable changes, but the future does not belong to them.

A third answer is the so-called Conservative revolution (Nietzsche, Spengler, Hans Freyer, Ernst Jüng, Arthur Moeller van der Bruck). They were optimistic about the capacities of human will and action, but presupposed the total loss of tradition. They opposed modernity and hoped to create a new man, new institutions, and a new order worth conserving. But is there any other option than to bury thinking and action based on tradition? Must today's Conservatives wily-nily follow the German 'Conservative revolutionaries'? Or is the politics of slowing down the only alternative? If Pangloss and Burke seem too acquiescent and too nostalgic, respectively, it hardly seems more sober to take up the standard of remaking the world in the pseudo-classicists image.

So What?

Once upon a time, the Hungarian born John Kekes asked Michael Oakeshott what could be done in a country where the existence of tradition, mainly a political one, was problematic. Oakeshott's semi-joking answer was, 'That's your problem.' Actually, that is our problem. But as I can see, and as I have mentioned, it is a rather common problem of the West, as well. As Oakeshott himself wrote, entertaining the thought of a crisis-point in a tradition at which everything seems lost:

> If, in order to meet this crisis, there were some steady, unchanging, independent guide to which a society might resort, it would be no doubt be well advised to do so. But no such guide exists; we have no resources outside the fragments, the vestiges, the relics of its own tradition of behaviour which the crisis has left untouched. (*RIP*, 50)

To turn to one of, if not the major crisis to which Oakeshott directed his attention, we should look at his well-known criticisms of the modern productivist state, and of mass society. Faced with what Ortega had labeled the 'revolt of the masses', emphasizing the revolutionary intent of the unconscious crowd and the civilizational stakes, and what others called, a little less uncalmly, the 'crisis of modernity', Oakeshott undertook to 'shore the fragments against our ruin', to gather the relics and dry bones of tradition, and to restate for contemporary ears the best of ancient and modern political wisdom. He faced 'our problem'.

May a nonreflective *quiet common sense* or the *plain man's practices* help guide human agents toward proper action? From Burke up to Oakeshott we may read many complaints about the evaporation of *Sittlichkeit* and the homeless mind, as Peter Berger[14] called it many years ago. Some explain the spread of rationalism in terms of the loss of certainty and the rise of an intellectual proletariat who may have only his chains to lose. But as Burke was forced by the French revolution, so the welfare state and New Left of the sixties forced the Conservatives to reflect on the world around them and on their presuppositions and prejudices. But one may stop here. It is not necessary to go further and to make a catalogue of tradition

---

[14] Peter L. Berger, Brigitte Berger, and Hansfried Kellner, *The Homeless Mind: Modernization and Consciousness* (Harmondsworth: Penguin, 1974).

or Conservatism, which seems to be a widespread tendency. The philosophical question is whether one is able to found and demonstrate universally a way of life and prejudices. But these efforts are against the old habits of Conservatives who valued prejudices *because they do not know their raison d'etre.*[15]

Is there any viable traditional knowledge at hand in the contemporary West or in the post-Communist countries that could steer a ship of state? Or is it necessary to become rationalist and ideological? In the latter case, it would not be a different epistemology, or a different mode of thinking and acting, but only different dogmas that would differentiate Conservatives from their opponents. Obviously, there must be some tradition at hand, and not only in museums and traditionalist communities. Of course, there are routines in everyday practices. But the real issue is the existence of moral and political traditions that may help us in making judgments in borderline cases.

In spite of centuries of critical destruction and reformulation of traditions, there are traditions in some islands of the lifeworld such as churches, libraries, vineyards, and families. These islands help us in everyday life where we do not stand alone, homelessly, in a barbaric, meaningless plurality not moderated by tradition. But it is not the answer I am looking for. The real issue is the existence of moral and political traditions, not simply vestigial traces of a past mode of life quaintly preserved, propped up by sentiment, tariffs, and sunk costs. How could the warmth of family life, the cool of the cellar, or the quiet of a library help actors in political situations? Before the spread of the rationalist ideal of political action as technical expertise using systematized knowledge, political education followed Polybius' ancient ideal, which used past events as a stock of experiences and examples out of which political actors might develop a tacit knowledge of situations and actors.

While contemporary situations and problems do not correspond in detail with the past, the practical skills for proper and reasonable action, and the keys for understanding current, non-routine situations, can be derived from learning about past situations. Of course, such derivation does not happen *via* explicit, conscious inference. Skillful apprehension of the past, like other skills, involves learning how to judge and not merely the assimilation of information. Because these skills exist only in practice, they can be learned only by personal participation. This 'participation' is an engagement to learn from the past, a question-and-response procedure as opposed to a merely personal reflection on first principles; but it is always *someone* reflecting and engaging *something* – in that sense, personal and direct.

The European, Greco-Christian tradition of authors is still at hand. We rely upon the same authors that past generations relied upon. Of course, just as we do not redesign the fire station during a fire, no one would be so crazy as to rush into a library and initiate his diligent study of the classics when he is facing a non-

---

[15] 'They are the product of innumerable human choices, over long stretches of time, but not of human design. And the choices from which they sprang were not responses to abstract beliefs, but to current situations.' Oakeshott, *Religion, Politics and the Moral Life*, ed. Timothy Fuller (London: Yale Univ. Press, 1993), 117. Hereafter: *RPML.*

routine situation, a 'crisis' or 'emergency'. In borderline cases our tacit knowledge springs to the fore; of course, this presupposes an already-acquired moral and political education. We must face the new already armed with the appropriations of the old.

This interpretive situation, broadly conceived, is becoming widely recognized as the starting point for grappling with the problem of prudence or practical wisdom today. While the meaning of tradition remains in dispute, tradition's importance does not. One might assert, (melo-)dramatically, 'we are all traditionalists.' During the recent decades historians of ideas have contributed – not only in Hungary – to public debates by their archaeological excavations of authors and texts. In the fields of political and social thought, scientism seems to me to be defeated, and the dominant mode of thinking is rather reflection on, or interpretation of, one author or tightly grouped subtraditions of several authors.

History is the history of situations, and the description of situations is always 'thick description,' to use Ryle and Geertz's phrase.[16] The description of situations or of experiences are thick, because they contain much more in a 'many-layered sandwich' than can be expressed openly, or discussed analytically: In another idiom, 'There are also many other things that Jesus did, but if these were to be described individually, I do not think the whole world would contain the books that would be written' (John 21:25).

 The great authors are great, partly, because of their rich and ineffable contents, of which some may be put into predicative statements, whilst many other elements will be reflected only in the studies, commentaries, and appropriations of later generations. But even the not yet reflected meanings are involved in the great authors' texts. Because of this 'thick' character of great authors' texts no one can argue for or against all the meanings imbedded in them. The subject of political or social learning is its own history.

To say that knowledge and experience come from tradition means that knowing and acting properly are never wholly a matter of present ideas; they are situated in a context of meanings originated from the past. Because of that, what is radically new cannot be reasonable, and what is reasonable cannot be wholly new. The boundlessly free man and his action cannot be understood by others; thus, what is presented as freed from all linguistic, social, or historic moorings must be heard as senseless babble.

Because the notion of tradition is usually connected to Conservatives, it may be important to point out, that the rediscovery of some past authors is not tradition yet. Leo Strauss and his method of 'close reading' supposes that the original meaning of texts can be found and reconstructed apart from both the time gap between us and the texts, and the commentaries concerning the authors. Strauss' methodology promises to jump over the tradition of commentaries. But this stretching back does not differ too much from the hope of radical enthusiasts and enlightened *philosophes*, who hoped to jump back to the original meaning of the Gospels, or to

[16] Gilbert Ryle, 'The Thinking of Thoughts: What Is *'Le Penseur'* Doing?' in *Collected Essays 1929–1968*, vol. 2 of *Collected Papers* (London: Hutchinson and Co., 1971), 480; Clifford Geertz, *The Interpretation of Culture* (New York: Basic Books, 1973).

understand directly what a Founding Father really intended. Thus, while Strauss himself was aware of traditions of thought, of commentary and interpretation, his approach tries to work back beyond these, to what seems alone sufficiently authoritative to meet present crises: the original. However, this risks lapsing into a rigidly technical way of handling texts.

Traditional understanding is a cultivated mental habit, not the application of a technique. Traditional knowledge is fused with a mode of life, with a kind of practice; therefore, traditional knowledge is personal. Thus initiation into a tradition is always character formation, too, implying the acceptance of authority as such. That is, the traditional learner apprentices with the great authors, submitting to them while being unsure where they will lead him. As MacIntyre wrote:

> The reader was assigned the task of interpreting the text, but also had to discover, in and through his or her reading of those texts, that they in turn interpret the reader. What the reader, as thus interpreted by the texts, has to learn about him or herself is that it is only the self as transformed through and by the reading of the texts which will be capable of reading the texts aright.... The person in this predicament requires two things: a teacher and an obedient trust that what the teacher, interpreting the text, declares to be good reasons for transforming oneself into a different kind of person – and a different kind of reader – will turn out to be genuinely good reasons in the light afforded by that understanding of the texts which becomes available only to the transformed self. The intending reader has to have inculcated into him or herself certain attitudes and dispositions, certain virtues, before he or she can know why these are to be accounted virtues. So a prerational reordering of the self has to occur before the reader can have an adequate standard by which to judge what is good reason and what is not. And this reordering requires obedient trust, not only in the authority of this particular teacher, but in that of the whole tradition of interpretative commentary into which that teacher had had earlier to him or herself to be initiated through his or her reordering and conversion.[17]

Conservatives are apt to think that the proper and reasonable moral and political action is the result of individual character and virtues rather than a pretended philosophical truth or scientific facts and laws. It is never certain that someone will act according to the models found in classic texts, but his understanding of situations presented in them, and of judgments and decisions made in them, will probably influence his practical knowledge, as well as his character. Therefore, as Oakeshott and our tradition say, education in the sense of character formation may be the answer for the dilemmas of tradition presented in this essay.

> What distinguishes a human being, indeed what constitutes a human being, is not merely his having to think, but his thoughts, his beliefs, doubts, understandings, his awareness of his own ignorance, his wants, preferences, choices, sentiments, emotions, purposes and his expression of them in utterances or actions which have meanings; and the necessary condition of all or any of this is that he must have learned it. The price of the intelligent activity which constitutes being human is learning. When the human

---

[17] Alasdair McIntyre, *Three Rival Versions of Moral Enquiry: Encyclopaedia, Genealogy, and Tradition* (London: Duckworth, 1990), 82.

condition is said to be burdensome, what is being pointed to is not the mere necessity or having to think, to speak and to act (instead of merely being like a stone, or growing like a tree) but the impossibility of thinking or feeling without having slowly and often painfully learned to think something.[18]

Today, to extol tradition is to swim against the tide. Although having to learn 'slowly and painfully' may eventually be a human predicament as widely recognized as our interpretive one, authors like McIntyre and Oakeshott are, at least for now, quite rare in being willing to tell us the price of becoming human in a world dominated by the flashy promises of fundamentalist rationalism on the one side, and on the other, a casual cynicism that calls itself 'post-modernism'. Traditional knowledge deals with forgotten, lost political and moral dilemmas, problems, and experiences. It is thanks to the continual resuscitation of authors out of textual entombment in dark and dusty archives, and their return to life's playing fields that we have notions – time-tested, if not eternally vouchsafed ideas – of good order, proper action, justice, freedom, and law. Although totalitarians, modern Enlightenment *philosophes*, and post-moderns have all promised our emancipation from the tormenting compulsions of the past, it is always the authors mediated to us in a tradition of thinking and acting who can liberate us from the simplifying limitations of contemporary intellectual and political fashions.

---

[18] Oakeshott, *The Voice of Liberal Learning*, ed. Timothy Fuller (Indianapolis: Liberty Fund, 2001), 5–6. Hereafter: *VL*.

18

Ivo Mosley

'A Dark Age Devoted to Barbaric Affluence': Oakeshott's Verdict on the Modern World

Introduction

'The beginning of a dark age devoted to barbaric affluence.' Oakeshott's assertion of where civilization was heading in 1972 struck some as unduly pessimistic. Now, thirty-seven years later, his diagnosis seems (to many) less like a gloomy prediction, more like a well-put observation.

I was drawn to Oakeshott's work because I felt he offered a convincing account of much that is puzzling in our modern world. He is particularly refreshing in one important respect: Whatever his shortcomings may be, an excessive reverence for sacred cows is not one of them. This lack of reverence is surely one reason for his relative obscurity. To have a good solid constituency, you must make obeisance to at least one sacred cow. If you would be an alternative guru à la Chomsky, you must believe in 'the people'; if you would be a free-market hero, you must worship the golden calves of affluence and corporate power; if you would be a progressive liberal, you must genuflect to rationalism and science.

Oakeshott is in thrall to none of these. In some ways, his outlook is closer to certain Eastern philosophers than to the mainstream European tradition. He is particularly fond of quoting the philosopher Chuang Tzu[1] and various features of his thought seem more familiar in the Eastern than in the Western tradition: to mention a few, his disdain for power; his non-religious spirituality; his respect for ritual;[2] his detachment from worldly ambition; and his recognition of story-telling as a means by which philosophy occasionally 'reaches the level of literature.'[3]

I mention these because they are all significant in the story of Oakeshott's

---

[1] See, for example, Oakeshott, *Rationalism in Politics, and other essays, new and expanded edition*, ed. Timothy Fuller (Indianapolis: Liberty Press, 1991), 14, 41 n, 236 n, 417, 480 n. Hereafter: *RIP*. Some, but (mysteriously) not all of the references to Eastern thinkers appear in the index.

[2] 'In short, the intimations of government are to be found in ritual, not in religion or philosophy; in the enjoyment of orderly and peaceable behaviour, not in the search for truth or perfection.' Hsün Tzu or Michael Oakeshott? (In fact, *RIP*, 428).

[3] His most expressive elaboration of this is the essay '*Leviathan*: A Myth,' in Oakeshott, *Hobbes and Civil Association* (1975; reprint, Indianapolis: Liberty Fund, 2000), 159-63. Hereafter: *HCA*.

preoccupation with the idea of a 'dark age of barbaric affluence.' The sentence in which this phrase appears is the following:

'The design to substitute 'socialization' for education has gone far enough to be recognised as the most momentous occurrence of this century, the greatest of the adversities to have overtaken our culture, the beginning of a dark age devoted to barbaric affluence.'[4]

I want to examine what he means by this sentence. My motive is not to find guidance or useful tips, just a bit of understanding. Oakeshott warned us repeatedly that philosophy has no practical use. 'If we seek guidance,' he wrote in an essay titled 'Political Philosophy,' 'we must hang up philosophy.'[5] And yet in the same essay he introduced a paradox. Philosophy, being 'radically subversive reflection,' questions the very assumptions we employ in practical living and so *may* have far-reaching practical consequences. Oakeshott compared the philosopher to a scientist investigating the nature of heat. The scientist is not trying to warm the room he inhabits, but his investigation may have huge implications for those who want to warm rooms in the future.

And Oakeshott certainly was radically subversive in his thinking. He put his position most forcefully in the final few pages of *On Human Conduct*[6] where he ridicules political opinion-makers as 'somnambulists' and 'jokers,' and states that our familiar political dualisms – such as left/right, progressive/conservative, pluralist/centralist – are insignificant compared to the manifestations of two fundamentally opposed human dispositions, which may for convenience's sake be abbreviated to individualism and collectivism. This opposition, and the tensions it brings to human activity, is the subject of most of his work.

Isaiah Berlin, taking an idea from the ancient Greek poet Archilochus, suggested that thinkers can be categorized as either foxes or hedgehogs. 'The fox knows many tricks,' wrote Archilochus in the seventh century B.C.E. 'The hedgehog only knows one, but it's a winner.'

Hedgehog-philosophers, says Berlin, 'relate everything to a single central vision, a single organizing principle in terms of which all they are and say has significance.'[7] Oakeshott made a similar observation about Hobbes some decades earlier; 'the coherence of Hobbes thought,' he said, 'lies in a single passionate thread that pervades its parts' (*RIP*, 236).[8] Surely Oakeshott too is a philosopher of this type, a hedgehog-philosopher.[9] He elaborates his single central vision in many manifestations: in politics, in law, in morality, in education, and in aesthetics.

Oakeshott's central vision is a polarity, and its political manifestation is familiar

[4] Oakeshott, 'Education: The Engagement and its Frustration,' in *The Voice of Liberal Learning*, ed. and with foreword and intro. by Timothy Fuller (Indianapolis: Liberty Fund, 2001), 99. Hereafter: *VL*.

[5] Oakeshott, *Religion, Politics and the Moral Life*, ed. Timothy Fuller (New Haven: Yale Univ. Press, 1993), 155. Hereafter: *RPML*.

[6] Oakeshott, *On Human Conduct* (Oxford: Clarendon, 1975), 318-20. Hereafter: *OHC*.

[7] Isaiah Berlin, *Russian Thinkers* (London: The Hogarth Press, 1978), 22.

[8] Oakeshott's metaphor of the 'passionate thread' comes, according to his footnote, not from Archilocus but Confucius.

[9] Curiously extending our mammalian theme, the metaphor Oakeshott uses to represent civil association (from Schopenhauer) involved porcupines huddling together for warmth (*RIP*, 460).

to all his readers. The political polarity is between two incompatible answers to the question, 'What role should the State play in our lives?' The collectivist says the state should be the overseer of a great common enterprise and involve us all in a great common purpose. This kind of state needs great power to realize its vision. The individualist believes the state should consist in an indifferent and impartial rule of law, accommodating our differences and mitigating conflict without imposing uniformity (*RIP*, 460). This kind of state needs a bare minimum of power.

Oakeshott's object of attention was the modern European state; but his analysis is important for the rest of the world, partly because various versions of the modern European state have been adopted by – or imposed upon – other nations of the world, and partly because the economic and military power of states built upon the European model have made them objects of desire and political aspiration.

Returning to our sentence, it concerns of course not politics but education, culture, and civilization.

At first sight it might seem surprising that he called 'the design to substitute socialization for education' 'the most momentous occurrence' of a century that had endured and seen off both Hitler and Stalin. It is an unusually passionate sentence for Oakeshott, who normally expresses himself with a calm and rather English reserve. To understand this large claim, we have to consider what he meant by 'socialization', 'education', 'culture', and 'barbarism'.

Oakeshott returned again and again to the theme that the words we use are full of ambiguities.[10]

Words such as 'freedom', 'rights', and 'democracy', he said, have long histories, and their meanings have shifted over time. Furthermore, when unscrupulous operators use them to rally supporters in some great cause, such words tend to become mere slogans, hazy promises of better things to come. The warm glow of anticipation they excite may be as deceptive as the witches' promises to Macbeth.

Education

Education is another such word with multiple meanings. It can mean practical or vocational training. It can mean getting any old qualification for earning a living – as Oakeshott puts it, a 'certificate to let one in on the exploitation of the world' (*VL*, 117). It can mean a child discovering who he or she really *is*. Or it can mean the business of transmitting our culture and civilization from one generation to the next.

Oakeshott meant something larger, more complex and more vital than all of these. Moreover, he felt that liberal education was under mortal threat; and in order to defend itself, it needed to understand itself clearly.

Liberal education, he said, is distinguished by its 'emancipation from the here and now of current engagements.' In it, we learn the languages of human self-understanding, the different languages of (for example) 'the natural sciences, ... the language of history, the language of philosophy, or the language of poetic imagination.' Oakeshott 'recognizes' these languages 'not merely as diverse modes

---

[10]   His fullest coverage of this is in 'Talking Politics' (1975) in *RIP*, 438–61.

of understanding the world but as the most substantial expressions we have of human self-understanding' (*VL*, 28, 29).

In one of his most resonant idioms, Oakeshott said these languages of self-understanding are themselves voices in a conversation. This conversation is 'an endless unrehearsed intellectual adventure in which we enter into a variety of modes of understanding the world and ourselves, and are not disconcerted by the differences or dismayed by the inconclusiveness of it all' (*VL*, 30). The flourishing of these voices is what constitutes our civilization. Barbarism intrudes when one voice wants to dominate the conversation, and it is victorious when one voice succeeds in suppressing all the rest. According to Oakeshott, it is the art of conversation that 'always distinguishes the civilized man from the barbarian.'[11]

Liberal education is the process of learning some of these languages and becoming acquainted with others. Oakeshott emphasizes *learning*: 'None of us is born human;' he says, 'each *is* what we *learn* to become' (*VL*, 6, italics added). This statement, of course, would stampede several varieties of sacred cow.

But the truth of the statement is surely evident when we consider how a child brought up by wolves is hardly what we call human at all, nor will it be able to learn this quality subsequently. Stories about feral children with happy endings – such as Francois Truffault's film *L'Enfant Sauvage* – have to alter the historical facts upon which they are based. Feral children do not in fact learn humanity. They remain savage.

So, education is part of a slow and sometimes painful process of learning to be human. 'For the teacher, it is part of his engagement of *being* human; for the learner it is the engagement of *becoming* human' (*VL*, 72, italics added). People who disparage this view of education as 'cultural conditioning' are talking rubbish, says Oakeshott: 'a man is his culture; and what he is, he has had to learn to become' (*VL*, 17).

Barbarians, by definition, are people who know nothing of a cultured way of life, and when a civilization weakens they gather to loot, and maybe destroy it. The kind of barbarians Oakeshott had in mind are not wild-eyed horse-riding types from the wastes of central Asia. They are barbarians within – like the ones Erasmus wrote about in his *Antibarbari*, also in defense of education, only five hundred years earlier. They are men and women who want to seize control of society in the name of some great vision, in order to impose that vision on the rest of us. In Erasmus' time, the barbarians were religious dogmatists; in Oakeshott's day, they were and are social engineers.

Socialization

'Socialization' is the process by which social engineers create a new kind of person who will be malleable material for their visionary dreams. Would-be social engineers are inevitably confronted with the question, what kind of citizen do we want to produce? Of course, the answer varies from time to time, from society to

---

[11] Oakeshott, *What is History? and other essays*, ed. with intro. by Luke O'Sullivan (Thorverton: Imprint Academic, 2004), 191. Hereafter: *WH*.

society, and it is a tribute to the versatility of the social engineer that the nature of the project is less important than the fact that there is a project to be getting on with. Oakeshott described socialization as 'the doctrine that because the current here-and-now is very much more uniform than it used to be, education should recognize and promote this uniformity.... Every learner should be recognised as nothing but a role-performer in a so-called social system' (*VL*, 20).

When socialization replaces education, what is offered to the next generation shrinks from the unknown and potentially infinite to the small and always shriveling. What could have been an adventure in self-understanding, its possibilities intimated but never known, becomes the business of accommodating to a contemporary culture that is already shrinking as its members grow unfamiliar with the notion that there is more to life than the petty concerns of the moment. Socialization, says Oakeshott, 'not only strikes at the heart of liberal learning, it portends the abolition of man' (*VL*, 20). What does Oakeshott mean by this astonishing phrase, the abolition of man?

I suppose it is fair to say of Oakeshott that he was not, in any sense of the word, a materialist, nor even a utilitarian. In this respect he quotes Paul Valery: '*Tout ce qui fait le prix de la vie est curieusement inutile*' (*VL*, 28).[12]

Affluence, of course, is not inherently barbaric. Aristotle was only the first to remind us that a certain amount of affluence is necessary for civilization to exist at all. Affluence becomes barbaric when all other activities are regarded as secondary or subservient to its pursuit – when society is permeated by what Oakeshott referred to, always in quotation marks, as 'the plausible ethics of productivity.'[13] In a book review of 1949, he attacked this ethic:

> The good life here is nothing other than the enjoyment by more and more people of more and more of everything ... So far as I am concerned it involves a revolting nothingness, which has only to be successful to reduce human life to absolute insignificance.[14]

The 'plausible ethics of productivity' produces slavery to wants. He wrote about this slavery to wants in various essays and from various points of view.

In his essay 'Work and Play,' for instance, he wrote:

> To be a creature of wants, desires which cannot have more than a temporary satisfaction because each satisfaction, however easily achieved, leads only to new wants – to be a creature of wants is itself a curse, a condemnation to a life in which every achievement is also a frustration .... It is an activity of getting and spending, of making and consuming, endlessly. (*WH*, 309)

---

[12] 'Everything that makes up the *value* of life is curiously useless.' A modern idiom for this would be, perhaps: 'No one's last words were ever, "I wish I'd spent more time at the office".'
[13] Oakeshott, *The Social and Political Doctrines of Contemporary Europe*, with foreword by Ernest Baker (London: Basic Books, by arrangement with Cambridge Univ. Press, 1939), xx, xxi. Hereafter: *SPD*.
[14] Oakeshott, 'Review of *Socialism and Ethics*,' by H. Selsam, *The Cambridge Journal*, 2 (1948–9): 693–4. [Oakeshott uses this phrase 'the plausible ethics of productivity' in several other places; for example, in 'John Locke,' *Cambridge Review*, 54 (1932-3): 73.– Ed.]

The dream of satisfying every want, says Oakeshott, has consumed our civilization. In the same essay, he describes the progress of that dream as it took hold in the West:

> I suppose that at no time in the history of the world has mankind been more determined to devote itself to exploitation of nature for the satisfaction of all its wants, less dismayed at the proliferation of wants to be satisfied, or more confident of success.
>
> This enterprise, I have suggested, is as old as the human race, as old as the emergence of man as a creature of wants rather than of needs. What is comparatively new is the faith and fervour with which it is being pursued and the manner in which all else tends to be regarded as subordinate to the happiness that comes from the satisfaction of wants. (*WH*, 307-8)

Oakeshott was fairly pessimistic about where this enterprise would lead.

> When what a man can get from the use and control of the natural world and his fellow men is the sole criterion of what he thinks he needs, there is no hope that the major part of mankind will find anything but good in this exploitation until it has been carried far enough to reveal its bitterness to the full. (*VL*, 124)

Oakeshott concludes his essay by saying that the defense against this 'barbarity' can only lie in education. Socialization provides no such defense; in fact, it prepares the citizen to be a working unit in this slavery to wants.

As a project capable of uniting society, 'enjoyment by more and more people of more and more of everything' proved to be a promising one. All the great powers – corporations, governments, trade unions – were happy to join in. By and large, democracies embraced the project with open arms, and in his essay 'The Masses in Representative Democracy' Oakeshott examined the process by which this occurred.

Here, Oakeshott explains what he means by a phrase we come across often in his work: 'the illusions of democracy.' The idea that democracy is to some extent an illusion is familiar, but as usual Oakeshott provides us with a more chilling insight.

> What in fact has happened, whenever the disposition of 'popular government' has imposed itself, is that the prospective representative has drawn up his own mandate and then, by a familiar trick of ventriloquism, has put it into the mouth of his electors: as an instructed delegate, he is not an individual, and as a 'leader' he relieves his followers of the need to make choices for themselves.... Thus ... was generated a new art of politics, the art, not of 'ruling', ... but of knowing what offer will collect most votes, and of making it in such a manner that it appears to come from 'the people'; the art, in short, of 'leading' in the modern idiom. (*RIP*, 380)[15]

---

[15] Oakeshott also referred to Marx as 'the German ventriloquist,' a phrase that can only delight anyone who has spent time listening to the rantings of some of the ventriloquist's dummies.

So, here we have two themes: the leader as ventriloquist, and the pursuit of affluence as a purpose popular enough to unite a democratic state. Oakeshott returned to both these themes in his magnum opus *On Human Conduct*, where we have the memorable sentence: 'The outcome of trying to make the state a paradise has always been to turn it into a hell' (*OHC*, 319 n. 1).

This sentence provided him with the theme of his last substantial work, titled *The Tower of Babel*. He approaches his theme in a somewhat unusual way – by re-telling an old myth.[16]

Myth

Oakeshott had a high opinion of myth. Hobbes' *Leviathan*, according to Oakeshott, is 'one of the masterpieces of the literature of our language and civilization' because it is an authentic re-telling of the myth that is the common dream of our civilization. When a work of philosophy reaches this level, he says, 'its gift is not an access of imaginative power, but an increase of knowledge; it will prompt and it will instruct. In it, we shall be reminded of the common dream that binds the generations together, and the myth will be made more intelligible to us' (*HCA*, 160).

Philosophy prompting? Philosophy instructing? Can this be Oakeshott talking? And myth and philosophy all scrambled up? Was not Oakeshott the great drawer of boundaries? Did he not insist that category errors are *the* great source of confusion? But consistency is the first victim of genius and one of Oakeshott's strengths is that he did not suppress contradictions.

The Tower of Babel

It seems to me that Oakeshott's retelling of the Babel story is even more illuminating of our present condition than of the time it was written; in other words, we have moved nearer to the model of human conduct he describes.

The citizens of Babel want not just affluence, but an end to any sense of deprivation. They resent the humiliating conditions imposed upon Adam and Eve when they were thrown out of the Garden of Eden. They want to transform their world of dirt and pain, of thorns and thistles and sweat and mortality, into a land of guaranteed plenty. They take *seriously* the old fantasy of a land where everything is for free: the land flowing with milk and honey, the peach-blossom fountain, the Big Rock Candy Mountain. They are going to make good their dreams by storming heaven; by taking away from God control of the satisfactions he doles out so stingily to humankind.

The city of Babel is in many ways recognizable to us. It is 'a city of Freedom; the home of every imaginable lib.'[17] Its people are self-absorbed and self-indulgent; they are rebellious, with the rebelliousness 'not of wild and passionate people, but of spoiled children.' They are 'not strikingly affluent,' but they are 'devoted to

[16] The essay is the second of two he wrote with the same title: *The Tower of Babel*. Had he read Lu Hsun's *Old Tales Retold*, I wonder?
[17] Oakeshott, *On History, and other essays* (Liberty Fund, 1999), 191. Hereafter: *OHist*.

affluence.' What they expect from life is the 'ready satisfaction of all their wants' (*OHist*, 192). But because their wants are unlimited, they experience a constant sense of deprivation. Indeed, this 'profound feeling of being deprived' (*OHist*, 196) is what they share in common.

The ruler of Babel is a charismatic leader. Like other Babelians he is a person of infinite wants. He rouses the people to communal action in the one project that can unite them all: putting an end once and for all to their sense of deprivation. They will build a mighty tower all the way up to heaven, displace God by force and 'appropriate for the enjoyment of all Babelians the limitless profusion of paradise' (*OHist*, 195).

The citizens of Babel are thus joined in a great collective enterprise, fuelled by enthusiasm for a better future. The leader is able to compulsorily commandeer resources (including 'human resources') for the great task in hand, and all that makes up a free society – institutions, professions, law are absorbed into the great task, their original purpose forgotten.

Because almost everyone is caught up in the enthusiasm, there is no need for political oppression. Skeptics go unheard except in their homes. The government is not guilty of 'the more scandalous charges which may be brought against collectivism in action' (*RIP*, 399): there are no concentration camps, no wars, and no torture camps. Babelians are not racist or intolerant. These obvious evils are not Oakeshott's theme. His theme is that the project itself is enough to create hell and eventually bring ruin upon them all.

As time goes on, what started off as 'a distant and precarious vision of limitless loot' turns into a monotony of hard work. Paradise seems as remote as ever. Moreover, the morally dubious nature of the undertaking has its effect upon the mood of the people. In a fascinating passage, Oakeshott describes the difference between living in a civilization of which one may feel proud, and being part of an enterprise that engenders misgivings – if not positive shame:

> Confidence in the nobility of a long and difficult enterprise may go far to sustain its pursuit and it may even make its collapse endurable. Indeed, an illusion of nobility may suffice. But those who invest all their energies and hopes in an undertaking even tinged with depravity are bound to its success and are apt to acquire an obscure self-contempt which qualifies their faith, first in their fellows, and then in themselves. (*OHist*, 205)

Discontent and paranoia become the norm. Enjoyment of the present dries up; everything is sacrificed to the vision of a plentiful tomorrow. The diverse small enjoyments of life are long forgotten and the citizens of Babel hang around listlessly waiting for the promised abundance, prey to all sorts of doubts. Are they being duped? When the ascent into heaven comes, will some be left out? Or will something go wrong, making a mockery of their lives spent in one huge effort?

Eventually, in a fit of mass paranoia, the citizens of Babel storm the Tower. Heavy with their weight and shaking with the thunder of their feet, the Tower comes crashing down. Everyone is destroyed, even the little crippled boy who could not keep up.

I said earlier that the theme of this essay was, 'The outcome of trying to make the state a paradise has always been to turn it into a hell' (OHC, 319 n. 1). Oakeshott appends a poetical version of this sentence at the end of his Tower of Babel essay:

Those who in fields Elysian would dwell
Do but extend the boundaries of hell.

This final collapse is only one moral of the story. The other moral, more pertinent perhaps to our present condition, is the hell it creates along the way. Long before it destroys itself, its citizens are living in a hell of dissatisfactions.

As a coda to this tracing of Oakeshott's ideas on the project of modernity, I want to quote from another late essay, 'A Place of Learning.' In this essay, first presented at Colorado College in 1974, under the invitation of Timothy Fuller, Oakeshott ties in the problems faced by educators with the problems we humans face more generally.

The world in which many children now grow up is crowded, not necessarily with occupants and not at all with memorable experiences, but with happenings; it is a ceaseless flow of seductive trivialities which invoke neither reflection nor choice but instant participation. A child quickly becomes aware that he cannot too soon plunge into this flow or immerse himself in it too quickly; to pause is to be swept with the chilling fear of never having lived at all.... This world has but one language, soon learned; the language of appetite' (VL, 33).

To that he might have added, quoting Shakespeare: 'And appetite, an universal wolf, must make perforce an universal prey, and last eat up himself.'[18]

---

[18]   Shakespeare, *Troilus and Cressida*, 1, 3, 121.

Index

www.ingramcontent.com/pod-product-compliance
Lightning Source LLC
Chambersburg PA
CBHW071838270326
41929CB00013B/2034